# GERONTOLOGY
## A Book of Readings

# GERONTOLOGY

# A Book of Readings

*By*

### CLYDE B. VEDDER, Ph.D.

*Professor of Sociology*
*Northern Illinois University*
*DeKalb, Illinois*

*With a Foreword by*

### Belle Boone Beard, Ph.D.

*Sweet Briar College*
*Sweet Briar, Virginia*

**CHARLES C THOMAS · PUBLISHER**
*Springfield · Illinois · U.S.A.*

*Published and Distributed Throughout the World by*
CHARLES C THOMAS • PUBLISHER
BANNERSTONE HOUSE
301-327 East Lawrence Avenue, Springfield, Illinois, U.S.A.

*With THOMAS BOOKS careful attention is given to all details of manu-facturing and design. It is the Publisher's desire to present books that are satisfactory as to their physical qualities and artistic possibilities and appropri-ate for their particular use. THOMAS BOOKS will be true to those laws of quality that assure a good name and good will.*

*Printed in the United States of America*

# CONTRIBUTORS

George F. Baier, III, M.D., Chief Medical Officer, California Men's Colony, Los Padres, California.

Milton L. Barron, City College of New York, Department of Sociology and Anthropology, New York, New York.

Belle Boone Beard, Ph.D., Professor of Sociology, Sweet Briar College, Sweet Briar, Virginia.

Zena Smith Blau, University of Illinois, College of Nursing, Chicago, Illinois.

Karl M. Bowman, M.D., Professor of Psychiatry, Emeritus, Department of Psychiatry, University of California School of Medicine, San Francisco, California.

Louis Carp, M.D., Consultant, Goldwater Memorial Hospital, New York, New York.

Ruth Shonle Cavan, Professor of Sociology, Rockford College, Rockford, Illinois.

Frederick A. Conrad, Department of Sociology, University of Arizona, Tucson, Arizona.

Wilma Donahue, Ph.D., Chairman, Division of Gerontology, Institute for Human Adjustment; Lecturer in Psychology, University of Michigan, Ann Arbor, Michigan.

Bernice Engle, Research Associate, Department of Psychiatry, University of California School of Medicine, San Francisco, California.

Margaret S. Gordon, Ph.D., Institute of Industrial Relations, University of California, Berkeley, California.

Robert M. Gray, Department of Sociology, University of Utah, Salt Lake City, Utah.

Robert J. Havighurst, Ph.D., University of Chicago, President, Gerontological Society, Chicago, Illinois.

Jere Hoar, Department of Sociology, University of Mississippi, Oxford, Mississippi.

Abraham Holtzman, Ph.D., Department of Government, Dartmouth College, Hanover, New Hampshire.

Jerome Kaplan, Executive Director, Mansfield Memorial Homes, Inc., Mansfield, Ohio.

Clifford Kirkpatrick, Ph.D., Professor of Sociology, Indiana University, Bloomington, Indiana.

Marvin R. Koller, Ph.D., Associate Professor, Department of Sociology, Kent State University, Kent, Ohio.

R. Grann Lloyd, Savannah State College, Orangeburg, South Carolina.

M. F. Nimkoff, Chairman, Department of Sociology, Florida State University, Tallahassee, Florida.

Charles T. O'Reilly, School of Social Work, Loyola University, Chicago, Illinois.

Raymond Payne, Department of Sociology and Anthropology, University of Georgia, Athens, Georgia.

Robert L. Peterson, Assistant Professor of Management, University of Illinois Bureau of Business Management, Urbana, Illinois.

Bernard S. Phillips, Sociology Department, University of Illinois, Champaign, Illinois.

Allan Rechtschaffen, Ph.D., Department of Psychiatry, University of Chicago, Chicago, Illinois.

T. Eric Reynolds, M.D., President, California Medical Association, Oakland, California.

Irving Rosow, School of Applied Social Sciences, Western Reserve University, Cleveland, Ohio.

Howard A. Rusk, M.D., Department of Physical Medicine and Rehabilitation, New York University, College of Medicine, New York, New York.

Nathan W. Shock, Gerontology Branch, National Heart Institute, National Institutes of Health, Bethesda, Maryland; Baltimore City Hospitals, Baltimore, Maryland.

Ansel P. Simpson, Department of Sociology, University of Missouri, Columbia, Missouri.

T. Lynn Smith, Chariman, Department of Sociology, University of Florida, Gainesville, Florida.

Clark Tibbitts, Sc.D., Chief, Program Planning, Special Staff on Aging, U. S. Department of Health, Education and Welfare, Washington, D.C.

Wayne E. Thompson, Department of Sociology, Cornell University, Ithaca, New York.

Irving L. Webber, Ph.D., Research Social Scientist, Pinellas County Health Department, St. Petersburg, Florida.

Ellen Winston, North Carolina State Board of Public Welfare, Raleigh, North Carolina.

# FOREWORD

THIS IS A TIMELY and opportune book. It appears at just the right psychological moment to fill a pressing and growing need. The mushroom growth of interest in aging is manifested by the attention given it by professional associations and by the space assigned to it by all the mass media — radio and television programs, syndicated columns and feature stories in daily newspapers, articles in popular periodicals and trade journals. Most significant perhaps is the emergence of gerontology as a scientific discipline in colleges and universities. This book will be a godsend to the teachers of such courses as well as to the students enrolled in them.

Dr. Vedder, by his sagacious choice of readings, shows not only the explicit steps whereby the scientific study of gerontology emerged and became enacted into professional circles, but also how this study has been enriched by progressive sophistication of research techniques and by critical evaluation of experts.

Some people erroneously refer to old age as an "age-old problem." This is incorrect. Old age may have been a personal problem to a few; but old age has become a social problem only very recently. The existence of millions of older people in the world is a new phenomenon. The tremendous change in average life span (largely due to the applications of technology) has presented society with an utterly new situation — a changed population pyramid. People are living longer. The old are getting older. The proportion of old to young is rapidly changing. Every social institution and every phase of activity and attitude will be affected by this change in the relative number of old people. This is not an isolated emergency calling for a temporary solution. The gift of longevity may be a mixed blessing but it seems destined to be given to increasing millions. A longer life span calls for drastic long time plans. Education, work, family life, recreation and social services will be revolutionized.

Gerontology is a new science which offers new life, new inspirations, new guidance to millions of aging people. It removes the study of aging from the category of mere social and health problems into a wider perspective of a life process which begins with birth and ends with death. Gerontology is a new science which beckons imaginative and scientifically minded men and women into new professions. Specifically it opens new avenues of research and new vistas of service to persons in the professions of biology, medicine and psychiatry, psychology, sociology and social welfare. More than fifty high level positions have become available in recent years for persons with specialized knowledge of gerontology and hundreds more will develop in the near future. No field in recent decades offers so much challenge.

The first half of the Twentieth Century was characterized by specialization in medical and social welfare services and by a similar splinteration of academic disciplines in the natural and social sciences. The second half of this century is seeing efforts at integration, coordination, cross-fertilization, and synthesis, seeking to view "the human organism," "personality," and "social organization" as complex constructs. Efforts to eliminate provincialism and monistic theories and to make knowledge more generally understandable and useful have been made by the Social Science Research Council, the National Science Foundation, National Institutes of Health, the Ford Foundation and other agencies and institutions financing and promoting research.

Gerontology is fortunate in that it began as an interdisciplinary study and as Clark Tibbits and Wilma Donahue point out has at all stages maintained its catholicity. No one can claim to be a gerontologist who knows just one discipline.

When one considers the long developmental history of other specializations in psychology, medicine and sociology, it is remarkable how much experimentation has taken place and how much synthesis has been achieved in gerontology in a few decades. True, attention to this field was long overdue. Outworn myths had to be exploded and prejudices against age eliminated. However, it is clear that rapid development was made possible by the unusual financial assistance that has been made available for the planning and promotion of training programs, research agencies, conferences and publications. Vast sums are needed for the encouragement of new approaches and new programs. Longitudinal and cross-cultural research programs are urgently needed. Although the emerging gerontologist will find in this volume striking evidence of the interdisciplinary approach with some cross-fertilization of ideas, he will see that real integration concepts and the development of a unified body of theory are still challenges to be met.

The selections presented in this volume are largely based upon empirical research. They raise more questions than they answer. This is healthy in a young science. Gerontology is in its infancy, but shows wholesome manifestations of growth. Gerontologists have from the beginning kept in close touch with each other, openly criticizing, testing, and re-testing each others' theories. Replication in different settings and under different conditions have enabled subsequent researchers to modify, clarify and redefine hypotheses. Another hopeful sign is the tendency to relate studies of aging to larger theoretical constructs as the life cycle, role indentification and change, self-image, social organization and the small group. Thus gerontological studies will no doubt lead to re-formulations of theory in sociology and psychology. They will also result in radical changes in medical and psychiatric practice and in welfare services. Indeed there are in the United States and in Europe scattered instances of thrillingly imaginative programs for "adding life to years." Unfortunately, the schools of social work and churches have lagged behind other professions in providing specialized professional personnel but there are indications that they are becoming interested and are catching up.

The aged are not a functional sub-group of society. Every study points out the differences to be found among older people —in capacity and interests, in rate of aging, in attitudes toward aging, and also differences in the patterns demanded of aging people by society. Thus it is evident that a study of aging involves not only steps in the aging process but also structural changes in society. Since our social structure has been evolved by people for meeting the needs of people, it is only reasonable to

assume that with changing population composition and a changing life span new structural patterns and changes in institutional
functions must result. Some may argue that the change of social
attitudes must anticipate structural changes. Others may argue
that social attitudes are developed only through functioning and
not as a prelude to it. Gerontologists will be concerned for some
time with priorities. For example, Nimkoff describes changing
family relationships in which the aged have fewer familial
pleasures and responsibilities, but Kirpatrick questions whether
society may not exert influence upon the family to change both
its attitudes and its patterns to increase family participation by
older people.

Since the responsibilities for social change to meet the needs
of a doubled average life span will rest largely on the shoulders
of younger people, gerontology should be of especial concern to
the present college generation. "Gerontology is for the young,"
said one of the oldest and most experienced gerontologists at a
recent meeting, "it is only by beginning when young to study
gerontology that one can profit by its wisdom."

This book will serve as a convenient compendium for the
initiated and as an orientation for the novice.

BELLE BOONE BEARD, PH.D.
*Professor of Sociology*
*Sweet Briar College*
*Sweet Briar, Virginia*

# CONTENTS

# GERONTOLOGY
## A Book of Readings

# Chapter 1

## DEVELOPMENT OF GERONTOLOGY

### SOCIAL GERONTOLOGY
### A NEW APPROACH TO UNDERSTANDING AGING*

CLARK TIBBITTS

T HE FIELD of social gerontology is finally emerging from more than three thousand years of recorded effort to extend the length of life and to enhance the circumstances of living in the later years. Two interests are said to have long dominated a good deal of human thought and striving: (1) the desire to change lead into gold and (2) to discover an elixir of youth. Many today insist that if we could achieve these two results we should rather promptly resolve all of the serious problems of aging.

### FORERUNNERS OF INTEREST

Evidence of efforts among primitive peoples to prolong life and preserve vigor in old age is found in magic and rituals, in reserving special foods for the old, in feeding breast milk and the blood of slain gladiators to the elderly, in various devices for warming old bodies, and in lightening the tasks assigned to the older members of the group. Later on, as empirical medicine developed, the range of medical and surgical treatments was extended, and scientific speculation began as to the nature and causes of aging and natural death.

In the psychologic area, some of the ancients made reasonably astute observations regarding the characteristics, potentialities, and limitations of older persons and undertook to describe the good life in retirement. Simmons has brought together observations made by anthropologists, travelers, and missionaries on seventy-one preliterate peoples and has shown that they were well aware of the presence and special needs of older persons. He has identified five

---

*Reprinted by courtesy of *Geriatrics*, Volume *15*, October, 1960. Presented at the Eleventh Annual Conference on Aging, University of Michigan, June 23, 1958. Revised.

universal desires: (1) to prolong life, (2) to conserve energy through rest and release from work, (3) to remain active participants in social life, (4) to safeguard such prerogatives as property, authority, and prestige, and (5) eventually, to depart life honorably and with a good prospect for a new existence in the hereafter. Stable, agrarian economies seem to have been well adapted to making use of the assets and residual capacities of the middle-aged and the aged with the result that the relatively few who survived into these years were accommodated without much difficulty, and, often, with real advantage of the community, at least as long as they could be functional.

Interest in aging has come rapidly to the fore within the present generation and has provided an increasingly favorable climate for research, if not, indeed, and insistence upon it. Pollak has suggested that the principal underlying factors have been the greater visibility of the aged due to their increasing numbers and to their growing detachment from the household and the work force, our value system with its stress on individual well-being, and the progress of research itself. Certainly, the advances of science and technology leading to a rapid increase in the numbers of older persons and their accumulation in urban industrial areas; the accelerated growth in average life expectancy; and, at least relatively, earlier completion of traditional adult roles without provision of adequate substitutes have greatly altered the proportion of older people and their position in society and served to focus attention upon them. A good many studies of social and economic aspects of aging were made during the twenties, thirties, and early forties but these were almost entirely in the nature of inventories, surveys, and strictly empirical researches designed to aid in the immediate solution of practical problems. No doubt they did serve, however, to call attention to the need for more basic, systematic, verifiable knowledge.

## THE RISE OF GERONTOLOGY

### Biologic Research

Beyond the largely speculative, theoretic formulations regarding the causes of biologic aging, MacNider has pointed out that the first real "contributions (to scientific knowledge) came about not primarily as previously planned studies on aging, but as the life of plants and animals was in the process of investigation, . . . factors of change with age insinuated themselves for detailed consideration. They forced the investigator to take an excursion into one of the many bypaths which develop during research and which if their significance is realized may lead to plateaus affording broad vision of problems that await solution of greater worthwhileness than the meticulous problem which prompted the original ininvestigation." At any rate, aging, as a generalized phenomenon or as a frame of reference for biologic research, is of recent origin. Thus, Lansing states that "Disciplined analysis . . . of the phenomena involved in the process of growing old, of the differences that exist between the young and the old, and the mechanisms associated with natural death, began with the opening of the Twentieth Century."

The advance has been most rapid since the late thirties when those biologic scientists who were interested in time-related changes in living cells, tissues, and physiologic mechanisms gave impetus to the development of a gerontologic science through the formation of mutual interest groups. In 1939, "a group of British scientists and professors of various branches of medicine decided to form an international Club for Research on Aging and, as a start, to establish the British Branch." Korenchevsky was dispatched to the United States later that year to inspire the formation of a similar club in the colonies. The publication of Cowdry's *Problems of Ageing* in 1939 foretold that Korenchevsky was destined to find fertile ground among the biologists in the United States, and, indeed, later that year, the American Research Club on Aging was organized under the aegis of the Josiah Macy, Jr., Foundation. The founding of the Gerontological Society, Incorporated, in 1945 and the increasing availability of funds have further stimulated research among those interested in the biologics of aging. It should be pointed out, however, that the biologists consider their progress to date as minimal and that they see much to be done before a firm body of systematized knowledge is established. Notwithstanding the gaps and limitations of current knowledge, a growing body of verified facts is emerging from which sooner or later an integrated system of biologic gerontology will be forged.

## Psychologic Aspects

The evolution in the area of psychologic research appears to have been much the same. Thus, Oscar Kaplan states that although "Interest in the psychological aspects of aging goes back at least several thousand years; . . . it is only with the last decades that comparative studies of adult age groups have put such interest on a scientific basis. Young human adults have been exhaustively scrutinized since the very inception of psychological science, but older individuals have failed to arouse curiosity on an equal scale." Older adults even now are much less readily available as subjects to the psychologist.

"A few scattered papers on later maturity appeared during the first thirty years of the present century, and in 1923 G. Stanley Hall published a book on senescence which was intended as a companion volume to an earlier work on adolescence.

The Stanford Later Maturity Research Project, a study which was conducted by Miles and his associates in the early thirties, was the first systematic attempt to investigate the subject." Miles summarized the results of his research and of other psychologic studies in Cowdry's first edition, but it was not until 1946 that the American Psychological Association set up a Division of Later Maturity and Old Age.

Like the biologic approach to gerontologic phenomena, the psychologic studies have been sporadic and have largely lacked a theoretic frame of reference. Most of the data, until very recently, were developed incidentally to investigations of other than age-related aspects of behavior. The only theoretic conceptualization has been found in the field of developmental psychology.

The application of this frame of reference to aging is, in part, a natural consequence of the fact that early populations studied in institutes of child welfare, for example, have matured, thus leading to an extension of these studies into the area of adult life. There are enough studies available now, however, to begin to formulate a behavioral science of aging.

## The Social Sciences

The social science pattern is similar to the others but has come even later. In the lead article in the first issue of the *Journal of*

*Gerontology* in 1946, Frank enumerated a large number of problems for social science and social action. Yet he was unable to report the existence of any significant amount of social science research or of any attempt to outline or organize the field, as he indicated the biologists had done. A year before Frank's article appeared, Simmons published his monumental work on *The Role of the Aged in Primitive Society* and thus provided a basis for evaluating the effects on the aged of the transition from an agricultural to an industrial culture. At about the same time, the Social Science Research Council had a committee drawing up a Research Planning Report on *Social Adjustment in Old Age.* In the report, which appeared in 1948, Pollak said that emerging sociologic interest in old age seemed to have had its origins in growing research interest in personality and interpersonal relations and in the developmental or case study approach which was beginning to carry over into later maturity and old age as additional stages of life. A comprehensive bibliography, prepared for the same report, listed a handful of research studies on the performance of older workers, on the age factor in mental illness, and on adjustment to aging, primarily among institutionalized populations.

From this time forward, however, social science research has begun to catch up. The University of Chicago began to direct more of its students toward research on aging, and Cavan and associates were developing instruments for measuring personal adjustment in old age. In 1950, eight sections of the first National Conference on Aging were devoted to social, economic, and related aspects of aging. In 1952, membership in the Gerontological Society was differentiated through the creation of a Division of Psychology and Social Science. And, in 1956, the Inter-University Training Institute in Social Gerontology was drawn up and given support.

## THE NATURE OF AGING

### Aging as a Process

The term aging is frequently used to imply the end result of a series of changes and often to suggest that individuals at particular ages or stages of life are homogeneous in their essential characteristics. While it is useful for some purposes to note the mean or modal characteristics and variations of those who have reached particular chronologic ages, gerontologic research is pointing increasingly to the conclusion that this approach is of limited value in arriving at an understanding of the true nature of aging.

Instead, it is becoming apparent that aging must be regarded as a *process* extending over the entire period from young adulthood onward, differentially manifested according to individual and social characteristics and situations which are relatively independent of chronologic age except as a limiting factor. Studies in all areas show that most aspects of aging may best be described in terms of a series of gradients, and this appears to be as true in the areas of role and personality changes as it is in biologic aging. Clearly, it is an error to regard the second half of life, or any part of it, as a unitary period and to fail to recognize the great variations among individuals. It should be noted, too, that studies of aging as a series of gradual alterations growing out of a complex of underlying processes and changing circumstances would seem to open the door to discovery of the factors which influence change and, hence, to the exercise of significant amounts of control.

## Aging as Development

There is another consideration which seems to have cogency at this point—namely, whether aging should be regarded entirely in terms of senescence or whether, in certain respects at least, there are not also clear positive or growth phenomena associated with it. Biologic gerontology has almost universally defined aging in the former terms. Lansing for example, says aging is "a process of unfavorable, progressive change, usually correlated with the passage of time, becoming apparent after maturity, and terminating invariably in death of the individual."

Psychosocial data suggest the presence of growth factors. Thus, Warthin postulated that cerebral functions have not completed their possibilities of development at the beginning of biologic senescence and that mental and spiritual evolution may continue in an ascending curve for twenty or more years while the biologic organism is weakening.

Linden has noted ". . . widespread tendency among people to regard progress through life as an uphill development from infancy to some vague plateau or prime called middle life, followed by a general decline." But he goes on to say that "This point of view fails to take account of the fact that different qualities and faculties of the human organism have different rates of achieving prime, and that—throughout most of life's course—for every faculty that has reached zenith of achievement there is another that has yet to reach its highest developmental goal.

"A generalized, indiscriminate decline is not a tenable notion," he continues, "for the reason that an individual's intellectual, emotional, and behavioral growth consists of countless separate trends, each having its own particular rate of development and its role in human action."

Psychologic studies support this view, for it has been found that some capacities maintain their efficiency or may even improve parallel in time to decrement in the biologic organism.

Subsequent controlled studies have shown that some aspects of intellectual functions may gradually increase until very old age. Thus, Miles states that while psychophysiologic capacities may show decrements with age, such traits as interpretation and imagination unrestricted by speed may decline very little over the life span. Wechsler urges that attention be given to the concept of sagacity and to the study of performance in adult roles. More recently, Peck suggested that "The ability to interpret perceptions farsightedly, foresee complex consequences, and make wise decisions . . . may require more lived-through experience than the years of youth permit." And Dennis has found very little decline in the productivity of creative workers between the ages of thirty and seventy, a point confirmed but not emphasized by Lehman in his classic studies. None of this is to say, of course, that decline does not come eventually, though certainly there are individuals who continue at high functional levels until death.

In the area of personality role, the case for continuous development may be even more clear. Situational changes, such as increases in free time resulting from tapering off or completion of parental and work roles, may lead to the establishment of new and more socially oriented goals and to expansion of interests. Interestingly, Valaoras reflects this point of view when he says that a population with "a sizable proportion of the persons surviving beyond their sixty-fifth birthday preserves mental and physical abilities which add immeasurably to the intellectual and material wealth of the community."

The social-psychologic person is a good deal more than a biologic and physiologic organism. Current research is pointing toward an approach to the biologic and sociopsychologic aspects of aging as more or less separable and distinguishable processes. Regardless of the nature of aging in the individual organism, most of the psychologic and sociologic processes must be viewed as possessing relatively independent characteristics within the limiting boundary of psychologic senility. Here it must be emphasized that, just as functional senility can occur independently of biologic senility, so social and psychologic growth may occur concurrently with biologic decline.

At any rate, it is clear that there is room for a good deal of sociopsychologic research on the actual nature of change during the later stages of the life cycle, with particular attention being given to the interrelation of different aspects of the aging process as a whole.

## The Onset of Aging

Aging is a part of the lifelong processes of development, change, and involution. All of these processes are known to occur simultaneously with respect to a single individual and at different rates within and among individuals. With respect to differing cultural definitions and societal interpretations, the relationship between the processes of the aging individual and the social definition of the aging person may vary considerably. These two analytically distinct but empirically interdependent processes of aging are, thus, differentially interrelated within societies, cultures, and subcultures—and even among various socio-economic and occupational strata. The delineation of the onset of aging represents an attempt to broadly characterize this range of individual and social gradients without in any way ignoring the problem of precise specification. Thus, identification of any particular point at which both individual and social aging may be said to begin is somewhat of an arbitrary matter. There is, however, an increasing tendency to depart from the earlier custom of focusing on the period beyond age sixty-five and to recognize early middle age as the turning point of maturity.

Considerable evidence apart from the obvious cosmetic changes supports this view. By the end of the fourth decade of life, there has been marked energy decline with increasing awareness of the need to depend upon mental activity as the source of ego rewards. Curves of the prevalence of chronic disease and impairment show inflection points during the fifth decade. Awareness of time appears to develop and of the fact that life does have length after all. Many people seem to feel during the 40s that they have reached a plateau in their careers. Parental roles are completed between forty-five and fifty-five years of age, when the majority of children have married and left home. Generally, at this time, there is a recognition that goals set in early adulthood are being completed and that it is time to find new ones.

The effective onset of both individual and social aging may thus be said to occur generally in early middle life. The changes which occur may well be as definitive as those which have occurred in the earlier years and which will occur later. Moreover, understanding of old age is dependent upon knowledge of what has transpired during the preceding decades of life. Some are now identifying three periods of later life: middle age, later maturity, and old age.

## THE AREAS OF SOCIAL GERONTOLOGY

Social gerontology may be said at the outset to have two major constellations of phenomena or foci of interest. One revolves around the changes which take place in the physiopsychologic capacities and performance of the individual as an organism and in the changes in his personality, which occur as a consequence not only of the changes in his basic capacities but also in response to the action of the culture and society upon him. This focus, then, represents the study of the individual in his behavioral aspects from the point of view of the psychologic and related sciences in which the specific characteristics and adjustments of the organism and the person are of central concern.

The other aspect of social gerontology is concerned with the manner in which the environment, including the society and the culture, acts upon older people and with how aging and aged people affect the system of group relationships within society, and, in turn, the organizational structure and the culture itself. The focus here is on the behavior of the individual as a social being, on the action of older people as aggregates, and on the action of the group both with reference to older people and in response to the needs which older people have and to their efforts to obtain these needs. This is the societal aspect and concerns all the social sciences, including anthropology, economics, political science, social psychology, and sociology.

It is obvious that the division between the individual and the societal aspects of the field is often essentially one of focus, for, as in any field of human behavior, the elements involved are mutually interacting and interdependent. To suggest one example, modern society's proclivity for chronologic age typing, responsibility for which is shared by older people, becomes part of the environment to which the older person is forced to adjust. And, his efforts at adjustment may, in turn, result in changes in the system of social relationships in the society. Thus, the individual is adjusting to an environment which he has helped to create and which he is also helping to modify, and it is essential to consider both aspects if the process is to be understood. Nevertheless, the analytic categorization of phenomena which has been suggested appears to be necessary if we are to achieve a systematic organization of the field.

## Aging and the Individual

In this area, social gerontology is accumulating knowledge concerning several broad types of phenomena. One set of problems has been identified with reference to changes in activity and speed, in perceptive and intellective abilities, and in the structure and physiology of the organism upon which they are presumably based. Another set of research problems is concerned with changes in motivation and performance in relation to such matters as learning, memory, efficiency, ability to integrate and organize experience, work, and retention of skills. A third area is building up around such matters as the development of criteria of adjustment to aging, assessment of reactions to illness and stress and to changes in the life situations, the development of abnormal behavior, and the discovery of procedures for off-setting unfavorable reactions. There is increasing recognition of the significance of environmental factors, of the socio-cultural background of the individual, and of previous modes of adjustment. There is interest not only in characteristics and performance at particular ages and stages in the life cycle but also in the processes involved in reaching successive levels.

A major research problem arises, of course, out of the interplay of the several factors in aging and out of multiple causes. For example, age changes in learning appear to be functions, in part, of organization of incoming material and of the strength of basic drives which may vary at different stages of life. The individual's concept of himself changes as he experiences declining energy and also when he is retired from work. Attitudes toward retirement may be conditioned by health status, range of alternative interests, values toward work, amount of income credit stored up, and many other considerations. Thus, the behavioral aspects of aging are seen as a complex of influences and processes involving biologic, psychologic, and sociocultural factors.

## Societal Aspects of Aging

The study of aging as a societal phenomenon is concerned, as indicated earlier: (1) with the role of the environment, including society and the culture in determining the position of older people; (2) with the changing roles and the interactive behavior of older people and other elements of the society in which they live; and (3) with the influences which older people exert on the system of social relationships and organizations of society and on the culture. The point of view is that the number, proportion, position, and so on of older people in any population are outgrowths, in considerable part, of the culture and of societal action and that, in the process of aging, adults' reactions to changes in

themselves and to society's expectations influence the societal
framework. The procedure in the present section will be to identify several categories of problems upon which research is needed,
most of which are arising out of the efforts of older people and of
other elements of society to adjust to the larger numbers of older
persons in a changing environment. A similar approach could be
employed with reference to the study of aging in any society. Studies
of aging in present-day civilizations are enormously complicated,
however, because of the rapid technologic and social changes, which
are largely responsible for the increase in the number of older people and greatly influence their position in society and necessitate
numerous adjustments on the part of society itself.

**Environmental Factors.** Individual and group behavior are
determined not only by the capacities and predispositions of the
individuals within a society but also, and probably to a greater
extent, by the environment which the society affords. The environment may be thought of as including the physical habitat; the tools,
machines, and other man-made surroundings which comprise what
is often called the material culture; the accumulated knowledge,
values, prescribed norms, and patterned ways of behavior developed
to meet life situations; and the society which serves as the agent in
transmitting the culture and in enforcing its requirements. Although man creates his culture and continues to modify it through
his participation in society, the culture, in turn, molds man. While
we are perhaps more accustomed to thinking in this context with
reference to the development and personality formation of children, the principle has equal applicability in determining the adaptations which adults make to their changing capacities and situations. Thus, one area of social gerontology is clearly that of discovering the factors in the total environment which define the
position and roles and influence the behavior of older people.

One of these factors is that of the role of the culture and society
in defining age itself. American society has developed fairly clear-
cut expectations on the basis of age. In primitive societies, role as-
signments appear to have been rather closely related to observed
changes in the individual, such as declining energy and accumulation of experience and knowledge and to the activities essential to

group survival. In our society, certain role expectations have been formalized in terms of chronologic age and sometimes appear to bear little relationship to the needs and capacities of individuals. This, together with the high value our society places on the qualities of youth, may well be powerful influences in determining the position of older people and their reactions to the process of aging.

The values which a society places on the right of older people to health and general well-being and the projected wishes or foresight of the younger generations will help to determine the share of national and personal income spent for research on aging; for provision of health facilities and services, housing, and other special requirements of older persons; and the amount of current expenditures we are willing to forego in order to provide adequate income in retirement. The long-time trend toward greater involvement of society in promoting individual welfare is certainly an important element in the environment of older people. At the same time, various developments in aging are influencing this trend, as will be discussed later, but how far and how rapidly they will go is at present unknown. Additional knowledge of the matters would be of great help to all who are responsible for major policies and programs with reference to older people.

The place of work in our culture is one of the major features in the environment of older people. Its value is determined by the need to survive, by consumption levels and aspirations, and by the values assigned to leisure. In the past, the availability of economic activity has been an important factor in both personal and societal adjustment to aging. In modern times, the phenomenal advance of industrialization and increasing expectation of life are adding many hours of free time to the lives of middle-aged people and freeing the majority of older persons from work altogether. Leisure is coming to be seen in a new light, as it offers both opportunity for and requires people to seek new roles in adulthood. Values and habits developed with reference to work in earlier periods have been abstracted, to some extent, from work itself. However, the persistence of these values and habits beyond the requirements of the economy for lifelong participation in the work force and the delay in offering alternative roles and in providing adequate income for retired people are creating some of the most serious of all of the personal and social problems of aging.

These are illustrations of the manner in which society, culture, and the environment act upon older adults. It should be pointed out, however, that the values and ideals which are generally characteristic of a particular culture may vary a good deal among groups within a population and hence call for subcultural studies.

*Social Interaction.* The concept of society also includes the area of social interaction—the system and processes through which individuals expresses their needs, through which society states and enforces its expectations, and through which balance or equilibrium is sought in harmonizing the interests of all elements within a population. It has been suggested by Simmons that such harmony appears to have been pretty well achieved in pre-industrial societies. It is perfectly clear, however, that, in a society characterized by rapid change, the system of patterned relationships is upset at many points and that new relationships and adjustments are required. The potentialities for research in this area will be illustrated with a few examples.

One area in which more knowledge is needed is that of how mature adults respond to the system of grading age, particularly when it carries implications of declining capacities; results in loss of status, as in retirement from work; and implies a sharp reduction in the need for income. There is considerable evidence of individual protest, though perhaps not much is on an organized basis. In this connection, Havighurst has recently developed an interesting hypothesis. Noting, first, that grading of an adult's age is related to performance; second, that certain capacities, particularly those in the psychologic area, do not decline as early or as rapidly as those in the physiologic area; and, third, that most older people are not, and not likely to be in the future, in the work force, he suggests that performance in work roles may lose much of its significance as a basis for grading age. His hypothesis is that, as society centers more attention on leisure, capacity for performance in nonwork roles may assume importance is social definitions of aging. This hypothesis certainly deserves to be tested.

Another area develops around the question of response to non-economic or free time roles, which take on new significance as society focuses more attention on leisure. What forms of activity and social participation are open to retired parents and retired workers? Will society offer sufficient ego rewards for roles in voluntary service, citizenship activity, self-development, pursuit of arts and crafts, and recreational use of leisure to make them attractive to older adults? Will they serve as bases for setting new goals in middle age? Will older people enjoy greater or less opportunity to serve in broader capacities as advisers and counselors to the community? Will they exhibit tendencies toward preservation of traditional values and modes of behavior in the face of the demands for change by the rising generations?

Somewhat related to this are the matters of how rapidly new concepts of aging and knowledge about the interests and potentialities of older people, about the rising productivity of the economy and its implications for work and free time, and about the significance of the changing nature of the family will be recognized by all members of society, including older people, and, particularly. social planners, legislators, and others who occupy key positions in making decisions.

A new question of pressing importance is whether or not older people wish separate facilities, such as geriatric clinics, retirement housing, and activity centers. To what extent do such facilities represent efforts to achieve efficiency and economy? To what extent are they supported or opposed by professional persons on the basis of their presumed relationship to cultural values? What are the effects of various types of facilities reflected in motivation, amount and kind of participation, and physical and mental health? To some extent, this is a part of a larger ecologic question of how older people distribute themselves throughout the community with particular reference to the availability of facilities and services.

***Aging and Social Organization.*** A third societal aspect of social gerontology is the impact of the aging population on the organizations and institutions of society. Members of all societies develop patterned ways of behaving and structural relationships in order to serve their common purposes. When these become long and universally established, they are called social institutions. Sociologists do not agree on the number of institutions there are, but most lists include family, state, economic organization, religion, education, and recreation. The purposes of institutions are carried out through countless formal and informal groupings, associations, and organizations, such as individual families; clubs; governments and government agencies; fraternal organizations; educational, recreational, and financial agencies; and many others, all of which are interrelated within a vast ideational and structural arrangement.

It is obvious that the increasing number of older people with new styles of living in a changing society will continue to have considerable impact on the social structure. Institutional patterns become deeply imbedded in the culture and change very slowly. Organizations, in contrast, are somewhat easier to create, modify, and disband. This is another area in which there is much room for research, as a few examples will reveal.

Storing up income credits for retirement in a wage-salary economy has become one of the principal concerns of the aging field. Members of agrarian and small shop economies, few of whom retired, were able to rely upon income derived from owning the means of production and upon support from the family, but these are minor sources of income today. For a number of years, a gradual shift has been underway from individual and family to community responsibility for providing retirement income. This change is raising numerous questions which social gerontology still have to consider.

Government functions have expanded widely as the population has increased, as society and the economy have become more complex, and as household functions have declined. In the field of aging, government at one or more levels has become involved not only in income maintenance but also in research and in the support of research, in helping to finance the cost of medical and rehabilitation facilities and housing, in payments for medical care, in employment services, in adult education, in recreation, and, most recently, in over-all planning. Questions have arisen concerning the optimum level of government for the performance of certain functions in relation to effectiveness and flexibility with regard to differentials in regional and local situations, financial support, and opportunity for citizenship participation; with regard to division of responsibility between statutory and voluntary agencies; and with regard to the most effective type of organization within any particular governmental structure.

Voluntary associations and agencies are being affected in similar ways, and similar questions are appearing along with others. Men's and women's service organizations, labor unions, and religious organizations are seeking ways to make their members conscious of the opportunities offered by free time and of the need to prepare for living in the later years and are also assisting in the development of programs for other groups.

What are effective technics for accomplishing these objectives? At least four new organizations have come into existence or have been greatly expanded as a consequence of society's concern for older people: namely, the club for older people, the multipurpose activity center, the commercial nursing home, and the interdisciplinary institute of gerontology within universities. All of them require special study and evaluation with reference to the effectiveness of the purposes they are trying to serve.

## SOCIAL GERONTOLOGY AS A SCIENTIFIC FIELD

Social gerontology may be seen as a striving to establish a body of verified propositions and systematic hypotheses with reference to the aging processes in the individual following early adulthood, to the societal factors in aging, and to the adaptations of society to older people. It represents a cross-sectional approach to the study of those aspects which the individual, the group, and the culture have with reference to aging. It is seen as a general scientific field, synthesizing approaches and knowledge and borrowing methods from an array of disciplines, including anthropology, biology, economics, political science, psychology, and sociology. Its unique attributes reside in its acceptance of aging as a reference point and in its effort to organize data within this framework. The forthcoming *Handbook of Social Gerontology* represents a major effort to systematize and organize existing scientific knowledge in the field.

Social gerontology is not necessarily concerned with aging as a problem. It has become important because aging is a problem, and it is as concerned with the problematic aspects of aging as it is with the natural aspects. The development of knowledge and principles with regard to any or all aspects of aging will have almost immediate practical usefulness. In the field of aging, the demand for scientific knowledge has preceded its availability, as has been indicated several times in the preceding sections. Most current planning and policy making has perforce proceeded on the basis of hypotheses or of attitudes, values, and patterns carried over from the preindustrial period. Thus, it may be assumed that there will be immediate effort to translate new knowledge into action as rapidly as it becomes available, and the field of applied social gerontology will be defined close upon the heels of social gerontology itself.

## A WORLD VIEW OF GERONTOLOGY*

### ROBERT J. HAVIGHURST

Gerontology as a special branch of science is very young, though it has roots which reach far back into the history of medicine. I do not propose to go into the past but rather to examine the present status and the prospects of gerontology in the United States and other countries.

A product of the efflorescence of science in the twentieth century, modern gerontology stated in this country about twenty years ago, when a small group of physicians, biologists, and sociologists formed the Club for the Study of Aging. Similar groups were forming in Europe, and soon an International Association of Gerontology was organized. This association has held four international meetings, and a Pan-American Congress of Gerontology met in Mexico City in 1956.

Gerontology is both an applied and a pure science. As an applied science it utilizes our knowledge of aging to make life longer and more satisfying. As a pure science it seeks knowledge about the aging of animals and men, both individually and in population aggregates.

*Reprinted by courtesy of *Journal of Gerontology*, Supplement No. 1, Volume *13*:2-5, October 31, 1957 as a Supplement to the April, 1958 issue, Volume *13*, No. 2.

The pure science of gerontology has been carried on wherever scientists have had time enough and resources enough to follow their own curiosity without having to solve some pressing practical problem. Thus we have had studies of the physiology, anatomy, and biochemistry of aging cells; of longevity in relation to diet; of the learning abilities of rats and of men in relation to their age; of changes of attitudes with age; and of the aging of human populations. In general, the pure-science aspects of gerontology have been produced by scientists of Europe and North America.

Work in applied gerontology is more widespread than work in pure gerontology. Applied gerontology appears wherever there is a problem that involves aging. Some of it is hardly science at all but is merely the application of common sense and human sympathy to problems of aging. The field of applied gerontology can conveniently be divided into two parts: medical and social. Each of these parts has three aspects, or stages of development. (We are seeking to look at gerontology in its broad features, without any attempt at historical balance, and consequently we shall not attempt to trace these stages of development in detail.)

Medical gerontology includes: (1) treatment of the elderly patient, (2) prevention of disease and disability in the elderly, and (3) preservation of vigor in the elderly. Social gerontology considers: (1) financial support of the elderly, (2) housing and living arrangements of the elderly, and (3) ego-support of the elderly.

## MEDICAL GERONTOLOGY

The first stage of medical gerontology, treatment of the elderly patient, is as old as the profession of medicine, but some of the twentieth-century developments make this as much a growing edge of science as are the later stages. Antibiotics have so reduced mortality that the chances of recovery from pneumonia and certain other infectious diseases have been multiplied many fold. Furthermore, the attitude of the medical profession toward surgery for aged patients has changed drastically. A patient of eighty or even ninety years is now regarded as a good risk for surgery, provided his general physical condition can be built up through diet and rest. No doubt most of us will live to see further major advances, such as a cure for cancer.

The second stage of medical gerontology, prevention of disease and disability, is essentially a twentieth century product. The early detection and treatment of cancer is its greatest triumph. Perhaps coronary heart disease and hypertension will be conquered in our lifetime. The multiple screening programs of some of the great clinics have demonstrated that lives can be saved on a broad scale by systematic screening of groups of people in late middle age. Another important development in this area is the application of physical medicine to the rehabilitation of persons who have suffered strokes and fractures.

The latest stage is the *positive* approach to physical aging, the attempt to help people preserve their full adult vigor as long as possible. The means used will probably be diet, supplemented perhaps by hormone and vitamin therapy. It is here that the medical scientists will make their greatest contribution to the basic aim of gerontology—to add life to the years.

Development of medical gerontology in the second and the third stages is discussed by Dr. Halbert L. Dunn, chief of the National Office of Vital Statistics, United States Public Health Service, who uses the concept of "positive health" to describe the attempt of society to help people achieve "high-level wellness." He says that this must be a joint project of medical and social gerontology.

## SOCIAL GERONTOLOGY

Social gerontology is much younger than medical gerontology. The only trace of social gerontology before the present century is found in the old people's homes which were established in Europe as a work of charity several centuries ago. The need for social gerontology arises when the traditional family breaks down and ceases to perform its function of caring for all the members of the family from the cradle to the grave. The transition from the traditional to the modern family was in full swing in the cities of Europe and the United States during the Nineteenth Century. By the end of that period it was clear that one of the major social problems resulting from this transition was the loss of economic and moral functions by the elderly members of the family.

The beginning of the first stage of social gerontology, financial support of the elderly, may be set around the year 1900, when various countries worked out old-age pension schemes. A growing population of older people was needing support because urbanization, industrialization, and family change had robbed them of their traditional means of livelihood. Society consequently devised schemes of pensions and old-age assistance, which have been extended to cover more and more older people in more and more countries. This is still a frontier sector of gerontology, as various countries experiment with, and adapt, their old-age insurance and pension programs to changing practices in retirement and to inflationary economic trends. Thus the first stage of social gerontology involved recognition of economic needs of older people and attempts to meet these needs.

The financial need was no sooner met than another need became evident, and with this came the second stage of social gerontology—consideration of the need by many elderly people for comfortable housing and living arrangements. With families and houses growing smaller, and with intrafamily attitudes changing, fewer and fewer old people could live with their children. Since many old people in the cities were not home owners, they were at a disadvantage in the competition for houses of their own and generally had to put up with the marginal housing, the least desirable. A variety of public and private housing schemes came into existence to help solve this problem, and a considerable body of expert knowledge has grown out of the experience with old people's homes, homes for infirm older people, public housing for couples and individuals, and private housing for people who can pay for good quarters. This sector of social gerontology is perhaps the most interesting today, with its variety of experiments involving architects, social workers, recreation experts, and nursing experts, as well as economists and real-estate specialists.

When these two needs for older people are reasonably well met, society discovers that there is still an unmet need, deeper and more baffling than the material needs. It is the need to be needed—the need to have a function in society, to have a respected place in the eyes of others, and to be doing something which is interesting and significant in one's own eyes. This *need for ego-support* is the province of the third stage of social gerontology.

Only a few societies have reached this third stage of social gerontology, though there are far-seeing, sensitive individuals in all societies who have discerned the need. It has been defined by the leading social gerontologists in Sweden, the country which has the keenest sense of society's responsibility for the individual and of the individual's responsibility for society. In a talk at a United Nations Conference in 1955, A. Helge Dahlström, director of the Swedish Social Welfare Office, described in one paragraph these three stages or tasks of social gerontology:

> Our basis for the measures for the aged is the conception that old people should be given the possibility to live a free and independent life to the same extent and with the same social amenities as the other age groups in society. To realize these aims it is at first necessary that old people should have financial security. . . . Furthermore and in the second place the old people must have access to good and appropriate dwellings and a social service which creates the possibilities for them to live in their own homes as long as possible. There also are to be measures which will help to make their lives pleasant and which break through the isolation from the outside world which so very easily becomes the lot of old people.

At this third stage of social gerontology it is recognized that helping old people to meet their material needs is not enough. They also need companionship, a sense of being wanted and needed by other people, and pleasant and interesting things to do in their many free hours. This is not a sentimental illusion of middle-aged people who project their own need for activity into the later years; it is a fact reported in many studies of people in their sixties and seventies. To meet these needs, a variety of devices have been developed, the most important being clubs or informal social groups of one kind or another. The activities of these senior citizens' organizations vary, from a simple monthly social meeting in a church hall or the community room of a neighborhood center, to a complex program including vacation bus tours, classes in landscape-painting, discussion groups on foreign and domestic social problems, handicraft shops, money-earning projects, and theater and concert parties.

In the development of this type of program, various kinds of organizations have been active: church groups in Holland and the United States; trade unions in Sweden; women's organizations in England and Holland; cooperative societies in Switzerland; municipal old people's welfare committees in England; organizations of senior citizens or older people in the United States, France, Holland, and Sweden; and social-welfare organizations in Germany, the United States, England, France, Sweden, and Denmark.

## SOCIAL GERONTOLOGY AND SOCIAL CHANGE

It is evident that the second and the third stages of medical gerontology are most highly developed in countries which are most urbanized and most industrialized and which have the largest proportions of older people.

This generalization applies also to social gerontology, which is most advanced in such countries as Sweden and England, and is hardly developed at all in the agricultural countries. Countries in transition toward urbanization and industrialization show the beginnings of social gerontology. For instance, when the Pan-American Congress on Gerontology met in Mexico City, a number of Mexicans presented papers in the social-gerontology field, all dealing either with Mexico's developing old-age-pension program or with old people's homes, while the papers by Americans and Canadians tended to deal with stage three of social gerontology but also to include developments at stages one and two. In Mexico, 3.5 per cent of the population is over sixty-five years of age, and the country is just beginning to become urbanized and industrialized. In Canada and the United States, over 8 per cent of the people are over sixty-five, and these countries are well into a phase of urbanization and industrialization.

Social gerontology does not exist at all, and is really not needed, in the nonindustrial, agricultural countries, with three-fifths of the world's population. It is just making its appearance in such countries as Mexico, Brazil, Russia, and South Africa, which have one-fifth of the world population. It is quite well developed and moving into the third stage in the industrial and urban countries with relatively large proportions of older people. These countries embrace another fifth of the world population.

## POPULATION FACTS AND SOCIAL GERONTOLOGY

The present and the probable future development of social gerontology and also of medical gerontology are closely related to the proportions of older people in the population and to the trends of these proportions. Figure 1 shows the trends in the proportions of people aged sixty-five and over in a number of typical countries during the past 50-100 years. These countries can be grouped as follows:

A. High proportion of older people, with rapid increases in the past one hundred years; population substantially industrial and urban: France, Great Britain, Sweden.
B. Slow increase of older population in the past one hundred years, reaching a moderately high present level; population slowly growing more urban-industrial: Germany, Switzerland.
C. Increasing proportion of older people in the past fifty years, which will reach the level of countries in Group A in the next twenty years; population rapidly growing more urban and industrial: Australia, Canada, United States.
D. Slow increase of older population in the past one hundred years, reaching a medium present level; population growing slowly more urban: Denmark, Holland, Italy, Portugal.
E. Low proportion of older people, with slow increase for the next twenty years; population mainly rural at present but growing slowly more urban-industrial: Brazil, India, Mexico.
F. Medium proportion of older people, with slight change in past fifty years; population growing slowly more urban-industrial, with high out-migration: Japan.

Social gerontology is most fully developed in the countries of Groups A, B, C, and D, with about one-fifth of the world's population. Social gerontology is less developed in the countries of Group E, which contain another fifth of the world's population. It does not exist at all, and is not relevant to the situation, in the agricultural, nonurban and nonindustrial countries which are often called "underdeveloped."

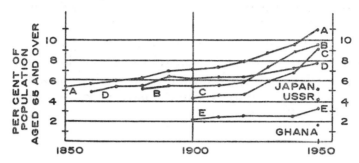

Fig. 1. Per cent of population aged sixty-five and over from 1850 to 1950 in typical countries of the world. Group A includes France, Great Britain, and Sweden: Group B, Germany and Switzerland; Group C, Australia, Canada, and United States; Group D, Denmark, Holland, Italy, and Portugal; Group E, Brazil, India, and Mexico.

As exceptions to the trend, certain of the countries of Groups A, B, and D have not pushed social gerontology much beyond its first stage. These exceptions are France, Italy, Portugal, and Switzerland. When compared with the other European countries, these are seen to be more rural and more Catholic, and to have stronger family institutions of the traditional kind which provide housing and ego-support for their elderly members. Even within these countries, as within mainly agricultural countries such as Brazil and Mexico and Russia, work is going on in social gerontology in the cities and industrial centers, as in Paris, Zurich, Rome, Milan, Mexico City, São Paulo, and Moscow.

## THE FUTURE OF GERONTOLOGY

From these considerations it is possible to predict the course of gerontology with assurance for the next twenty years, and with a fair probability for fifty years. The frontier developments, both in medical and in social gerontology, will occur in those countries which are most prosperous, most urban-industrial, and which have the largest proportions of older people. At the same time there will be a slow development of both second and third stages of medical and social gerontology in such countries as Brazil, India, and Mexico. In the remaining three-fifths of the world, which is essentially agricultural and nonindustrial, little gerontological activity will appear before the beginning of the twenty-first century.

The countries with the least activity in gerontology will, nevertheless, be adding years to human life during the remainder of this century; while the countries with the most activity in gerontology will be adding life to the years.

## TRAINING IN SOCIAL GERONTOLOGY*

### Wilma Donahue

At the 1955 annual meeting of the Gerontological Society, Inc., the Section on Psychology and Social Sciences appointed an ad hoc research committee to explore a means for more clearly defining the role of the social sciences in gerontology. The committee met and agreed that the most compelling need was for university instruction in the psychosocial aspects of aging. All three members— Dr. James Birren, Dr. Clark Tibbitts, Dr. Wilma Dohahue—had been impressed with the paucity of college courses in the field of aging revealed by Dr. Dale Harris' survey in 1947, with the increasingly insistent demands for personnel trained in both the scientific and the applied fields of social gerontology, and with the growing number of individuals seeking opportunities for training. The crucial question seemed to be that of how to augment the number of college and university teachers equipped to train others in the psychologic, social science, and applied aspects of aging in order that they, in turn, might insure through their own teaching an adequate supply of persons to fill the mushrooming requirements of the field. The problem was referred to the Research Committee of the Gerontological Society itself with the request that a subcommittee be established to devise a plan for dealing with this pressing situation. The committee was appointed and included, in

*Reprinted by courtesy of *Geriatrics,* Volume *15,* November, 1960.

addition to the original three members Robert W. Kleemeier, Ewald W. Busse, M.D., John E. Anderson, and Ernest W. Burgess.

The destiny of social gerontology was undoubtedly cast when these first steps were taken in the long chain of events which were to lead eventually not only to the Inter-University Training Institute in Social Gerontology but also to the development of other types of programs aimed at increasing the number of persons trained to teach and to serve in the burgeoning field. Examples of these subsequent efforts include the two training seminars held in June, 1956, as a part of the University of Michigan's Ninth Annual Conference on Aging, the special Ph.D. training programs with specialization in aging at Washington University in St. Louis and the University of Chicago, which admitted their first trainees in September, 1958, and a six-day conference at Aspen, Colorado, in the fall of 1958 on the preparation of social workers for work with the aging sponsored by the Council on Social Work Education.

The second phase of the development of the Inter-University project got underway when Dr. Robert Kleemeier was asked to convene a group under the auspices of the newly appointed research subcommittee to develop a specific plan for a training program. The National Institute of Mental Health made a grant in support of the working conference, and the University of Florida served as the fiscal agent. The meeting was convened in Palm Beach, Florida, July 26 to 31, 1956. A full report of the deliberations and recommendations of the distinguished group of conferees has already been published in full; thus, only the following summary of the major recommendations of the group is required here:

(1) that a training institute in social gerontology be established to further the training of social scientists in the field of aging in order to help increase the number of educators prepared to offer instruction and direct research in social gerontology.

(2) that the training institute be organized on a cooperative inter-university basis involving the widest possible geographic spread of educational institutions, thus bringing to all parts of the country gerontologically trained teaching personnel and insuring that the effort is national in scope and impact.

(3) that the University of Michigan be the coordinating agency for the project and that Dr. Wilma Dohahue be its director.

(4) that the program of the institute include:

a. the preparation and publication of systematic technical summaries of existing scientific knowledge in the psychological, social, economic, and political aspects of aging.

b. that special surveys of problems and preparation of materials related to the introduction of gerontology into the curriculum and the support of graduate students and of research be undertaken.

c. that an intensive four-week training institute be offered to selected college faculty members interested in preparing to teach gerontology in their respective universities and colleges.

## THE INTER-UNIVERSITY TRAINING INSTITUTE IN SOCIAL GERONTOLOGY

The third phase of the Inter-University project began when grants were made January 1, 1957 to the University of Michigan in support from the National Institute of Mental Health and the National Heart Institute. At that time 16 universities—California, Chicago, Connecticut, Cornell, Duke, Florida, Illinois, Iowa, Michigan, Minnesota, Pennsylvania State, Pittsburgh, Purdue, Syracuse, Washington (St. Louis), and Wisconsin were invited to become sponsors of the project. Subsequently members of an Inter-University Council* were named, and an Executive Committee* was selected to represent the Council.

Definitive plans for the Inter-University Training Institute in Social Gerontology whose central headquarters were established at the University of Michigan were evolved at the meeting of the Council and Executive Committee held in Ann Arbor, April 17 to 19, 1957. The primary purposes of the Institute were (1) to shape

---

*J. E. Anderson, (Minn.), H. W. Braun, (Pittsburgh), J. H. Britton, (Penn. State), M. E. Bunch, (Wash. at St. Louis), F F. Fauri, (Mich.), R. W. Fleming, (Ill.), E. A. Friedmann, (Wisc.), H. C. Hunsaker, (Purdue), H. E. Jones, (Calif.), D. P. Kent, (Conn.), R. G. Kuhlen, (Syracuse), L. Saville, (Duke), G. F. Streib, (Cornell).

*J. E. Anderson, J. E. Birren, E. W. Burgess, E. W. Busse, M.D., W. W. Morris, Bernice L. Neugarten, C. Tibbitts, I. Webber, R. C. Wilcock, Wilma Donahue, chairman.

the scientific field of social gerontology through the collection and systematization of existing scientific knowledge in the psychologic and social aspects of aging; (2) to disseminate this knowledge through publication and through the training of social science faculty in colleges, universities, and professional schools; and (3) to increase the number of social scientists trained to teach, carry on research, and offer service in the field of social gerontology.

## PROGRAMS OF THE INSTITUTE

To fulfill its purposes, a series of related programs were undertaken in three broad categories:

(1). Those devoted to the preparation and publication of systematic technical summaries of existing scientific knowledge in the psychologic and social aspects of aging.

(2). Those relating to the problems involved in introducing and establishing social gerontology as a part of the university curriculum.

(3). Those directed to the training of university and college faculty prepared to offer instruction in the field, and to increasing interest in and promoting the development of opportunities for research in social gerontology.

All three of these categories are seen as integrally related to the basic problem of determining the nature and content of social gerontology and of meeting the need for personnel trained to teach and direct research in the field.

## INSTRUCTIONAL MATERIALS

The development of the field of social gerontology as a proper area of education and research required that existing scientific knowledge be gathered and organized to provide a comprehensive reference work on the subject which, in turn, would furnish a basis for instruction. Accordingly, preparation of the following three volumes was undertaken under the editorships of three outstanding gerontologists.†

*Handbook of Aging and the Individual: Psychological and Biological Aspects of Aging* systematizes the biologic and psycho-

---

†Two of these volumes have been published by the University of Chicago Press. The remaining one will be available in the fall of 1960.

logic factors related to the aging of the individual. Its editor is Dr. James Birren. The material of the book is organized in four sections: the theoretical and empirical foundations of gerontology, the biologic bases of the behavioral aspects of aging, aging and environmental settings, and psychologic characteristics of aging individuals. There are twenty-four chapters in the book, each of which has been prepared by an outstanding biological or behavioral scientist.

*Aging and Society: Handbook of Social Gerontology*—deals with the social phenomena of aging as manifested through the impact of cultural and societal determinants of aging and their interrelationships on the individual, and through the impact of older people on the cultural, social, and institutional organization of society. The nineteen chapters are organized under three headings: the basis and theory of societal aging, the impact of aging on individual activities and social roles, and aging and the reorganization of society. Dr. Clark Tibbitts is editor of the volume, and distinguished scholars in the social sciences have contributed the various chapters.

The third book—*Aging in Western Culture: A survey of Social Gerontology*—offers a comparative interpretation of the impact of aging and the methods employed to promote the welfare of older people in various countries of Western Europe and the United Kingdom. Much of the data and information were gathered at first hand by the individual authors of the ten chapters of the book. Dr. Ernest Burgess is editor of the volume.

## AIDS OF ACADEMIC DEVELOPMENT OF SOCIAL GERONTOLOGY

The second program of the Inter-University Training Institute was concerned with surveying the current status of university instruction in social gerontology and identifying the major sources of support for training and research in the field. The program also included the preparation of a series of course syllabi and annotated bibliographies in the several aspects of social gerontology.

*The survey of university instruction in social gerontology* was prepared under the chairmanship of Richard C. Wilcock and a committee made up from members of the Inter-University Council and with the assistance of Harold L. Orbach, assistant director of the project. A summary of the data collected in the winter of 1957-58 indicates that, although there is undoubtedly growing interest in providing training for graduate students in the field of gerontology, course offerings are still very limited.

Out of 312 institutions returning the survey questionnaires, only fifty were offering credit courses or seminars in some area of social gerontology; many of these courses had been initiated only within the prior year or year and a half. Departments or schools offering credit courses were distributed as follows:

| | |
|---|---|
| 17 sociology | 4 public health |
| 18 psychology | 2 nursing |
| 4 social work | 2 medicine |
| 5 education | 2 home economics |
| 5 economics | 1 psychiatry |

Thirteen other institutions reported that they were planning credit courses or seminars in one or more areas of social gerontology. Research in social gerontology appeared to be receiving somewhat more attention than instruction. Seventy-two institutions out of the 312 reporting listed a total 184 research and thesis studies under way or currently planned in social gerontology.

Noncredit extension courses, workshops, and conferences on some aspects of social gerontology were being offered at forty-one institutions.

Considering credit courses, research, and noncredit offerings together, there was a total of eighty-seven institutions at the time of the survey where some activity in social gerontology was being carried out.

The survey will be repeated in the spring of 1960 and a comparison of these findings with those obtained in the earlier survey will be made in order to determine what, if any, change has occurred to the amount of instruction and in the fields offering such training.

*The survey of government and foundation support* for social gerontology was planned by a committee of the Inter-University Council under the chairmanship of Dr. Woodrow W. Morris. Since the results of this study have already been published, there is no need to report the findings here beyond making a comment on the almost total lack of fellowships and traineeships in social gerontology. With the exception of those being provided by the National Institutes of Health, only one organization was supporting a fellowship at the time of the survey. Funds for research were in somewhat larger supply, but such funds without the supplementation of traineeships or fellowships are not likely to result in the training of large numbers of students.

*Preparation of five course syllabi in social gerontology* was carried out under the editorship of Dr. Irving Webber with the assistance of a committee of Inter-University Council members. In the editor's foreword to the syllabi, Dr. Webber says that preparation of the syllabi and annotated bibliography "was undertaken in order to meet the need for teaching materials in social gerontology . . . the introduction of courses into the curricula of colleges and universities has been hampered . . . by the paucity of textbooks and of study guides except those of a rather general character." The syllabi were prepared to aid in filling this void in instructional materials. They are intended for use only as possible foundations of materials and aids in the several fields covered and not as final and definitive course outlines.

The syllabi have been published and are being distributed by the Institute in Social Gerontology, University of Michigan. Syllabi and annotated bibliographies are listed below.

| Title | Authors |
|---|---|
| I. The Economics of An Aging Population | Walter H. Franke |
| | Richard C. Wilcock |
| II. The Psychology of Aging and the Aged | Raymond Kuhlen |
| | Woodrow W. Morris |
| III. The Sociology of Aging and the Aged | Irving L. Webber |
| | Gordon Streib |
| IV. Social Welfare and the Aged | Gordon J. Aldridge |
| | Fedele F. Fauri |
| V. An Interdisciplinary Course in Social Gerontology | Bernice L. Neugarten |
| | Robert J. Havighurst |
| | Claire F. Ryder |

## SUMMER INSTITUTES IN SOCIAL GERONTOLOGY

The foregoing programs were part of the over-all preparation for the Council's basic objective of training faculty for the teaching of social gerontology. To this end, two summer institutes in social gerontology were held which offered a month's intensive training to established university and college faculty members in the psychologic and social sciences and allied professional fields.

The first summer institute was held under the auspices of the University of Connecticut at Storrs, August 3 to 29, 1958; the second one was sponsored by the University of California at Berkeley, August 3 to 28, 1959. Members for the two Institutes were chosen from among the applicants who responded to the announcement by the Inter-University Council of the availability of training fellowships. The fellowships provided travel, living expenses, and a $500 stipend.

That interest is current among teaching faculties in various social sciences and related fields as evidenced by the fact that each year there were 130 fellowship applicants. (Approximately 100 other applications and requests were received each year after the deadline for consideration.) These applicants represented from ten to fifteen fields (Table 1). The largest number of applications were made by sociologists, and the selection committee of the Inter-University Council nominated to fellowship a total of 39.5 per cent (or 30 persons) from this field. Psychologists constituted another 25 per cent (or 19 persons) and the remaining third (or 27 persons) were scattered over twelve other fields. Thus, although the group was inter-disciplinary in composition, it was heavily weighted in favor of psychology and sociology.

TABLE 1
DISTRIBUTION BY PROFESSIONAL FIELD

| Field | Number of Applicants | | Number of Nominees | |
|---|---|---|---|---|
| | 1958 | 1959 | 1958 | 1959 |
| Sociology | 50 | 38 | 15 | 15 |
| Psychology | 29 | 15 | 10 | 9 |
| Education | 13 | 5 | 1 | 0 |
| Economics | 11 | 9 | 3 | 4 |
| Social work | 10 | 21 | 2 | 4 |
| Political science | 5 | 1 | 3 | 1 |
| Social science | 4 | 0 | 0 | 0 |
| Nursing | 3 | 3 | 0 | 1 |
| Anthropology | 1 | 0 | 1 | 0 |
| Medicine | 1 | 3 | 0 | 2 |
| Psychiatry | 1 | 0 | 1 | 0 |
| Pharmacy | 1 | 0 | 0 | 0 |
| Home economics | 1 | 6 | 0 | 3 |
| Public health | 0 | 1 | 0 | 1 |
| Total | 130 | 130 | 36 | 40 |

## The Fellows

The seventy-six nominees (36 in 1958 and 40 in 1959) selected represented thirty-six states and the Commonwealth of Puerto Rico, and came from 64 different educational institutions. Academic rank of the nominees is shown in Table 2. The interest of well-established faculty personnel (21 fellows were heads of departments or deans of schools) indicates a probability that instruction in aging will have a favorable climate in which to develop if one can assume administrative involvement as a factor in gaining acceptance of new teaching fields and courses.

TABLE 2
DISTRIBUTION BY ACADEMIC RANK

| Rank | Number of Applicants 1958 | 1959 | Number of Nominees 1958 | 1959 | Total |
|---|---|---|---|---|---|
| Professor | 38 | 20 | 19 | 9 | 28 |
| Associate professor | 29 | 27 | 12 | 14 | 26 |
| Assistant professor | 28 | 51 | 4 | 13 | 17 |
| Instructor | 20 | 14 | 1 | 3 | 4 |
| Other title | 15 | 18 | 0 | 1 | 1 |
| Total | 130 | 130 | 36 | 40 | 76 |

Approximately 60 per cent of the fellows were under age forty (Table 3). In 1959, the Selection Committee gave special consideration to the selection of younger applicants in the belief that fewer young faculty men would have already made life-long commitments to other fields.

TABLE 3
OTHER CHARACTERISTICS OF APPLICANT AND NOMINEE GROUPS

| Item | Nominees 1958 | 1959 | Applicants 1958 | 1959 |
|---|---|---|---|---|
|  | (N = 130) | (N = 130) | (N = 36) | (N = 40) |
| Number of states represented | 39 | 40 | 25 | 27[1] |
| Age range | 28-61 | 21-61 | 27-55 | 27-59 |
| Number 40 yrs. of age or under | 65 | 70 | 20 | 27 |
| Sex—number of males | 109 | 72 | 36 | 32 |

[1]Puerto Rico was also represented.

A number of the applicants had already done some work—research, teaching, or both—in gerontology; but of those selected for fellowships, only six in 1958 and seven in 1959 had offered any instruction in the field prior to making application to the Summer Institute. Almost without exception, the future aims of the applicants and nominees included teaching courses in gerontology at the graduate level and carrying on research in aging and/or directing the research of degree candidates specializing in aging.

## The Summer Institute Curriculum

The development of a curriculum for the Summer Institutes in Social Gerontology was necessarily a pioneering effort since the Institutes were a unique endeavor. In general, it was decided that the curriculum should be so organized as to provide a rich exposure to contemporary scientific thinking in social gerontology and first-hand acquaintanceship with leading investigators in the field. Further it was planned to apply the scientific data to the practical problem of aging through discussion, project development, and field trips. For the first Institute (1958) it was assumed that no special emphasis need be given to the planning of specific programs of research and training for use at a later time. Experience, however, showed this to be an unwarranted assumption; and, at the suggestion of the 1958 fellows, special research seminars and project committees were included in the 1959 Institute.

Two basic seminars constituted the major part of the Institute curriculum. One, *Behavioral Aspects of Aging,* encompassed the biologic, psychologic and psychiatric aspects of the aging process and their impact on the aging individual: the nature of physical aging and physical health in the aged; the character of sensory, perceptual, and psychomotor changes with age; learning, memory, and intellectual and motivational processes; age changes in personality, interests, attitudes, and social adjustment; and mental health, mental disorders, and the psychiatric treatment and care of the aged. The other seminar, *Social Gerontology,* offered a systematic presentation of the field covering the demographic, health, and cultural factors in aging: the changing position, roles, and social adjustment of individuals in the later states of the life cycle, including family and associational relationships; the impact of aging on the social, economic, and political structure of society; and societal measures to promote and support the health and well-being of the older population and of society.

Following are the topical outlines of the two seminars indicating the organization of the material.

## SEMINAR ON BEHAVIORAL ASPECTS OF AGING

**Orientation**

Introduction to Behavioral Aspects of Aging

**Physiology and General Biology of Aging**

Physical Aging
Physiological Aging
Health and Activity Levels
Aging in the Central Nervous System

**Psychology of Aging**

Sensory and Perceptual Changes
Psychomotor Performance and Work Output
Learning and Memory
Intellectual Changes
Creativity
Interests and Activities
Emotions, Motivation, Attitudes, and Values
Personality Changes with Age

**Mental Disorders and Psychiatric Changes with Age**

Reactions to Illness and Disability
Neurotic Patterns of Adjustment
Psychosomatic Disorders
Psychosis Related to Age
Psychiatric Care

**Training in Behavioral Gerontology and Applied Fields**

General Curricula and Special Courses

## SEMINAR IN SOCIAL GERONTOLOGY

**Orientation**

Introduction to Social Gerontology
Background of Aging as a Social Phenomenon

Cultural Factors in Aging

## Sociology of Aging: Social Psychologic Aspects
Roles and Status of the Aging
Work Roles and Retirement
Leisure Roles
Roles of Older People in Associations

## Sociology of Aging: Aging and Social Structure
The Changing Population Structure
Evolving Family Relationships
Impact on Organizations and Institutions
Role Choice and Aging

## Aging and the Economic Structure
Aging and the Labor Force
Economic Status and Sources of Income
Programs for Financial Security

## Aging and the Political Structure
Impact on Government and Political Behavior

## Programs of Social Action for an Aging Population
Health Facilities and Services
Housing the Elderly
Developing Organizations and Services

## Training in Social Gerontology and Applied Fields
General Curricula and Special Courses

The Behavioral Aspects Seminar was organized by Professors Ewald W. Busse and John E. Anderson in 1958, and by Professors Busse, Robert W. Kleemeier, and Harold E. Jones in 1959. The Social Gerontology seminar was directed by Dr. Clark Tibbitts and Professors Bernice Neugarten and Ernest Burgess in 1958, and by Dr. Tibbitts and Professors Robert J. Havighurst and Burgess in 1959. Other special lecturers included some of the country's most distinguished scientists. The two *Handbooks on the Survey of*

*Western Cultures* were available in draft form and constituted the basic reference works for the seminar.

One may ask, how did the fellows respond to the obviously rigorous academic fare. Many said that it was a stimulating, informative, intellectual experience. Many said they enjoyed the rare privilege of working in a truly interdisciplinary situation, and that, as a result, they had achieved a new and comprehensive view of the field of gerontology. Several indicated that they had achieved a firm commitment to gerontology as a life work. All agreed the Handbook materials were of incalcuable and enduring value as reference works. All expressed a strong sense of participation in a unique and historic undertaking and predicted that the full impact of the Summer Institutes on the field of Social Gerontology could not be measured for several years since the seeds planted would take a number of years to fully mature. It is the considered opinion of the Institute faculty and of the Inter-University Council that the seventy-five fellows trained in the Summer Institutes represent the initial cadre of instructors in the new field of social gerontology and that, because of their strategic locations in every region of the country, they will constitute nuclei from which further development of the field will emanate.

The experience gained from the two training institutes, the clear emergence of social gerontology as a scientific field of study which the Inter-University Institute has helped bring about, the increasing requirements for trained teaching and research personnel in gerontology, and the pressing demands for practitioners for the aged suggest the direction and nature of further training efforts. First, the number of requests from qualified social science and professional faculty for short-term, intensive training in the field makes obvious the need for additional training institutes similar to those already held. Second is the need for the development of regional institutes at universities having well-established research and training centers where post-doctoral students may enroll for training in some specialized aspects of the field. Finally, there is need for gerontologic fellowships which will encourage the entry of young doctoral students and professional workers in the field and which will become a realistic goal only with the expansion of research opportunities.

The growth of social gerontology as a new area of scientific endeavor carries with it the need for an assessment of research frontiers and a coordinated program of research training to supplement the programs of instructional training as the next major step in the development of the field. The need for such research training programs has been the most consistent response from the fellows of the Summer Institute to the question of the character of future training programs.

## RECOMMENDED CURRICULA IN SOCIAL GERONTOLOGY*

### Marvin R. Koller

Among the stimulating experiences provided by the second Summer Institute in Social Gerontology held in 1959 under the auspices of the Inter-University Council in Social Gerontology at the University of California, Berkeley, was the opportunity for a committee of fourteen Institute fellows to develop a recommended curriculum for training in social gerontology. This paper summarizes the discussions of the committee.

### RESOURCES NOW AVAILABLE

A few university and interuniversity programs for training in gerontology have already been organized, and many more will ensue in the next few years. At this time, however, while instructional materials and scientific data are accumulating, the general picture of gerontologic instruction is one of a small number of colleges and universities offering courses in some phase of the subject according to individual interest in this instruction. Out of an approximate 2,500 higher educational units in 1957, about fifty had a total of seventy-two courses. Thirteen additional schools reported plans to offer courses in social gerontology in the near future. Over the past five years, twenty-nine masters and nineteen doctorates were reported to have concentrated upon gerontologic problems.

A scarcity of university teachers in this field has led to two sum-

---

*Reprinted by courtesy of *Geriatrics*, Volume *17*, April, 1962.

mer training institutes in social gerontology and to the publication of three reference handbooks in various phases of social gerontology and to a series of instructional syllabi in the areas of psychology, sociology, economics, social welfare, and an interdisciplinary approach. The latter was published by the Division of Gerontology, University of Michigan, Ann Arbor.

While there is a need for more teachers in social gerontology, there is also need for the best students possible to avail themselves of current offerings for study in this field. Colloquies, seminars, and projects with a gerontologic content lend themselves well to programs offered on numerous American campuses. The complex nature of aging, with all its ramifications, offers a real challenge to the best minds being trained in our universities and colleges.

## OBSTACLES HINDERING PROFESSIONAL TRAINING

The members of the committee concurred that one of the major obstacles to the development of professional training in aging is the firm entrenchment of specialists devoted to particular disciplines. A strong reluctance to depart from an established field to identify with the new and growing interest in social gerontology was noted. It seems paradoxic to talk in terms of "youth" when one deals with the field of "aging," but it appears that the very youthfulness of social gerontology attracts only a few of the more hardy souls. Comparatively few seek the role of pioneer or leader, and many prefer to take a "wait and see" attitude.

A second real obstacle to the development of gerontologic courses or curricula within universities is the attitude which many hold that the further proliferation of courses can only harm the academic scene. An inventory of what courses are serving their purposes and what courses may be omitted with profit is needed if we are to make room for new programs in keeping with the changing society. Educators must be willing both to remove and to add courses. If proliferation of courses continues after this process, it only reflects the growing needs of our complicated society. Social gerontology may be one of the areas to be added.

The committee noted the time demands made upon both students and professors when new curricula offerings appear. The recommendations made by the group were therefore not intended to place more time requirements upon students and faculty but rather to suggest alternative courses.

An additional obstacle was noted in the manner in which new curricula is administered. The committee preferred to keep within academic departments or within established schools. The creation of an interdisciplinary committee to supervise gerontologic courses was considered a possibility, but it was recognized that this demanded greater skill and coordination than was possible in many universities. It was recognized, of course, that some universities had successfully carried on such programs and that this particular obstacle would present no hazard to them.

## GENERALIST VERSUS SPECIALIST

The one issue that stood out in the discussions was the question of fostering curricula leading to a generalist in gerontology or to a specialist who remains within his field but with a strong interest in gerontology as it applies to his work.

The committee described the future prototype of gerontologist as a person who has achieved his PhD., or even his M.A., in gerontology. Such a person does not now really exist, but the serious question remained as to what he would be doing if he did and what his occupational pursuits would be. Such a gerontologist was described in the following manner:

1. He would have *breadth* of gerontologic knowledge but not necessarily *depth* in a given discipline. Accordingly, he would serve as a utility man and fit his services into an interdisciplinary team wherever and whenever a gap occurred.

2. He would keep in close touch with developments within the field of gerontology and bring these to the attention of operating or appropriate agencies.

3. He would conduct studies of older people and take into account resources available to them within a given area.

4. He would be in a position to identify specialized personnel for those agencies wanting particular services.

5. He would increase awareness to aging by means of talks, conferences, and other communication media.

6. He would serve as a resource person to advise in designing content, organization, and development of gerontologic courses and programs of training.

7. He would advise community leaders whose work would not permit them to probe deeply into gerontology but who would be in need of enough briefing to develop an over-all policy which would take aging into account.

8. He would serve as an administrator or assist in the administration of homes and other facilities for older people.

9. He would be of service in adult educational work with vocational and avocational training for older people.

10. He would be a counselor in "living" in one's later years.

11. He would be an asset to voluntary associations which include or planned to include aging within the scope of their organizations.

### Recommendations for the Generalist

If such a generalist is to be developed, the training should begin early in his academic experience and continue late into postgraduate years. While a broad exposure to substantive knowledge in many fields having some relevance to gerontology is needed as background preparation, courses within biology, anthropology, economics, sociology, health and physical education, psychology, social administration, and philosophy have particular value to the study of aging. These courses would be taken at the undergraduate level and would provide a comprehensive base from which the student would move to graduate study where core courses that would integrate scattered gerontologic data into a meaningful whole would be taken. These courses would preferably be divided into those which emphasized social aspects and those which concentrated upon the biologic and psychologic phases of aging. The generalist in gerontology should be thoroughly grounded in both aspects, although specialization in a specific discipline or field should be encouraged at the advanced graduate level.

It was recommended that some courses be offered which would be of value to professionals and other specialists who are past their academic training period and are currently employed in their respective fields. The graduate student would thus be informed of outcomes when application is made of knowledge gained in an academic setting. For the professionals themselves, the university experience would add to their fund of knowledge and provide an orientation for those who might serve as field supervisors or trainees.

The capstone of academic training of the student planning to become a generalist would be his research experience. While it is traditional for a degree candidate to work alone and to confine himself to an established scientific field, the interdisciplinary nature of social gerontology suggests that it might be acceptable and perhaps desirable to permit the candidate to select a thesis topic which crossed interdisciplinary lines.

## Recommendations for the Specialist

Because the specialist in social gerontology was seen as a more realistic result of training in aging than a generalist, the group considered in some detail the nature of specialized courses in sociology, psychology, political science, child development and family relations, and social work which would prepare individuals for specialization in aging within each field.

Within the disciplines of sociology and psychology, opportunities were seen for the development of Ph.D. programs, with a concentration in gerontology through both pure and applied research and a core series of courses and seminars. These would supplement a broadening of general offerings in various specialties to encompass gerontologic material and the establishment of a basic specialized course in aging at the advanced undergraduate level. Such courses would also serve as the nucleus for the development of interdisciplinary programs serving the other fields.

For example, a program in sociology might offer an introductory course in social gerontology or an advanced course at the undergraduate level in the sociology of aging. Such a course would not only be an appropriate companion course to sociology of childhood, which is a standard course in many departments, but would broaden the students' sociologic knowledge and orient the undergraduate toward specialization in social gerontology at the graduate level.

For this purpose, the course might be best geared to the senior year, when it might carry either undergraduate or graduate credit.

Departments of sociology would do well to scrutinize their current offerings to ascertain if appropriate emphasis is being given to aging. It would appear that courses in social problems; cultural anthropology; family; demography; community; rural, urban, and medical sociology; sociology for nurses; and educational and industrial sociology lend themselves to the inclusion of gerontologic subject matter.

Any graduate program in sociology that specializes in gerontology would assume an adequate base in undergraduate sociology as well as a broader foundation in biology, psychology, economics, political science, anthropology, mathematics, and statistics. Within the conventional set of undergraduate courses in sociology, specially recommended were social problems, family demography, social psychology, minority groups, medical sociology, and industrial sociology. These plus a graduate seminar or research course in gerontology and a thesis involving an investigation of a particular problem of aging would probably constitute the maximum of specialization possible at the master's level.

Within the Ph.D. program, the following courses or seminars might well be developed:

- The social psychology of aging, covering the influence of physical aging on personality, personality changes with age, social roles, and maladjustments of aging.
- The demography of aging, including trends in population composition, inter-relationship of demographic factors relating to aging, and the impact of demographic changes upon society.
- Aging in various cultures, consisting of a cross-cultural study of roles and statuses of the aged in different cultures and the social and cultural factors related thereto.
- Aging and the family, including historic study of familial roles of the aged, current roles and variations, conflicts and maladjustments, housing patterns related to family roles and composition.
- Aging and social institutions, including the impact of demographic changes upon economic, political, religious, and educational institutions and consequent adjustments in those institutions.

The Ph.D. program in psychology, with concentration in gerontology, would follow similar lines. Training would be in terms of the core concepts and research methods of psychology. There would be additional specialized training and experience in a particular area of psychology, such as clinical or social, with further concentration within the context of a special field in the area of aging.

The specialized courses particularly recommended would be a course in psychology of aging and in the biology of aging and a seminar on the social and economic aspects of aging. A practicum or internship experience with an older population for clinical, counseling, and industrial students would be recommended. The Ph.D. dissertation would be concerned with aging in one of the relevant psychologic areas.

In political science, this would take the form of offerings in governmental administration and basic elements of political behavior and power structure in the United States. The family relations and child development courses emphasizing family relations in the later years would be a logical extension of the emphasis on the life cycle study. In social work, a course on aging would be in effect a further development of the human growth sequences which are now a basic part of the curriculum. In all of these areas, emphasis would be on professional training for the problems facing the practitioner in gerontology. In addition, interdisciplinary research opportunities would be utilized for the development of needed research in those areas, with special emphasis on problems of policy development. The relation of the social work profession to the social security program is one such area.

## SUMMARY

The committee felt that, at this time, there are practical and conceptual obstacles to the development of courses to train Ph.D. candidates in gerontology, per se. The time and circumstances may yet come and, indeed, may already be present on certain campuses to devise doctoral programs to create a new professional called a gerontologist. The glimpse of the future that the group could see ahead was as follows:

1. A large corps of professors will remain who will prefer only a nodding acquaintance with gerontology and continue as before.

2. A second group of professors and administrators will introduce, add, and integrate gerontology into their current offerings.

3. A much smaller number will be willing to foster, create, and develop new courses that will give rise to an academic generalist in gerontology who can span, master, and contribute to the related materials culled from the widest range of source material.

*Chapter 2*

# THE SOCIOLOGY OF AGING
## SOME THEORETICAL APPROACHES TO THE SOCIOLOGY OF AGING*

### Raymond Payne

T HIS PAPER considers some sociological aspects of aging within contemporary society and is concerned most specifically with the process by which the aging male assumes and maintains (or fails to assume and maintain) appropriate statuses and roles in his social world.[1] The task is, then, one of theoretical formulation, however tentative the result must be.

Before proceeding, two asumptions must be stated.[2] First, a person, as a member of society, *must* progress during his life through a *series* of more or less sequentially compatible and harmonious social statuses. For example, a person must move, socially as well as physically, from the status of infanthood, through those of childhood, young-adulthood, maturity, into that of the aged, and, further, the society must provide the means by which a person not only learns what statuses he will be expected to assume, but it must also provide the motivations for the assumptions of those statuses by the person at the appropriate times and in the appropriate manner.

The second assumption which must be stated is that in a rapidly changing society such as ours, the role requirements of the status series are changing, not static, so that much, if not all, that is

---

*Reprinted by courtesy of *Social Forces*. Volume *38*:359–362, May, 1960. Paper Presented at the Southern Sociological Society meeting in Gatlinburg, Tennessee, April 18, 1959.
[1]The concepts *social status* and *social role* are applied here as they were conceived by Ralph Linton: *The Study of Man*. New York, D. Appleton-Century Company, 1936, pp. 113-131.
[2]Cf. Alfred R. Lindesmith and Anselm L. Strauss: *Social Psychology*. Rev. ed.: New York, The Dryden Press, 1956, p. 579 ff.

learned concerning a particular status *prior to the assumption of that status,* would be considered inappropriate when the person finally finds himself in the status. Thus, it must be recognized that not only must children learn how to be adults, but *adults must learn how to be adults.*

Therefore, an adequate theory of aging would be a dynamic theory, because it must take into account (1) changes in the individual as he moves from status to status within the social organization, and (2) changes in the social organization itself.

The present effort to outline an adequate dynamic sociological theory of aging is based upon empirical findings from several newer researches, including the author's study now in progress, and integrates some convergent theories of (1) socialization,[3] (2) prestige age groups,[4] (3) decisionmaking,[5] and (4) social roles.[6] The product, while perhaps not radically new, is certainly an extension of existing systems.

In this case application is made to the male situation only because it was supposed that the contrast between active and retired statuses of the male would be more clear-cut than changes in female statuses with aging, and would provide for greater ease at the beginning stages; work will continue, however, which will allow for hypotheses concerning the female and combined situations.

In this formulation the concept of socialization is central and basic. Socialization is here conceived in its basic essentials, i.e., as the process by which a person acquires as a member of society the understandings, attitudes, and skills with which and upon which to construct his behavior in the situations (statuses) in which he finds himself or expects to find himself. When thinking of the

---

[3]This formulation is based upon the concept of socialization as it was set forth by Bennett and Tumin over a decade ago. See, John W. Bennett and Melvin M. Tumin: *Social Life: Structure and Function.* New York, Alfred A. Knopf, 1948, pp. 50-52.

[4]Paul H. Landis: *Introductory Sociology.* New York, The Ronald Press Company, 1958, p. 324 ff.

[5]"Decision making" here refers to the process by which the individual mobilizes for action to satisfy his functional needs.

[6]For a statement of the function of roles in social structure, see, Ronald Freeman *et al.: Principles of Sociology.* Rev. ed.; New York, Henry Holt and Company. 1956, p. 204-214.

socializing individual (the *object* of the socialization process) it must be recognized that he is performing *two* activities: (1) he is reaching out, so to speak, and taking on new knowledge, information, understands, and the like; and (2) he is integrating the new material into his personality organization in the form of new or altered responses. Most materials so acquired (learned) come to the person in experience situations involving other people, either directly or indirectly, and such other people serve as the sources of the materials, whether so preceived by the person or not. These "others," to use Mead's term, in the learning situation of the infant or small child are typically the parents or parent surrogates, and are spoken of as the "agents of the child's socialization." [7]

Note that it was stated that integration of new material by the person is an *active* process, involving an expenditure of energy; therefore, it is necessary to speak of integration and re-integration as *achievements*, since they do not emerge automatically as some psychological theories might imply. Instead, before a person will proceed with his own process of integration (that is, either create new structures or amend existing ones) he must have become convinced of the relatively greater value of the new over the old material in relation to his own self-system and its situation, either current or in the hypothetical future. For help in this evaluating process (support, reinforcement, etc.) the small child must look *outward* almost entirely, asking the "other" to provide the bases for deciding to accept or reject the new material. However, as the child grows older he can provide some of his own value support, because he will have internalized "the other," as Mead has pointed out. The person then achieves—theoretically, at least—a condition in which he can make decisions involving value judgment without requiring specific or immediate reinforcement or support from outside himself.

The condition just described—functional self-containment or

[7]George Herbert Mead: *Mind, Self, and Society.* Chicago, The University of Chicago Press, 1934, Part III, "The Self," p. 135 ff. An excellent summary and interpretation of this portion of Mead's theory may be found in Francis E. Merrill and H. Wentworth Eldredge: *Society and Culture: An Introduction to Sociology.* Englewood Cliffs, New Jersey, Prentice-Hall, Inc., 1957, chap. 8, "Personality and the Group," p. 158 ff.

self-sufficiency in decision-making—would be the person's greatest departure from the socially dependent state; if his most dependent state (socio-psychologically speaking, and not necessarily physically) be that of infanthood, then at what point in the life cycle is he the fartherest from that state? Does he progress from the fully dependent stage, in which he cannot or does not trust his own decisions but must look to significant others for not only information but value support, also, through increasing degrees of independence, into the fully independent state at the last stage of the life cycle? Common observation would indicate otherwise in our society, and the author suspects that this is not true to the extent we have been led to believe even in those societies which honor their aged much more than we.

Can it be posited, then, that independence of decision making is the characteristic antithesis of infant socio-physical dependence? If so, then the question becomes: When *does* man typically reach the stage in which he will place relatively the greatest amount of confidence in his own—vis-a-vis others'—value judgment?

To investigate this and to develop and refine hypotheses for additional phases of the study, certain research steps have been taken. Central to the procedure has been the development of twenty-six case studies of men over seventy years of age, each of whom is not an invalid and has at least as much available money as social security payments would provide. These two criteria were applied so as to yield subjects who are neither physically nor financially dependent, and who have, therefore, some decision-making latitude.

One tentative conclusion from the first phase of the study is that each of our subjects has experienced, since retirement, a decreasing confidence in his own decision-making ability. This decrease was reflected not only (or even primarily, in some cases) in the direct statements of subjects, but in the following manner: each subject was asked to examine two folios of eight pictures each. Each spread included four males and four females, the individuals of each sex differing in no major respect except age, according to the unanimous agreement of fifteen sociologists and psychologists at the University of Georgia. There was one male and one female in each of the major age groups above childhood—teen-age, young adulthood, maturity, and the aged category. The subject was asked to select from each folio that person whom he considered best able to give him (the subject) the "best advice and the most help" in solving the kinds of problems, he, the subject, has to face these days; then he was asked to make a second choice from each folio.

Choices were predominately of the *mature males;* secondly of the mature females. Only rarely would a subject select one of his own age-mates, and *never* did a subject select a teen-ager or young adult, while adhering strictly to our instructions.

When asked why mature persons had been chosen, rather than others, the following comments were made:

> I chose him because he looks old enough to be in the know, but not too old to know what it's all about.
>
> I wouldn't go to any of those old foggies for help; they wouldn't know any more about what's going on than I do.
>
> That [mature] man is still working; still going to meetings; keeping in touch. These old men haven't been able to keep in touch.

Their selections, together with their supporting statements, indicated that the oldsters recognized that the more responsible, significant, and "knowing" social statuses are now occupied by *mature,* not aged persons, and that persons of the mature ages would be more capable of serving as sources of valuable information on the oldsters' problems than would be the oldsters, themselves. Also granted to the mature (rather than the aged) was the support or value reinforcement capacity.

This conclusion was supported by other parts of the case studies. For example, each subject was asked to document the process by which he had solved some of his own problems in the weeks or months immediately preceding the interviews. One question asked in reference to each problem was, "To whom did you go for information, advise, or support for your tentative decision?" Almost without exception, if someone other than the wife had been consulted, the consulted person had been in the *mature* age category, regardless of the nature of the problem and regardless of whether he had been consulted for information or for value support or decision reinforcement.

Next, we applied the picture selection to other age categories, with this general pattern of results: high school and college youngsters chose young adult and mature persons in about equal proportions, never choosing oldsters, and only rarely choosing members of their own age category. On the other hand, mature subjects chose mostly *mature* pictures, only rarely selecting young adults or aged persons, and *never* choosing teen-agers.

Thus, we found youngsters "looking up hill" toward persons whom they usually identified with older siblings or parents, their choices and comments reflecting a willingness to use these persons in preference to others as sources of information and value judgment. On the other hand, oldsters, while also "looking up hill," were looking upward along the age route they had *already* traveled; hence, *they* were looking *backward* to an age group from which they realized they had already departed. In the third place, mature persons were looking to their own age group members, and identifying with them as sources of information and value support. In terms of prestige age group theory it is possible to say, therefore, that our informants of all ages tended strongly to agree that a member of our society reaches maximum prestige levels during maturity, then loses prestige as he grows older. This is certainly not a new point emerging from our study, but the significance here lies in the facts that our oldsters recognize and can express this, and that they can admit that they would need to look to other than themselves or their age contemporaries for advice or support. Further, it would seem significant that the age category to which they would first turn is *that of their own children.*

Now, expressed in terms of socialization theory, youngsters accept as agents of socialization those persons who are older than themselves and who are presently occupying statuses they, themselves, expect eventually to occupy, and relatively soon. On the other hand, the oldsters were accepting as agents of their own socialization, either their own children or their children's surrogates. To do so represents a direct and complete role reversal, carrying with it no doubt the necessity of drastic revisions of self-concepts and definitions.[8] Throughout the infanthood, childhood, and young adulthood of the person's children, the parent (now our aged subject) has been the *agent* of his children's socialization. Recently, however, as the person had moved into the aged status, he had accepted the fact that his own child (or child's age mate) had become the agent of his (the oldster's) continuing socialization process.

The ease with which the infant or small child plays the dependent role inheres in his relative helplessness and lack of alternatives. The older child or young adult is motivated to continue in status because of eagerness to qualify for assumption of subsequent statuses, currently occupied by older sibling or parent. In contrast, certainly part of the difficulty with which the oldster accepts reversal of role inheres in the fact that to do so requires admission of *decreased* abilities and surrender of power and authority, as well as surrender of personal autonomy over achieved personality organization, as the admission that the specific other (the child) who was for so long his inferior-subordinate, has indeed become his superior. Further, the child accepts authority or superordination expecting it to be temporary, whereas the *oldster* can see nothing ahead but further submergence of his own will to that of others. There is also this point: the child has no reason to defend his own decision-making ability, that ability being largely untried and unneeded by society; the aged man has ample reason to be concerned about his, however; now having a lifetime of successful performance behind him, it is humbling and demoralizing to be forced outside one's self and outside even one's own age category for information and value-support necessary to making one's day-to-day life decisions.

## SUMMARY

This has been an attempt to approach the phenomenon of aging in contemporary society through theories of socialization,

---

[8]It is assumed that Lindesmith and Strauss were indicating this conclusion by their statement, "Personality is still in the making, even at advanced ages," although they did not develop their analysis to this point. See: Lindesmith and Strauss, *op. cit.*, p. 585.

decision making, prestige age groups, and social roles. Especially fruitful, it would appear, has been the application of the concept of *socialization* to later life stages, and the exploration of the significance of self-other role-reversal of socializing *agent* and *object* (parent and child) in terms of necessary revisions in the oldster's self-definitions, concepts, and evaluations of his status.

# A ROLE THEORY APPROACH TO ADJUSTMENT IN OLD AGE*

### BERNARD S. PHILLIPS

Aged populations must adjust to conditions that are not generally characteristic of other stages of the life cycle, namely, the increased probability of illness and impending death. To these conditions any society imposes additional ones with which the aged must come to terms. In our own society, and in many others, the changes experienced by the aged often include (1) retirement from full-time employment by men and relinquishment of household management by women, (2) withdrawal from active community and organizational leadership, (3) breaking up of marriage through the death of one's mate, (4) loss of an independent household, (5) loss of interest in distant goals and plans, (6) acceptance of dependence upon others for support or advice and management of funds, (7) acceptance of a subordinate position to adult offspring or to social workers, (8) taking up of membership in groups made up largely of old people, and (9) acceptance of planning in terms of immediate goals.[1]

Cavan and her associates maintain that these changes may be classified under two broad headings: the relinquishment of social relationships and roles typical of adulthood, and the acceptance of

*Reprinted by courtesy of *American Sociological Review*, Volume 22:212-217, April, 1957. Paper read at the annual meeting of the American Sociological Society, September, 1956.

[1]Ruth S. Cavin, Ernest W. Burgess, Robert Havighurst, and Herbert Goldhamer: *Personal Adjustment in Old Age,* Chicago, Science Research Associates, 1949, pp. 6-7.

social relationships and roles typical of the later years. This suggests the possible utility of a role theory framework for understanding the adjustment of the aged individual, an approach outlined by Cottrell.[2] The present study attempts to explore this possibility, giving particular attention to aspects of the relation between an individual's self-conceptions and his social roles. It is felt that adjustments may be best understood when these two categories are examined together.

Data are based on interviews with 500 respondents in the Kips Bay-Yorksville Health District of New York City and 468 respondents in Elmira, N. Y.[3] The Elmira field work was done between mid-1951 and early 1952, with respondents constituting a random sample of non-institutionalized individuals sixty years of age or older. The Kips Bay interviewing took place during late 1952 and early 1953. As in the case of the Elmira study, a probability sample of the non-institutionalized aged individuals sixty or over was drawn.[4]

Although the two interview schedules are not the same, a large proportion of the items are identical. The present study is based on the items common to the two studies. The purpose of utilizing samples in two areas is essentially one of replication, although the environments are not replicated. The premise is that factors affecting the adjustment of the aged in a very large city vary to some extent from those in a relatively small city. If a role theory frame-

---

[2]Leonard S. Cottrell, Jr., "The Adjustment of the Individual to his Age and Sex Roles," *American Sociological Review,* 7:617-620 October, 1942.

[3]The Elmira data were collected by the Department of Sociology and Anthropology, Cornell University, under the direction of John Dean and with the assistance of Milton Barron, Bernard Kunter, Gordon Streib, and Edward Suchman. The research was supported by grants from the Rockefeller and Lilly Foundations. The Kips Bay data resulted from a co-operative venture by the Department of Health of the City of New York, the Cornell University Medical College, the Cornell University Social Science Research Center, and the Russell Sage Foundation, and were secured under the direction of Bernard Kutner, David Fanshel, Thomas Langner, and Alice Togo.
[4]The sample design in the Kips Bay study involved an area sample that weighted the population in low-rental areas. City blocks were classified into three rental groups: $90 per month and over, $40-$89 per month, and $20-$39 per month. Approximately 10 per cent of the sample were drawn from the high-rental group, 30 per cent from the middle-rental group, and 60 per cent from the low-rental group.

work provides a useful tool for predicting adjustment in cities of varying size, then it is that much more generalizable.

Before defining adjustment, it is important to point out that no value judgment is intended. Adjustment to a given socio-cultural setting may or may not be a "desirable" goal for a given individual, depending largely on his own value premises.

Pollak defines adjustment as "the efforts of an individual to satisfy his personal needs as well as to live up to the expectations of others." [5] He goes on to state that "the well-adjusted person is able to satisfy his needs quickly and adequately as they arise; a poorly adjusted person is unable to satisfy certain of his needs." [6] Cavan and associates define maladjustment as "behavior which does not completely satisfy the individual and social needs of the person, even though it may reduce his drive tensions. . . . Maladjustments, because they represent partial satisfactions of the wishes and needs of the person and because certain of them become ingrained as habitual behavior, impede readjustment." [7]

The index of adjustment is, therefore, based on the degree to which there is a patterned lack of alignment between the needs of the individual and the rewards he obtains, i.e., the existence of a relatively durable state in which needs are not satisfied. This state may be indicated by the individual's degree of habitual involvement in the world of fantasy. Absentmindedness, daydreaming about the past, and thoughts of death are the three items constituting our operational definition of degree of adjustment. These items are referred to in the question, "How often do you find yourself doing the following things? Would you say often, occasionally, hardly at all?" They form a Guttman scale for both samples, and this scale may be dichotomized into "mal-adjusted" and "adjusted" categories. [8] This measure of adjustment was found to be related to

---

[5]Otto Pollak: *Social Adjustment in Old Age: A Research Planning Report,* New York, Social Science Research Council (Bull. 59), 1948, p. 8.
[6]*Ibid.,* p. 33.
[7]Cavan *et al: op cit.,* p. 15.
[8]The Coefficient of reproductibility is 91 per cent for the Kips Bay sample and 89.5 per cent for the Elmira sample. A response of "often" or "occasionally" on any of the items is scored +1. Those who scored +3 and +2 were combined to form the "maladjusted" category, with +1 and 0 forming the "adjusted" category. It should

———————————————————→

a number of items such as expressions of unhappiness and nervousness which would be expected to be related to it if it were a valid measure.[9]

It should be noted that the data utilized were not originally collected for the purpose of testing the utility of role theory for understanding adjustment. Consequently, there are limitations to the conceptual distinctions that can be made. We will utilize Rommetveit's definition of a social role as "a system of . . . social norms directed toward one and the same individual as member of a group or representative of a psychologically distinguishable category of individuals,"[10] with social norm defined as "a pressure for a pattern of behavior existing between two or more participants in a category of recurrent situations." Our basic premise is that behavior that conforms to these pressures is generally rewarded; to the extent that the pattern of reciprocal behavior is disturbed, the rewards are neither sent nor received. Since role changes may not only result in a temporary disturbance of rewards but also in a lasting reduction, definite consequences for adjustment may be expected.

Two of the four role changes to be considered are relatively easy to delimit. It is postulated that changes in role due to the death of one's spouse or to retirement tend to involve an overall reduction in the degree of reward associated with conforming behavior in the new as opposed to the previous roles.[11]

A third role change is indicated by a "yes" answer to the question, "Do you think people treat you differently because you are

---

[9]Bernard S. Phillips: "A Role Theory Approach to Predicting Adjustment of the Aged in Two Communities," Ph.D. dissertation, Cornell University, 1956, pp. 44-50.
[10]Ragnar Rommetveit: *Social Norms and Roles,* Minneapolis, University of Minnesota Press, 1955, p. 85.
[11]The statement is made in this form because there is no direct evidence for it in the data collected.

---

be noted that the items scale in different orders for the two samples. For Elmira, the order from highest to lowest marginal frequency of "maladjusted" responses is (1) absent-minded, (2) daydreaming, and (3) thoughts of death; the order for Kips Bay is (1) daydreaming. (2) thoughts of death, and (3) absent-minded. This difference in scaling order poses interesting and difficult questions about the factors in each community responsible for it but the problems will not be treated here. However, in spite of the difference, the fact that the same items scaled in both studies provides additional support for their unidimensionality.

older?" In this case, the role is not so circumscribed as in the previous ones but concerns the entire matrix of roles within which the individual behaves. Furthermore, it is indexed by directly examining the respondent's perception of role change.

The fourth role change is indexed by whether or not the individual has reached the age of seventy. Changes in chronological age are important for their direct and indirect effects on a multitude of roles. Although it is difficult to point to definite changes in role prescriptions, role expectations or role behavior accompanying, for example, a change from age sixty to age seventy, the fact is that the combined effects of this change on various roles make it significant for the present study. It is posited for this role change, as in the case of the previous three, that the overall reward associated with conformity to the changed role prescriptions tends to be reduced.

The final aspect of the theoretical framework has to do with the "self-image," which may be regarded as a complex of self-conceptions. One of these is self-conception of age and is measured in this study by the item, "How do you think of yourself as far as age goes—middle-aged, elderly, old, or what?" The "old" and "elderly" categories may be combined to include respondents who identify themselves as old, in distinction to those who identify themselves as middle-aged or young, or who have made no clearcut identification.[12]

Age identification is conceived as a relatively high-order generalization from various social roles as well as from relatively subtle ongoing physiological and psychological processes. Unfortunately, there are no data on these processes, and thus we are limited to considering the interrelations of the above-mentioned roles and age identification.

It is hypothesized that a self-conception as old is related to maladjustment. Because our society values youth over age, the indi-

---

[12]Twelve per cent of Elmira respondents and 2 per cent of Kips Bay respondents used euphemistic expressions to indicate their age rather than selecting one of the three structured categories. These individuals, who were not willing to commit themselves to a definite identification as old or elderly, were combined with the middle-aged category and other individuals who had not made a transition from a younger age identification.

vidual who identifies as old to a degree accepts a negative cultural evaluation of himself. In so doing, he deprives himself of many of the rewards accompanying the adult status, rewards which are associated not only with specific social roles but also with behavior outside of narrow role contexts.

We may now present evidence on the interrelations among the variables of adjustment, role change, and age identification. In the general model age identification is conceived of as an intervening variable between role changes and adjustment, i.e., a variable which specifies conditions under which role changes affect adjustment. The remainder of this paper presents data on (1) the relations between each role change variable and adjustment, (2) interrelations among the various role change variables, (3) the relation between role changes and age identification, (4) the relation between age identification and adjustment, and (5) combined effects of role changes and age identification on adjustment.

Table 1 reports data indicating the relationship to maladjustment of each of the four role changes. All differences in the proportion of maladjusted respondents among those who have and have not undergone role changes are significant at the .01 level with one exception, which is significant at the .05 level.

We may now ask whether or not these relationships are main-

TABLE 1
PER CENT MALADJUSTED RESPONDENTS BY ROLE

| Role | Elmira Per Cent | N† | Kips Bay Per Cent | N |
|---|---|---|---|---|
| Employed | 22 | (171) ** | 27 | (161) ** |
| Retired | 42 | (98) ** | 40 | (200) ** |
| Married | 27 | (173) ** | 30 | (221) ** |
| Widow or widower | 40 | (217) ** | 47 | (180) ** |
| Age 60-69 | 29 | (277) ** | 31 | (254) * |
| 70 or over | 52 | (187) ** | 40 | (233) * |
| Not treated differently | 34 | (366) ** | 32 | (355) ** |
| Treated differently | 53 | (87) ** | 48 | (118) ** |

†In this table and in the following ones, N refers to the total number in each category. The sum of those in the employed and retired categories, as well as those who are married or widowed, is somewhat less than the total number of respondents in each sample. In the former case housekeepers are omitted from the samples, while in the latter instance respondents who never married are excluded.

*Difference is significant at the .05 level.

**Difference is significant at the .01 level.

tained when control variables are introduced. With respect to the employment role, controls on marital status, age, and age identification were introduced. Thus, for example, the age control allows a comparison of employed and retired who are age sixty to sixty-nine as well as employed and retired who are seventy or over. Consequently, there are six comparisons of employed and retired, two for each control variable, or a total of twelve for the Elmira and Kips Bay samples. Of these, eleven are in the expected direction, i.e., there is a higher proportion of maladjusted respondents among the retired than among the employed, while two of the differences are significant at the .05 level.

With respect to the marital role, controls on employment, age, and age identification result in eleven of the twelve differences between married and widowed in the expected direction, of which five are significant at the .01 or .05 levels. Controls on employment status, marital status, and age identification, when introduced into the age variable, produce results similar to those obtained with respect to the marital role, except that only three differences are significant. Finally, four controls are introduced into the differential-treatment variable, resulting in sixteen comparisons in the expected direction, of which nine are significant at the .01 or .05 levels.

It may be concluded that each of the four variables in Table 1 to a degree is independently related to maladjustment. However, since a high proportion of the differences are not statistically significant after introducing the control variables, one suspects that combinations of various role changes would not greatly increase the proportion of maladjusted respondents. This does not in fact prove to be the case. For example, among those respondents with all of the first three role changes in Table 1, the highest proportion of maladjusted respondents is only 52 per cent for the Elmira sample and 47 per cent for the Kips Bay sample, which is no greater than that for certain role changes taken individually.

The next aspects of the data to be taken up are the interrelations among the role change variables. Our approach is to view the differential-treatment variable as dependent, with the remaining three variables considered as contributing to effecting differential treatment, whether directly or indirectly. From general knowledge of how these changes occur, it would be difficult indeed to imagine feelings of differential treatment as effecting any of the other three role changes in a high proportion of instances. The differential-treatment variable is representative of a large number of dependent variables, other examples of which might be changes in various types of activities and in social participation.

Table 2 indicates a relationship between each of the three role changes and the dependent variable of differential treatment, a relationship that seems to be less pronounced in the Kips Bay sample. This perhaps is due to a greater degree of anonymity in a large city and consequently a degree of compartmentalization of any role change, resulting in reducing its possible influence on other role changes.

TABLE 2
PER CENT RESPONDENTS TREATED DIFFERENTLY BY ROLE

| Role | Elmira Per Cent | N | Kips Bay Per Cent | N |
|------|------|------|------|------|
| Employed | 13 | (170) * | 24 | (160) |
| Retired | 23 | (95) * | 28 | (187) |
| Married | 14 | (219) ** | 20 | (169) * |
| Widow or widower | 27 | (176) ** | 30 | (206) * |
| Age 60-69 | 13 | (271) ** | 23 | (244) |
| 70 or over | 30 | (185) ** | 29 | (230) |

*Difference is significant at the .05 level.
**Difference is significant at the .01 level.

We will now consider the relation between the three relatively independent role changes and a self-conception as old, the primary data for which are presented in Table 3. This relationship is strongly indicated by five .01 level differences and one .05 level difference.

If, for each role change variable, the other two are introduced as controls, the following results are found: (1) for the employment role, all of the eight relationships between this role change and identification as old are positive, with seven being significant at the .01 level; (2) these results are identical to those obtained with the age role; and (3) with respect to the marital role, all differences are in the expected direction, and three of these are significant at the .01 or .05 levels.

TABLE 3
PER CENT RESPONDENTS WHO IDENTIFY AS OLD BY ROLE

| Role | Elmira Per Cent | N | Kips Bay Per Cent | N |
|------|-----------------|---|-------------------|---|
| Employed | 12 | (172) ** | 23 | (154) ** |
| Retired | 42 | (96) ** | 50 | (195) ** |
| Married | 18 | (220) ** | 35 | (167) * |
| Widow or widower | 35 | (178) ** | 45 | (217) * |
| Age 60-69 | 11 | (273) ** | 27 | (246) ** |
| 70 or over | 47 | (186) ** | 55 | (240) ** |

*Difference is significant at the .05 level.
**Difference is significant at the .01 level.

These data indicate a considerable degree of independent relationship to age identification for each of the three role variables.
This is substantiated upon examining the cumulative effects of the
above three role changes on age identification. For the Elmira
sample, the proportion of identifications as old for three role
changes is 56 per cent; for the Kips Bay sample, it is 65 per cent.
These proportions are somewhat above the analogous percentages
for any one role change taken by itself.

The fourth aspect concerns the relation between age identification and adjustment. The evidence presented in Table 4 shows
that a significantly higher proportion of maladjusted respondents
are found among those who identify as old as opposed to middle-
aged. This is found to hold when controls on employment status,
marital status, and age are introduced. All of the twelve differences
are in the same direction and eleven of them are significant at the
.01 or .05 levels.

Finally, combined effects of role changes and age identification
on adjustment may be considered. Table 5 compares the proportion of maladjusted respondents among those who identify as

TABLE 4
PER CENT MALADJUSTED RESPONDENTS BY AGE IDENTIFICATION

| Age Identification | Elmira Per Cent | N | Kips Bay Per Cent | N |
|--------------------|-----------------|---|-------------------|---|
| Middle-aged | 31 | (343) ** | 28 | (287) ** |
| Old | 58 | (118) ** | 49 | (199) ** |

**Difference is significant at the .01 level.

middle-aged and have undergone a given role change with the proportion among those who identify as old and have not undergone this role change. Although none of the differences are significant, they are all in a direction indicating that age identification can reverse the expected relation between a given role change and adjustment. This is striking in view of the fact that the role change variables were previously shown to be significantly related to adjustment.

TABLE 5
PER CENT MALADJUSTED RESPONDENTS BY AGE IDENTIFICATION AND ROLE

| Age Identification | Role | Elmira Per Cent | N | Kips Bay Per Cent | N |
|---|---|---|---|---|---|
| Middle-aged | Retired | 39 | (56) | 31 | (97) |
| Old | Employed | 57 | (21) | 37 | (38) |
| Middle-aged | Widow or widower | 40 | (116) | 31 | (119) |
| Old | Married | 54 | (41) | 36 | (58) |
| Middle-aged | Age 70 or over | 44 | (99) | 28 | (104) |
| Old | 60-69 | 48 | (33) | 42 | (66) |

It is possible to carry this type of analysis one step further due to the size of the samples under consideration. For example, one might compare respondents who identify as middle-aged and have undergone any two of the three role changes with respondents who identify as old and have not experienced these role changes. There are three different combinations of two role changes for each sample. The data here indicate a turning point, for in five of these six comparisons age identification does not reverse the expected relation between the role changes and adjustment; in fact, the expected relation is statistically significant in two of the six comparisons.

This paper has outlined a theoretical framework that may be utilized in predicting the degree of adjustment of the aged. In this approach, age identification is conceived of as an intervening variable between each role change and adjustment. The five aspects of the data may be summarized as follows:

1. The role changes considered are significantly related to maladjustment, although there is little tendency for multiple role changes to cumulate and result in a closer relation to the adjustment variable.

2. The differential-treatment role change, conceived of as representative of a number of variables influenced by employment, marital, and age role changes, generally is significantly related to these role changes.

3. The role changes considered are significantly related to identification as old, and there is some tendency for multiple role changes to cumulate, resulting in a closer relation to age identification.

4. Identification as old is significantly related to maladjustment.

5. Age identification can reverse the expected relation between any one of the role changes considered and adjustment. Where two role changes are combined, however, this reversal does not generally take place.

It is hoped that future studies of adjustment will further specify the relatively crude variable of role change. In addition, the significance of the age-identification variable for adjustment indicates a need for further investigation of this and other aspects of the self-image.

# SUCCESSFUL AGING*

### Robert J. Havighurst

The science of gerontology has the practical purpose, as we often say, of "adding life to the years" of the latter part of the human lifespan. By the phrase "adding life to the years" we mean helping people to enjoy life, and to get satisfaction from life.

One of the major aims of gerontology is to provide society and individuals with advice on the making of societal and individual choices about such things as retirement policy, social security policy, housing, where and with whom to live, how to relate oneself to one's family, what to do in free time. In order to provide

---

*Reprinted by courtesy of *The Gerontologist,* Volume *I*:4-7, March, 1961. Presidential address given to the Division of Maturity and Old Age, American Psychological Association, Chicago, Illinois, September 2, 1960.

good advice, it is essential that gerontology have a theory of success-ful aging.

A theory of successful aging is a statement of the conditions of individual and social life under which the individual person gets a maximum of satisfaction and happiness and society maintains an appropriate balance among satisfactions for the various groups which make it up—old, middle-aged, and young, men and women, etc. The latter part of this definition serves to emphasize the prin-ciple of the greatest good for the greatest number, which is a useful principle in considering the question of the success of any segment of a society. No segment of a society should get satisfaction at a severe cost to some other segment.

The modern American society is rich enough in material goods to provide the material basis of successful living to all ages and all segments of its population. However, this society may not be rich enough to meet the needs of all its members for intangible goods, such as prestige, opportunities for interesting and challenging new experience, friendship, opportunities to be of service to others, and provisions for other human wants. This is difficult to believe, how-ever, since these intangible goods do not seem to have any arbitrary limits to their production.

At any rate, we shall assume that the American society can pro-vide adequately for the material and non-material needs of all its groups and, therefore, that the older segment need not be deprived of satisfactions through the needs of other age groups. This leaves us with the question posed in the first part of the definition of a theory of successful aging—what are the conditions of individual and social life under which the individual older person gets a maxi-mum of satisfaction and happiness?

## Two Theories of Successful Aging

There are two contrasting theories of successful aging. They are:

*1. The Activity Theory.* Successful aging means the mainten-ance as far and as long as possible of the activities and attitudes of middle age.

*2. The Disengagement Theory.* Successful aging means the acceptance and the desire for a process of disengagement from active life.

*The Activity Theory* is favored by most of the practical workers in the field of gerontology. They believe that people should maintain the activities and attitudes of middle age as long as possible and then find substitutes for the activities which they must give up —substitutes for work when they are forced to retire; substitutes for clubs and associations which they must give up; substitutes for friends and loved ones whom they lose by death.

However, as Henry and Cumming (1959) have pointed out:

> Our conceptions predispose us to use the middle-age status as a model of desirable social and personal development, and hence to see any deviation from this model as negative and undesirable. This may perhaps result in a failure to conceive of old age as a potential developmental stage in its own right, having features qualitatively different from middle age.

*The Disengagement Theory* is based on the observed facts that as people grow older they generally curtail their involvement in the activities of middle age. As stated by Cumming and McCaffrey (1960):

> This theory starts from the common-sense observation that in America, the old person is less involved in the life around him than he was when he was younger and proceeds without making assumptions about the desirability of this fact. Aging in the modal person is thought of in this theory as a mutual withdrawal or disengagement which takes place between the aging person and others in the social systems to which he belongs. He may withdraw more markedly from some classes of people and remain relatively close to others. This withdrawal may be accompanied from the outset by increased preoccupation with himself. When the aging process is complete, the equilibrium which existed in middle life between the individual and his society has given way to a new equilibrium characterized by a greater distance and an altered type of relationship. In a previous report, we have presented data which suggest that one of the early stages of disengagement occurs when the aging individual withdraws emotional investment from the environment. We have thought of the inner process as being an ego change in which object ca-

thexis is reduced; this results in an appearance of self-centeredness, and an orientation to others which betrays less sense of mutual obligation. This is accompanied by a somewhat freer and more expressive manner. The fully disengaged person can be thought of as having transferred much of his cathexis to his own inner life; his memories, his fantasies, and his image of himself as someone who *was* something, and *did* accomplish things.

There is no doubt that disengagement does take place with aging, but proponents of the Activity Theory regard this as a result of withdrawal by society from the aging person, against the will and desire of the person. However, the Disengagement Theory stated by Cumming and her colleagues regards the disengagement process as natural, the aging person accepting and desiring it, and they speak of the disengagement process as being "primarily intrinsic, and secondarily responsive."[3]

For example, Lady Astor, on the occasion of her 80th birthday, is supposed to have said. "Years ago, I thought old age would be dreadful, because I would not be able to do all the things I would want to do. Now I find there is nothing I want to do." A seventy-four year old woman in the Kansas City Study, when asked what were the best things about being her age, said:

> The change—over a period of several years—freedom— from petty conventions, children, husband. A sense of relief from petty fears about jobs, finances, social position, new clothes. Freedom to accept or decline invitations and appointments without strain on my husband's business or hurting my children, or the Victorian standards of my parents."

Yet she expressed some of her ambivalence about disengagement when she answered the question about the worst thing about

---

[3]It is important to make a distinction between a theory of successful aging, and a theory of process of aging. In a theory of process of aging, one is concerned only with generalization about the processes which go on, in the body, in the personality, and in the social environment, as a person ages. No assumptions about value are made. One does not take into consideration the questions of happiness or success. The Disengagement Theory of Process of Aging has recently been stated and tested by two of my colleagues, Elaine Cumming and William E. Henry (1961). They have also noted some of the implications of this theory for a theory of successful aging. In a theory of successful aging one must make some assumptions about value.

her being her age, as "the realization that for better or for worse, the job is done, and there is no chance to make any more contributions to your generation."

## DEFINITION AND MEASUREMENT OF SUCCESSFUL AGING

It should be possible to choose between the theories of successful aging, by finding whether older people who remain rather fully engaged are more or less successful than those who are disengaged. All that is required is an operational definition of successful aging and a method of measuring the degree to which people fit this definition. However, this has not proved easy.

There are a number of procedures for the measurement of successful aging, and all of them have been criticized. We shall summarize them. First, though, let us state the characteristics of a good procedure for measuring successful aging. It should be based upon an operational definition of successful aging, and it should not assume that either activity or disengagement is desirable. If it is based upon such an assumption, then it cannot be used to test either of these theories of successful aging.

### A Way of Life that is Socially Desirable for this Age Group

One way of defining successful aging is to say that it consists of a way of life that is regarded by the society as appropriate for older people. If there is a fair consensus within a society concerning what is appropriate behavior for older people, it should be possible to develop an instrument to measure the social acceptability of a person's behavior and consequently the degree of his success in aging.

This was attempted by Havighurst and Albrecht (1953) on the basis of a study of public opinion concerning the activities of older people. A social approval scale was developed which could be applied to any particular person's life as he reached the period of later maturity. The particular items on the scale represented various degrees of activity and disengagement in various areas of life, and their scale values were determined by a public opinion study. A person's score for successful aging depends on the degree to which his behavior matches what the public in general regards as desirable for older people in general.

This method has two shortcomings. In the first place, it assumes that public opinion is the criterion of successful aging, regardless of the feelings of the individual older person. In the second place, it assumes that public opinion in inflexible, whereas in fact public opinion is rather tolerant with respect to the behavior of older people in the United States, and allows and even rewards exceptional behavior in some individals.

## Maintenance of Middle-age Activity

Successful aging may be defined as maintenance of the level and range of activities that characterize a person in his prime of life with a minimum downward adjustment. A measurement which uses this definition is illustrated by Havighurst and Albrecht (1953) in the Prairie City Study and by Havighurst (1957) in the Kansas City Study. Here success was defined as competent behavior in the common social roles of worker, spouse, homemaker, citizen, friend, association member, and church member. A set of rating scales was created to measure a person's performance against the societal norms in these role areas.

Another measure of this type is the activity score on the schedule entitled "Your Activities and Attitudes" developed by Cavan. Burgess, Havighurst, and Goldhamer (1949), which sums up a person's participation in a variety of activities.

These methods provide a measure of what Havighurst has called "social competence." They do not necessarily measure successful aging unless we define successful aging in this way. They cannot serve as a test of the activity theory of successful aging.

## A Feeling of Satisfaction with One's Present Status and Activities

Successful aging may be defined as a condition in which a person feels satisfied with his finances, family, friends, work, clubs, and church activity. A widely-used measure of this type is the Chicago Attitude Inventory, first described by Cavan *et al.* (1949), revised by Havighurst and Albrecht (1953), and adapted for use with middle-aged people by Havighurst (1957). This method relies partly upon activity and social participation of a person, and therefore should not be used as a test of the activity theory or of the disengagement theory of successful aging.

## A Feeling of Happiness and Satisfaction with One's Life

This method assumes that a person who is aging successfully feels satisfaction with his present and his past life and asks him as skillfully as possible to report on his feelings about his life. It does not ask him how active he is, or what his health or financial status is—it simply asks him how he feels about himself.

A good example of measurement of successful aging using this "inner" definition is given by Kutner's "morale" scale which was derived from the Elmira Study conducted by the Department of Anthropology and Sociology of Cornell University. Kutner (1956) says:

> "Morale refers to a mental state or a set of dispositions, while adjustment refers to behaviors that stem from these dispositions. Hence, we may assume that an attitude or evaluation scale of morale measures life adjustment.

The morale scale employed by Kutner consists of the following items:

1. How often do you feel there's just no point in living?
2. Things just keep getting worse and worse for me as I get older.
3. How much do you regret the chances you missed during your life to do a better job of living?
4. All in all, how much unhappiness would you say you find in life today?
5. On the whole, how satisfied would you say you are with your way of life today?
6. How much do you plan ahead the things you will be doing next week or the week after—would you say you make many plans, a few plans, or almost none?
7. As you get older, would you say things seem to be better or worse than you thought they would be?

My colleagues and I have not been completely satisfied with Kutner's morale scale, which is supposed to be a one-dimensional scale of the Guttman type, because we believe that life satisfaction it likely to have more than one dimension. Consequently we have worked out new scales for the measurement of successful aging based upon our analysis of satisfaction with present and past life into five components.

This was done by examining the measures of adjustment and morale that have been used by ourselves and others in previous studies and by analyzing a set of intensive interviews made in the Kansas City Study of Adult Life. Eventually we produced an operational definition of *Life Satisfaction* in terms of five components which are defined below. Rating scales have been worked out for these components.

**1.** *Zest vs. Apathy.* To be rated here are enthusiasm of response, and degree of ego-involvement—in any of various activities, persons, or ideas, whether or not these be activities which involve him with other people, are "good" or "socially approved" or "status-giving." Thus the person who "just loves to sit home and knit" rates as high as the person who "loves to get out and meet people." Physical energy is not to be involved in this rating. A low rating is given for listlessness and apathy, for being "bored with most things," for "I have to force myself to do things," also for meaningless (and unenjoyed) hyper-activity.

**2.** *Resolution and Fortitude.* Here we are concerned with the extent to which respondent (here-after called R) accepts personal responsibility for his life; the opposite of feeling resigned, or of merely condoning or passively accepting that which life has brought him; the extent to which R accepts his life as meaningful and inevitable, and is relatively unafraid of death. This is Erikson's (1950) "integrity."

This is not to be confused with autonomy or the extent to which R's life has been self-propelled or characterized by initiative. R may not have been a person of high initiative, but yet he may accept resolutely and relatively positively that which life has been for him. He may feel it was a series of hard knocks, but that he has stood up under them (this would be a high rating) .

There are two types of low ratings, the highly intropunitive, where R blames himself overly much, and the extrapunitive, where R blames others or the world in general for whatever failures or disappointments he has experienced.

**3.** *Goodness of Fit between Desired and Achieved Goals.* Here we are concerned with the extent to which R feels he has achieved his goals in life, whatever those goals might be; feels he has succeeded in accomplishing what he regards as important.

High ratings would go, for instance, to the man who says, "I've managed to keep out of jail" just as to the man who says, "I've managed to send all my kids through college."

Low ratings would go to the R who feels he's missed most of his opportunities, or who says, "I've never been suited to my work" or "I always wanted to be a doctor, but never could get there." Also to R who wants most to be "loved," but instead feels merely "approved." Expressions of regret for lack of education are not counted in this connection.

**4.** *Positive Self-concept.* Here we are concerned with R's concept of self—physical and psychological attributes.

High ratings would go to R who is concerned with grooming and appearance; who thinks of himself as wise, mellow (and thus is comfortable in giving advice to others) , who feels proud of his accomplishments, who feels he deserves whatever good breaks he has had, who feels he is important to someone else.

Low ratings to R who feels old, weak, sick, incompetent; who feels himself a burden to others; who speaks disparagingly of self or of old people.

**5.** *Mood Tone.* High ratings for R who expresses happy, optimistic attitudes and mood, who uses spontaneous positively-toned affective terms for people and things, who takes pleasure from life and expresses it.

Low ratings for depression, "feel blue and lonely," for feelings of bitterness, for frequent irritability and anger.

Here we consider not only R's verbalized attitudes in the interview; but make inferences from all we know of his interpersonal relationships, how others react toward him, etc.

The Life Satisfaction Rating requires at least one long interview with a person, and is too cumbersome to be used on a large scale. Consequently, we have produced two self-report instruments which can be filled out by a person in a few minutes and which have correlation coefficients of .58 and .71 with the Life Satisfaction Rating.

One instrument, called the *Life Satisfaction Index A,* is an attitude scale of twenty items selected from existing scales or invented so as to get four or five items representing each of the five components. This instrument contains four items rather similar to Kutner Morale Scale items and several items from the Happiness scale of the Chicago Attitude Inventory.

The other instrument, called *Life Satisfaction Index B,* is a combination of six open-ended questions and six check list items, which are scored on a three-point scale, from 0 to 2. Four of the twelve items are from Kutner's Morale Scale, and others come from various sources.

The correlation coefficient between forms A and B is .73 for ninety cases. Their combined score has a correlation of .62 with the Life Satisfaction Rating.

Since Life Satisfaction can be measured scientifically in these ways, these methods might be used to test the Activity and the Disengagement theories of successful aging.

## The Validity of the Various Measures of Successful Aging

The measures which have been discussed all have a face validity. That is, their content obviously is related to one or another definition of successful aging. Some researchers simply accept this fact as sufficient. For example, Kutner (1956) assumes that his morale scale measures life adjustment and lets it go at that, and others have been content to follow his lead. Other researchers, like Havighurst (1951) have sought an acceptable criterion of adjustment or successful aging to use as a test of the validity of their instruments. Havighurst has used some form of rating by experienced judges as the criterion against which to validate self-report measures, such as the Chicago Attitude Inventory. Self-report instruments are vulnerable to conscious and unconscious psychological defenses and should be tested for validity against something more objective.

As a test of the validity of the Chicago Attitude Inventory, the Cavan Adjustment Rating Scale has been used. This is a rating by judges based on an interview with a person. The rating takes into account the person's association with family, friends, formal and informal groups, his feelings of importance and satisfaction, and his emotional stability. The Attitude Score has a correlation coefficient of .73 with the Cavan Adjustment Rating.

As a test of the validity of the Life Satisfaction Indexes, the Life Satisfaction Rating has been used in the Kansas City Study of Adult Life. Correlation coefficients of the Life Satisfaction Rating with Life Satisfaction Indices A and B are .58 and .71, respectively.

The Life Satisfaction Rating depends on scoring by judges who have read interviews with the respondent but have not seen him or interviewed him. Possibly a more valid rating can be obtained from a clinical psychologist who interviews the respondent. This is being done at present in the Kansas City Study.

### How to Use the Various Measures of Successful Aging

As long as there is disagreement as to what constitutes successful aging, caution must be used in selecting measures of successful aging. At present a theory of successful aging is an affirmation of certain values. Persons with different values of life in the later years will have different definitions and theories of successful aging. One who believes in the activity theory will be satisfied with a measure of successful aging based on activity. One who believes in the disengagement theory of successful aging could not be satisfied with such a measure.

There is much to be said in favor of procedures for measuring Life Satisfaction which depend upon an "inner" or psychological definition of successful aging. They may be used to study the effects of various social and economic conditions on people and also the relations between various life-styles and life satisfaction.

In gerontology it will probably be useful to use several different measures of successful aging, always being explicit about their relations to operational definitions of successful aging. In this way we are likely to learn more than if we limit ourselves to one theory and one definition of successful aging, with its appropriate measure.

## THE RELATION OF PERSONALITY TO SUCCESSFUL AGING

If life satisfaction or happiness is taken as the sign and the product of successful aging, it is not likely that successful aging, thus defined, will be associated with only one particular life-style, whether it be one of activity or one of disengagement. Life satisfaction will probably be associated with active involvement for some kinds of people and with disengagement for other kinds.

Persons with an active, achieving, and outward-directed life style will be best satisfied with a continuation of this style into old age with only slight diminution. Other persons with a passive, dependent, home-centered life style will be best satisfied with disengagement.

Reichard, Livson, and Peterson (1961) in a study of working-class men found three types of "successful agers," one of them active, one passive, and a third "mature." These were three personality types, who were rated by clinical psychologists on the basis of lengthy interviews as "well-adjusted" older men. They would probably have all scored high on our Life Satisfaction indices. According to the activity theory of successful aging, the active type should show signs of satisfaction and happiness, the passive group should be unhappy and dissatisfied and the "mature" group should be happy and satisfied in so far as they are active. According to the disengagement theory of successful aging, the situation would be reversed, with the men who are most disengaged showing the greatest satisfaction and happiness.

Thus it appears unlikely that any simple theory of successful aging will account for all the people who are happy and satisfied in their later years. Undoubtedly there is a disengaging force operating on and within people as they pass seventy and eighty. But they will still retain the personality-life style characteristics of their middle years; those who were happy and satisfied by being active and productive then will continue to be happy and satisfied if they can maintain a considerable part of their activity and productiveness; and those who were happy and satisfied by being relatively passive and dependent in their middle years will be happy and satisfied if they can become even more disengaged in their later years.

# CHANGES IN STATUS AND AGE IDENTIFICATION*

## Zena Smith Blau

The conceptions individuals have of themselves as young, middle-aged, or old are, of course, related to their actual age. People in their sixties are certainly more likely than people in their thirties to think of themselves as old. But the variations in age identification between persons in the same age group and the similarities between those whose actual age differs indicate that chronological age is only a limiting condition and does not fully explain the changes in age identification that occur in the course of the individual's life span.

In this paper two topics will be discussed: first, the relative influence of chronological age and age identification on other aspects of the self-image of older persons, and second, some of the social factors that hasten or forestall changes in age identification among older people.

A representative sample of 468 people sixty years old and over in Elmira, New York, were asked: "How do you think of yourself as far as age goes—middle-aged, elderly, old or what?" Fully 60 per cent of the respondents considered themselves middle-aged, 38 per cent described themselves as old, elderly, or used an equivalent euphemism, and 2 per cent gave no answer to the question.

Of course, the likelihood that people consider themselves old

*Reprinted by courtesy of *American Sociological Review,* Volume *21*:198-203, April, 1956. Paper read at the annual meeting of the American Sociological Society, September, 1955. The data presented in this paper are part of a seris of studies in social gerontology being conducted by the Department of Sociology and Anthropology at Cornell University under the direction of M. Barron, J. Dean, B. Kutner, G. Streib, and E. Suchman, aided by grants from the Rockefeller and Lilly Foundations. I wish to express my gratitude to all concerned for the use of these data.

rather than middle-aged steadily increases as they grow older. Under sixty-five, only 18 per cent define themselves as old, between sixty-five and seventy, 37 per cent do so, but in the age group of seventy and over this proportion rises to 59 per cent. Old age is, after all, something more than a state of mind, since the aging process is marked by objective physical and behavioral changes. Although these changes usually occur gradually and, therefore, do not immediately intrude upon the consciousness of the individual, one might expect that they become increasingly apparent to him and his associates as the years pass and thus finally bring about identification with old people. Indeed, when asked "How much have you changed in the past ten or fifteen years—would you say hardly at all, somewhat or a good deal?" less than a fifth of those under seventy, compared to a third of those who are seventy and over, feel that they have changed "a good deal" (see Table 1).

TABLE 1
PER CENT WHO PERCEIVE "A GOOD DEAL" OF CHANGE IN SELF BY AGE IDENTIFICATION AND AGE

| Age | Age Identification Middle-aged | Old | Total |
|---|---|---|---|
| Under 70 | 15 (206) | 42 (31) | 18* (273) |
| 70 and over | 22 (73) | 40 (88) | 33* (175) |

*This difference is significant on the .01 level. Numbers in parentheses in all tables are the number of cases on which percentages are based.

However, if age identification is held constant, this relationship between chronological age and perceived change in oneself tends to disappear. These findings suggest that while objective changes mark the aging process, a shift in age identification is a crucial intervening variable for perceiving them. Not all older people, but only those who have shifted their age identification, are likely to perceive these changes in themselves.[1] It seems that neither the

[1]Although it is not known whether the shift in age identification or the perception of changes in self occurs first, there is some indirect evidence on this point. It was shown in the text that the relationship between chronological age and perception of changes in the self disappears when age identification is held constant. But if perceived change in self is held constant, the relationship between age and age identification persists. This suggests that a shift in age identification precedes and produces an increased awareness of change in the self, and not vice-versa. For a discussion of this method of inferring the direction of influence between two variables see Peter M. Blau, "Determining the Dependent Variable in Certain Correlations," *Public Opinion Quarterly, 19:*100-105, Spring, 1955.

knowledge of their years, nor even their white hair and wrinkles, induce older people to preceive that they have changed. As Proust writes:

> It does no good to know that the years go by, that youth gives way to old age, that the most stable thrones and fortunes crumble, that fame is ephemeral—our way of forming a conception—and so to speak, taking a photograph of this moving universe, hurried along by time, seeks on the contrary to make it stand still.[2]

And so, to borrow Proust's metaphor, it is the conception of himself as old and not the weight of his years as such, that constrains the older person to relinquish the photograph and reluctantly to substitute the mirror.

A similar phenomenon can be observed in respect to the older person's beliefs about the image his significant others have of him. The older people are, the more frequently do they answer affirmatively when asked, "Do you think that the people you see and care most about think of you as an old man (woman)?" Only about one-eighth of those under seventy, but a third of those who are seventy and over feel that their close associates consider them old (see Table 2). This relationship, however, also tends to disappear if the age identification of respondents is controlled. In other words, regardless of their actual age, people come to believe that *others* consider them old only if they consider *themselves* old.[3]

In sum, various mental states that characterize older people,

### TABLE 2

Per Cent Saying That Significant Others Consider Them Old by Age Identification and Age

| | Age Identification | | |
|---|---|---|---|
| Age | Middle-aged | Old | Total |
| Under 70 | 7 (206) | 45 (31) | 13* (276) |
| 70 and over | 14 (73) | 50 (88) | 32* (187) |

*This difference is significant on the .01 level.

---

[2]Marcel Proust: *Remembrance of Things Past*, New York, Random House, 1927, Vol. 2, p. 1063.

[3]If, instead of controlling age identification, the beliefs respondents hold about the attitudes of their significant others are controlled, the relationship between age and age identification remains, which indicates that the sequence suggested in the text is the correct one.

and distinguish them from others are actually precipitated by shifts in age identification from middle-aged to old. The important question consequently becomes: What are the social conditions that hasten or forestall such shifts in age identification? The rest of the discussion will be devoted to an examination of this question.

In youth and middle-age, the loss of one social status is generally accompanied by entry into another. For example, the status of student is relinquished for a position in the occupational structure, or the young women may give up her career to become a wife and mother. In contrast, retirement and widowhood, the two major status changes that typically occur in old age, designate the permanent loss of two crucially important social roles and the activities and relationships that define them.[4] It could be expected that these changes in social status of older persons are responsible for shifts in age identification among them, but the data only partly confirm this expectation.

TABLE 3
PER CENT IDENTIFIED AS OLD BY AGE AND EMPLOYMENT STATUS

| Employment Status | Under 70 | | Age 70 and over | | Total | |
|---|---|---|---|---|---|---|
| Employed | 18 | (136) | 41 | (37) | 24 | (170) |
| Retired | 37 | (41) | 67 | (57) | 57 | (93) |

All differences are significant on the .05 level.

Retirants, at each age level, do indeed consider themselves old more frequently than those who are still employed, but the widowed are not significantly different from the married in this respect. Under seventy, less than a fifth of the employed, but more than a third of the retirants identify themselves as old. Among those who are seventy and over, 41 per cent of the employed, but fully two thirds of the retired, regard themselves as old (see Table 3). In contrast, at each age level, widowed people consider themselves old hardly more often than those who are still married. (see Table 4).

---

[4]For a brief, but suggestive discussion of this point see Talcott Parsons, "Age and Sex in the Social Structure of the United States," *American Sociological Review*, 7:604-616, October, 1942.

TABLE 4
PER CENT IDENTIFIED AS OLD BY AGE AND MARITAL STATUS

| Marital Status | Under 70 | Age 70 and Over | Total |
|---|---|---|---|
| Married | 22  (160) | 55  (65) | 33  (218) |
| Widowed | 26  (81) | 60  (99) | 46  (173) |

The remark of a retirant suggests one of the reasons why retirement predisposes the older person to define himself as old.

When did I start to feel old? Why when I stopped working. I was always real proud that I'd come to Chicago and got a job and supported myself. Then when I couldn't work anymore, why I wasn't good for anything.[5]

Retirement is a *social* pattern which implies an invidious judgment on the part of others in the society about the lack of fitness of *old* people to perform a culturally significant role, whereas the death of the marital partner, being a natural event, and not a socially induced one, does not have such implications in our culture. Thus, the retired individual, but not the widowed one has reason to believe that he is socially defined as old.

Furthermore, retirement removes the individual from a social peer group and thereby disrupts the informal relations developed on the job. The death of the marital partner, on the other hand, disrupts a single, albeit a very significant, social relationship.[6] In other words, the hypothesis is suggested that loss of membership in a peer *group* has more pronounced effects on the self-image of older people than the loss of an intimate interpersonal relationship, and that this helps to explain the differential effect of retirement and widowhood on age identification.

This hypothesis can be tested by determining whether membership in a friendship clique is, indeed, more significant for age identification than relationships with individual friends.

---

[5]From an interview in William H. Harlan, "Isolation and Conduct in Later Life," Ph.D. dissertation, University of Chicago, 1950.

[6]Of course, under some conditions, widowhood may also have a determental effect on group memberships of the individual. For example, the surviving marital partner may drop out of those friendship groups in which the marital couple had participated jointly, or discontinue membership in "auxiliary" organizations, that is where participation of the wife is contingent on that of her husband.

Respondents were asked three questions about their social participation: "How many really close friends do you have here in town that you occasionally talk over confidential matters with?" "Now think of the friend that you know best here in town—how often do you get to see that friend?" and "Would you say you go around with a certain bunch of close friends who visit back and forth in each other's homes?"

Neither the number of friendships nor the frequency of contact with the closest friend is significantly related to age identification. But older people who belong to a friendship clique consider themselves old significantly less often than those who do not participate in such a group. Only 29 per cent of the members, in contrast to 41 per cent of the non-members regard themselves as old (see Table 5). However, this relationship may be a spurious one, since, as they grow older people tend to participate less in friendship groups, and they also are more likely to think of themselves as old.

Indeed, when age is controlled, the relationship between clique membership and age identification disappears among those who are under seventy. The vast majority under seventy still define themselves as middle-aged whether or not they belong to a friendship group. But among people who are seventy and over clique membership makes a considerable difference for age identification. Only half of those who participate in a friendship group, but nearly two thirds of the others consider themselves old.

TABLE 5

PER CENT IDENTIFIED AS OLD BY AGE AND MEMBERSHIP IN A FRIENDSHIP GROUP

| Friendship Group | Under 70 | | Age 70 and Over | | Total | |
|---|---|---|---|---|---|---|
| Member | 20 | (115) | 49 | (53) | 29* | (168) |
| Non-member | 24 | (164) | 63 | (136) | 41* | (300) |

*This difference is significant on the .05 level.

The fact that participation in a friendship clique makes no difference for age identification in the younger group only *appears* to refute the hypothesis that group memberships are more effective in forestalling old age than single relationships. Actually, this hypothesis helps to explain why participation in a friendship clique is less important in the younger than in the older age group. People under seventy are likely to have alternative group memberships. For example, since a majority of the men in this age group are still employed, they participate in work groups and other occupational groups. Younger women, as well participate more in clubs and organizations than those who are older. Thus, it makes little difference whether or not they also participate in a friendship group as such. But after seventy, when participation in these other social groups is the exception rather than the rule, the person's position in a friendship group becomes more important in forestalling a shift in age identification.

Similarly, the belief that his close associates consider him old is influenced by the individual's participation in a social peer group, but not by the number of friends he has. Regardless of their age, those who belong to such a group less often hold this belief than those who do not (see Table 6). Indeed, among people seventy and over, two thirds of the clique members, compared to less than half of the others, deny that their associates consider them old.

TABLE 6
Per Cent Denying That Significant Others Consider Them Old by Age and Membership in a Friendship Group

| Friendship Group | Under 70 | Age 70 and Over | Total |
|---|---|---|---|
| Member | 87 (115) | 64* (53) | 80† (168) |
| Non-member | 73 (164) | 45* (135) | 60† (300) |

*This difference is significant on the .05 level.
†This difference is significant on the .01 level.

These indications that participation in a social group more effectively forestalls the psychological changes that mark old age than participation in a number of dyadic relationships can be explained by the emergent properties that characterize social groups. Studies of various types of small groups by Roethlisberger and Dickson, Whyte, Homans and Bales,[7] show that recurrent interac-

---

[7]See F. J. Roethlisberger and William J. Dickson: *Management and the Worker,* Cambridge, Harvard University Press, 1930: William F. Whyte: *Street Corner Society,* Chicago, University of Chicago Press, 1943; George C. Homans: *The Human Group,* New York, Harcourt Brace and Company, 1950; and Robert F. Bales *et al.:* Channels of Communication in Small Groups," *American Sociological Review,* 16:461-468, August, 1951.

tion between individuals tends to fix the role of each member relative to the others in the group. The images and expectations that arise among the group members tend to persist and to influence their subsequent behavior toward one another. This stability of the network of relationships within a group of friends or co-workers prevents mutual awareness of gradual alterations that take place in each of the participants, particularly if these changes in the person do not interfere with his ability to share in the activities of the group. Consequently, the recurrent gatherings of the same people lend a sense of continuity to the life of each participant. An incongruous but revealing manifestation of this feeling of immutability provided by the groups is the practice of people who have grown old together to continue to refer to themselves as "the boys" or "the girls."

Participation in a friendship group does, indeed, serve to postpone shifts in age identification, and this provides support for the hypothesis that loss of the work group is one of the reasons why retirement influences the age identification of older persons more than widowhood. Further clarification of these relationships can be achieved by simultaneously comparing the relative impact of widowhood and retirement on age identification among those who do and do not participate in the friendship group.

TABLE 7

PER CENT IDENTIFIED AS OLD BY MEMBERSHIP IN A FRIENDSHIP GROUP AND MARITAL STATUS

| Marital Status | Member | | Friendship Group Non-member | | Total | |
|---|---|---|---|---|---|---|
| Married | 29 | (85) | 35* | (133) | 33 | (218) |
| Widowed | 34 | (53) | 51* | (121) | 46 | (173) |
| Difference | 5 | | 16 | | | |

*This difference, as well as that between proportions among totals, is significant on the .05 level.

Table 7 shows the relationship between friendship group, marital status, and age identification. Among those who are part of a friendship group, widowed people consider themselves old, hardly more often than married ones—34 per cent as against 29 per cent, a difference of 5 per cent. However, among those who are not clique members, the widowed define themselves as old considerably more often than the married—51 per cent as against 35 per cent, a difference of 16 per cent. The death of the marital partner, even though it is a natural event, is more likely to precipitate "old age," if the elderly person does not participate in a friendship group.

Membership in a friendship clique has similar implications for age identification following retirement (see Table 8). Among those who do not belong to a friendship group, nearly two-thirds of the retired, compared to only a quarter of the employed consider themselves old, a difference of 37 per cent. Loss of employment status makes less difference if people are members of a friendship group: 42 per cent of the retired and 21 per cent of the employed feel that they are old—a difference of 21 per cent. Thus, either change in social status is less likely to produce identification with the "old" if the older person maintains his position in a group of peers. However, the friendship group is less effective in preventing the consequences of retirement than those of widowhood. Among those who have a group of friends, twice as many of the retired of the employed consider themselves old, but hardly any more of the widowed than of the married do so.

TABLE 8

PER CENT IDENTIFIED AS OLD BY MEMBERSHIP IN A FRIENDSHIP GROUP AND EMPLOYMENT STATUS

| Employment Status | Friendship Group | | | |
|---|---|---|---|---|
| | Member | | Non-member | Total |
| Employed | 21 | (66) | 25* (104) | 24 (170) |
| Retired | 42 | (24) | 62* (69) | 57 (93) |
| Difference | 21 | | 37 | |

*This difference, as well as that between proportions among totals, is significant on the .01 level.

Thus, the data that support one of the two explanatory hypotheses advanced to account for the finding that retirement influences the age identification of older people more than widowhood, furnish indirect evidence for the other one as well. Group memberships are indeed more effective than even intimate dyadic relations in postponing identification with the old, but this factor alone does not account for the differential effects of retirement and widowhood on age identification. Loss of employment status, as a socially induced event, implies a judgment on the part of others that an individual is old, and this is an additional reason why it influences his age identification more than does widowhood, which, as a natural event, is devoid of such a social judgment in our culture.

*To summarize:* The socio-psychological and physical aging processes can be analytically distinguished. Age identification rather than actual age constrains older people to recognize changes in themselves and to perceive that the attitudes of others toward them have changed. Analysis revealed that of the two major changes in social status that commonly occur in old age—retirement and widowhood—only retirement appears to hasten the onset of old age. Two hypotheses were advanced to explain this difference: one, retirement implies a social judgment that the person has become old, whereas widowhood, because it comes about through a natural event, does not have this implication for the older person; two, retirement has more serious consequences for age identification because it removes the individual from a significant peer group, whereas death of the spouse directly disrupts only a single, albeit a highly significant, relationship. The finding that participation in a friendship group serves to forestall a shift in age identification, but that the number of close friends and the frequency of contact with one's closest friend do not, provides support for the second hypothesis. However, the fact that participation in a friendship group appears to be less effective in retarding shifts in age identification among the retired than among the widowed indicates that the loss of the work group only partially explains the greater influence that retirement exerts an age identification. It, therefore, furnishes inferential evidence for the first hypothesis that the cultural evaluation implied by retirement, but not by widowhood, tends to force the person to recognize that he is socially defined as old.

# SOCIAL CLASS CORRELATES OF OLD AGE*

## Ansel P. Simpson

However the social classes are delimited, one finds significant differences in style of life, values, aspirations, etc. Not only are there "between-class" differences, but there are also "within-class" differences. One dimension in terms of which "within-class" differences are revealed is stage in life cycle: infancy, childhood, adolescence, adulthood, middle life, and old age. One dimension in terms of which "between-class" differences are revealed is differential social environment. It is the purpose of this paper to investigate "between-class" differences with respect to old age. Accordingly, we formulate the hypothesis that position on the social scale has differential adaptive consequences for older people, both psychological and social.

Our method will be to extrapolate from existing research findings conclusions which are relevant for our hypothesis. At the end of this paper, we will introduce a consideration which research in gerontology has hitherto ignored.

Despite the fact that between 1936 and 1956 some 18,000 articles were published on the subject of old age, one must look hard and long to find a treatment of old age and social class. The subject seems to have been almost entirely neglected in sociological literature; and where it is dealt with, it is decidedly tangent to some more central issue.

Friedmann and Havighurst report on a series of six studies of old people, roughly between sixty and seventy years old, in different occupational groups. The investigators were principally concerned with the relative importance which these people ascribed to certain aspects of their occupations such as income, expenditure of time and energy, personal identification and status, interpersonal relations, and source of meaningful experience, i.e., giving purpose to life, creativity and self-expression, new experience, service to others, etc. The occupational groups represented in these studies

*Reprinted by courtesy of *Sociology and Social Research*, Volume 45:131-139, January, 1961.

were unskilled and semiskilled steelworkers, rank and file coal miners, retail salespersons, skilled craftsmen, and physicians. These occupational groups are grossly representative of the social classes: lower (steelworkers and miners), middle (skilled workers and retail salespersons), and upper (physicians). If we can accept this extension beyond the actual data, the findings of these investigators are significant for our own hypothesis.

It was found that the steelworkers and miners (representing the lower class) were "more likely to see their work as having no other meaning than that of earning money. Skilled craftsmen and salespersons (representing the middle class) were found to view their occupations as avenues of self-expression, purposeful activity, and new experience. Physicians (representing the upper class) were found to regard their occupation primarily as an opportunity to serve others. These represent significant variations among the several social classes with respect to occupational image and old age.

As one might expect, it was found by Pressey that older people work in the type of jobs characteristic of their social class. He reports on a group of 1,280 persons aged sixty-five and older, whom he describes as "largely [middle] social class." Extrapolating his data one derives the following occupational distribution: professional and managerial, 30 per cent; service, 21 per cent; skilled, 13 per cent; clerical, 12 per cent; agriculture, 11 per cent; owners and partners, 6 per cent; semiskilled, 4 per cent; unskilled, 3 per cent. These data confirm the expected conclusion that middle-class older people are heavily represented in occupations carrying higher prestige.

Weinberg in discussing the emotional problems of the aged lists the following principal factors: (1) loss of capacity in mastery of the environment and one's physical self and (2) increasing isolation. He states that these deficiencies are met through (a) selectively excluding certain stimuli, a conscious or unconscious process, (b) conservation of energy by following old patterns rather than learning new techniques, and (c) regression.

However, loss of capacity in mastery of the environment and one's physical self seems to be directly related to the nature of the environment, that is, whether it is supportive or nonsupportive.

Andrus in an experiment using eleven college graduates, aged sixty and over, conducted a study designed to test the hypothesis that appreciable and significant change would occur in older persons in a cooperative, stimulating, and supportive environment. The hypothesis grew out of the philosophy that "productive change and growth are possible throughout life." Through a program of lectures and discussions, rhythmics and movement, art, creative writing, work in gardens and greenhouses, etc., and through healthful, appetizing, and attractive meals, positive changes were effected among these older people. These changes included greater alertness, more vigor, higher self-esteem, and the development of a more hopeful attitude toward the future. The image of "old age" was shattered, and in place of the "debilitated old man" was substituted a picture of the functioning person. Parallel physiological changes accompanied these psychosocial improvements. Improvements in agility, strength and energy, dietary deficiency, and circulatory ailments were observed; cases of hypertension and anemia were significantly relieved.

If we can accept "college graduates" as a category having class dimensions, conclusions of the Andrus experiment are significant for our own hypothesis.

On Weinberg's point of increased isolation, some older people prefer domestic isolation as long as they can maintain frequent social contact with nearby friends and relatives. Townsend, in a study of over 200 families in England with members aged sixty and over, found that many old people with relatives nearby preferred to live alone and maintain "supported independence," seeing their families everyday but not sharing a roof with them. Nearly twenty-five years ago, Morgan, in a study of 381 older people primarily from the working class, drew this conclusion: ". . . the ideal arrangement was to live in your own home, near enough to your own children to see them and the grandchildren frequently; go and make a little visit and then come home again to your own concerns."

To a given point, it can be safely maintained that education is class related, both in terms of amount received and in amount desired. Anderson, referring to Friedmann and Havighurst, points out that adjustment in retirement is functionally related in education. Education "increases an individual's repertoire of skills and interests with the results that when he meets a difficult transition period, he has a greater variety of activities to which to turn and can, therefore, make a better adjustment." This latter conclusion was found to apply from steelworkers and miners with little education all the way up to professional people with "a considerable amount" of education. Education is therefore functionally significant for social class, and this relationship manifests itself in a higher coefficient of adjustment for the better educated and socially privileged. Beckman, Williams, and Fisher corroborate this point when they conclude that "the greater a person's education, the better prospect he appears to have for favorable adjustment in later maturity," and " . . . poor adjustment is associated with low socioeconomic status as gauged by income and occupational level."

Steiner and Dorfman report on a study of 3,600 men and women aged sixty-five years and older. They found a number of instances in which the aged in the several social classes differ. Variation in median income was as follows: proprietary and professional, $2,361; white collar, $2,111; skilled, $1,385; semiskilled, $1,304; unskilled, $1,262; and farm classes $944.

These authors found that whereas there was a common interest in working among the several classes, there were significant differences in physical ability to work. Physical ability to work clearly favored the professional and technical occupations, and it was thereafter followed by a sharp and rather consistent decline.

As far as reasons for retirement are concerned, health reasons accounted for only 21 per cent of those in the professional and technical category; 38 per cent for the clerical category; and for occupations lower in the stratification structure, these rates increased sharply. These authors found no significant association between size of medical payments and size of income. However, it would be very profitable to investigate the relationship between need for medical care and social class.

The emergence of retirement communities is a fairly recent development. Granick summarized surveys of six primarily middle-class retirement communities; he found a number of correlates of social class indicated by amount of education. Size and source of income were found to vary with educational attainment. The principal sources of income for persons with little education were small pensions, old-age assistance, part-time work, and savings. On the other hand, the primary sources of income for the "well-educated" groups were pensions, annuities, investments, trust funds, real-estate rentals, and substantial savings. Granick's findings with respect to "type of work" also confirm the conclusions of Pressey and others to the effect that jobs of greater prestige are held by persons in the higher social classes.

Further, Granick reports that "Social activities . . . consume a good deal of the time and energy of the elderly group. Major pastimes are visiting with a variety of friends, attending parties, and simply passing the time of day with casual acquaintances." Also, he found relatively high church attendance, with only 25 per cent rarely or never going to church.

Cavan and associates report on the social participation of 1,258 men and women aged sixty and over. In the age groups between sixty and seventy-four, nearly half of the persons studied participated in seven or more selected activities such as hobbies, attending group meetings, attending church, etc. The percentage was more closely half for the women than for the men. But Cavan's data are not reported in a manner such that class correlates of social participation may be extrapolated.

The most recent study which aims directly as investigating socio-economic factors in the life of the aged is *Five Hundred over Sixty*. Occupation, income, and interviewer's rating were used in determining the socioeconomic rating. Scales were designed for each of the three determining variables, and each respondent was rated thereon, producing three scores for each person which were then summed. The scores so derived ranged from 3 to 20, with the lower numerical scores signifying higher socioeconomic status.

In this work, a large number of relationships between socio-economic status and selected variables are studied. We have selected those of broader significance for coverage here.

Persons scoring 3 to 8 were classified as High socioeconomic status; 9 to 13, Middle; 14 to 20, Low. In the total sample, there emerged 55 Highs, 148 Middles, and 297 Lows. Oftimes, the Middles and Highs were combined, resulting in simply a dichotomy of socioeconomic status, High and Low.

With respect to morale, it was found that high socioeconomic status and high morale were positively correlated. State of health, which might be thought to influence morale, did not alter this basic relationship. Morale was also associated with marital status: the married in the high status group ranked much higher in morale than the married in the low status group; 60 per cent of the high status married had high morale as compared with only 32 per cent in the low status group. Also, employment status was found significantly related to morale, as within each status group the employed were found to have the higher morale rating.

Satisfaction with retirement was found in a higher degree among the higher status group members as compared with the low status group members, 59 per cent and 24 per cent, respectively.

Self-image, defined in strict sociological rather than psychological terms, was studied. It was found that 55 per cent of those in the high status group had a positive self-image as compared with 38 per cent in the low status group. In addition, positive self-image was found to be associated with morale: high status group members with a positive self-image were found to have morale significantly higher than high status group members with negative self-image. Of course, low status group members were found to have positive self-images less often, but when they did, this tended to be positively associated with higher morale.

The amount of social contacts was measured by a scale based on such items as how often visits from children, relatives, and friends occurred, how often new friends were made: 58 per cent of the high status group members maintained relatively wide social contacts as compared with only 35 per cent of the low status group members. At the same time, the groups maintaining greater interpersonal relations also had higher morale.

This study also found that "residential isolation" does not necessarily portend social isolation. This finding concurs with findings made by Peter Townsend in his study of 200 families in England.

A definite and clearly positive association between socioeconomic status and health was found: the favored status group enjoyed good health to an appreciable extent over and above the lower status group. This would undoubtedly remain true despite the fact, recognized by the investigators, that ill people in high status groups tended to be shielded from being interviewed; this was not the case with the lower socioeconomic status groups.

Whereas there was found a significant difference between state of health and socioeconomic status, on the one hand, and expressed concern with state of health, on the other, still a significant percentage of low status persons in poor health expressed little concern over their actual physical condition. Concern with state of health seems to be under-reported.

The question of health care for older people is currently a matter of great national concern. From the social psychological point of view, a good question is would older people use community facilities for their care if they were available. The low status group was found to be more favorably disposed to use these facilities than the high status group. However, appreciable discrepancy was found between disposition to use health facilities and actual use of these facilities. Among both the high and low status groups, poor health was found positively associated with favorable attitudes toward use of health facilities.

On the question of the use of age-specialized health centers, the low status group showed more favorable attitudes, but more than half of both groups were favorable. This status group relationship to attitudes was maintained for those in both good health and poor health, but was more pronounced for those in poor health.

The high status group individuals are joiners, while the low status group members are less so. Further, almost "three times as many high as low status individuals would join a club of mostly young people"; the percentages are 25 and 9, respectively.

This study of *Five Hundred over Sixty* is an important work. Its methodology is insightful, and the data analysis is a particular tribute to the authors and especially to Kutner, who wrote the report. A substantial portion of this work deals with medical and health aspects of old age, which are admittedly a very significant consideration in old-age research. Sociologists, however, would be interested in two major improvements in a subsequent study. The first is a greater coverage of "purely social facts" such as aspirations, values, attitudes (political, social, and economic), class consciousness, role image. The second improvement would be a greater number of native-born individuals in the sample. A little less than 30 per cent (153) of the present sample was native-born. To be sure, foreign-born respondents would have experiences in early American life which could appreciably affect their adjustment in old age, and which could also significantly differentiate them from native-born Americans.

Any complete understanding of a major social role must take into account the total social situation and the whole matrix of interaction whose forces impinge upon the influence the role under investigation. It is informative, of course, to learn what self-images older persons have of themselves, what their needs, desires, wants, and longings are, and how well they are being met. However, only a partial understanding of these phenomena can be obtained as long as the older persons alone are investigated. Heretofore, studies of the aged have relied completely on the responses of the aged person alone, thus ignoring the fact that self-image, identity, self-validation, and role performance are products of the social situation and the dynamics of group interaction; that they are defined and developed by the reciprocal responses of the group. This fragmentary approach can only produce partial and perhaps misleading results.

If our understanding of the aged is to be complete, we must employ a more comprehensive approach and our design must be more inclusive. No aged person is a complete social isolate in the final sense. Always there are other persons of whom he must take very serious account. Very often these include people with whom the oldster lives, his relatives, friends, children, neighbors. Can these people be systematically excluded and we still get a substantial understanding of his domestic life, family relations, his friendship and social relations? We would submit that a comprehensive understanding of the aged must take cognizance of the attitudes and responses of these other people.

This proposal may at first glance appear to suggest an impracticable and unwieldly extension of old-age studies. One may inquire, "Is it not too difficult to identify the individuals who should be studied in addition to the old person?" "How may one know whom the old person takes into account?" We answer, "With two devices: (1) by inspection of the social situation and (2) by inquiry of the old person. Haven't these been our tools in the past?"

As much as any other, the purpose of this study has been to focus attention on the need for a broad and comprehensive investigation of the sociological and the social psychological aspects of old age. The deficiencies of this study and its failure to reach its goal in the manner desirable are but a clarion call that such a study be undertaken with all deliberate speed.

# MINORITY GROUP CHARACTERISTICS OF THE AGED IN AMERICAN SOCIETY*

## MILTON L. BARRON

For the most part sociologic research on the aged has lacked a theoretic framework. In an earlier article one possible framework was offered with special reference to the problem of occupational retirement. Another possibility is now suggested, namely, the study and analysis of the aged in American society as an emerging quasi-minority group. An attempt will be made to demonstrate that the social psychology of older people in the labor force as well as of retirants (and to a large extent the situation of the aged as a whole in urban, industrial society) resembles that of the ethnic groups with which the concept of minority is usually associated. To regard the aged as an emerging quasi-minority group may not only contribute to the understanding of the aged, but new insights for the fruitful examination of the traditional minorities may emerge in the process.

*Reprinted by courtesy of *Journal of Gerontology, Volume* 8:477-481, October, 1953. Presented at the Second Institute on Aging, April 17-18, 1953, Washington University, St. Louis, Missouri.

A fundamental question, of course, is whether or not it is sociologically valid to proceed even further by considering the aged as a full-fledged minority. Why, one may ask, should they be conceptually confined to the quasi-minority level? Are they not stereotyped by younger age groups and do they not suffer from subordination, prejudice, and discrimination? Is it not true that they demonstrate such typical minority group reactions as hypersensitivity, self-hatred, and defensiveness as far as their age is concerned? Some scholars have already stated emphatically that ethnic groups are not the sole proprietors of minority and majority characteristics and experiences. They have argued, for example, that most of the essential defining aspects of majority-minority group interaction apply to women in our society in their social relations with men as readily as they apply to such intergroup relations as are true in the case of American Negroes and whites. Therefore, they claim, it is unwarranted to think of minorities and majorities exclusively in terms of racial, religious, and nationality groups.

In criticism of this argument, however, one may say that it is insufficient to show that women and the aged, the alleged minorities, share the traditional minorities' experiences of subordination and frustration from total and equal participation in those opportunities which the values of American culture theoretically extend to all members of the society. Unlike the traditional minorities, neither women nor the aged are socially organized as independently functioning subgroups in American society. On the contrary, they are found within the same families as the alleged majorities so that intergroup relations cannot possibly be involved in the full sense of the term. Hence the avoidance of the minority concept and the utilization of "quasi-minority" seem justified in the case of the aged as well as women.

Another basic distinction should be made between the aged as a quasi-minority, on the one hand, and as the source of interest or pressure groups on the other. Like the membership of other minorities, quasi-minorities, and even majorities, it is common knowledge that some of the aged have organized themselves into pressure groups, the most conspicuous of which are the Townsend and Mc-Lain movements. Pressure groups are seldom synonymous with the

larger groups from which they are derived. Nevertheless, they seek
to represent the larger groups in their contention for power, exert-
ing their influence at any level of government, and directing their
points of pressure at whatever centers of power may be present.

## MAJORITY ATTITUDES AND BEHAVIOR
## TOWARD THE AGED

Attitudes of prejudice and stereotyping as well as discriminatory behavior against the aged by younger adults are easily discernible. One student of the American labor force has gone so far
as to assert that older workers are the most vulnerable group in the
labor market in terms of discrimination. "Many persons," says
Bancroft, "can live out their working lives untouched directly by
the factors that adversely affect the employment of women, of
Negroes, of the foreign-born, or other minority groups, but none
can escape the effects of age—as it influences both his own employment and that of someone to whom he is closely related."

*1. The Aged as a Menace.* An extreme yet useful example of
majority feelings of threat and menace concerning the aged quasi-
minority is to be found in the following statement:

> The new class war between the young and the old will mani-
> fest itself in several ways. First, there will be heavy pension taxes
> that may eventually absorb more than one-fourth of the income
> of both workers and employers. This new class war may progress
> so far that we will see workers and employers . . . standing
> shoulder to shoulder against the hard-driven politicians who
> promise our senior citizens impossible pensions and encourage
> the older worker to exploit the younger worker, the older farmer
> to exploit the younger farmer, the older businessman to exploit
> the younger businessman, the older professional men to exploit
> the younger professional man. . . . Let us remember that these
> pension leaders will soon have the votes. Karl Marx and others
> have taught us that mass movements are rarely rational: they
> spring from broad social changes. These basic changes in the
> population pattern started recently and slowly; the resulting
> mass movement has not yet matured. Townsendism may be as
> important in the next fifty years as were the doctrines of Karl
> Marx during the last half century. . . May I put the proposition

quite bluntly? "Cradle to the grave" is a scheme whereby those close to the grave would fasten themselves on the pay-checks of those closer to the cradle, and ride piggy-back (or piggy-bank) to the grave.

Has our aging population condemned us or entitled us to an age-conscious future rather than a class-conscious future? Will the increased voting power . . . of older people be used to exploit youth to such an extent that a revolt of youth will become inevitable? Should the state constitution be amended to provide a maximum voting age?

The aged so far have provoked relatively few feelings as hostile and fearful as this. Today, fear of the aged by younger adults is still more or less subdued, and the majority action taken is considerably less drastic than that suggested in the quotation above. An illustration is the following defense of the practice of compulsory retirement and the rationalization for the pre-retirement counselling offered by an oil company:

All of the working population over sixty-five, and to a lesser degree those who have passed the forty-five-year mark, are conscious of the idea of compulsory retirement. They are aware of the difficulty in obtaining employment and are doubly concerned about their uncertain future.

If a sizeable portion of this group were to band together . . . the weight of their combined support would be the most powerful political force the country has ever known . . .

There is another possibility inherent in this problem, however. Conservatism and age are companions. Thus is is possible that the peak of political support for radical changes in our government's economic system has been reached. Preservation of property rights and individual security are of more personal importance to the elder citizen than experimental radicalism. If industry can convince the aging industrial population that it is doing something concrete about their uncertain future, socialistic remedies might well wither for lack of support.

This situation also holds the possibility of unfavorable repercussions of industry. Consider the community aspects. If a man is retired from business and goes into the community feeling that he is no longer useful to himself, to industry or to anyone else, his degeneration tends to be rapid. . . . A defeated, apathetic attitude on the part of retired individuals soon permeates the community and it isn't very long before members of the community point to the company from which Jones was retired with such statements as "They certainly killed poor Jones retiring him like that." The cumulative adverse effect of such reaction is obvious.

Esso feels that retirement is something earned by faithful service, a form of "graduation" into a new phase of life rather than a "casting out" process. Retirement should be the opportunity for the employee to enjoy the fruits of his labors in freedom, leisure and relaxation as well as an opportunity to serve himself, his family and his community in ways not open to him during his working career.

In seeking to help its employees approach retirement in this way, Esso feels that individual counseling and help are basic prerequisites. . . Thus the concept developed of a seminar or discussion-type approach, wherein a group of employees approaching retirement is offered the opportunity to gather and explore some of the problems and requirements of a successful retirement.

**2. *Prejudice and Stereotyping in Employers' Rationalization for Discrimination.*** Many of the reasons which employers give for discriminating against older workers in hiring and retirement policies involve the same process of stereotyping which is an integral part of prejudice against ethnic minorities. Pigeonholing, premature generalizations, and unwarranted economizing of thought are found in the reasons given for the arbitrary retirement and the reluctance to hire older workers. Employment agencies may be used to illustrate this point. A survey of ninety-four agencies in New York City found that the agencies believed that the older job-seeker was "his own worst enemy," destroying his chances for employment by such alleged personality deviations as "talking too much, being too hard to please, too set in his ways, and lacking poise and grooming."

Before considering these reasons, it should be noted that an implicit factor underlying many of such discriminatory policies is the provocation given to employers by insurance companies. They warn employers that to hire men over forty-five and women over forty, or to retain employees beyond sixty-five, would result in the request for payment of higher premiums on workmen's compensation and other forms of insurance in effect in the company, such as disability and accident insurance. Another real, underlying factor is the development of pension plans. If a company is committed to paying a pension at a fixed chronologic age, such as sixty-five there is likely to be an aversion to hiring people fifty or fifty-five years of age. If it were to hire such people, the company must then set aside enough money to provide them with pensions comparable to those which ordinarily go to employees whose service in the company has extended over a greater number of years.

Aside from the arguments that younger workers need to be given a chance to advance into better jobs and that "the organization needs new blood," one of the major reasons given by employees for discriminating against older workers is that the latter are poor physical risks, thereby disrupting production. While it is true that the likelihood of sickness, disability, and death increases noticeably after forty years of age, there is considerable variation among individuals and between types of employment in these respects. For example, vigorous and productive septuagenarians among manual laborers are not unusual. Furthermore, the Bureau of Labor Statistics' study of work-injury and absenteeism has indicated that older workers, as a group, fare relatively well. Industrial accident rates, on the average, were found to be lower for workers forty-five years of age and over than for younger workers. Once injured, however, the disability of older workers lasts longer. Older workers were also found to have been absent from work less frequently, the lowest rates of absenteeism being among workers fifty-five to sixty-four years of age.

Another major argument usually given by employers who discriminate is that older workers produce less than younger people. But statistical data are almost entirely lacking regarding the productivity of older compared with younger employees working at the same tasks. The argument, too, ignores individual differences. It overlooks the observation that persistence of efficiency beyond forty years of age is largely related to the amount of skill and experience required for a job. Although most older workers probably cannot exert themselves as much as they did in their younger years, it is widely acknowledged that most of them waste less material, seldom damage machines, and are steadier in production than younger workers.

A third major reason given for discrimination against older workers is that they are resistant to change; they are so "set in their ways" that they fail to adjust to new ideas and techniques of organization and production. Actually, however, the association between old age and conservatism is probably given undue emphasis. Older people are frequently more adaptive than they are reputed to be. Much of their alleged inflexibility could be the result of unnecessary, tactless practices of management.

### MINORITY GROUP REACTIONS OF THE AGED

In order to merit serious consideration as a quasi-minority group, the aged, especially older workers, should manifest typical minority-group reactions. These include such things as marked self-consciousness, sensitivity, self-hatred, and defensiveness about their traits. Williams asserts that militant forms of these reactions are most likely when the group's position is rapidly improving, or when the position is rapidly deteriorating, especially following a period of improvement. Young has suggested as a probable hypothesis that the harder minorities are pressed to earn a living, the more they tend to be defensive about their minority qualities and traditions. This hypothesis is likely only when minority individuals find it impossible to "pass" and identify with the majority.

The bitterness, resentment, and self-hatred of older workers who experience discrimination in employment and re-employment represent minority group reactions. Consider, for example, the following unsolicited comments of a Midwesterner:

> I am in my middle fifties and want to state that I regard myself a pretty good person and able to do a good day's work, a veteran of World War I. Some of the punishment I go through from persons twenty years up regarding my age is sickly. Such remarks as "you old S. O. B. you're all washed up," at times makes me want to do some harm. I am the oldest in my department. I help the new employees who lack experience with my knowledge

of certain types of work, and after they gain the experience, they give you the brush. One thing I notice when a younger person has authority over an older person, there seldom is any consideration...

## A Southerner writes:

I am a construction man and have handled thousands of men as general labor foreman. But what's killing off the elderly people is being told "you're too old." The government and the employer are to blame. When a man reaches the age of forty, from then on there is the same tune until sixty-five. Right here in the U. S. A., think of the millions of men who are willing to work but cannot get work. It rings in their ears, "you are too old."

## A Westerner says:

No one except a man who has worked regularly for thirty or forty years at one kind of work and very suddenly at the age of sixty-five is thrown out of work on one-third his regular pay, can realize or understand the depressive mental effect or the worry brought by the fact that he is old and not wanted in a country he worked so hard to build. Eleven months ago at the age of sixty-six and in good health after forty-eight years of railroad work, I was taken out of service. I accepted my annuity, $97.31 per month. By living conservatively the wife and I could get by on $160 per month. I have tried many times to secure work with no success. I would be glad to work. Retirement as it is today is a death sentence, by worry, depressive feeling of being useless and an insufficient annuity. I was compelled to drop my lodge dues. I may drop my insurance. I worry almost continually and sometimes feel that I'd be glad to know that I will not awaken tomorrow to a useless and idle life.

### LEGISLATION AGAINST DISCRIMINATION

Increasingly, an American societal reaction to majority discrimination against minority groups is to enact legislation for the purpose of punishing or deterring such behavior. In view of the fact that, alongside "FEPC" laws against ethnic discrimination, one state has already enacted such legislation with regard to age discrimination, and other states show signs of following suit, another type of evidence is available in behalf of the feasibility of utilizing a modified majority-minority-group framework in dealing with problems of the aged.

Massachusetts in 1937 passed a law to the effect that discrimination in employment against older workers would be contrary to public policy. The law had virtually no enforcement provisions, with the result that only two cases developed during the thirteen years of its existence. In 1946, Massachusetts passed a fair employment practices act. When the bill was originally drawn up, it had included age as well as race, religion, color, creed, and national origin among the defined social categories deserving protection from discrimination. However, the age provision was dropped. Ultimately, in 1950, a separate bill was passed which included age in the coverage of the Fair Employment Practices Act.

Enforcement of this law resembles that used for the protection of ethnic minorities. The agency administering the law endeavors to "conciliate and persuade" in cases of violation or alleged violation. Educational techniques are also available to prevent age discrimination. If these various methods and techniques fail, a penalty up to $300 for a violation may go into effect. The law also provides that the victim of discrimination may secure from the violator between $100 and $500 in reimbursement. As a result of this law the Massachusetts Commission Against Discrimination has ruled that pension plans with a compulsory retirement age of less than sixty-five are inoperative and in violation of the state law.

In July, 1952, it was reported that the question of amending the New York State Anti-Discrimination Law to include a ban on age bias in employment was about to be reexamined by the Joint Legislative Committee on Problems of the Aging.

## SUMMARY

It is a widely held theory that whenever there are serious external threats, internal societal distinctions are minimized and, among other things, discrimination against minorities is held in abeyance. The exact extent to which this applies to the aged is unknown. There is little doubt, however, that in recent war emergencies, the urgent need for man power in industry has induced a noticeable degree of relaxation in the otherwise stringent restrictions against the hiring or retention of older workers as well as against ethnic minorities.

We have seen that although the aged in modern, industrial society do not comprise a functioning subgroup, nevertheless they meet many of the criteria of a minority as defined in sociologic theory of majority-minority group interaction. Evidence has been presented that in the out-group they are looked upon as a threat to the power structure. Prejudiced attitudes against the aged are not uncommon. Stereotypes and rationalizations for discrimination by younger adults assume the same properties as they do in technic intergroup relations. The aged have many of the reactions of a minority group. Lastly, legislation against discrimination has begun to be enacted in behalf of the aged which parallels that for the protection of ethnic groups.

One may conclude, therefore, that there is considerable justification in utilizing the quasiminority concept and framework in collecting and analyzing data on problems of the aged in urban, industrial situations.


# SOCIAL AND PERSONAL ADJUSTMENT OF RETIRED PERSONS*

## R. Grann Lloyd

Supporting the interview with a check list composed of semi-structured questions (response structured, stimulus free) , the investigator made a study of the personal and social adjustment of 140 retired individuals in Orangeburg County, South Carolina— sixty males and eighty females. These persons represent all the retired Negroes that could be located in Orangeburg County over a five-week period by a team of twenty interviewers. The respondents ranged from 50 to 108 years of age, the modal or most frequent age

*Reprinted by courtesy of *Sociology and Social Research,* Volume 39:312-316, May, 1955. This is the first of two reports on a socioeconomic study of retired individuals. The second paper will be concerned with the Social and Economic Circumstances of Retired individuals.

being seventy-two. Of the 140 retired individuals cooperating in this study twenty-two or 15.7 per cent had been to college and one had a master's degree; fifteen or 10.7 per cent of the others attended high school; eighty-four or 60 per cent reported that the extent of their education ranged variously from the first through the ninth grade, with the most frequent maximum education in this group being the fifth grade; nineteen or 13.6 per cent had no education.

The 140 individuals involved in this study retired during the thirty-two year period from 1918 to 1950. The thirty-three or 23.6 per cent that retired in 1950 were the largest number to retire in any one year; eighty-three or 59.3 per cent retired during the 1940's. Hence, 116 or 82.9 per cent retired during the period 1940-50.

One unexpected revelation of the inquiry was that so few of the respondents had planned their retirement. Prevailing economic thought favors the systematic removal of older workers from the labor force in order to increase the availability of jobs for younger workers. Hence, it is surprising to discover that of the 136 individuals responding to the inquiry only twenty-six or 19.1 per cent had made plans to retire, whereas 110 or 80.9 per cent had not. It is highly possible that the retired individuals who made no plans for retirement merely failed to accept the inevitability of old age until it was upon them. Then, too, it seems that they were not only unaware of or indifferent to the changes in human relationship with relatives and friends that accompany old age, but failed to develop interests and/or avocations to comfort them, occupy their time, and give them a feeling of wholesome satisfaction after retirement. Conversely, the few who did not expect to continue working until death report that they made plans to retire which included the following: (1) saved their money and (2) made plans for other support to supplement retired income, such as acquiring houses to subrent and establishment of contacts with public relief agencies with a view toward public assistance.

Only eight or 5.7 per cent of the respondents in this study retired voluntarily. The findings clearly indicate that the remaining 94.3 per cent believed that retirement was forced upon them by circumstances beyond their control. This supports and is supported by the negative response given by 80.9 per cent of the interviewees to the question "Did you make plans to retire?" Unquestionably, the overwhelming majority of these subjects expected to continue actively in the labor force until death. Apparently, that was a virtue in the days of their fathers, and perhaps in the days into which they were born, but it is not the philosophy of the present. And yet, believing their plight unusual, fifty or 35.7 per cent gave poor health as the reason for their retirement, twenty-eight or 20 per cent cited poor eyesight as the reason for retirement twenty-seven or 19.3 per cent blamed bad nerves, and one said personal prejudice forced retirement. Whereas only twenty-six or 18.6 per cent gave old age alone as the reason for retirement, fifty-eight or 41.4 per cent gave old age together with one or more of the other factors just mentioned as concomitant reasons.

Of the 104 retired individuals responding to the question, thirty-nine or 37.5 per cent reported that economic difficulties constituted their greatest problem in making the shift from the labor force to retirement; thirty or 28.8 per cent said ailing health was their greatest problem upon retiring; seventeen or 16.3 per cent were beset with varying adjustment problems; worry was the greatest problem irritating sixteen or 15.4 per cent; two or 1.9 per cent were disturbed most by the rural-urban transition that accompanied their removal from the labor force.

It is interesting to observe that forty-five or 32.1 per cent of the retired individuals involved in this study stated that if they could relive their lives, they would live them as they had, and forty or 28.6 per cent said they would change their lives only "a little bit." On the other hand, thirty or 21.4 per cent stated that an opportunity to relive their lives would result in considerable change in the patterns of their lives, and twenty-five or 17.8 per cent indicated they would live their lives altogether differently. It is perhaps not without significance to note that, whereas forty-five or 32.1 per cent would relive their lives as they had if given the opportunity, ninety-five or 67.8 per cent would seize upon an opportunity to change the pattern of their lives in varying degrees.

The "happiest years" in the lives of fifty-four or 42.5 per cent of these involved in this study responding to the question were when their "children were young"; the years of "married life" were happiest for thirty-five or 27.6 per cent; the days of their youth when they were carefree were happiest for thirty or 23.6 per cent; five or 3.9 per cent stated that they have been happy all their lives; two persons report that they are happier now than ever before. In this connection, it is interesting to discover that sixty-two or 44.9 per cent of the 138 retired persons responding to the inquiry are reportedly "about as happy" now as they were before their retirement; twenty-eight or 20.3 per cent indicate that they are happier since they retired. On the other hand, thirty-three or 23.9 per cent said they are "somewhat less happy"; and fifteen or 10.9 per cent stated that they are "much less happy" since retirement. Hence, whereas retirement seems to have adversely affected the happiness of forty-eight or 34.8 per cent, of those answering this particular question, such is not the case with ninety or 65.2 per cent of them.

The church and religion hold more meaning since retirement for seventy-seven or 57 per cent of those replying than formerly; for fifty-seven or 42.2 per cent they hold about the same meaning now as before; only two persons say that they hold less meaning for them now than formerly. Furthermore, seventy-two or 52.6 per cent of the 137 retired persons answering say they never worry about death, whereas twenty-eight or 20.4 per cent worry no more now than formerly about it. Conversely, twenty-nine or 21.2 per cent indicate that they worry somewhat less, and eight or 5.8 per cent say they worry much less now than formerly about death. Thus it seems that at least 80 per cent of those involved in this study have made satisfactory adjustment to their situations and the possible nearness of death. Indeed, sixty-seven or 48.2 per cent of the respondents indicate that they would welcome death; sixty-four or 46 per cent are indifferent toward death; while only eight or 5.5 per cent actually fear death.

Another indication of satisfactory adjustment can be seen in the feeling of 131 or 93.6 per cent of the retired individuals involved that they are welcome and liked by their neighbors; only nine or 6.4 per cent felt unwelcome and disliked. Whereas ninety-four or 67.1 per cent feel that they have about as many friends since retirement as before, thirty-seven or 26.4 per cent believe they are acquiring more friends; nine or 6.4 per cent feel they have fewer friends since retirement. Furthermore, eighty-one or 58.7 per cent see their friends about as much since retirement as before; thirty-four or 24.6 per cent see them more often now; only twenty-three or 16.7 per cent see their friends less since retirement.

It is revealing to note that fifty-two or 38.2 per cent of the 137 retired respondents to the question claim dependents; eighty-four or 61.8 per cent replied in the negative. Of the respondents replying in the affirmative thirty-five or 67.3 per cent of them claimed their wives as dependents; furthermore, a total of twenty children and grandchildren were claimed as dependents. It was perhaps to be expected that most, if not all, of those involved in this study would be in a less advantageous position financially after their retirement than formerly. It was not surprising, therefore, that fifty-five or 40.1 per cent of the 137 persons answering report that they are in worse position now than they were ten years before retirement; forty-three or 31.4 per cent feel that their position now is about the same as before; thirty-nine or 28.5 per cent feel they are in a better position now than ten years prior to retirement. Although 40.1 per cent reported that they are in a worse position now than they were ten years before their retirement, 55.3 per cent indicate that they have not had to alter their level of living since retirement because of low income or lack of income. On the other hand, 44.7 per cent report that the low income or lack of income accompanying their retirement has deprived them of necessities, insurance, home repairs, social activities, and many other things including the loss of home ownership and the inability to pay church dues. Nevertheless, 66.7 per cent of the respondents feel assured of permanent security.

The 140 retired persons cooperating in this study indicate that their major hobbies, interests, and activities—given in the order of decreasing frequency are—gardening and farming, the church, sewing, reading, social activities and recreation, hunting and fishing, singing, talking, preaching, cooking, housewifery, bricklaying, radio listening, and relaxation.

Relative to the future, 68.9 per cent of these retired persons had no plans for the future; 11.2 per cent plan to "live for good" for the remainder of their lives; the future plans of others include visiting their children and relatives, finding remunerative work, repairing their homes, raising chickens, and assisting children through college.

## RECAPITULATION

If the findings of this study have been presented with reasonable accuracy, some degree of intuitive insight, and a fair degree of perspicacity, the presentment will carry with it self-revealing implications and self-evident conclusions. However, restatement of several of the major findings seems appropriate.

1. In order of decreasing frequency, the greatest problems associated with the shift from the labor force to retirement are economic difficulties, ailing health, varying adjustment difficulties including worry, and rural-urban transition.

2. Whereas, if given the opportunity, 32.1 per cent of the respondents would relive their lives as they had, 67.8 per cent would seize upon such an opportunity to change the pattern of their lives in varying degrees.

3. Retirement seems to have adversely affected the happiness of only 34.8 per cent of those responding to the inquiry, in contrast to the 65.2 per cent who report just the opposite.

4. At least 80 per cent of those involved in this study seem to have made satisfactory adjustment to their situation and the possible nearness of death. Incidentally, it might be significant to note that 80.1 per cent have no real plans for the future.

5. Positive indication of favorable adjustment is revealed in the feelings of the cooperating retired persons relative to their neighbors and friends—93.6 per cent feel welcome and liked by their neighbors; 93.5 per cent feel that they have as many or more friends now than before retirement; 83.3 per cent see their friends as often or more often now than before retirement.

6. A substantial majority of the participants in the study responding to the inquiry—66.7 per cent—feel assured of permanent security.

7. Although most of the retired persons involved in this study made no plans to retire, practically all of them have developed

hobbies, interests, and activities providing varying degrees of physical, mental, and emotional outlets.

8. Most of the persons involved in this study have made favorable social and personal adjustments to their retirement.

# CHANGING FAMILY RELATIONSHIPS OF OLDER PEOPLE IN THE UNITED STATES DURING THE LAST FORTY YEARS*

## M. F. NIMKOFF

The family relationships of older people have a number of facets: 1) the marital relationship; 2) the relationship of the aged and their children; 3) the relationship of the aged and their grandchildren; and 4) the relationship of the aged and their siblings and other kinfolk. A comprehensive review of my topic should encompass all of these facets, but unfortunately the paucity of available data does not permit this.

## THE MARITAL RELATIONSHIP

There are now relatively more males and females in the United States, sixty-five years of age and over, who have never married than there were in 1900 (Table 1). We do not know what family context these single persons have but we probably can assume that their increase means more aloneness, if not more loneliness. Our reason for thinking so derives from the fact that in 1900 somewhat better than one in two of the older population lived on farms, compared to one in seven in 1950, a very radical reduction. The probabilities that an unmarried person will live in a household with relatives are greater on the farm than in the town or city. The reduction in the number of farms is of course linked to the increase

*Reprinted by courtesy of *The Gernotologist*, Volume 1:92-97, June, 1961. Presented at the Fifth Congress of the International Association of Gerontology, San Francisco, August 7-12, 1960. This paper will also be published in *Aging around the world, Vol. III, Social and psychological aspects of aging.* Proceedings of the Fifth Congress of the International Association of Gerontology.

in celibacy. In an urban-industrial environment there is less social pressure to marry and the alternative to marriage is less unattractive than in a rural setting.

There are also relatively more married males and females and relatively fewer widowed and divorced persons among the aged now than in 1900 (Table 1). The causes are mainly the longer length of life and the higher rates of remarriage in middle and old age. The latter reflects a more favorable, more permissive public attitude toward the remarriage of divorced and widowed persons.

In the last half century one of the more significant changes in the marital relationship is the lengthening thereof. Both sexes marry earlier and stay married to each other longer. On the average, the gain is about ten years of married life. Modern couples have fewer children and the last child marries sooner. In 1890 the last child married on the average two years after the death of one of his parents, whereas in 1950 the last child married from thirteen to fourteen years before the death of one of his parents. This means an increase of from fifteen to sixteen years in the length of marriage without unmarried children living at home. Since married chidren now seldom live with their parents, wherease in 1900 they often did, the result is an appreciable increase in the length of married life without children at home. The marital component has expanded and the parental component has shrunk.

TABLE 1

MARITAL STATUS OF THE POPULATION, 65 YEARS OF AGE AND OVER,
UNITED STATES, 1900 AND 1958[a]

| Year | Single | Male Married | Widowed | Divorced |
|------|--------|--------|---------|----------|
| 1900 | 6.0 | 67.1 | 26.4 | 0.5 |
| 1958 | 6.7 | 69.4 | 22.6 | 1.3 |
| | | Female | | |
| 1900 | 6.2 | 34.2 | 59.3 | 0.3 |
| 1958 | 7.5 | 36.0 | 55.3 | 1.2 |

[a]*Twelfth Census of the United States, 1900, Vol. II. Population*, Part II. Table XLIX. Also *Statistical Abstract of the United States, 1959*, Table No. 39, p. 40.

The quality of marriage has changed as well as the quantity. The change is in the direction of equalitarianism. In 1900 the division of labor between the sexes was sharper than it is today, and more was made of the distinction between men's work and women's work. The home was more exclusively the woman's domain, and the man had his job. Since then, the trend has been for wives to take jobs away from home and for husbands to share more in household duties. So far, to be sure, only token integration in domestic roles has been achieved, since the husband's help is often only symbolic and minor, But the prejudice against domesticity for men has broken down, and those who will may engage in housekeeping without public disapproval. Retirement of the bread winner provides the occasion for stepping up his domestic role. On the farm, the male's occupational role was continuous, with adjustments made as health and age required. Now, with compulsory retirement, the occupational role of the male is discontinuous. The adjustment of males in retirement is, then, facilitated by the availability of a social approved domestic role to compensate for the loss of the occupational role.

## THE RELATIONSHIP OF THE AGED AND THEIR CHILDREN

So far as children are concerned, two crucial variables are number and location. One of the more important changes, already mentioned, is that families are smaller, which means that there are fewer children to look after parents in old age. "Looking after" has an economic aspect and a sentimental one. If there are many children, the probabilities that they will collectively be able to support their aged parents is greater than if there are few children. This is the rationale that one very commonly finds in old agricultural societies like India, where the large joint or extended family exists. If you ask them why they prefer the large family, they will tell you that it provides more protection in old age. This rationale may be reasonable in a static agricultural society, but in a dynamic industrial society like the United States, with a rising standard of living, having fewer children may mean that the parents can accumulate more capital and be less dependent on their children in old age.

Where the children of the aged live is important both for economic and sentimental reasons. We have the data for recent years on the living arrangements of old people. If aged couples, un-related males and unrelated females are combined, then in April, 1952, a little over half of them (53.5%) lived alone; about one in six (17.6%) were heads of households and had children 21 years old and over living with them; an additional one in six (17.6%) lived with their children. This picture, then, is primarily one of the aged in our time living alone, apart from their children or other relatives.

Some students have raised a question as to whether the residential picture just presented is significant. Yes, they say, independent residence is the vogue for the aged, but they have relatives living nearby. In one sample of the aged, 50 per cent reported that all their children live close enough so that they can see them whenever they wish.

In this paper we are interested not just in the present situation but how it compares with the situation half a century ago. Unfortunately there are no data on living arrangements by age groups for this earlier period. But from our knowledge that better than 50 per cent of the aged lived on farms in 1900 we can probably safely make certain inferences. One is that there was less independent housing for the aged than now and more living with relatives. Another is that the aged parent, usually the father, was more often the head of the household, and more rare than now would be the arrangement of aged parents living in the household of a married child. Lacking census data, we cannot measure the extent of the change, but such knowledge as we do have disposes us to think that the changes are appreciable.

One reason for thinking so is the considerable increase in physical mobility which has the effect of separating members of families one from another. In 1900, there were only 8,000 registered automobiles and 144 miles of paved road in the United States, compared to 52,000,000 cars and over 2,300,000 miles of surfaced roads in 1955.

A recent study reports that 65 per cent of the aged expect their children to live nearby. We do not have comparable data for 1900, but it seems safe to assume that a larger percentage had such expectation at the turn of the century. Where children are separated from their parents, the expectation that their children will write their parents replaces the expectation that their children will visit them. It would be interesting to know whether, when separated, children write as often as they used to visit. It is unlikely that they do, since when they live nearby, daily visits are common, and daily correspondence is not so common. A letter, besides, is ordinarily not so satisfying as a visit in person.

One result of the greater separation is an increase in what may perhaps be called routine visiting. Many oldsters are modern circuit riders, visiting their married children in turn. The visits are usually short because living space is limited, and the visits, if protracted, are hard on both young and old. The periodic visit is a compromise on the part of the aged who wish to keep their independence and separate residence and yet maintain personal ties with their married children. The children may reciprocate by paying visits to the parental homestead, but usually with less frequency than the converse because the children are less free. In fact, a not so minor purpose of the children's visits may be to deposit the grandchildren for safe keeping while the children take off on an unfettered vacation.

What the changes involve is a radical modification in the status of aged parents and their children. In a farming economy the young married sons are more often than not dependent upon their father for support. As unpaid family labor, at least one of the sons may remain with his parents after his marriage, with a view eventually to taking over the farm. Other sons may settle nearby on land provided by the father, or they may be given a cash settlement and may migrate to town in search of jobs. The situation is very different in our industrial society where non-family employment is the rule and wages are in money, a highly individualizing commodity. Moreover father and son on the land are engaged in a common occupation, and the son is likely to respect his father for his knowledge of farming, which comes with long experience.

Now things are very different. Ours is a time of great change. The proliferation of new occupations and new knowledge creates gaps between the generations. It creates different universes of discourse so that the generations cannot communicate with each other in these fields. To see how modern changes favor the young, one has only to see how young are the leading contemporary physicists of the United States. They tell us that if you visit the missile launching site as Cape Canavaral, you are impressed first of all by the youth of the men in charge. These are the authorities in the new space age.

The aged recognize this change. It may be one reason why they over-whelmingly prefer to maintain independent households. They were household heads in 1900 and want to remain so. In 1900 they did not object to having their married children in the household; indeed, they preferred it. Meantime, with industrialization, the norm has gained favor that married children should have households of their own and that they should not live with their parents or in-laws, if they can help it. This norm the aged now respect. They do not want their children to live with them, although they would like to have them nearby. Nor do they want to live with their married children, if they can help it. The spatial separation is a concomitant of the social distance between the generations.

Parenthetically, an interesting point in this connection is that in agricultural society a married son often remains with his parents, and a married daughter seldom does, if she is living with her husband. Today, however, if an old parent lives with his or her relatives, the chances are 55:45 that it will be with a daughter rather than with a son (Glick, 1957). Apparently if an aged parent has to be dependent, it is safer to be dependent on a daughter than on a son. Or to state it differently, since the woman usually sets the tone of the home and has the major responsibility for the management of the home, it is more satisfactory to be dependent on a daughter than on a daughter-in-law.

In comparing residential arrangements of 1900 with those of 1950, we probably err if we place too much emphasis on living together, as opposed to not living together, in the same domicile. In 1900, when a married couple lived with the husband's parents, a separate addition was often built into the house for the newly weds; or the parents might occupy the new addition. The point is that the two conjugal units often had separate dwelling space, even though adjacent. It was not much different from living nearby,—

only somewhat more nearby. The residential arrangement is less important than the functional arrangement, although place of residence is not without bearing on function. What matters most in any case is the functional unity of the group. In the past, the extended family was a more highly integrated economic unit, with the aged parent as head. Now the economic integration of the family is much less, even when children contribute to the support of their aged parents. Further, the demand upon children to help with this support is lessened by programs of social security in industry and government.

Litwak (1960) has recently sought to establish the idea of the "modified extended family" in contemporary United States. He thinks it is a mistake to believe that the American family is organized on a nuclear or conjugal basis. He tries to show that although the conjugal units are no longer characterized by propinquity, occupational similarity, and control, they are nevertheless still tied together by mutual aid. We may note, however, that in using the phrase, modified extended family, he acknowledges the fact of change. The scientific question is: precisely how much modification has occurred in the extended family since 1900? It would be unrealistic to ignore the ties that bind together the members of the extended family. The nuclear family seldom if ever operates in complete independence of kin. But if one is interested in the direction of social change in our time, it would be equally unrealistic to ignore the increasing individualism which expresses itself in attentuation of the ties of kinship, and for that matter, even in greater separation of the members of the conjugal family itself.

## THE RELATIONSHIP OF THE AGED AND THEIR GRANDCHILDREN

The grandparents of 1960 have fewer living grandchildren than the grandparents of 1900, but the grandchildren of 1900 had fewer living grandparents than the grandchildren of 1960. The reason for the former is, of course, the lower birth rate; and the reason for the latter, the increase in the span of life.

Since grandparents now have fewer grandchildren, perhaps the grandchildren are more precious than they used to be, on the basis of the law of supply and demand. But we do not know this to be true. Another conjecture is that since grandchildren are fewer, each gets more attention than formerly. We have had many studies of the only child, who is the recipient of undivided parental attention. We need some studies of the only grandchild. But grandparents in 1900 were more likely than now to live near their grandchildren. Now there is more separation. It is more difficult to have an intimate relationship at a distance.

One thing is clear. More grandchildren now have association with a grandparent than was true in 1900. And this association should have the effect of giving the children more of a sense of family tradition. Grandparents are characteristically chroniclers of the past and help to keep the family history alive. This may offset somewhat the loss of interest in things familial, which is the result of the increased individualism of our time.

When grandparents live with or near their grandchildren, the grandparents take over some parental functions. In a recent study, 50 per cent reported baby-sitting and child care. We do not know what percentage of grandparents performed these functions in 1900 but we surmise that the number was low. Recreation and social life away from home have greatly increased in recent decades. The term baby-sitter did not come into our vocabulary until relatively recently. In 1900, only one in twenty-five married women had a paying job outside the home, whereas at present the ratio is nearly one in three, and is expected to increase further. The number of employed mothers is of course less than the number of wives, but it too has increased. If the grandmother is nearby and not infirm, she may assist her daughter with the responsibilities of child care. And the grandfather who has retired is pressed into service as a baby-sitter. The parental roles of grandparents have accordingly been strengthened.

The family status of grandparents in 1960 is lower than it was in 1900. They are not so often heads of the households in which the grandchildren live and do not have the authority that goes with economic control. Also, owing to accelerated change, the cultural gap between grandparents and grandchildren has widened even more than that between parents and children, because the new generation is the principal vehicle of change.

Grandparents in 1960 in the United States have the reputation of being highly permissive with reference to their grandchildren. The arguments usually advanced in explanation of this fact are that the old folks have mellowed, that they have learned to put first things first, and that moreover they are relaxed in dealing with their grandchildren because they are not principally responsible for them. These are all more or less constant factors, hence we should expect to find them also in 1900. But the relationship of grandparents and grandchildren are not so permissive then. In fact it was quite authoritative. Henry Seidel Canby in his illuminating memoir, *The Age of Confidence,* describes his boyhood in his home in Wilmington, Delaware, around the turn of the century. He writes that in the big sprawling house where three generations resided, "it was the grandparents you had to watch out for." He mentions particularly the thimbled finger with which his grandmother would rap him when she thought he needed disciplining. The children went about on tiptoe for fear of disturbing the peace and quiet of their elders; they always addressed them as "sir" or 'm'am"; and they never contradicted them. Lest it be thought that Canby's experience was unique, may we mention that a favorite series of books for children in the early 1900's was *The Prudy Books,* in which the heroine, little Prudy, was disciplined by her grandmother by the same method of the thimbled finger.

If the grandparents were more authoritative in 1900 than they are now, the reason was that they had more authority. "It was the grandparents you had to watch out for," even more than the parents, because the family home belonged to the grandparents. The sprawling house was only one part of the family property, which is so important a key to an understanding of the extended family. Now the big sprawling house is largely a thing of the past, and the less ample house of today more often belongs to the parents, not the grandparents. The greater permissiveness of grandparents in 1960 reflects their decline in status within the family.

We have said the home now usually belongs to the parents. Why, then, do the children not show deference to their parents, as they did to both their parents and grandparents in 1900? Canby says in those days children showed deference to their parents and grandparents even when they profoundly disagreed. His explanation is that the children showed more respect for authority because the authority was a responsible authority. The parents were held to account for their children's behavior and expected to be held responsible. They expected also to hold their children responsible. Now there is more shrugging off of the family responsibility, because that responsibility is shared by the school bus driver, the teacher, the playground director, the Boy Scout leader, the Sunday School teacher, the music teacher, the librarian, the doctor, the nurse, the employer, the sitter, and others *in loco parentis.*

## THE RELATIONSHIP OF THE AGED AND THEIR SIBLINGS AND OTHER KIN

This paper would not be complete without some discussion of the relationship of old people and their siblings and other relatives. Unfortunately the students of the family have given little attention to these relationships, perhaps because they are more removed than those already considered.

The relationship of siblings, especially that of brothers, is generally more unstable than that of parent and child. The experience in India is instructive on this point. There the traditional joint family, when organized around the household of the head and two or more married sons and their families, often breaks down when the father dies. The estate is divided up, contrary to the ideal of the joint family. The basic reason is the competition or jealousy existing among the brothers. It is easier to maintain the joint family when it is organized vertically, in terms of three or more generations than when it is organized horizontally, in terms of siblings. In the towns and cities, the vertical joint family is taking the place of the horizontal joint family of the village. It is easier to maintain the unity of the group when the members have a clearcut relationship of superordination and subordination than when the members have a relationship of equality. In a joint family of brothers, the elder brother has authority over the younger but the fact that they are all brothers makes their status more nearly equal than in the case of father and son. Whatever the explanation, the fact seems to be that parents and children usually live more harmoniously than siblings.

In the light of the foregoing, it seems reasonable to conclude that the relationship of siblings of aged persons, especially the relationship of brothers, would have changed more since 1900 than the relationship of parent and child. The parent-child relationship has become attenuated and we surmise therefore that the sibling relationship has been weakened even more.

We conclude with an observation on the changing relationship of the aged and other kin, such as uncles, aunts, nephews, nieces, and cousins. The increased individualism and physical mobility of the last half century have increased the social distance between kin. One important manifestation of this change is that the limits of responsibility have been modified. In 1900, there was more willingness to assume responsibility, financial and other, for cousins than there is today. The limits of acknowledged responsibility are now being drawn more closely. The effect of this on the aged is that the web of effective or functional relationships is not as wide and complex as it used to be. There are fewer relatives on whose support—material and psychological—the elders can count.

## CONCLUSION

In 1900, in an era still agricultural, the aged were generally persons of considerable power in the family because they controlled property and occupations, and they were greatly respected for their knowledge and ability. Since then, with the growth of our industrial society, property and jobs have moved away from family control. The increased physical mobility separates the aged more often from their children and other kin. The relationship of aged husband and wife has been strengthened by its prolongation and its more equalitarian nature, but the older people now depend less on kin than in 1900, and more on government, industry, and philanthropy. The loss by the aged of economic power, authority, and deferences within the family is probably the most importnat change in their family situation during the past half-century. This loss is being offset by the growing public benefits for the aged resulting from their increasing political power which in turn flows from their proportional increase in the population.

# SELF AND ROLE IN ADJUSTMENT DURING OLD AGE*

### RUTH SHONLE CAVAN

The concepts of self-conception, role-taking, and role-playing —as developed by George H. Mead, Charles Horton Cooley, and others—have possibilities for a significant analysis of adjustment to old age.* They are here applied, first, to retirement from occupation, which is commonly accepted as the most acute adjustment that the older man has to make. The concepts are further tested in brief analyses of the adjustment of the retired man to his family, the adjustment of the widow, and adjustment to grandparenthood. These situations should be regarded as illustrative of the way in which the three concepts may illuminate adjustment in old age.

## RETIREMENT

Both self-conceptions and the social roles through which they find expression are culturally determined. Moreover, some conceptions and roles have higher public esteem than others. For example, the "ideal" male self-conception is the mature adult who is at the height of his powers in a position that he has reached competitively through his own efforts. The self-made man in general is more highly respected than the one who steps in at the top because of family contacts; the employed man out-classes the unemployed or the retired; the self-supporting man has a higher status than the one who depends upon some form of assistance or pension, unless he has earlier contributed to the pension. These different valuations are extremely important at the time of retirement.

At the point of retirement, we may make a generalized picture of the male. He has a well-ingrained self-image as competent, successful at some level of work, usefully productive, self-supporting,

*Reprinted by courtesy of Arnold M. Rose, Editor, *Human Behavior and Social Processes, An Interactionist Approach.* Houghton, Mifflin, New York, 1962, pp. 526-536.

*The present paper was read at the Twentieth Groves Conference on Marriage and the Family, May 1, 1957, East Lansing, Michigan.

and able to provide for his family. This image has been built up over years of time by the favorable reactions of his family, friends, co-workers, and those segments of society whose opinion he values. He has, moreover, found a kind of work—a social role—that permits him to express his self-image satisfactorily, and he is firmly incorporated into a physical environment and a group of co-workers which make it possible for him to carry out his role.

Using the concepts employed above, let us consider what happens at the point of compulsory retirement.[1] First, the means of carrying out the social role disappears: the man is a lawyer without a case, a bookkeeper without books, a machinist without tools. Second, he is excluded from his group of former co-workers; as an isolated person he may be completely unable to function in his former role. Third, as a retired person, he begins to find a different evaluation of himself in the minds of others from the evaluation he had as an employed person. He no longer sees respect in the eyes of former subordinates, praise in the faces of former superiors, and approval in the manner of former co-workers. The looking glass composed of his former important groups throws back a changed image: he is done for, an old-timer, old fashioned, on the shelf. Fourth, he cannot accept this new evaluation for several reasons. He has had the old self-image for so many years that it has become part and parcel of him and is no longer dependent upon the current reflection of himself that he sees in the words and gestures of others. Long ago he internalized satisfying group reflections which now form a kind of independent self-conception. His self-image therefore is in conflict with the reflection he now finds in the attitudes and actions of others. Any movement toward solving the conflict is made difficult because the new self-image offered by those around him is of lower valuation than his internalized self-image.

Therefore at retirement we have a man still motivated by his old self-conception, but separated from his previous roles and many of his previous evaluative groups. He is a true social isolate. Moreover, the faint traces of a new self-image that he sees reflected

---

[1]For additional light on retirement, see Dubin (5), Havighurst and Albrecht (6, Chapter 7), and Streib (9).

in old and perhaps new groups is distasteful and unrewarding. His emotional reactions are likely to be distressing.

We will not go into the changes in this general sequence made by such factors as ill health, voluntary retirement, or retirement of the person who dislikes his work.

Let us look rather at what would be necessary to give a retired person a satisfying adjustment experience.[2] The same concepts are involved as in the original building up of a self-image. First, there would need to be a culturally approved set of values for old age as the basis for a new self-conception. At present, old age is more or less of a vacuum; culturally, it has few real values. Second, these values would have to be accepted and respected by society itself and by the specific groups to which the retired person belonged. Without these two steps the retired person is almost helpless to change his self-image in a constructive manner. His new self-image will develop as his original self-image developed—through finding in others an evaluation of himself as a retired person which he can internalize. Third, new roles are needed through which the retired person may find expression for his new self-image.

Two difficulties exist at present. (*a*) To be satisfying, the new self-image offered by society should be the equivalent in respect of the one he has lost through retirement. A solution is found in partial retirement or in the transition from active worker to consultant. The old self-image may then be retained. Other solutions are less happy. One new self-conception offered to the retired man is the man of leisure who makes a career of leisure-time activities. While recreation has a definite value, to make a career of recreation, hobbies, and the like goes against deeply instilled values. The playboy has never held the respect given to the industrious producer. Another new conception offered by society is the image of oneself as old—that is, identification with old age itself. The names of clubs often suggest simply an old age self-conception: Golden Age Club, Borrowed Time Club, Three-Quarter Century Club, Senior Citizens, and so on. Thus the lawyer, doctor, philanthropist,

[2]The article by Becker and Carper (1) on the process of identification of young men with an occupation has implications for retirement adjustment, since some of the same processes are involved.

shop superintendent, and foreman are all invited to stop being their former selves and to become generalized old age selves.

(*b*) The second difficulty is that many retired men have no real social group to replace their former co-workers. Many recreational and other programs are offered to the retired by social welfare or recreational workers, who make up a group in which the retired man does not have membership. Recall that the self-image is created by the evaluation of a group in which the person has membership. In time, the recreational club may form its own social group exclusive of social workers and may create some new self-conceptions. Such self-conceptions are often limited, however, in that they may not be capable of expression in any group except the club itself.

The present rush to find activities to fill leisure time for old people will not solve the problem of retirement adjustment satisfactorily. The two basic ingredients for adjustment are a culturally approved concept of an old age self held in respect by groups that are meaningful to the old person, and provision to express overtly the implications of the self-image. These elements usually are not present in the present programs devised for the old.

## ADJUSTMENT OF THE RETIRED MAN TO HIS FAMILY

An important adjustment that the retired man has to make is to his family. At the time a man retires his immediate family usually consists only of his wife. The wife, like the husband, has a long established self-image. For a woman now in her sixties, the basic self-image is usually that of wife, mother, homemaker, with a peripheral self of church or community worker, which is in reality but an extension of the homemaker self. Her image has been reflected with approval by family, friends, and community. Her overt role has consisted in establishing the tone of the home, doing or managing the housework, planning and purchasing, giving her husband sympathy and support in his work, and in earlier years rearing children. She has already made one change in her self-image when her children married and left home. Although this change is difficult for some women, it actually is less difficult than the retirement adjustment of the husband. The wife still receives a favorable reflection of herself from those around her, for her married and self-supporting children are a credit to her; and she retains much of the old self-conception and attendant role in continuing as homemaker and companion for her husband. Moreover, society has provided a new self-image for the woman who finds her life too constricted after children leave. The middle-aged employed woman now is socially accepted, and many types of work are open to her. She may devise some mixture of the old and new selves or she may discard the old homemaker self-image and develop a new employed-woman self-image. However, with the present group of retired husbands, the percentage of working wives is low, and the self-image usually is that of wife, homemaker, and retired mother.

Before the retirement of the husband, the self-images and the social roles of husband and wife were neatly dovetailed. It was conceded that the husband's role had slightly higher social status and that he was the head of the family. In her own home, however, the wife reigned supreme. Her self-conception included her queenship in the dominion of the home.

When the retired husband finds himself without his usual means of expression of his self-conception through his work role, he may try to work out a new role at home, without materially changing his self-image. Like a bull in a china shop, we have a man whose self-conception tells him to be competent, decisive, and productive, electing to express this self in a situation in which the available roles are already well filled by his wife, who, within her home, visualizes herself as competent, decisive, and productive. The husband's entrance into the situation tends to create tension in the former coordination between himself and his wife with respect both to their self-images and their roles. The husband sometimes attempts to express his superior status by assuming the decision-making roles in the home; or he may become a self-appointed expert, either criticizing or making suggestions regarding the way in which his wife manages the home. In thus attempting to give expression to his self-conception, he threatens his wife's image of herself. The wife is not opposed to having help in her housekeeping, but her self-conception calls for subordinates who take directions from her. Here, then, is a serious conflict between husband and wife in terms of their self-conceptions and roles. The problem is not one of what housework the husband will do, but of how the self-conceptions of husband and wife will be readjusted. If she retains her superior status and its self-image, his self-conception is damaged; if the husband takes control, the wife's self-conception is damaged.

Often husband and wife go through a period of incipient or actual conflict while self-images and roles are adjusted to a new orientation. Often these adjustments work out very well, especially if increasing age diminishes the desire of both husband and wife for full-time work. In other families, however, little change occurs in the self-images. Accommodation may be made only in roles, as some functions are assigned to the husband and the two overtly carry out coordinated roles. But each may feel dissatisfied and frustrated, with the result that there is bickering between the two.

## WIDOWHOOD

Eventually each family dwindles to one person, and this person is more likely to be the wife than the husband. Only the widow will be discussed.

Instead of looking at widowhood only in terms of loneliness and lack of support, it is helpful to consider it also in terms of self and role. As we have just seen, the self-conceptions as well as the roles of husband and wife become well coordinated during the period when the husband is working; after the husband's retirement, and a transitional period of tensions, the coordination may become even closer with a new orientation. The death of the husband therefore severely disturbs the self-image of the wife. In a sense the two-images have come to form one unit, a kind of family self-conception carried out jointly by husband and wife. Must the widow expand her self-image to include that of her husband, or must the family concept shrink to match her self-image? One may surmise that sometimes one thing happens and sometimes the other. Some widows seem to acquire the attributes of their former husbands; other widows never seem to recover from the bisecting blow of death. The widow may assume the overt roles or tasks of her husband, but this move may be because of necessity. It is in the intangible adjustment of self-image that the heart of the problem of adjustment lies.

If the widow is to modify her self-image, we must go back again to the conditions under which new self-images arise—the culturally acceptable pattern for self-conceptions, and groups of which the widow is a member which will help her achieve a new self-image through their approving evaluation of her change. Fortunately in the case of widowhood, the culture has devised several appropriate self-conceptions. It is important also to recall that the widow usually retains at least some of her old group memberships. She will receive a favorable reflection from her groups if she is courageous, if she attacks practical problems realistically, if she increases her civic or church work, and so forth.

It is at the point of widowhood that adult children often enter the picture, sympathetically offering the mother a home with the family of one of them. If the shock of death has been severe or if there are not sufficient financial resources for continued independence, such a move may be wise. It involves, however, some serious changes in self-conceptions for all concerned. We will consider primarily the situation of the widow. She is now very much in the position of the man who has experienced compulsory retirement. She retains her former self-image as competent housekeeper, companion to her husband, and so forth. But she has no way in which to enact the appropriate roles to give expression to this self-image. As in any well-coordinated household, the members of the younger family have developed self-images and roles that fit together to produce a unified family. It often seems impossible for each a unified family to open to admit an old relative in any except a subordinate—and, to the old person, almost disgraceful—status. Moreover, if the move has carried the widow into another city, she loses her supporting group of friends. Her children's friends are kind to her but do not accept her as an important person with a self of her own. She is Charlie's aunt or Ida's mother. Hence the widow who moves into a younger functioning family in a new community has none of the elements for the construction of a satisfying new self-image. Unless the family is wise enough to help her find a new and respected self-image and accompanying role, she is likely to deteriorate rapidly in personality or to become chronically complaining and disgruntled. It should be emphasized here that the step needed is not to provide love and activities alone, but also to provide a new and valued self-conception which will receive approval and which may be appropriately expressed.

## GRANDPARENTHOOD

Finally, a word about the grandparent self-conception. Often this self-conception has been absorbed into the personality during the fifties or early sixties, especially on the part of women. In fact, some women visualize themselves as grandparents before a child is born and eagerly await the birth of a grandchild so that they may express the grandmother self-image in an appropriate role.

During middle age, men may be proud of their grandchildren, but perhaps do not savor the role completely until after retirement. At first, the man may have some difficulty in accepting the grandfather self as the culture defines it. In the patriarchal and to some extent in the patri-centered family, the grandfather self-image was one of authority and responsibility. Now, however, change has swept away this often satisfying self-image. As the culture defines the grandfather self-image and social role they are maternal in nature. The approved grandparent self is really a grandmother self-conception, whether the holder is the grandfather or the grandmother. Unless the child's own father is dead or not functioning in his role, the grandfather has little opportunity to function in the father role, which is one of financial supporter and source of authority as well as teacher and friend. The child's father guards his self-image and role jealously because they contribute to his conception as head of his family. The maternal role is less precisely defined and may be filled concurrently or successively by a number of different people, each of whom may develop some degree of maternal self-image. In this array of people who fill a maternal role toward the child the retired grandfather takes his place. He must see himself in relation to his grandchild not as a secondary father but as a minor form of mother. His role is to baby-sit, spoon in food, and trundle the baby around in its carriage. If he resents the role, he may arouse some resentment in turn from the baby's mother, who is often pressed for a responsible subordinate. If he accepts the role and develops a slightly masculine grandmother self-image, he may receive an emotional experience that he missed when his own children were young and his time was absorbed in earning a living for them. But to enjoy it he must genuinely be able to acquire a grandparent conception of himself and discover the values in the conception, for the self-image and the role differ widely from the man-of-affairs self and role which dominated his earlier years. Fortunately, the elements for developing a grandparent self are present in the culture. Since children are highly valued in the United States, the mere possession of a grandchild brings respect (or even envy) from friends and from society in general. Since the maternal type of grandparent image is virtually the only one in existence in the United States, the retired man trundling the baby carriage does not feel out of place. The baby comes to love the kindly man who helps to care for it, and the hurried mother adds her thanks. Thus the members of the man's social group approve of the self-image and he sees himself reflected on all sides as a good grandfather filling a valued position.

## CONCLUSION

This essay has attempted to point out the way in which the concepts of self-conception based upon role-taking (Mead) and social role-playing can be helpful in analyzing certain kinds of adjustment in old age and in suggesting how better adjustment could be manipulated. The necessary elements for forming, maintaining, or modifying self-conceptions are socially approved self-images and social roles for their expression, and a group that supports these self-images and roles. To achieve or modify a self-image, the person must be a member of one of these groups and must value the group's evaluation of himself. He will then incorporate within himself the self-image approved by the group. He will need continued membership and the opportunity to enact an appropriate role. These elements are all present at the point of original formulation of self-images in youth, but are partially or completely lacking at the point of reformulations in old age.

# STRUCTURAL CONSTRAINTS ON FRIENDSHIPS IN OLD AGE*

## ZENA SMITH BLAU

Traditionally, survey research has confined itself to interpreting patterns of conduct in terms of differences between individuals, ignoring the ways in which these patterns are conditioned by the different structural contexts in which they occur. In recent years, however, a number of sociologists have become concerned with the problem of using survey data in the systematic investigation of the effects upon conduct of social structures, as distinguished from the social or psychological characteristics of individuals.[1]

The present paper examines how major changes in social status among older people—specifically, widowhood and retirement—affect their friendships, and particularly, how differences in the structural context modify, and sometimes even reverse, the impact of widowhood or retirement on the friendship ties of older persons. Survey data are used to study these influences of social structures.

The data from two surveys of people sixty years old and over—one covering a sample of 468 persons in Elmira, New York, and the

*The present analysis is an extensively revised and condensed version of a paper read at the annual meeting of the American Sociological Society, Washington, D.C., August, 1956. I wish to acknowledge here the many helpful suggestions for revisions offered by Peter M. Blau. The data presented here are part of a series of studies on aging conducted by the Department of Sociology and Anthropology at Cornell University under the direction of Gordon Streib aided by grants from the Rockefeller and Lilly Foundations. Reprinted by courtesy of *American Sociological Review*, Volume 26:429-439, June, 1961.

[1]For example, Samuel Stouffer, *et al.*, *The American Soldier*, Volume I, Princeton: Princeton University Press, 1949, p. 252; Wendell Bell and Maryanne T. Force, "Urban Neighborhood Types and Participation in Formal Associations," *American Sociological Review*, 21 (February, 1956), p. 31; Elihu Katz and Paul F. Lazarsfeld, *Personal Influence*, Glencoe, Ill.: Free Press, 1955, pp. 249-252; S. M. Lipset, M. Trow, and J. S. Coleman, *Union Democracy*, Glencoe, Ill.: Free Press, 1956, pp. 338-363; and James Coleman, "Adolescent Subculture and Academic Achievement," *American Journal of Sociology*, 65 (January, 1960), pp. 337-47. For a discussion of some methodological implications of the use of individual and group data in survey research see Patricia L. Kendall and Paul F. Lazarsfeld, "Problems of Survey Analysis" in *Continuities in Social Research*, edited by Robert K. Merton and Paul F. Lazarsfeld, Glencoe, Ill.: Free Press, 1950, p. 194, and more recently, Peter M. Blau, "Structural Effects," *American Sociological Review*, 25 (April, 1960), pp. 178-93.

other composed of 500 respondents residing in the Kips-Bay York-
ville Health district of New York City[2]—strongly indicate that extensive association with friends becomes an important mechanism
of adjustment in old age following either widowhood or retirement.[3] It is therefore important to discover what social conditions
influence social participation in old age and, in particular, how
differences in the structural context alter the significance that each
type of status change has for the formation and maintenance of
friendships among older people.

In both communities, the extent of friendship participation
declined with age.[4] Thus, in Elmira, 65 per cent of the respondents
still in their sixties had extensive association with friends, compared to 58 per cent of those seventy and over, and in Kips-Bay the
corresponding proportions were 46 per cent and 32 per cent.[5]

---

[2]Although the Elmira survey (1951-52) was an exploratory study of the problems
of older people and the Kips-Bay study (1952) was focused more specifically on their
health problems they contained many of the same questions to make the results in
the two communities comparable. However, some differences between the two
samples deserve mention. For example, people of low socio-economic status were
deliberately overchosen in the Kips-Bay sample, and consequently it contains twice
as many low SES respondents as the Elmira sample. The majority of the Kips-Bay
respondents are foreign born (70 per cent), whereas in Elmira the majority are
native born (87 per cent). Finally, the Kips-Bay sample contains a significantly
higher proportion of respondents seventy years old and over (49 per cent) than in
Elmira (40 per cent), and correspondingly higher proportions of widowed (44 per
cent) and retired people (33 per cent) than in Elmia (38 per cent and 21 per
cent, respectively).

[3]See Zena Smith Blau, "Old Age: A Study of Change in Status," unpublished Ph.D.
Dissertation, Columbia University, 1957.

[4]The index used to measure the extent of friendship participation of respondents
in both communities is a score based on the following three items: 1. "How many
really close friends do you have here in town that you occasionally talk over confidential matters with?" (dichotomized: none [coded 0], one or more friends [coded
+1]; 2. "How often do you get to see the friend that you know best here in town?"
(dichotomized: less than once a month [coded 0], more than once a month [coded
+1]; 3. "Would you say that you go around with a certain bunch of close friends
who visit back and forth in each other's houses?" (No [coded 0], Yes [coded +1]).
A combined score of +2 or more indicates "high" friendship participation. These
three items from a Guttman scale with a Coefficient of Reproducibility of .95.

[5]It is interesting that the proportion of respondents with extensive friendships is
considerably lower in each group in Kips-Bay than in Elmira. These differences, it

———————————→

The likelihood that an individual will have experienced a change either in his marital status or employment status also increases, of course, as people grow older. Thus, in Elmira the proportion of widowed is only 29 per cent among people still in their sixties, but this proportion increases to 52 per cent among those seventy and over, and in Kips-Bay the corresponding proportions are 35 per cent and 53 per cent. The situation with respect to changes in employment status is similar. In Elmira only 15 per cent of the people still in their sixties are retired, but this figure rises to 30 per cent among people seventy and over. In Kips-Bay the corresponding proportions are 31 per cent and 51 per cent.

TABLE 1

PER CENT WITH HIGH FRIENDSHIP PARTICIPATION BY MARITAL AND EMPLOYMENT STATUS IN ELMIRA

| Marital Status | | | Employment Status | | |
|---|---|---|---|---|---|
| Married | 65 | (225) | Employed | 68 | (173) |
| Widowed | 54 | (180) | Retired | 58 | ( 98) |
| Difference | 11 | | | 10 | |

Retirement and widowhood each represent the loss of a major institutional role and it could be expected that each implies some changes in the extent and nature of the social activities among older people. Indeed, a comparison of the extent of friendship participation in Elmira among the married and the widowed, on one hand, and the employed and retired, on the other, suggests that a change either on marital or employment status tends to have an adverse effect on friendships. Table 1 shows that in Elmira widowed respondents associate less with friends than the married and that the retired do so less than the employed. In Kips-Bay retirants also have less association with friends than the employed (see Table 2), but contrary to expectation, the widowed do not participate less in friendships than the married.

will be seen, tend to persist whatever sub-groups are compared in the two communities. Although based exclusively on responses of older people, these findings seem to provide support for the belief that the metropolis is less conducive to the formation and maintenance of extensive close friendship ties than the smaller community.

TABLE 2

PER CENT WITH HIGH FRIENDSHIP PARTICIPATION BY MARITAL AND EMPLOYMENT
STATUS IN KIPS-BAY

| Marital Status | | | Employment Status | | |
|---|---|---|---|---|---|
| Married | 34 | (174) | Employed | 47 | (161) |
| Widowed | 38 | (220) | Retired | 36 | (202) |
| Difference | −4 | | | 11 | |

The problem is to account for these relationships between age, status loss, and social participation. Starting with an examination of the social effects of widowhood in the Elmira community, the discussion will examine similarities and differences in the Kips-Bay data and conclude with an analysis of the social effects of retirement in the two communities.

## AGE-SEX STRUCTURE AND EFFECTS OF WIDOWHOOD

It was noted earlier that association with friends tends to decline and the incidence of widowhood rises as people grow older. A pertinent query at this point is whether the increase in widowhood accounts for the decrease in social participation. In other words, the greater social isolation of people over seventy may be due to the fact that there are more widowed among them than among those in their sixties and that the widowed have disproportionately few friends. Alternatively, it may be that social participation decreases with age regardless of marital status.

TABLE 3

PER CENT WITH HIGH FRIENDSHIP PARTICIPATION BY MARITAL STATUS AND AGE AMONG
MEN AND WOMEN IN ELMIRA

| | Men | | | | Women | | | |
|---|---|---|---|---|---|---|---|---|
| Marital Status | Under Seventy | | Seventy or Over | | Under Seventy | | Seventy or Over | |
| Married | 72 | ( 96) | 65 | (40) | 64 | ( 64) | 44 | ( 25) |
| Widowed | 47 | ( 17) | 67 | (24) | 63 | ( 64) | 52 | ( 75) |
| Difference | 25 | | −2 | | 11 | | −8 | |
| Per cent widowed | 13 | (130) | 33 | (72) | 43 | (149 | 65 | (116) |

Table 3, which compares the social participation of married and widowed men and women under seventy and over, indicates that widowhood does not account for the decline in friendships as people grow older. Although the widowed of both sexes associate significantly less with friends than the married in the younger group, this difference disappears in the older group. Only the participation of the married declines with age; that of the widowed does not. In short, the hypothesis that the higher proportion of widowed persons accounts for the decline in the friendship associations. of people seventy years old and over must be rejected. Widowhood has no detrimental effects on the social participation of people seventy and over, but it has detrimental effects on the friendships of those still in their sixties. How can one explain this unanticipated finding that the *same* change in status has *different* consequences for the individual's social participation depending on whether he is under or over seventy years old?

There are, of course, more widowed persons among older than younger people, and this furnishes an important clue, as an examination of the last two rows in Table 3 reveals. Among men in their sixties, very few are widowed (13 per cent), and the social life of the widowed suffers in comparison with that of the married. However, among men over seventy, a greater proportion (33 per cent) are widowed, and widowhood no longer has adverse effects on social participation. The same difference exists among women; as the proportion of widows increases with age (from 43 per cent to 65 per cent), widowhood ceases to have an adverse effect on friendships. The positive difference between the married and widowed turns into a negative one.

Widowhood appears to have an adverse effect on social participation only when it places an individual in a position different from that of most of his age and sex peers. People tend to form friendships with others in their own age group, and to the extent that this occurs, the widowed person under seventy is likely to be an "odd" person at social gatherings, since most of his associates are probably still married and participate with their spouse in social activities. This difference in his marital position may very well have a detrimental effect on his participation. But after seventy, married couples who continue to participate jointly in social activities become the deviants since most of their friends in this age group are likely to be widowed. A social gathering of septuagenarians, for example, most of whom are by now widowed, will often be composed largely of people of the same sex, and the married couple does not quite fit in. Moreover, continued association on the part of a widow (or widower) with couples whose company she and her spouse used to enjoy together serves as a recurrent reminder of the loss she has suffered, and this may well discourage her from associating frequently with her married friends.

Sex as well as age influences the formation of friendships and consequently it could also be expected to condition the effect of widowhood on participation.[6] Widowhood has a detrimental effect on the friendships of both men and women in their sixties, but, in this younger group, loss of spouse is likely to have a more adverse effect on the participation of men than on that of women (see Table 3). Thus, among people in their sixties, the difference in the proportion of high participants between married and widowed *men* is 25 per cent, while that between married and widowed women is 11 per cent. Married men associate more with friends than married women; widowers, at least under seventy, do so less than widows.

This difference can also be explained in structural terms. In the age group under seventy there is a very marked difference in the proportion of widowed persons among men (13 per cent) and women (43 per cent). Since loss of spouse is especially rare among younger men, the widower occupies a more deviant position with reference to his age-and-sex group than the widow. In concrete terms this means that the overwhelming majority of the male friends of the widower in his sixties are still married and consequently tend to participate in social activities with other couples, since their wives can be expected to find friendly "get-togethers" where other women are also present more enjoyable than visits with a widower friend with whom they, if not their husbands, are likely to have few shared interests. To be sure, younger widows would encounter similar problems in their social relations with married friends. But widowhood is less detrimental to the par-

[6]Newly formed friendships, for example, are restricted to persons of the same sex in more than four-fifths of the cases in Kips-Bay.

ticipation of women under seventy than to that of men in the same age group, because the woman in her sixties is more likely to have some associates who are widowed too. The younger widow, therefore, is not in as deviant a position socially as the younger widower, although widowhood probably decreases her social contacts with *married* friends as much as it does that of men. Hence, widowhood does not affect the participation of younger women to the same extent as that of younger men.

Table 3 shows further that among people seventy and over, where there is a far larger proportion of widowers (33 per cent), the difference in the participation of married and widowed men disappears (−2 per cent). In other words, as this change in marital status becomes more prevalent among age and sex peers, widowhood ceases to have an isolating effect upon widowers. By this time, a number of his friends have also become widowers, oldsters in "the same boat" as he on whom he can rely for social companionship. Indeed, older widowers associate more with friends (67 per cent) than younger ones (47 per cent), while older married men tend to do so less (65 per cent) than younger ones (72 per cent).

The social participation of women reveals the same pattern. The proportion of high participants among married women drops from 64 per cent in the younger group to 44 per cent in the older one, but there is no such drop among the widowed. Among women over seventy, two thirds of whom are widowed, it is the married person who occupies a deviant position, and as a result, she tends to associate somewhat less with friends than the widow in the same age group.

In sum, these findings suggest the following hypothesis: the effect that changes in major status have on the friendships of older people depends on the *prevalence* of these changes in the social structure. A change in status which places the individual in a deviant position in his age or sex group interferes with his opportunities to maintain old friendships. For if a change in a major status places an individual in a minority position among his peers, it differentiates his interests and experiences from theirs and thereby reduces the mutual bonds that serve as the basis for the formation and persistence of friendships. But if the same status change becomes predominant in a social group, then it is the individual who retains his earlier status who becomes the deviant, and consequently it is his social participation that suffers.

## TESTS OF THE HYPOTHESIS[7]

Several methods of testing the hypothesis that the prevalence of widowhood conditions its effect on the friendships of older people could be pursued. First, a replication of the foregoing analysis could be undertaken in another community to determine whether the findings differ and whether these differences could be accounted for in terms of the hypothesis. Second, since class structure presumably provides an important boundary for friendship choices, it might be expected that the prevalence of widowhood in different socio-economic status levels would also condition the effects that widowhood exerts on the friendship associations of older people. Third, since retirement as well as widowhood is a major status change characteristic of old age, it is pertinent to inquire whether the prevalence of this type of status loss in the age, sex, and class structures occupied by the older person also conditions its effects on friendship participation. Space limitations force us to eliminate a step by step analysis of the replication in Kips-Bay, and of the significance of class boundaries in the two communities. Instead, we proceed directly to examine simultaneously the implications of all three structural variables—age, sex and class—for the friendships of widowed and married people in both communities.

---

[7]The use of statistical tests of significance in survey research has become a subject of controversy in recent years. The assumptions underlying their use are perhaps particularly open to question in the case of the kinds of relationships under examination here—the interaction effects of the distribution of a variable in a population and the same variable as it characterizes individuals on another attribute of these individuals. It has been decided, therefore, not to use statistical tests of significance in this paper, but to rely on the recurrence of an expected pattern in various subgroups and independent samples as the criterion for accepting or rejecting a hypothesis. For a discussion of the uses and abuses of statistical tests, see S. M. Lipset, M. A. Trow, and J. S. Coleman, *Union Democracy*, Glencoe, Ill.: Free Press, 1956, pp. 427-432 and Hanan C. Selvin, "A Critique of Tests of Significance in Survey Research," *American Sociological Review*, 22 (October, 1957), pp. 519-527.

TABLE 4

PARTICIPATION BY MARITAL STATUS AND AGE-SEX-CLASS-POSITION IN ELMIRA
AND KIPS-BAY

| | | | | | Elmira | | | | |
|---|---|---|---|---|---|---|---|---|---|
| | | | | | | Per Cent High Friendship Participation Among | | | |
| Class | Sex | Age | Per Cent Widowed | N | Married | N | Widowed | N | Difference |
| High | Men | Under 70 | 17 | (58) | 76 | (41) | 50 | (10) | +26 |
| | | Over 70 | 36 | (25) | 77 | (13) | 78 | ( 9) | − 1 |
| | Women | Under 70 | 42 | (89) | 62 | (36) | 88 | (37) | −26 |
| | | Over 70 | 70 | (59) | 27 | (11) | 56 | (41) | −29 |
| Low | Men | Under 70 | 10 | (72) | 69 | (55) | 43 | ( 7) | +26 |
| | | Over 70 | 31 | (47) | 59 | (27) | 60 | (15) | − 1 |
| | Women | Under 70 | 46 | (61) | 64 | (28) | 43 | (28) | +21 |
| | | Over 70 | 60 | (57) | 57 | (14) | 47 | (34) | +10 |
| Total | | | | | | (468) | | | |
| | | | | | Kips-Bay | | | | |
| High | Men | Under 70 | 3 | (38) | 47 | (30) | .. | | .. |
| | | Over 70 | 25 | (19) | 47 | (15) | 0 | ( 5) | +47 |
| | Women | Under 70 | 51 | (42) | 60 | (15) | 76 | (21) | −16 |
| | | Over 70 | 64 | (39) | 0 | ( 7) | 28 | (25) | −28 |
| Low | Men | Under 70 | 19 | (68) | 21 | (47) | 43 | ( 7) | −21 |
| | | Over 70 | 39 | (63) | 23 | (26) | 38 | (24) | −15 |
| | Women | Under 70 | 56 | (109) | 44 | (25) | 43 | (60) | + 1 |
| | | Over 70 | 63 | (122) | 50 | ( 8) | 28 | (76) | +22 |
| Total | | | | (500) | | | | | |

## SOCIAL STRUCTURE AND EFFECTS OF WIDOWHOOD IN TWO COMMUNITIES

Table 4 compares the differences in the proportion of married and widowed respondents with high social participation in eight age-sex-class[8] categories in Elmira (top) and in seven corresponding categories[9] in Kips-Bay (bottom), and shows the proportions of widowed in each of these fifteen categories. These data permit an

[8]A score based on interviewer ratings, on educational level, and on class identification of respondents was used as the index of socio-economic status in the Elmira study. In Kips-Bay a more refined scale of interviewer ratings served as the index of socio-economic status.

[9]One category in Kips-Bay, that of men under seventy in the higher class, is omitted from the analysis, because it contained only one widowed male.

over-all test of the hypothesis that widowhood tends to exert a detrimental effect on friendships in those structural contexts where it is
relatively rare but not in those where it becomes more prevalent.
In order to carry out this test, however, it is necessary to define
operationally the terms, "prevalence," and "detrimental effect."
Widowhood is considered prevalent if a third or more of the people
in a category have experienced this change in status.[10] And widowhood is considered to exert an adverse effect on friendships if the
proportion of respondents with extensive friendship participation
among the married exceeds that among the widowed by at least
five per cent.

Inspection of Table 4 shows, looking first at the Elmira data,
that in two of the three categories where less than a third of the respondents are widowed this change in status has adverse effects on
friendships. In the third category—males over seventy in the lower
class—widowhood does not exert a detrimental effect. On the other
hand, in three out of the five categories where the widowed constitute over a third, widowhood does not have an adverse effect on
friendships. In the remaining two categories—younger and older
lower class women—widowhood has detrimental social effects despite its prevalence.[11] In Kips-Bay a similar pattern is found. In
one of the two categories where widowhood is not prevalent it has
adverse effects on friendships but in the other—lower class males in
their sixties—widowhood is not detrimental to friendships. On the
other hand, in four out of the five categories where widowhood is
prevalent it does not have adverse social effects. But in the remaining category, that of women over seventy in the lower class, widowhood is detrimental to friendships despite its prevalence.

In sum, the results in ten out of fifteen comparisons confirm the
hypothesis that the effects of widowhood on friendships vary inversely with the prevalence of this type of status change in the social

[10]This proportion was selected as the cutting point simply because it provided the
"best fit" among the various alternatives that were tried.

[11]To be sure, in Elmira widowhood makes more difference for participation among
the lower class women under seventy where 46 per cent are widowed than among
those over seventy where 60 per cent are widowed, but these must still be considered negative cases since in both the widowed participate less socially than the
married.

structure. It is worth noting that all five negative cases involve lower class respondents in the two communities. Indeed, if the lower class and higher class categories are tabulated separately, as shown in Table 5, it is seen that the postulated relationship between the prevalence of widowhood and the nature of its effects of friendships is confirmed without exception in the higher class categories in the two communities but not in the lower ones. Thus, among the higher classes, in all five age-sex categories in the two communities where widowhood is prevalent the widowed associate as much or more with friends than the married, and conversely, in the two categories where it is not prevalent the widowed associate less with friends than the married.

Among the lower classes, in contrast, the findings in five out of the eight categories are opposite to those predicted. Moreover, a reexamination of Table 4 shows that lower class women constitute three of the five deviant categories. In all but one of the categories of women in the lower classes in the two communities widowhood has an adverse effect on friendship participation despite the prevalence of this status change in all of them.

These interesting, albeit unanticipated findings suggest that class position operates as a contingency factor in the relation between the prevalence of widowhood and its social effects. Among the higher classes differences in the prevalence of widowhood account for its varying effects on the social life of older people but in the lower classes, particularly in the case of women, other factors seem to block the individual from taking advantage of the social opportunities created by the prevalence of widowhood among her peers. As a result, widowhood usually has an isolating effect on her social life.

TABLE 5

PREVALENCE OF WIDOWHOOD AND EFFECTS ON FRIENDSHIPS BY CLASS POSITION IN ELMIRA AND KIPS-BAY

| | Class Position | | | |
|---|---|---|---|---|
| | Higher | | Lower | |
| Prevalence of Widowhood | Detrimental | Not Detrimental | Detrimental | Not Detrimental |
| 34-100% | 0 | 5 | 3 | 2 |
| 0- 33% | 2 | 0 | 1 | 2 |

Differences in the patterns of participation of working class and middle class wives prior to the advent of old age may partly explain the differences in their social position in widowhood. There is reason to believe that the social life of the working class woman is limited largely to visits with relatives and some joint participation with her spouse in social activities. The social life of the woman in the higher classes, on the other hand, is more likely to include more extensive association with other women. As a result of more varied organizational activities and social pastimes which bring her into frequent contact with age-sex peers, she is likely to accumulate over the years a relatively wide circle of friends and acquaintances. To be sure, her participation in these activities may become more limited as she grows older. She may see less of her old friends and acquaintances and devote herself more to activities that she can share with her husband. But the death of her spouse generates a need for alternative sources of companionship, and she is likely, after the first shock of grief has passed, to welcome the solicitude of old friends and to take advantage of opportunities to reestablish closer ties with them, particularly with other widows who, like herself, also want social companionship. In other words, in widowhood the middle class woman is likely to reestablish, with some modifications, of course, her earlier pattern of shared social activities—bridge, shopping, attendance at cultural events, visits, travel—with other women whom she had known before. Thus, her pattern of shared social activities with other women of like status prior to widowhood constitutes a "reservoir" of social opportunities that the middle and higher class woman can draw on after the death of her husband, particularly if several of her old friends are also widows and equally disposed to strengthen old social ties. In contrast, the lower class woman, who is not as likely to have participated in this pattern of shared social activities with other women in middle age while her husband was alive, is less apt to have this reservoir of social opportunities to draw upon when widowhood deprives her of the social activities that she had shared with her husband.

The economic deprivation occasioned by the death of her husband in all probability constitutes another factor that limits the social opportunities of the lower class woman regardless of the prevalence of this change in status among her peers. To be sure, for the middle class woman widowhood also often entails some reduction in income, particularly if her husband was still in the labor force, but her financial resources are generally greater than those of the lower class widow, who is often subject to the stringent economies imposed by Old Age Assistance grants. No matter how modest the scale of social activities, they usually involve some expenditures of money—the carfare required to pay visits, the refreshments offered to a guest, the cost of a ticket to the movies—and these costs of participating in social life may constitute a formidable barrier for the lower class widow but not for the one in a higher class position.

## SOCIAL STRUCTURE AND RETIREMENT IN TWO COMMUNITIES

An analysis of the effects of occupational retirement on friendships in Elmira and Kips-Bay, paralleling that on widowhood, provides an opportunity to test and extend the scope of our hypothesis.

A preliminary comparison of the over-all participation of employed and retired respondents in the two communities indicates that in each of them retirants associate less with friends than people who are still employed. In Elmira the proportion of people with high friendship participation scores is 68 per cent among the employed and 58 per cent among the retired (see Table 1), and the corresponding proportions in Kips-Bay are 47 per cent and 36 per cent (see Table 2). However, as Table 6 shows, when the respondents in the two communities are divided into the same sixteen age-sex-class categories used in the analysis of widowhood, it becomes evident that the social effects of retirement, like those of widowhood, are not consistently detrimental.

In the case of men the findings lend support to the hypothesis that the social effects of retirement, like those of widowhood, vary according to the prevalence of this change in status among others occupying a similar position in the social structure. These results can be more readily seen if the data in Table 6 are classified according to the sex of respondents and ordered on the basis of more precise operational criteria.

Retirement is defined as prevalent if more than a third of the

**TABLE 6**

FRIENDSHIP PARTICIPATION BY EMPLOYMENT STATUS AND AGE-SEX-CLASS POSITION IN ELMIRA AND KIPS-BAY

*Elmira*

| Class | Sex | Age | Per Cent Retired | N | Per Cent High Friendship Participation Among Employed | N | Retired | N | Difference |
|---|---|---|---|---|---|---|---|---|---|
| High | Men | Under 70 | 30 | (58) | 75 | (40) | 59 | (17) | +16 |
| | | Over 70 | 56 | (25) | 82 | (11) | 79 | (14) | + 3 |
| | Women | Under 70 | 9 | (89) | 65 | (23) | 63 | ( 8) | + 2 |
| | | Over 70 | 9 | (59) | 40 | (5) | 40 | ( 5) | 0 |
| Low | Men | Under 70 | 21 | (72) | 71 | (58) | 60 | (15) | +11 |
| | | Over 70 | 63 | (47) | 78 | (18) | 50 | (30) | +28 |
| | Women | Under 70 | 2 | (61) | 47 | (17) | .. | | .. |
| | | Over 70 | 14 | (57) | 60 | ( 5) | 60 | ( 8) | − 3 |
| Total | | | | (468) | | | | | |

*Kips-Bay*

| Class | Sex | Age | Per Cent Retired | N | Employed | N | Retired | N | Difference |
|---|---|---|---|---|---|---|---|---|---|
| High | Men | Under 70 | 11 | (38) | 55 | (33) | 25 | ( 5) | +30 |
| | | Over 70 | 50 | (19) | 30 | (10) | 40 | (10) | −10 |
| | Women | Under 70 | 15 | (42) | 63 | (16) | 67 | ( 6) | − 4 |
| | | Over 70 | 19 | (39) | .. | ( 3) | 43 | ( 7) | .. |
| Low | Men | Under 70 | 53 | (68) | 28 | (32) | 33 | (36) | − 5 |
| | | Over 70 | 81 | (63) | 33 | (12) | 36 | (50) | − 3 |
| | Women | Under 70 | 31 | (109) | 67 | (33) | 45 | (33) | +22 |
| | | Over 70 | 46 | (122) | 47 | (19) | 29 | (55) | +18 |
| Total | | | | (500) | | | | | |

respondents in a category are retired, otherwise, it is considered not to be prevalent. The effects of retirement on friendships are defined as detrimental if the proportion of people with high friendship participation scores is at least 5 per cent larger among the employed than among the retired. If the differences are smaller or negative retirement is not considered to have adverse social effects.

Table 7 shows the relationship between prevalence of retirement and its effect on friendships in all eight categories of men and in six of the eight categories of women[12] in the two communities.

---

[12]Two categories, lower class women under seventy in Elmira and higher class women over seventy in Kips-Bay, are omitted from the analysis owing to the fact that the first contained fewer than five retirants and the second less than five employed.

Among men, in all three categories where retirement is not prevalent retirants associate less with friends than the employed, indicating that this change in status has adverse effects on participation. On the other hand, in four out of the five categories where retirement is prevalent no adverse effects on friendships are noted. In the fifth category, that of lower class men over seventy in Elmira, retirement, despite its prevalence, is detrimental to friendships. In short, among men the data, with one exception, support the hypothesis that the effect that retirement has on the social life of the older individual is contingent on its prevalence among others occupying a similar position in the social structure.

TABLE 7

PREVALENCE OF RETIREMENT AND ITS EFFECTS ON FRIENDSHIPS BY SEX IN ELMIRA AND KIPS-BAY

| | Men | | Women | |
|---|---|---|---|---|
| Prevalence of Retirement | Detrimental | Not Detrimental | Detrimental | Not Detrimental |
| 34-100% | 1 | 4 | 1 | 0 |
| 0- 33% | 3 | 0 | 1 | 4 |

These findings can readily be explained. Retirement, whatever the age of the man, reduces his opportunities for contact with co-workers. But early retirement is also apt to disturb those social ties that the individual has established with age peers outside the work situation, since in most cases of men in their sixties the majority are still employed (see Table 6). Even when employed friends who are not co-workers come together socially their experiences on their jobs color their conversation in various ways. They may exchange amusing stories that originated in the work situation. They may relieve tensions that arose on the job by telling their friends about conflicts with co-workers and superiors, and, in turn, listen sympathetically to the work-connected problems of their friends. In the company of intimate friends they may permit themselves to talk about their successful experiences on the job and thereby heighten the gratification derived from these achievements.

Retirement deprives the older individual of the run of common experience that is shared by people who work. As a result he can no longer fully participate in the conversational "give-and-take" of his employed friends.

The individual who retires while most of his friends are still employed becomes a deviant in his social group, an "outsider." The conversation about "business" in which he had been able to join freely when he had still been working become after retirement a sign of his no longer being in the in-group and a barrier to continued association with his employed friends. In short, the very pattern that serves as a means of interpersonal integration for the individual who is in the same position as the majority of his friends operates as a mechanism of exclusion when his position becomes different from theirs.

The retirant over seventy is less likely to encounter this problem. The majority of his age group are retired, and a good many of his friends are in the same position as he. Thus, Table 6 shows that among men over seventy at each class level in the two communities at least half the respondents have experienced this change in status. As a result the older retirant ceases to be at a social disadvantage compared to the man who is still employed. Indeed, in Kips-Bay where retirement is generally more prevalent than in Elmira it is the employed man over seventy who tends to occupy a deviant position with respect to his age and sex peers and consequently associates less with friends than his retired counterpart. In short, the fact that the majority of his age and sex peers have experienced a similar change in status more than compensates the retirant for the loss of social contacts with his co-workers on the job.

Table 7 indicates that the effect that retirement exerts on the friendship participation of women follows no discernible pattern. Retirement is, of course, generally less prevalent among women than among men since many women have not been gainfully employed during their married life. The proportion of retirants, as shown in Table 6, is under a third in all but one of the categories of women in both communities. In four of the six groups, nevertheless, retired women associate as much or more with friends than the employed. Clearly, among women the prevalence of retirement is not inversely related to whether retirement is detrimental for friendships. These findings serve to emphasize the profound difference in the significance of gainful employment for men and women in our society.

For the married woman marital duties, rearing children, and management of the household are culturally defined as the obligatory social roles. To be sure, there is a growing acceptance of employment for women, particularly after their children are grown, but the prevailing attitude is that the job for women constitutes a secondary role that must not be allowed to interfere with the discharge of their primary responsibilities, that of wife and mother. As a result, the patterns of association among women, whether they are gainfully employed or not, are conditioned primarily by their marital status and, in their child-rearing years, also somewhat by their maternal status. Indeed, the married woman who seems unduly concerned with her job is apt to be an object of criticism not only among her own sex but among men as well.

The secondary nature of the employment role for women is perhaps most clearly visible at social gatherings. Since the prevailing status among married women in most social circles in this society is that of housewife, the woman who holds a job is constrained at social gatherings to converse about matters of common interest to others of her own sex—that is, to engage in "women's talk." Although women may jokingly disparage their tendency to engage in this pattern, just as they exhort their husbands to stop "talking shop," they nevertheless tend to persist in it. The occasional woman who deviates from this dominant pattern of interaction risks criticism from her housewife friends, who are typically in the majority and can effectively impose negative sanctions upon such deviants. However, most married women who work willingly give precedence to their feminine roles and rarely allow their jobs to become a basis for differential association with others. In other words, the social life of the married woman is conditioned more by her marital status than by her employment status. Since the status of wife is the focus of her social life, widowhood rather than retirement has the major impact. The social life of men, on the other hand, is strongly conditioned by their work role and, consequently, also by retirement.[13]

[13]In an analysis of how retirement affects personal adjustment in old age it was found that retirement also makes considerably less difference for the adaptation of women than for that of men. See Zena Smith Blau, *op. cit.,* p. 47.

## CONCLUSIONS

Comparison of the friendship participation of married and widowed people in Elmira suggested the hypothesis that the effect of widowhood on friendships depends on its prevalence in a given structural context among older people. Since friends tend to be of the same sex and in a similar age group, a change in marital status that places an individual in a deviant position among his age and sex peers and differentiates his interests and experiences from theirs is likely to have an adverse effect on his friendships. When, on the other hand, widowhood becomes prevalent among others similarly located in the social structure it is the individual who is still married who occupies a deviant position and who, therefore, often sees less of his old friends.

In Elmira, loss of spouse is the exception rather than the rule among both men and women under seventy, but it is especially rare among men in this age group, and consequently, widowhood has a more detrimental effect on the participation of men than on that of women. After seventy, the prevalence of widowhood increases among men, and as a result the differences between married and widowed men decrease. But only among women over seventy, where the widowed are in a majority, do widowed women tend to have more association with friends than the married.

An examination of the effects on friendships of the varying prevalence of widowhood in the sixteen age-sex-class categories in Elmira and Kips-Bay suggested that class position operates as a contingency factor. In the higher classes in both communities the social effects of widowhood varied with its prevalence among the various age-sex categories, but in the lower classes in the two communities, particularly in the case of women, widowhood had consistently adverse effects on friendships, regardless of its prevalence. Two reasons for these differences were suggested: (1) the middle class married woman, in contrast to the working class woman, tends to engage in a pattern of shared social activities with other women, supplementing those shared with her husband, and these previously established social ties constitute a reservoir of social opportunities in widowhood which is less available to the working class woman, because she is less likely to have had during her husband's lifetime an extensive social life independent of him; and (2) widowhood for the working class woman, more often than for the middle class woman, imposes severe economic deprivations which operate to drastically limit her social activities. Finally, analysis of the social effects of retirement, another major type of status loss in old age, constituted an additional test of the hypothesis and an opportunity to extend its scope. It was found that among men the effects of retirement on friendships vary according to its prevalence among the age-sex-class peers of the individual. Thus, in all structural contexts where retirement was not prevalent, this change in status had adverse effects on the friendships of men. On the other hand, in all but one of the categories where retirement was prevalent it did not have adverse social effects for the individual. However, among women, as might be expected, retirement does not exert any patterned effect on friendships, because in contrast to its major significance for men, gainful employment for the married woman constitutes a secondary role, and therefore, is rarely a basis for differential association whether she is employed or retired.

A methodological implication of this paper is the suggestion of a procedure for using survey data to infer selected characteristics of the group structures in which respondents are located when no direct information about these peer groups is available. The proportion of widowed and retired among each respondent's associates and potential associates is not known. But since it is known that people tend to associate with others in their own sex, age, and class position, the proportions of widowed or retired among the respondents themselves in these categories were used to infer the proportions among their associates. To be sure, it would be preferable to have direct evidence on the characteristics of each respondent's peer group. But if such data cannot be readily collected, the attributes of these peer group structures can be roughly inferred by the procedure here employed.

The basic substantive finding of the present paper—that the *same* status may have different consequences depending on its prevalence in the social structure—calls attention to the importance of taking the structural context into account in sociological analysis.

For when the conduct of individuals is analyzed not simply in terms of their own social status, but also in terms of the structural context in which they are located an explanation of observed differences in conduct among people of *like* status is more likely to be forthcoming. Thus, the analysis of the friendships of widowed and retired individuals in terms of the prevalence of widowhood and retirement in those social contexts within which friendships are likely to occur helped to explain why widowhood and retirement, which constitute the major changes in status in old age, sometimes have an adverse effect on the friendships of older people, but at other times do not. What had appeared, at first, as a number of idiosyncratic exceptions was discovered to be, once structural analysis was introduced, a new social pattern.

# Chapter 3

## DEMOGRAPHIC CHARACTERISTICS OF THE AGED

### THE RELATION OF SOCIOLOGICAL TO BIOLOGICAL RESEARCH IN GERONTOLOGY*

BELLE BOONE BEARD

IN SEVERAL AREAS of gerontology, the biologist and sociologist have mutual concern; and research in one area may suggest hypotheses in the other. In addition to raising some questions regarding longevity and fertility, I shall discuss four ideas which have had wide acceptance, but which, in the light of research findings, warrant continuing re-examination. They are:

1. that longevity is chiefly a matter of heredity—that is, of "choosing the right ancestors";

2. that the span of life is fixed and cannot be changed by health practices—"the expectation of life has been changed but not the life span";

3. that senescence consists of automatic changes related to age; and

4. that aging is a process which cannot be retarded or reversed.

It is my belief that acceptance of the first two notions may lead to undue optimism and of the last two to undue pessimism or apathy.

Most studies of longevity, from Galton to Rockstein treat longevity as an hereditary trait. Although there is considerable evidence that there are long-lived and short-lived strains among both people and lower animals, none of the earlier studies attempted to differentiate between genetic factors and social and economic factors. Richardson's study comparing the life spans of children with those

---

*Presented at the annual meeting of the Gerontological Society, Philadelphia. November 7, 1958. Reprinted by courtesy of *Geriatrics*, Volume *14*, October, 1959.

of their parents and grandparents shows striking differences, but no allowance was made for nonhereditary increase in the average age of death that had taken place between generations. A difference in death age of even ten years seems very impressive until we compare it with increments of life span due to medical, social, and economic factors. The table, taken from Mayer's and Hauser's study of class differentials in expectation of life, shows wide divergencies in life expectation for white and nonwhite in Chicago for the highest and lowest of five economic groups. If the mortality rates of all persons in Chicago in 1920 had been as low as that of the highest economic class of the white population, the number of deaths would have been 34 per cent less.

TABLE 1
EXPECTATION OF LIFE AT BIRTH BY COLOR, SEX AND ECONOMIC CLASS

|  | White | | Nonwhite | |
| --- | --- | --- | --- | --- |
|  | M | F | M | F |
| Lowest Economic Class | | | | |
| 1930 | 51.3 | 56.2 | 38.6 | 42.5 |
| 1940 | 52.8 | 62.7 | 47.3 | 52.7 |
| Highest Economic Class | | | | |
| 1930 | 63.0 | 67.1 | 47.9 | 50.9 |
| 1940 | 65.4 | 70.3 | 53.3 | 58.5 |

The tenth anniversary report of the World Health Organization cites phenomenal gains in expectation of life. For example, Puerto Rico's expectation of life rose from 46.0 years in 1939-41 to 63.8 in 1955. In Ceylon there was a gain of 17.1 years in an even shorter period—from 42.8 in 1946 to 59.9 in 1954. This report attributes these gains largely to "use of penicillin and other antibiotics, use of vaccines, better diagnosis and treatment of illness, more hospital facilities, better child and maternal care, advances in surgery, and the spraying of large areas with insecticides."

What are the prospects for further increase in the average expectation of life? Biologically is there any reason to believe that expectation of life has reached a plateau around seventy? Or, can it be expected to reach seventy-five, or eighty, or ninety years? By what means can we establish valid projections for the future?

Louis Dublin, who has been consistently conservative in his estimates of future life expectation, predicted in 1942 that advances in science might prolong life appreciably. He predicted that at least a year might be added if the problem of cancer is solved and another if heart and circulatory impairments are understood. He concluded that modern social and medical science might create a level of human vitality so high that even the life span itself might be raised.

How long can the average life be extended without increasing the maximum span? The idea of a fixed upper limit, predetermined and immutable, seems still to be taken for granted by many biologists, physicians, psychologists, and sociologists. For example, Dr. Carl V. Weller's oft-quoted theory holds that the life pattern of each species is indelibly stamped into the living nuclear substance which determines heredity. He contends that the ultimate life limit of people will not be extended by the efforts of the health sciences and that there is no scientific basis for dreams of a life limit of 125 years.

On the other hand, a few biologists are now making cautious statements regarding modification of the life pattern. Comfort, after examining numerous studies dealing with senescence of specific biological factors, concludes that there is no "inherent" factor which determines the maximum limit of life span. Moreover, Dublin and other students of longevity have found no one demonstrable external agent known to affect the life span. If then there are neither inherent nor external factors known to determine man's maximum life span, barring radioactive fallout and drunken drivers on the highways, is it not possible that he may avoid more or less indefinitely lethal conditions? If Dr. James B. Rogers at the University of Louisville can increase the life span of guinea pigs from the average of 2.3 years to eight years, why is it not possible to double the life span of man?

Doubt regarding the validity of a fixed life span arises from such factors as the following:

1. Discoveries regarding the viability of human cells, cultures which seem immortal.

2. The known variability in ages of many species and the ex-

treme cases which double or triple the accepted norms for the species.

3. Years added by the conquest of smallpox, tuberculosis, pneumonia, and other diseases, and the predictions of years to be added by conquest of cancer, heart disease, and so on.

4. Indications of the possibility of maintaining a state of health and vigor or of preventing deterioration of specific functions by diet, exercise, and so on.

5. Evidence that such measures as use of vitamins, hormone therapy, blood transfusions, and organ replacement may extend life.

6. The replacement of worn parts by artificial aids, such as nylon arteries, silver pins and hip hinges, ear trumpets, iron lungs, and heart pumps.

Three types of evidence may be considered in answering the question of whether the life span has increased: (1) the percentage of centenarians in a given population at successive time intervals; (2) the number of persons living to 110 or beyond; and (3) the changing shape of the population pyramid.

In neither of the first two do we have clear-cut evidence. Two decades ago Walter G. Bowerman, an actuary of the New York Life Insurance Company, predicted that the proportion of centenarians would decrease. He based his predictions on census reports: "In 1850 there were eleven centenarians reported per 100,000 population. In each successive decade this proportion decreased until in 1910 there were only 4 per 100,000; in 1930, 3.2."

According to the U. S. Bureau of the Census, there was in the United States in 1940 only 1 centenarian to 37,000 population or less than 3 per 100,000 population. Yet the number of centenarians in the United States rose from 3,679 in 1940 to 4,475 in 1950, an increase of 21.6 per cent, while in this same period, the total population of the United States increased by only 14.5 per cent. Estimates on the basis of spot studies indicate the number of centenarians will exceed 5,000 by 1960. Does this mean that the same factors which have been responsible for the increase in the average expectation of life will continue to operate to increase markedly the number passing the century mark? If so, what is to prevent this carry-over from being extended for another twenty, thirty, or forty years?

### Age Composition of the Population: 1880 and 1955

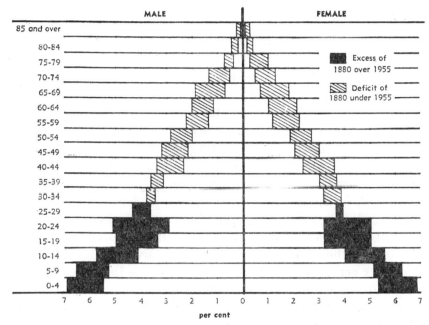

Source: Taeuber, Conrad, and Irene B. Taeuber, 1958,
The Changing Population of the United States., page 32.

Verification of ages beyond 110 to seldom possible. Our only reliable sample today is the much publicized veterans of the Civil War. Of the approximately 4 million men who took part in the Civil War, 137 are known to have survived to 100 or more. Rulon Williamson, actuary of the Federal Security Agency, after careful analysis of mortality tables, devised an ingenious formula of 40 per cent loss each year after 100. If this rule had been applied to the 137 veterans, none would have survived beyond 108. You will recall the embarrassment of the GAR when Albert Woolson of Duluth survived the estimated date for final demise of Union vets and a special appropriation had to be granted him.

At least five of the 137 Civil War veterans reaching 100 lived beyond 110. James Hard, who lived to be 111, was the oldest GAR veteran, and there are today two surviving Confederate Veterans, John Salling, 112, and Walter Williams, who was 116 on November 14, 1958. Obviously, the 40 per cent formula is not correct. If the same percentage (3.6 per cent) should apply to the approximately 4,500 centenarians living today, 162 people should reach 110. If 162 of the present centenarians reach 110 years of age, what are the chances that some of these 162 will live to be 120 years old?

While the above data may be selective and therefore not typical, the third type of evidence—the changing shape of the population pyramid—relates to the total population. Changes in the population pyramid from 1880 to 1955 are shown in the figure, which is adapted from Taeuber's *Changing Population of the United States*. It will be seen that, even with our current baby boom, the percentage of persons under twenty-five has markedly decreased; whereas, the percentages in the age brackets beyond forty have increased. For example, the percentage of population from fifty-five to sixty-five has doubled; whereas, from sixty-five upward, the percentages have tripled. In other words, more people are living longer and the older they get the larger the differential. If the increases in older age groups shown by these pyramids continue, what are the prospects for pushing up the maximum age limit? There is no doubt such findings plus their traditional mortality tables have led insurance companies to change the recovery limit on life policies from 96 to 108 years and now to 116 and 120 years of age.

## Longevity and Specified Biological Factors

In the passage quoted above, Dr. Weller referred to the "indelibly stamped life pattern" as "that most successful for the perpetuation of the species." This raises questions concerning the relation between longevity and biological factors associated with reproduction. The sociologist has observed many phenomena about longevity and fertility but must turn to the biologist for explanations.

All studies of longevity in man and animals show sex to be the most universal and persistent differential. In all nations, in all social classes, and in all historical eras, females outlive males. Why? Numerous studies have shown that married women have lower mortality rates than single, divorced, or widowed women. How does the biologist account for the differential longevity of married women? Does the married woman live longer because she is married or does the potentially long-lived woman get married? Is there a life-giving effect accruing from giving life? Do females who perform their biological function of procreation thereby complete more adequately some predetermined life pattern or is increased longevity of married women a socially determined factor? Many studies have shown that the happy person tends to live longer than the unhappy. Can it be argued that marriage increased happiness, and thus the life span? If so, what is the biological explanation of the fact that single women after eighty seem to be practically indestructible? In Beard's unpublished study of sex and mortality of 563 female centenarians, there was almost one-third larger proportion of single women than found in their population cohort at age sixty.

What is the relation between age of puberty and longevity? Between age at menopause and longevity? Between fertility and longevity? Do the survivors of mankind have larger families than those who die younger? Is there any biological evidence of a relation between a long reproductive span and longevity? In two recent investigations of fertility, the Indianapolis study made under the auspices of the Milbank Foundation and the Puerto Rico study sponsored by the Population Council, Inc., interruption of the reproductive sequence seems to influence future fertility. Can this be explained biologically? Does cessation of reproduction before menopause shorten life? What effect will early childbearing have on the future of women's longevity? If, as has been pointed out before, there is a relation in most species between end of productivity and age at death, will the early cessation of pregnancies tend to decrease the life span?

## Factors Characterizing Senescence

To the sociologist, the important question is not "How long can the human organism be kept alive and breathing?" but rather "How long can the human mechanism continue to function in such a fashion that life is enjoyable?"

In the planning of sociological research, the experimental designs might be considerably altered if the biologist could supply us with answers to such questions as: How automatic is senescence? Is there an unalterable pattern to changes associated with senescence? To what extent are variations in senescent changes due to biological differences? We hear much today about the prime of life being extended and we have all seen men and women sixty and seventy years of age who look and act more like people twenty years their juniors. Is there a pleateau that is reached after growth it attained before senescence begins? Or is it true, as has been so frequently stated, that senescence begins with conception and ends with death?

Comfort defines senescence as "a change in the behavior of the organism with age, which leads to a decreased power of survival and adjustment." Do changes proceed at a different rate at various ages, under various conditions?

It is pertinent to speculate on the fact that 175 million people might, through the various means of prolonging life described above, increase life expectancy by five years. This would mean a total of 875 million years and 318,375 million days added to life. When we consider the constantly increasing costs of medical and hospital care, we realize that extra years might impose a staggering burden. We are not training enough social workers, nurses, physicians, or psychiatrists to meet present needs. Do we subconsciously rely upon a maximum age limit to save us the distress of senescence? Perhaps too much emphasis on maximum upper limit has lulled us into a false sense of security. Unless we can offer freedom from disabling illnesses, additional years may be a mixed blessing.

There are literally thousands of studies in biology, psychology, and sociology which record age related changes in physical and mental capacity and in social adjustment. At first glance these studies seem to offer irrefutable proof of the inevitability of physical and mental decline and deterioration with age, and yet, if one examines the range of ability in each category, it will be found that some persons of 100 have as good eyesight as others of sixty, that the kidneys of some eighty year olds function as well as those of fifty. Are these differences due to social factors or are they due to biological variation? Can the two be separated?

The sociologist cannot presume to evaluate the multiplicity of hypotheses advanced to explain senescence. Sooner or later, no doubt, the biologist will be able to rank in order of importance current explanations of the cause of senescence as: the decrease in pituitary function, depletion of the enzymes, deterioration of irreplaceable structures, commercial hydrogenation of dietary facts resulting in decrease of linoleic acid, decreased cellular division, development of connective scar tissue instead of elastic tissue, the accumulation of lipids in the arteries, the inhibiting factor of cholesterol in the blood, decreased hormone activity, and so on.

In a list of factors contributing to senescence: Dr. Comfort mentions; "previous injuries which are imperfectly repaired." Dr. Hardin Jones of the University of California's Donner Laboratory has a similar dramatic theory of aging. He believes that aging is "a result of impairment of metabolism by the usual diseases and the cumulative effect of countless little ailments that chip away at the body's defenses in the course of a lifetime." In support of this thesis, he cites the relation of disease and death rate in France, England, and the Scandinavian countries, where the so-called childhood diseases have been reduced to a minimum as contrasted with Finland which has the highest childhood disease rate in Europe and the shortest life span.

These two experts seem to agree on the deterimental effect of diseases, accidents, and so on, which may retard growth or weaken the organism. Does this mean that we may add additional years to our lives by inoculating ourselves against every known kind of bacteria or virus? Is the implication that people who are brought up and live in hothouse conditions of regulated temperature and freedom from shock or illness more likely to have long lives than those persons who showed the ability to combat diseases by the development of natural processes of immunity? Is the old theory of struggle as a means of strengthening not applicable in this field? Again, we are reminded of the "survivors of mankind." Few centenarians were vaccinated even for smallpox and most of them react negatively to inoculations of any kind. They frequently attribute their longevity to the fact that they "didn't fill up their bodies with vaccines and other poisonous substances."

What conclusions regarding long time effects of taking antibiotics, hormones, and so on, do biologists draw from what appears
to the layman contradictory evidence?

There is perhaps no field in which biological and social factors
are so intertwined as in eating. Numerous studies have shown the
relation between psychological and nutritional problems. Since
eating is frequently a form of compensatory behavior and related
to deep emotional drives, food habits of the neurotic are not easily
changed. There are, however, today millions of aging persons who
are becoming interested in the preservation of health and vigor
and who believe that they are willing to follow any prescribed plan
in order to remain healthy. No doubt the majority hope for a pill
which will solve all their problems, but many would be willing to
revise eating habits if they were sure that advice available to them
is authentic.

The sociologist is interested in the communication of knowledge. How can the biological findings regarding nutrition and
health needs be channelled to the masses of aging people? At present the chief avenue is through the medical profession which pro-
verbially is not interested in the well person and usually does not
see a patient with nutritional problems until serious damaging
results are apparent.

Studies by social scientists have shown senescence to be correlated with death of spouse, neglect by children, retirement or loss
of job, loneliness or social rejection, loss of sight or hearing, neurotic history, loss of friends, institutionalization, isolation, loss of
income, decrease in social status, fear of illness, and various motivation factors.

The wide variations in ability and performance at any given
age suggest that factors other than chronological age determine
senescence. What are these factors? To what extent can they be isolated and controlled? Is it not possible that with more attention to
social factors many millions of people may retard the onslaughts of
senescence?

There is much evidence that social attitudes of acceptance, or
shall we say expectation, of physical and mental decline have
thwarted personal and social efforts at adjustment and rehabilita-

tion. Perhaps this is not surprising. After reading hundreds of studies conducted within a frame of reference of "optimum life span," normal involutionary processes," "increased decrements of function," "progressive deterioration," and so on, it is indeed refreshing to have Dr. Shock and his research associates assert that contrary to common belief, not all functions show decrements with age.

Senator Thomas C. Desmond, whose persistent efforts in behalf of New York's aging population are well known, concluded his years of service with the Legislative Commission with this optimistic note: "No longer do surgeons deem all old folks poor risks. No longer do psychiatrists refuse to accept patients merely because they are old—or, as they used to tell me—'have no hope; therefore we can't do anything for them.' No longer do rank and file employment service personnel relegate the 40-plus job applicants to the 'file and forget' folders."

Senator Desmond's optimism is documented by numerous studies indicating the successful treatment of mental disease in old age. Patients who twenty years ago would have been considered hopeless respond to treatment as quickly as younger persons.

The effects of isolation, social rejection, loneliness, and discouragement upon measured intelligence and mental acuity have thrown considerable light upon mental states previously diagnosed as senility. Certainly in the field of mental health it is impossible to separate biological and social factors.

In summary, it seems that the whole field of gerontology would profit from:

1. a more open-minded and flexible attitude regarding the increasing life span and the consequences thereof;

2. more attention to the variants instead of concentrating on the "averages";

3. more consideration of causal factors and preventive measures rather than mere cataloging or measuring of degrees of decrement as related to age;

4. more detailed studies of the effects of age on bodily functions, especially studies of decrease of function in senescence similar to studies of increase of function in the growth stages;

5. more longitudinal studies in which control and experimental subjects are more clearly defined; and

6. more interdisciplinary studies such as are now in progress at Duke, at the Presbyterian Village in Detroit, at National Institutes of Health, and elsewhere.

## SOME CURRENT TRENDS IN PROBLEMS OF THE AGED*

KARL M. BOWMAN and BERNICE ENGLE

The United States has a population of 175 million persons, of whom about 15 million, or 8½ per cent, are aged at least sixty-five years. The people in this age group make up the highest proportion of a country's population in history, and they are now increasing at about twice the rate of the over-all population.

### Longevity

The average length of life for white people in the United States reached in 1956 a new high of 70.2 years, a gain of ten years in the past two decades and double the average life of thirty-four years at the end of the century. The increases in average longevity, however, may now be nearing their limit, according to Woodhall and Joblon, unless the mortality rates in later adult life fall, as they would with the conquest of cardiovascular-renal diseases or of cancer.

The proportion of aged persons, however, is expected to continue to increase, though at a less rapid rate. According to a U. S. Bureau of Census forecast, by 1960 there will be nearly 16 million aged sixty-five and over, and by 1975 almost 21 million, or about 9.5 per cent of the population.

### Male Versus Female Longevity

So far the gains in average longevity have favored women above men. The life expectancy at birth is now about seventy-three years

---

*Reprinted by courtesy of *Geriatrics*, Volume *14*, March, 1959.

for white females and sixty-seven years for white males, a difference of six years in favor of women. In the age group of sixty-five and over, women have long outnumbered men. The disparity is expected to increase, with nearly 3 million more women than men forecasted by 1970. Some demographers are said to point "to the prospect of 'a nation of old ladies.' "

## The Vulnerable Male

Bond's recent article in *Geriatrics* on the "fragile male" contains many interesting facts. Female death rates in the U. S. white population since 1900 have declined 65 per cent, men's, only 50 per cent. For all ages, the age-adjusted death rates in white males that in 1953 were 56 per cent higher than for females were only 10 per cent higher in 1900. The excess in male mortality is now highest for the two age groups of fifteen to twenty-five and forty-five to sixty-four. Men of fifty have a 74 per cent chance of living to age sixty-five, whereas women have an 84 per cent chance. Bond quotes a prediction that by 1975 there will be a 4 per cent excess of women in the total population and a 40 per cent excess in the age group of sixty-five and beyond, if the present trend continues.

Why this male vulnerability? Bond considers the theory that excessive male mortality "is due to biologic differences . . . rather tenuous." He gives greater weight to certain sociocultural pressures. An extensive study by Madigan, however, points to biologic factors as the main causes of women's greater longevity.

## Biologic Factors

Madigan studied the life records for the period 1900 to 1954 of more than 41,000 Roman Catholic native white celibate educational workers (9,813 male, 32,041 female) in this country. He selected this homogenous group of both men and women in order to eliminate such differential stresses as male service in the armed forces; the social, economic, and physical strains of marriage and parenthood (no subjects had been married) ; and occupational diversity and hazards. In this way Madigan planned to "observe the operation of biological factors in comparative isolation."

In general, the life expectancies of the celibate men at all ages except for the very oldest proved to be "considerably greater than those of white males of the general public," but the rates of the celibate women also exceeded those of women in the general public, though not so much.

When the celibates were compared with each other, the women, with two exceptions, "consistently exhibited greater expectations of life, and Brothers shorter expectations." In the one exception, the men at ages fifteen to thirty-four had had some-what longer life expectancies than had the women, a gain Madigan attributed to the men's cloistered protection from traffic and industrial fatalities, as compared to men of these ages in the general public. In the other exception, the life tables of the celibates showed that, for the period 1900 to 1919, the men outlived the women, who evidently "had extremely high rates of tuberculosis." For the period 1950 to 1954, however, the life tables showed at age fifteen and again at age forty-five a six-year greater expectancy for women than for men. Indeed, with the two exceptions noted, the female advantage was consistent in the celibate persons for the entire study period. From age forty-five on, the women had a clear advantage over the men in all decades of the study and after 1939, they had it at all ages.

To Madigan, these results point to a biologic factor as the chief cause in the differential death rates of the two sexes in the general public. Young women as a class had the poorest mortality records in the period from 1900 to 1919, but after 1939 they improved so rapidly as to have by far the best records. These facts suggest that *"under conditions of equal stress* women may be no more resistant to the *infections* and *contagious* diseases than men—perhaps even less so" therefore gains of women over men in this century may be chiefly due to "a greater constitutional resistance to the *degenerative* diseases." The considerably greater female longevity of recent years would thus be a result of the change from one set of major diseases to another as a major cause of death. Madigan seconds Wiehl's earlier recommendation of medical specialization in the care of men equal to the gynecologic care of women. He suggests that careful studies of the specific biologic factors associated with female longevity may yield results for the treatment of middle-aged and elderly men.

## Cultural Factors

Against the facts of excessive male mortality in many species of lower animals and in a human population as far back as 1763, Bond cites the steady change in the past fifty years in the U. S. ratio of male to female deaths. These ratios also vary in other countries— for example, in nineteen North American, European, and British Commonwealth nations, the ratios go from 1.2 to 1.5, with the highest ratio in the United States and the lowest in Scandinavia. To be valid, the biologic changes would have to be selective for the U. S. male. Perhaps Madigan's results, if confirmed, may point to some factors of selectiveness.

Bond finds that men stand social stresses less well than do women. He points out that, in the past twenty years, the rates for cardiovascular renal diseases and ulcers for the age period, forty-five to fifty-four years, have risen more than 30 per cent in men while falling about 30 per cent in women. At about age forty-five in men, heart disease becomes the major cause of the higher male mortality, with suicide and tuberculosis next. At age sixty-five, cancer heads the list of diseases with higher male mortality rates.

In the age range of forty to seventy-four, twice as many U. S. men as women die of heart diseases (872 men and 437 women per 100,000 of each sex). In other advanced countries, more males than females die from heart disease during the life span, but the male to female ratio varies considerably and the death rates from heart diseases are lower.

In his review of the problem, Scheinfeld lists a few clues to some inherent elements that discriminate against males. First, the fact that female adults have an average normal blood pressure (156/84) higher than that of males (145/82) suggests greater female tolerance for high pressure. Studies by Master and co-workers of blood pressure in a large sample of healthy persons aged sixty-five or more indicate the need for separate sets of blood pressure standards, since healthy women on the average have higher pressures and yet have longer life expectancies than do men.

Some evidence indicates that female hormones may help to prevent the clogging of arteries and that estrogens, until after the menopause, may protect against heart damage from blood clots.

Certain biochemical elements apparently figure in such discriminatory diseases as gout, slanted against men, and as diabetes, more common in women.

Women are said to be biochemically better adjusted to withstand bodily stresses, perhaps because of the female need for adaptation to "the great hormonal and other biochemical" changes during menstruation, childbearing, and menopause. Men's heavier musculature may be a liability in modern psychologic stresses. Women also seek medical attention earlier than do men and take better care of themselves. According to a recent survey, women make 5.5 visits a year to physicians, compared to 3.9 for men. Women aged sixty-five and over average 7.6 visits a year, and men of the same age group, 5.8 visits.

In an analysis of annuity mortality, Bowerman found in 1950 that the male-female differential in death rates had increased every decade for at least thirty years, with the greatest change in 1940 to 1947. He noted the two peaks of excess male death at ages fifteen to twenty and fifty to sixty and saw a secular trend in the male-female mortality ratio, in that the females "have benefited more" than males "at the very ages where death rates themselves have declined."

These figures ran parallel with five events—great decline in deaths from tuberculosis, infections and parasitic diseases; increased urbanization; decreased family size; greatly increased use of machinery; and freer, more athletic life of women. He concluded that women do better with urbanization and men with rural life, in general. He cited as evidence the comparative mortality data from Canada, still largely a rural country, and from England, largely an urbanized country. Blair, a discussant of the analysis, equated the two mortality peaks and their sex differentials to violence and accidents at around twenty and to circulatory diseases plus accidents at fifty to fifty-five in men; the trough between (ages 18 to 45) he assigned to pregnancy, childbirth, and the puerperium —the causes of death in women of these ages.

Shettles in 1958 reviewed extensively the chromosomal, hormonal, constitutional, and other biologic sex differences with special reference to disease, resistance, and longevity. He concluded that, although in every population fewer females are conceived, after conception the biologic differences favor the female. In utero and in every age group, more males succumb. But females, more resistant to disease and strains of life, are better operative risks and have fewer postoperative complications; in general, "their biological existence is more efficient . . . ."

Testosterone, according to evidence gathered by Shettles, contributes to male fragility. Observations on human and animal castrates show that testicular secretions increase male metabolism and radiosensitivity and have other widespread bodily effects. Castration promotes the male's survival value. The XY chromosomes of the male may lack factors for longevity carried in the female's XX chromosomes. The human male, "with beard and functioning testes pays the higher price."

One of the first research plans to attack the problem is "The Fragile Male Project," organized sometime ago by Wilson T. Sowder, Florida State Health Officer. An interesting approach is a survey of about eighty mothers of unlike-sexed twins aged five to sixteen to determine any significant sex differences in the twins' records of accidents and illnesses and also in the mothers' attitudes, expectations, and repression-expression toward the behavior of their boy and girl twins.

The need for extensive studies in the comparative biology of aging in the lower animals has been emphasized by Bourlière, who points out the far longer life span in precisely those mammals with a poor temperature control and normally low rate of metabolism, and the long life span in all mammals with reduced energy metabolism and low fecundity. These data suggest a comparison with human beings and the fact that women habitually have a lower metabolic rate than do men. There are no extensive data, however, on large numbers of lower mammals living in nature.

## HEALTH IN OLD AGE

At the Nuffield Foundation in Great Britain, Sheldon's findings on certain things important for a healthy old age include other differences in the sexes. Vision and hearing aids are ranked first, in that 90 per cent of people over sixty-five need spectacles and 66 per cent by age eighty have serious hearing difficulties. Weinberg, however, observes that the elderly tend to shut out various stimuli, and that this cause of many so-called defects of hearing or memory is amenable to therapy.

Sheldon ranks good feet second, because ambulation is so important. Falling is termed "a true old age phenomenon." In Great Britain 90 per cent of fatalities from falls occur in the old, and 65 per cent of domestic accidents occur in people over sixty-five. The liability to tumble, which begins in the sixties and is worse by the eighties, is linked with a decline in postural skill. The elderly person's gait, with its lower ground clearance (similar to the gait in a person with disease of the brain nuclei), increases his liability to trip and fall. Of course, little children also fall often, but their falls are not usually serious in result.

The other main cause of falls is any excessive strain on postural skill, especially the act of reaching up, with the head thrown back. Another type of fall, a sudden collapse during standing or walking, is "undoubtedly due to a complete cutting off of all the stream of postural impulses flowing from the brain." Sheldon therefore suggests that the brain nuclei begin to lose their function quite clearly.

In the tendency of the old to trip and fall, a sex difference turned up. By age eighty only 40 per cent of men but 75 per cent of women have suffered from vertigo. About 90 per cent of elderly women and 65 per cent of men have trouble getting around in the dark; evidently they cannot coordinate the information from the labyrinth with that from the eyes, which with age "steadily become more independent of the kind of information coming from inside the body." Other observers attribute this difficulty to arteriosclerosis.

Slowness of reaction time, part of the same process as the decline of postural skill, accounts in Sheldon's opinion for many pedestrian accidents; the elderly person's decision as to oncoming traffic is already obsolete by the time he starts across the street. Vertigo and falls may go together and have "a particular female incidence," although Sheldon notes that young girls have much better coordination than do boys, and much less dizziness.

In his wide clinical experience, Freeman finds that better-pos-

tured persons have better health and live longer than do poor-pos-
tured ones. In older persons, shifts in blood volume, dilated vascular tree, and reduced vessel elasticity are reflected in the motor
agitative features of cerebral anoxia-findings too often interpreted
as a primary cerebral impairment instead of a generally compen-
sated state of chronic brain syndrome unmasked, for a time, by a
temporary physiologic inadequacy.

The Kallmann studies on twins mark genetic factors at the base
of some individual differences in aging. All measurable similarities
between aging identical twins, even those raised apart, are consistently greater than are those between fraternal twins and between
other siblings; they include physical and mental signs of aging,
type of intellectual performance, with its rate of decline, and social
adjustment. Hence the need for an individual approach to these
problems in the elderly. In the total number of both identical and
fraternal elderly twins, the women outnumber the men as expected.
The biologic factors considered most favorable to aging are healthy,
longevous parents and good use of one's genetic potentials for
health and emotional adjustment before senescence.

## PSYCHOLOGIC CHANGES

Very little is known regarding the actual changes in personality
and mind in the old. Cultural comparisons are difficult. Elderly
persons in the societies that honor the old are said to keep their
abilities practically intact and to have no mental illness. However,
Mayer-Gross and co-writers consider that these elderly persons comprise the relatively few healthy, resilient survivors in their societies
and therefore cannot be easily compared with the aged in Western
urban communities.

One of the few attempts to measure personality changes with
age was a Rorschach study made by Ames and co-workers on 200
reasonably healthy subjects (140 women and 60 men) aged seventy
to 100 years, only eight of whom proved to be available for retest-
ing after two years. In general, the aged normal subjects were within normal limits, with some persons having extremely well integrated personalities. The presenile subjects tended to follow test
suggestions less well and to be forgetful and garrulous, using the

examiner as an audience. The senile subjects' responses were as a rule 'extremely restricted, underproductive, stereotyped, intellectually and emotionally impoverished, uncritical, and insecure.' The subjects had to be interrupted and reminded to resume the test.

A few sex differences were noted. The women's responses were more practical and detailed, with the subjects more emotional and creative and more concerned with themselves and their bodily processes; the men took a more intellectual, generalizing approach, with more accurate perceptions and greater interest in others.

The problem of determining mental and personality changes is complicated by the fact that comparisons of mental tests, for example, in persons of all ages usually do not allow for widely different kinds of education. Mental tests given in both World Wars showed for adults a very similar positive correlation between the highest grade reached in school and the measure of intelligence.

Longitudinal studies have some advantages over cross-testing in that they follow the same persons over a period of time. Two noteworthy studies, one by Owens and the other by Bayley and Oden, describe intellectual function, through age fifty, in persons of superior intelligence. To summarize these findings—the Owens study showed a significantly increased total Alpha score on the Army Alpha Form 6 test and no significant decreases in any subtest in 127 men tested on their college entrance in 1919 and retested in 1949, a thirty-year interval. Similarly, Bayley and Oden found that the type of intelligence tested by the Concept Mastery Score continued to increase from age twenty through fifty in 768 persons followed since the 1921-23 Terman study of gifted children and in 355 spouses.

Jones reported on a group of eighty fairly well educated persons, now about thirty-three, recently retested by the Terman Group Test, and representative of the 200 who from ages ten to eighteen had been given ten tests (5 were the Terman Group Test) between the fifth and twelfth grades in the Oakland, California, public school system. More than half the men were college graduates. In the sixteen year period, the group gained about twelve to thirteen months on the test scores—a gain which may have been gradual or may have held since age twenty. A small sex difference favored the men in two of the ten subtests that involve problem solving—the arithmetic and the number series, wherein the women had small average losses and the men, negligible gains. Both men and women made more than half their net gains in two subtests on vocabulary; similar results are reported for people in the fifties and sixties, who keep or improve their scores in vocabulary and information. Wechsler's preliminary report also shows little if any decline on verbal tests in people in the fifth decade or even beyond, but a constant decline on the speed-performance measures.

Lorge believes that middle-aged or elderly persons can learn the same things they could have learned in the teens or twenties, allowing for reduced speed and sensory acuity. The British study of Goulds and Raven on long staying employees in a public utility company illuminates this topic. In the top groups, the vocabulary score rose with age and was still going up at the man's retirement in the sixties; it held in the middle occupational group but dropped in the unskilled group. In all three groups the performance test went down with age, and was lowest in the unskilled group.

A few comparative results for persons beyond age sixty are available. Kallmann and co-workers in 1947 began a study of the intellectual functions of 300 senescent twins. These 150 like-sexed pairs were healthy, testable persons living at home, whose homes were within a certain radius. They were selected from a New York state sample of about 2,000 white, native-born twins over age 60, whom they represented in distribution of sex (the preponderance of female pairs accorded with statistical expectation) and proportion of identical to fraternal pairs.

Three rounds of a 6-test psychometric battery, all but two from the Wechsler-Bellevue test, were given within an eight year period: one in 1947-48, the same battery a year later, 1948-49, and the third in 1955. The test group quickly shrank from 150 to 127 pairs at the first test round, sixty-two at the second, and thirty-six at the third. The thirty-six pairs of the final sample were composed of twenty-six identical and ten fraternal pairs, twenty-one female and fifteen male, with an average age of seventy-four and one-half years. At the time of the report the age range was sixty-eight to eighty-seven years.

Compared with the test results of the first round, the mean re-test scores for the same subjects declined on all tests, significantly so on three performance tests. But when scaled scores were made from the raw scores of the four Wechsler-Bellevue subtests, "the mean scores of the retest series are found to be consistently higher than those of the standardization group." Moreover, the rate of decline over the eight year interval was "smaller than that inferred from cross-sectional studies." Within the group, individuals varied considerably, some making either the same or a higher score than earlier. The tests gave no significant differences between the sexes.

Intelligence may be linked with survival. Compared with the original total test population, "the retest series of survivors achieved higher mean scores on all original tests." The differences, though small, "may reflect a measurable degree of selectivity with respect to biological survival values." On four tests the decreased group had lower (though not significantly) mean scores than did the survivors. These differences, which need to be confirmed, may point to the fact that those in the superior test group live longer than do the others.

In the comparisons between twin pairs, the identical pairs had test scores with consistently smaller mean intrapair differences than did the fraternal pairs on all three test rounds. This points to genetic factors as a cause of measurable variations in intellectual functions and their decline, a fact "clearly demonstrable during the period of senescence."

Clay's comparative studies on British subjects in the twenties to seventies showed that the greater the complexity of task items and the greater the load on short-term memory, the poorer were the test performances of the elderly. The aged stopped their tasks because of confusion and inability to make corrections, rather than for lack of motivation. Clay compares these results with those of Lashley's maze-learning tests on rats with varying amounts of brain lesion, especially the increase in errors with the increase in the animal's age and the difficulty of the task. These comparisons suggest a possible relationship in human beings between loss of brain cells in old age, impairment of short-term memory, and decreases in test performance.

Other analogies to human intellectual functions can be drawn, again from experimental studies on aging rats. For example, some subjects in each test group learned and recalled mazes within the normal limits of younger rats, whereas others of the same age and training could neither learn a new maze nor recall or relearn an old one. No biologic signs differentiated them— old looking, thin, weak rats recalled a maze perfectly to the day of death, while other, seemingly healthy ones could not do so.

A few longitudinal studies have been made on animals. Actuarial data now exist for some laboratory rats and mice and other small rodents, according to Comfort. According to Shock, Wisconsin University workers have set up a long-term study on the effects of radiation in a group of monkeys, and the effects of normal aging can be observed in the control group.

From the evidence thus far collected, Shock considers that human intellectual capacity increases up to age thirty-five or forty, and thereafter the impairment with age is greater in the less rather than in the more intelligent. With age, performance decreases more in new than in well-practiced tasks, and previously learned material may interfere with new learning.

In general, new psychologic tests for measuring age changes should be devised and standardized. One difficulty is the rapid decreases in numbers—for example, from 300 to 72 persons in eight years, in a Kallmann study, and from 200 to 8 subjects in two years, in the Ames study. Another difficulty is that, in longitudinal tests, repeating the same tests means a possible confusion between effects of aging and improvements due to learning, which thereby impugns the validity of longitudinal researches using intelligence tests, according to Heim and Wallace.

## SEXUAL LIFE

Elderly persons are often expected to have no sexual needs. Although the sex drives change with age, they do not disappear. Comments in a recent editorial, "The Sex Life of the Aging Individual," are pertinent. The second Kinsey volume pointed up the differences between male and female in sex desires and capacities. Whereas most men by age forty have markedly decreased sexual capacity and a considerable number by age sixty-five may be impotent, women retain more or less their full capacity into the fifties and sixties. This may pose a difficult problem, especially for women, about half of whom are widows by age sixty-five, and the rest of whom are either single or married to husbands with less sexual drive and capacity than their wives.

Some writers, Stokes for example, have suggested that a franker attitude toward sexual enjoyment in maturity would prolong male functional potency and vigor and stave off the depressions and hostile behavior that often develop in aged, impotent men. Other reports, as in case histories, emphasize that well-adjusted elderly persons still have and enjoy a certain amount of sex life.

Peck states that the powers of physique and active sex belong biologically and socially to the first half of life, and therefore, biologically, older people may feel many other drives more strongly than the sex drives. Those who feel especially frustrated by waning sexual potency are still trying to work out their unfulfilled needs from an earlier age. They view the climacteric as a tragedy because they still value themselves by their sexual powers.

Those people age most successfully who view the sexual climacteric as a crossroads to new kinds of value that Peck terms socializing versus sexualizing. These values consist of useful skills, to be gained only by a certain amount of life experience. A comparison of the role of sex activity in early and later life points up its primary importance in the years of courtship, marriage, and child-rearing and its lesser role thereafter.

This is not to say that sexual activity has no value or importance in old age or that the elderly person must renounce it, but only that the elderly person cannot expect to attain various sexual satisfactions he has missed or feels he has missed in earlier life. Indeed, Peck would construct and use developmental rather than age criteria for the study of stages in later life, somewhat along the lines of the present Kansas City study of middle and old age, with the aim of rating the individual's success in mastering the various steps in life, from "Wisdom versus Physique, through Ego Transcendence."

In her study of a series of old persons, "potential centenarians," Dunbar found that 98 per cent had been married, 30 per cent more than once, and the record of divorce was low. They enjoyed being married and contrived to make marriage into "a healthy state of living." If a spouse died they married again, even in the nineties.

## WORK

Very little concise material has been gathered regarding problems of work for the aged. The industrial test measurements of intelligence, guidance, placement, and performance have mostly been standardized on young workers. These penalize older persons in regard to their education, test "wiseness" and anxiety, speed of reaction, visual and auditory acuity, cultural background, and so on, as compared to younger workers.

Such tests do not test actual job performance, in Odell's opinion. He reports that a recent chance test throws some light on the problem. An employer of toy assemblers who wished to continue his plan of hiring older persons requested a scale of test selection standards. Analyses of the data available on sixty-five workers, about half of them over forty-five, who used small hand tools or small power tools and presses in assembling, showed no significant differences in job performance in these workers. The two groups differed significantly, however, on 7 mean scores of the USES General Aptitude Test Battery, and were similar only on three tests (General Intelligence, Verbal Facility, and Numerical Ability). Test norms based on the older worker group failed to screen out the younger groups, and vice versa. Odell therefore considers that separate norms need to be constructed for older workers.

Emphasizing the need for suitable tests and evaluations of men's and women's actual industrial production at different age levels, Brozek would set up miniature work situations, to bridge the gap between laboratory tests and actual job performance. Middle-aged and elderly persons may often hesitate to take tests and participate in theoretical studies that do not allow for their experienced judgement or the compensations they develop in job performance.

## ECONOMIC STATUS

A study by Steiner and Dorfman, poses some of the socioeconomic problems involved in the excess of elderly women, a disproportion slated to increase strikingly in the next few decades. Marital status, for example: In April 1952, only 35 per cent of women over age sixty-five lived with their husbands, as compared with 74 per cent of women aged twenty to sixty-five who did so. From ages twenty to sixty-five years, 78 per cent of men lived with their wives as compared with only 66 per cent over sixty-five who did so. That is, so-called unrelated females, those living alone, made up the largest single group in the aged population. In the immediate future, only about one-third of the women over sixty-five, compared with two-thirds of the men, will be married persons, again a disparity slated to increase greatly in another fifty years. Soon the majority of persons over age sixty-five will be lone females (many of them widows), in a bad economic position because they lack employable skills. The authors note that most women past age forty find it hard to get a job.

For older men, retirement is the great problem, often with poor health and obsolescent skills the main factors. Continuous education rather than re-education is now considered the better way to mitigate the difficulties connected with the obsolescence of skills.

## HEALTH

The question of health is an important one. There is the common statement that many men die very soon after retirement and that the arbitrary retirement hastens the man's death. The fact is that ill health forces some men to retire who in any event would die soon. Brown and co-workers recently reported on a detailed medical examination of 1,062 Birmingham men (458 above age 65) representative of the male population aged sixty to sixty-nine, at a time of full employment. In brief, three in every four men were still working full time in the sixty-sixth year, and one in two in the seventieth year, with financial need the main cause for continuance at work. In the age group sixty-five to sixty-nine, unfitness for work was sharply related to social class (rated Class I-V, top to bottom) —that is, about one in ten in the two top classes, compared to one in five in the two lowest classes, and an even higher proportion in these classes if fitness for the man's original work was assessed. These British authors question whether a pension age of sixty-five is realistic when "at least three in every four men work beyond it" if they need to and can get work, "and nine out of ten are physically capable of doing so."

We might also question the present emphasis, in the literature, on the planning for retirement and the need for hobbies, travel, avocations, and club sociality. Such activities, in Barron's opinion, may well represent a typical bourgeois norm, in their appeal to middle-class rather than to lower-class people. Some foreign-born and semiskilled persons look on hobbies as made-work or childish play; indeed, the idea of preparing and planning for various life periods belongs more to middle-class than to industrial class psychology. Among older people, the working classes out-number the higher social classes. Some evidence on the operation of the four-day work week shows that many industrial workers did not use the leisure for an avocation but quickly took up a second job.

People react to aging according to the norms of their social group, according to Riesman. The aged constitute no homogeneous group in such important problems as widowhood, illness, obsolescence of skills, and retirement. Nor have attempts so far been made "to bridge the organic, psychological, and social aspects of aging."

## EXERCISE

Authorities agree on the lack of information about exercise and hard work as an aid to physical mental fitness throughout life. White considers exercise beneficial for aging persons, though admitting that a very small number need almost no exercise. Maintenance of good muscle tone by exercise helps to keep blood vessels elastic and thus aids the heart in the work of circulation. Exercise benefits digestion and controls obesity by increasing the metabolic requirements. Not just fat here and there, but a few grams in the wrong places such as the important arteries cause the damage. Psychologically, exercise helps to drain off nervous tension and to promote mental concentration. Exercise is beneficial even in the presence of disease; in various heart diseases, except for the most severe cases, a careful program of regular exercise "as in the President's case," may both improve health and help retard "the further progress of increase of coronary atherosclerosis."

Bortz also recommends purposeful activity up to the limits of the person's physical and mental optimum as "the most potent factor in the fight against premature human deterioration." Brozek states that physical exercise, without preventing the deposit of fat, "seems to retard or eliminate the atrophic changes noted in the process of aging."

According to a British study, heavy workers aged forty-five to sixty-four had half the mortality for coronary disease than did light workers and a study of Swedish workers indicated the same relationship between hard physical work and the low incidence of symptoms of coronary disease. However, there have also been examples to the contrary. Brozek notes that a cluster of factors, including nutrition, may operate in the upper social classes and that these and other occupational factors have not been at all carefully investigated.

## WHAT IS OLD AGE?

Simmons made an historical review of the attitudes and habits of seventy-one world-wide peoples regarding old age. The recurring interests of the aged are summed up under five main heads: (1) to live as long as possible and still remain fairly efficient; (2) to safeguard waning energies; (3) to participate in some group affairs; (4) to preserve and even strengthen acquired skills; and (5) to withdraw, when necessity compels, "as honorably and comfortably" as possible. Metraux emphasized the evidence, in the Simmons studies, that very few single irregularities as to behavior, belief, and so on, in old age are "absolutely related to it." That is, one's ideas about old persons, their behavior and relationships, are largely man-made and learned from one's society and can therefore be modified through new learning. Metraux points out that in China not the young but the old scholars achieve originality, and this is expected of them.

# A COMPARATIVE STUDY OF THE AGE DISTRIBUTIONS OF THE POPULATIONS OF MAJOR CITIES IN THE UNITED STATES*

### T. LYNN SMITH

In the course of the last twenty years the writer and some of his associates have had occasion to note, in an incidental manner, the extreme differences between the age distribution of certain cities in the United States.[1] It is not strange, therefore, that he developed an interest in examining in some detail the similarities and differences between the age profiles of all the principal cities in the United States. As time permitted these studies have been under way since 1953, when the data for the nation's major cities gathered in the 1950 Census became available. This paper is the first attempt to report the results of those studies. The analysis involves all of the cities, 113 in number, having 95,000 or more inhabitants at the time of the 1950 Census. (The "cut-off" point was set at 95,000, rather than 100,000, in order to include St. Petersburg, Florida, and Albuquerque, New Mexico, in which the writer has a special interest, along with Jackson, Lincoln, Lowell, Madison, and San José.)

As suggested above, even the most casual examination of the age data for these cities reveals great variation from one city to another. No exhaustive search has been made in order to determine exactly which cities represent the extremes with respect to each

*Presented at the annual meeting of the Population Association of America, Providence, Rhode Island, April 24-26, 1959. Reprinted by courtesy of *Social Forces*, Volume *38*, March, 1960.

[1]See, for example, T. Lynn Smith, *Population Analysis* (New York: McGraw-Hill Book Company, 1948), p. 106; T. Lynn Smith and Homer L. Hitt, "The Characteristics of the Populations of Southern Cities," in T. Lynn Smith and C. A. McMahan, *The Sociology of Urban Life* (New York: The Dryden Press, 1951), pp. 230-236; T. Lynn Smith and Homer L. Hitt, *The People of Louisiana* (Baton Rouge: Louisiana State University Press, 1952), p. 54; T. Lynn Smith, "The Migration of the Aged," in New York State Joint Legislative Committee on Problems of the Aging, *Growing with the Years*, Legislative Document No. 32 (Albany, 1954), pp. 76-78; and "The Changing Number and Distribution of the Aged Population," *Journal of the American Geriatrics Society*, III, No. 1 (1955), pp. 9-11.

age group, but enough study was done to determine definitely that
the proportions of young children, adolescents, young adults, those
in the prime of life, persons nearing the retirement ages, and of the
aged differ sharply from one city to another. For example, in San
Antonio, Baton Rouge, and Salt Lake City, the 1950 Census indicated that children less than five years old made up 13.5, 12.7,
and 12.2 per cent, respectively, of the population, whereas in Wilmington (Delaware) and Richmond (Virginia), the corresponding percentages were only 8.5 and 8.6. Likewise, in San Francisco
the age group ten to nineteen comprised only 9.5 per cent of the
population, while in El Paso persons in these ages constituted 15.7
per cent of the inhabitants. If attention is centered on the age
group twenty to twenty-nine, the cities of a single state (California)
had proportions ranging from only 13.8 per cent in Pasadena to
23.7 per cent in Berkeley, and even greater extremes are apparent
if one compares St. Petersburg, Florida (10.5 per cent), and Madison, Wisconsin (26.0 per cent). In Washington, D. C. 18.2 per cent
of the population were aged thirty to thirty-nine, but in Salt Lake
City only 14.2 per cent were in the corresponding age group. If one
considers those who were aged forty to forty-nine, he may note that
in Madison only 11.2 and in El Paso 11.4 per cent of the population
were so classified, while in New York and San Francisco the corresponding percentages were 15.6 and 15.9, respectively. The next
older group, those fifty-five to sixty-four, accounted for only 6.8
per cent of the population of Savannah, but they formed 12.4 per
cent of the residents of Pasadena and 11.1 per cent of those living in
San Francisco. Finally, the proportions of those who had passed the
sixty-fifth birthday ranged from only 3.7 per cent in Corpus Christi
to 22.2 per cent in St. Petersburg.

## METHOD AND PROCEDURES

Demographers have, of course, developed and utilized a considerable number of devices and techniques for bringing the
masses of data pertaining to the ages of various populations into
focus so that meaningful generalizations and comparisons may be
made. For the purposes of the present comparative study of the
age distributions of the major cities, the present writer found the

most useful of these to be simple charts based on index numbers which show for each five-year age group the extent to which each city contained in 1950 more or less than its pro rata share of the national total (see Fig. 1). The computation of the indexes may be illustrated with some of the data for New York City. In 1950, the 7,981,957 persons enumerated in the nation's largest city were the equivalent of 0.5236 per cent of the population of the continental United States. Therefore, if New York City had contained exactly its pro rata share of those less than five years of age in the nation, who totaled 16,163,571, there would have been 846,235 children of these ages in the city. The actual count, however, showed only 665,889, indicating that New York City had only 78.7 per cent of its proportionate share of the nation's very young children. Similarly, on a strictly proportionate basis this great city should have had

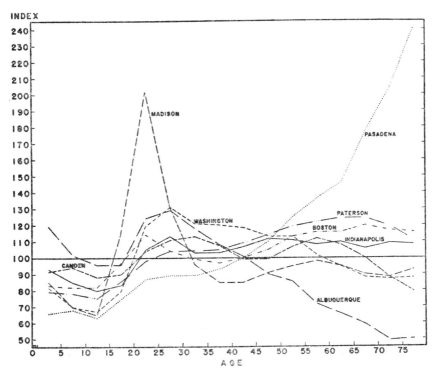

Fig. 1. Indexes showing the extent to which selected cities contained more or less than their pro rata shares of each age group in the United States, 1950.

464,930 of the 9,070,465 persons in the United States aged forty-five to forty-nine. Actually, though, the number enumerated in New York was 590,622, so that the city had an index of 124.4 or almost 25 per cent more than its pro rata share of this particular age group.

After the indexes had been computed showing the extent to which in 1950 each of the 113 major cities in the United States contained more or less than its pro rata share of each age group, from zero to four, to seventy-five and over, the data for each were charted as in Figure 1. In all of the 113 charts the age factor was plotted on the horizontal scale and the index numbers on the vertical one. In order to facilitate observation and study, a horizontal line was drawn across each chart at the point on the vertical scale corresponding to the index of 100, so that all portions of the curve that are above the line indicate a concentration of the respective age groups in the city represented by the chart and the portions below the line depict a relative scarcity of the age groups involved.

The 113 charts were then studied with care for the purpose of identifying and describing the various types of age distributions found in the major cities of the United States, and then all of the cities were classified according to the type or category in which it appeared most appropriate to place them. A description of each of these types or categories and the names of the cities classified in each are given in the following section. Before turning to this, however, it seems well to comment briefly upon two features of the curves which appear on nearly all of the 113 charts. The first of these is the uniform tendency for the portions of the curves representing persons of less than twenty years of age to fall below the base line. This is merely a reflection of two well-known facts, namely, that the birth rate in the cities is lower than that in the rural portions of the nation, and that the net movement of population is from country to city, with the bulk of the migrants being in the ages from about seventeen to thirty. The second feature is the general tendency for the indexes for the age groups ten to fourteen and fifteen to nineteen to be lower than those for children zero to four and five to nine. In all of the 113 major cities in the United States, there are very few exceptions to this rule. This is a reflection of the fact that the rise in the birth rate in the United States during the decade 1940 to 1950 was more rapid in the urban than in the rural portions of the country.

## TYPES OR CATEGORIES OF AGE DISTRIBUTIONS

All except five of the age distributions of the major cities in the United States, as portrayed on the charts described above, fall into seven rather distinctive types or categories. These are described briefly in the following paragraphs, and in each case a list is given of the cities designated as corresponding to the respective type.

*Type 1: Cities Whose Age Distributions Correspond Most Closely to the National Pattern.* Many cities have age distributions that correspond about as closely to that prevailing for the nation as a whole as it is possible to expect in an urban population. They are characterized, of course, by somewhat less than their pro rata shares of persons under eighteen years of life, and, in compensation for that, by slightly more than their proportionate numbers of people in most of the other age groups. They do not, however, attract extremely large proportions of the youth, as do university cities and defense centers, who will move elsewhere as soon as their immediate objectives are attained or their military obligations satisfied. Their growth is steady, even though it may be rapid, and not by spurts, such as those taking place during the first and second world wars, which gave the distinctive features to the age distributions of the cities which have been designated as belonging to Type 5. Nor do such cities attract inordinately large proportions of those near or in the retirement ages, the factor which overweighs all others and makes it evident that certain cities are genuine "retirement centers," the Type 4 of this classification.

As a result, the indexes showing the extent to which they contain more or less than their pro rata shares of the persons in the various age groups do not fall below eighty, remain above 100 for all ages between twenty and seventy, do not fall below ninety for the most advanced age-groups, and never exceed 120 at any point on the curve.

Indianapolis is a good selection to represent cities with this type of age distribution, (see Fig. 1). Note especially that the lowest point to which the curve for it descends is the index of eighty corresponding to the age-group ten to fourteen, and that the highest index is 113 for the age-group twenty-five to twenty-nine. From about the age of twenty-three the curve stays above the 100 line, with the slight dip corresponding to the ages thirty to thirty-nine probably reflecting a slowing down during the depression years in the stream of migrants flowing to it from the surrounding areas. The peak mentioned above, on the other hand, attests to an influx of young adults during the decade of the second world war. In this connection, it should be noted that the population of Indianapolis rose from 233,650 in 1910 to 427,173 in 1950, with the percentage increases for the decades ending with the stated years being as follows: 1920, 34.5; 1930, 15.9; 1940, 6.3; and 1950, 10.4.

The other cities which should be designated as Type 1, on the basis of the criteria described above, are as follows: Evansville, Fall River, Louisville, Philadelphia, Pittsburg, and Wilmington (Delaware). In addition Allentown, Dayton, Little Rock, Phoenix, Tampa, Toledo, and Waterbury each fails to meet all the specifications for inclusion only in one slight respect, and also probably are best characterized as having age distributions of Type 1.

*Type 2: Cities with Heavy Concentrations of Those in the Productive Ages and Low Proportions of the Young and of Those Approaching or in the Retirement Ages.* Whenever a city grows rapidly for two or three decades by attracting migrants from the surrounding areas or immigrants from abroad its population comes to be heavily concentrated in the ages twenty to fifty-four and its inhabitants will include relatively few of the young and of those who have passed the prime of life. In 1930, the entire urban population of the United States exhibited this type of an age distribution,[2] and, although this study has not extended to all the large cities as of that date, it is likely that a large majority of them did likewise. Even in 1950, when the persons who had flocked to the large cities during the first quarter of the century were pretty well advanced up the age ladder, there were many cities in which a rapid growth during the preceding quarter of a century had produced this type of age distribution.

[2]Cf. T. Lynn Smith, *The Sociology of Rural Life* (New York: Harper and Brothers, 1940), pp. 71-77.

The nation's capital, Washington, D. C., exhibits well most of the characteristics of this type of age distribution (see Fig. 1). But Houston, Texas, also had in 1950 an age distribution closely approaching the ideal of this type. It should be kept in mind, in this connection, that any substantial halt in the migration to a given city during the depression years of the early 1930's and a consequent lag in its rate of growth during the decade involved, may have weighed heavily enough to bring about the exclusion of that city from the Type 2 category.

In addition to Washington and Houston, the other cities whose age distributions are of Type 2 are as follows: Atlanta, Baltimore, Birmingham, Charlotte, Chicago, Dallas, Detroit, Fort Worth, Gary, Jacksonville, Jersey City, Memphis, Miami, Newark, New York, Oklahoma City, Richmond, Shreveport, South Bend, Tulsa, Wichita, and Yonkers. In the cases of Chicago and New York, however, it should be mentioned that the highest indexes are for the age groups fifty-five to fifty-nine and fifty to fifty-four, respectively; and for Detroit and Jersey City the indexes for the age groups thirty-five to forty-nine are considerably lower than those for the groups immediately above and below.

*Type 3: Cities with Inordinately High Proportions of Persons Eighteen to Thirty, and Consequently, Low Proportions of Those in Other Age Groups.* Certain cities, for two different reasons, regularly include in their populations such large proportions of persons in the ages between eighteen and thirty that all other features of the age distributions are overshadowed or obscured by that fact alone. Most of these are the university cities, but some of them are defense centers. In cities such as Austin, Baton Rouge, or Madison, the presence of a very large university in a comparatively small city is responsible for the exceedingly high proportion of young adults in the population, whereas in Norfolk a closely similar age distribution is determined, in the last analysis, by that city's importance as a defense center. Madison has been selected as the case to represent this Type 3 distribution in Figure 1. Other cities definitely exhibiting the characteristic features of this Type are as follows: Austin, Baton Rouge, Knoxville, Nashville, and Norfolk. Berkeley, Cambridge, and San Diego also probably should be placed in this group, even though Berkeley and Cambridge have relatively high proportions of persons above the age of sixty, and in San Diego the ages thirty to forty also are heavily represented.

*Type 4: Cities with Exceedingly High Proportions of the Population in the Older Age Groups.* There are a few cities in the United States in which residence for those who have reached or are nearing the age of retirement is so important that the high proportions of those beyond fifty-five years of age is the dominant feature of their age distributions. St. Petersburg, Florida, in which the 1950 Census showed that 22.2 per cent of the population was aged sixty-five and over and 7.6 per cent above seventy-five is the extreme case of this Type 4. Since in 1950 St. Petersburg had 292 per cent of its pro rata share of the nation's population aged seventy-five and over, in order to keep the dimensions of Fgure 1 within more reasonable limits, Pasadena, for which the maximum index rises to 240 was selected for representation in connection with this illustration.

In addition to St. Petersburg and Pasadena, the other cities with Type 4 age distributions are as follows: Long Beach, Portland (Oregon), Spokane, and Tacoma. It should be emphasized, however, that in none of these do the indexes showing the concentrations of the aged rival closely those for St. Petersburg and Pasadena.

*Type 5: Cities in Which Concentrations in the Ages Twenty-five to thirty-four and fifty to sixty-four Are the Dominating Features of the Distribution.* Apparently many cities in the United States owe the distinctive features of their age distributions to the fact that much of their growth came in two spurts, one during the first world war and the other during the second. In many cities the first period of rapid growth extended through the decade 1920 to 1930, and in some of them there was a loss of population between 1930 and 1940. Since most of the migrants who were responsible for these two periods of rapid growth were in the ages eighteen to thirty at the time, these two influxes are reflected in the 1950 age distributions by high indexes for the age groups twenty-five to thirty-four and fifty to sixty-four, respectively. It has been deemed advisable, however, to divide the cities in which these features predominate into subtypes, namely: Type 5-A, consisting of the ones in which the two marked concentrations appear and in which there were less than the pro rata shares of those under twenty years of age, those between forty and forty-nine, and those above the age of seventy; and Type 5-B, made up of those having age profiles similar to those of Type 5-A, except for the fact that the proportions of the aged were relatively high.

The curve representing the age profile of the population of Camden (New Jersey), as shown in Figure 1, corresponds closely to the ideal for Type 5-A cities, and that for Boston is fairly representative of those designated as belonging in the Type 5-B group. In the case of Camden, it is pertinent to note that the population of the city rose from 94,538 in 1910 to 124,555 in 1950, with the percentage increases for the decades ending with the stated years being as follows: 1920, 23.0; 1930, 2.1; 1940, —1.0; and 1950, 6.0. In Boston, the population increased from 670,585 in 1910 to 801,444 in 1950, and the percentage increases for the decades ending with the stated years are: 1920, 11.6; 1930, 4.4; 1940, —1.3; and 1950, 4.0.

Other cities rather clearly of Type 5-A are Akron, Bridgeport, Canton, Chattanooga, Cleveland, Erie, Flint, Kansas City (Kansas), Milwaukee, Trenton, and Youngstown. Elizabeth, Fort Wayne, Hartford, and New Orleans also have age distributions resembling in most essentials those of this subtype. In addition to Boston, the other cities whose age distributions are of Type 5-B are Cincinnati, Des Moines, Grand Rapids, Minneapolis, New Haven, Omaha, Peoria, Providence, San José, Seattle, Springfield (Massachusetts), Somerville, St. Louis, St. Paul, and Syracuse. Denver and Kansas City (Missouri) also have populations with age profiles so similar in almost all essential respects that they, too, probably are best designated as being Type 5-B.

*Type 6: Cities in Which High Proportions of Young Children and of Young Adults Are the Dominant Features of the Age Profile.* Interestingly enough in 1950 there were in the United States a few cities in which indexes showing considerably more than the pro rata shares of young children and of persons aged twenty to twenty-nine determined the basic nature of the age profile. Albuquerque, with the distribution represented as Type 6 on Figure 1, shows these features to a high degree, but Corpus Christi, El Paso, Jackson, Mobile, Montgomery, Salt Lake City, San Antonio, and Savannah also correspond closely to type. In contrast to the situation in most of the other cities of the United States, where migration seems to have been the principal primary factor responsible for the age profiles as they were in 1950, it is likely that the high birth rates known to be characteristic of the Spanish Americans and the "Mormons" have been of basic importance in giving rise to age distributions of five of the Type 6 cities, and it may be that further study will produce an explanation of why Jackson, Mobile, Montgomery, and Savannah also have age distributions of this type.

*Type 7: Cities Marked by Relatively High Proportions of Persons in All the Ages Above forty.* Some cities have grown little or not at all since 1920, although they developed rapidly prior to that time. As a result, the curves depicting the manner in which their age profiles compare and contrast with that of the nation, show high indexes for all ages beyond forty. As may be observed by comparing in Figure 1 the curve for Paterson (New Jersey) selected to illustrate the age distributions of this type, with that for Pasadena, the age distributions, with that for Pasadena, the age distributions of these two types differ substantially. As a matter of fact, in most of the cases the curve depicting Type 7 age distributions usually drops as the very oldest groups are reached.

In addition to Paterson, the age distributions of Duluth, Lowell, New Bedford, Reading, Rochester, Scranton, Utica, and Worcester definitely are of Type 7; and, although the factors responsible are different, the distributions for Albany, Buffalo, and San Francisco exhibit so many of the characteristic features of the class, that it probably is justifiable to designate them as being of this Type.

*Five Cases That Are Difficult to Classify.* The cities mentioned above whose age distributions have been designated as belonging to one or another of the seven types described above total 108 of the 113 major cities in the United States. The other five cases, however, do not conform closely to any one of these Types, and it seems advisable to leave them in a miscellaneous category. Three of these cities are in California (Los Angeles, Oakland, and Sacramento), and they have age distributions corresponding closely to Type 1 except for the fact that the proportions of persons aged five to nineteen are considerably too low. Lincoln, capital of Nebraska and home of the University of Nebraska, is the fourth of the miscellaneous group. Its distribution is featured by the exceedingly high proportion of persons aged twenty to twenty-four, characteristic of Type 3, but the curve also ascends to an index of 140 for the age group seventy-five and over, indicating that the city contains far more than its pro rata share of those in the most advanced ages. Columbus is the other city that is difficult to characterize. The proportions of those aged five to fourteen are too low and of those aged 20-24 too high to permit it to be designated as having a Type 1 distribution, and, on the other hand, the proportion of those twenty to twenty-four is not high enough to justify characterizing it as Type 3.

## FACTORS AFFECTING THE AGE PROFILES

At a few points in the preceding section, incidental mention has been made of the factors responsible for some of the variations in the age profiles of the principal cities in the United States. It will be necessary, though, for considerably more research to be done before the ways in which the three primary factors (fertility, mortality, and migration) function to produce these variations will be thoroughly understood, and even more work will be necessary to give thorough insight with respect to the secondary factors and the roles they play. It is evident that various types of migration are greatly involved, so that it is particularly unfortunate that the data on migration are so unsatisfactory. It is clear, too, that population growth or decrease (the net result of balancing the three primary factors) also is of prime significance, and with respect to this no one can legitimately claim the lack of adequate data. As a next step the writer, himself, proposes to move to a thoroughgoing study of the patterns of urban population growth during the twentieth century. This endeavor he believes will assist in determining associations between these patterns and the age profiles of the principal cities of the United States. This knowledge should also throw some light on the manner in which the various age profiles have come into being and the manner in which they may be expected to change.

# THE EFFECT OF MIGRATION ON THE NUMBER AND DISTRIBUTION OF THE AGED IN FLORIDA

Irving L. Webber

Although it is generally recognized by demographers that older people are the least migratory of all age groups, it is known also that in recent decades there has been a considerable interstate movement of elderly persons. This stream of migration has flowed mainly from the Northeast and North Central Regions to states on the Gulf and Pacific coasts.

The movement of large numbers and proportions of persons in the older ages into a few states which are made attractive by their mild climate and by other factors has importance from a number of points of view. Basically, the migration necessitates personal readjustments on the part of the older people who move and social readjustments on the part of the communities in which they take up residence. These readjustments have social, economic, and political aspects. Moreover, a relatively heavy influx of the aged may change, to a greater or lesser extent, the ethos or distinguishing cultural patterns of a community.

Earlier studies have suggested that older migrants to Florida have settled in disporportionate numbers in certain sections of the state. The purpose of the present investigation is to measure, as accurately as the data permit, the volume and relative importance of movements into the state and its sixty-seven counties during the decade ending in 1950.

## METHOD

Official census data do not lend themselves to the direct determination of the size and direction of streams of migration during 1940-1950. Accordingly a technique employed earlier by Smith and Hitt has been utilized to obtain presumptive evidence. The method involves the following computations:

*Reprinted by courtesy of *Journal of Gerontology*, Volume *11*:323-327, July, 1956. Presented at the annual meeting of the American Sociological Society, Washington, D.C., September 2, 1955. Published on a grant from the Forest Park Foundation to the *Journal of Gerontology*.

1) The population aged fifty-five and over on April 1, 1940, when the sixteenth census was taken. This population should comprise, when allowance for mortality has been made and in the absence of migration, the group aged sixty-five and over in 1950.

2) The expected population aged sixty-five and over in 1950. The assumption is made that mortality in the state and its counties is the same as that in the nation. For the whole aged population the rate of attrition between 1940 and 1950 was 37.4 per cent; for the white population, 37.6 per cent; for the Negro 34.5 per cent.

3) The population aged sixty-five and over actually enumerated on April 1, 1950.

4) The difference between the expected and the enumerated population. It is assumed that this figure represents net gain or loss due to migration between the two census dates of persons who were sixty-five years of age in 1950.

### RESULTS

*Absolute Changes, 1940-1950*—The application of the above procedure to the census data indicates that Florida had, in 1950, 66,484 more elderly residents than would have been the case had there been no migration. The vast majority of these persons were white. The net increase due to migration of 2,665 Negroes represented only 4.0 per cent of the gain in total aged population experienced by the state. Since the movement of white persons so far overshadows the incoming stream of nonwhites, the results are presented only on the basis of race, a procedure which permits a more discriminating analysis.

Fifty-four of the state's sixty-seven counties gained older white people as a result of migration during the decade. However, in fifteen counties the increases amounted to less than 100 persons. To lessen the possibility that errors in enumeration or other factors will influence the findings, only the thirty-nine counties in which the net increase was 100 or more white persons aged sixty-five or over in 1950 are considered for further analysis.

Pinellas County, in which the well-known retirement city of St. Petersburg is located, experienced by far the largest gain through migration, 15,290 persons. Dade County (Miami) was next, with 12,853 more aged residents attributable to migration. Both of these counties were in a class of their own with respect to net gains due to migration. As the accompanying figure indicates, three other counties realized increases in excess of 3,000. These are Orange (Orlando), 4,427, Hillsborough (Tampa), 3,720, and Palm Beach (West Palm Beach), 3,190.

In seven other counties, from 1,000 to 3,000 more aged white residents than would have been found in the absence of migration were counted. These were Broward (Ft. Lauderdale), Duval (Jacksonville), Lake (Leesburg), Manatee (Bradenton), Polk (Lakeland), Sarasota, (Sarasota), and Volusia (Daytona Beach).

Although thirteen counties are shown by the method used to have lost older white residents during the decade, none decreased by as many as 100 persons. The largest decrease was that of Gilchrist County, a jurisdiction without urban population according to the census definition, in which the loss was only fifty-three persons. Since these net decreases were so small, they merit no detailed consideration.

Of the thirty-eight counties which gained elderly Negro residents during the decade, only thirteen had increases of 100 or more persons. Four counties were the recipients of from 200 to 450 migrants: Duval, 444, Polk, 316, Hillsborough, 219, and Pinellas, 200. The nine other counties whose gains supposedly due to migration fell between 100 and 200 were Alachua (Gainesville), Bay (Panama City), Broward, Dade, Escambia (Pensacola), Leon (Tallahassee), Orange, Palm Beach, and Seminole (Sanford).

As in the case of the aged white population, no one county in the state lost as many as 100 elderly Negroes during the decade. Twenty-seven counties sustained slight losses, the largest being that of Monroe (69 persons).

*Relative Changes, 1940-50*—The magnitude of gains or losses due to migration may be assessed by relating the enumerated population aged sixty-five and over in 1950 to the expected population as computed. For the aged population of the state, the ratio of enumerated to expected population was 138.9; for the white aged, it was 144.7; and for the Negro aged, 108.5. In the discussion which follows, only those counties which experienced a net gain of 100 or more persons putatively through migration are considered.

For the white population there were thirty-nine counties for which the ratios were in excess of 100. Twenty-six of these had ratios of 125 or above, indicating that one-fifth or more of the older persons counted by the Census Bureau in 1950 had migrated into the county during the preceding decade.

Pinellas County, in which the ratio of actual to expected population was 212.3, ranked all other counties in the state. Only one other county, Sarasota (210.3), owed more than half of its 1950 aged white population to migration during the ten year period.

In eleven counties ratios were between 150 and 199: Broward, 193.4; Orange, 169.2; Manatee, 169.0; St. Lucie, 161.9; Highlands, 160.1; Osceola, 159.1; Brevard, 157.1; Dade, 155.6; Clay, 153.1; Palm Beach, 152.9; and Charlotte, 150.5.

Relative gains in the aged Negro population of the counties were decidedly lower than those for the white population. Bay County, with a ratio of 147.9, far outdistanced the others. Polk, for which the ratio was 130.3, was next. The only other counties for which ratios were higher than 120 were Broward and Pinellas, in both of which the increase due to migration during the decade amounted to 124.1.

## DISCUSSION

The available evidence indicates that two states, California and Flordia, have during the last two decades received the largest numbers of aged migrants. Smith has calculated that in 1940 California had 57,000 residents and Florida 33,000 residents aged sixty-five and over who had moved into the state during the preceding decade. The comparable figures for other states which received a substantial number of older migrants during the 1930-1940 decade are: Texas, 21,300; Tennessee, 8,676; Louisiana, 8,076; Mississippi, 7,535; Washington, 7,115; Oklahoma, 6,913; Missouri, 4,413 Minnesota, 4,419; and Oregon, 3,875.

Using a similar method, Hitt found that from 1940 to 1950 migration accounted for the movement of 130,000 persons into California and 66,000 persons into Florida who were sixty-five and over on April 1, 1950. Other states which realized fairly large increases in their aged populations due to migration during the most recent intercensal period are Texas (32,000), Washington and Louisiana (12,000), Arizona (8,900), Alabama (8,100), and Oregon (7,000).

The states which lost older residents in the greatest numbers

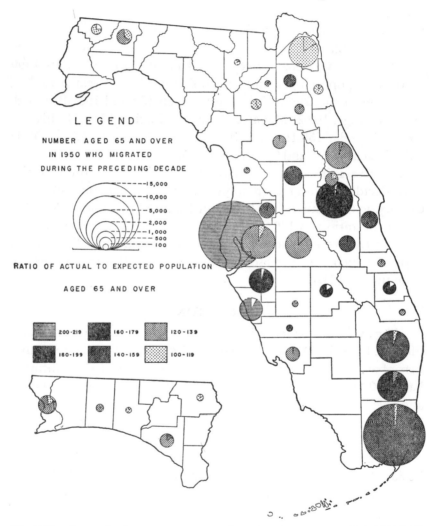

Fig. 1.Number and relative importance of aged migrants to Florida, 1940-1950, by County. (Starting at 12 o'clock on the circles and reading clockwise, the first segment represents Negro migrants and the second white migrants. For method and sources of data, see text.)

between 1930 and 1940 were Pennsylvania (33,239), New York (25,800), Illinois (12,780), New Jersey (11,370), Indiana (10,597), Massachusetts (10,139), and Ohio (9,702). Those which sustained the heaviest losses of older persons between 1940 and 1950 (4) were New York (55,900), Pennsylvania (52,500), Illinois (31,200), Ohio (15,800), Massachusetts (14,400), Iowa (13,300), Indiana (12,600), Missouri (11,000), and Minnesota (10,000).

These gains and losses take on greater significance when they are related to the aged population that would have been found in the various states had there been no migration. In this respect Florida was a special case; its increase between 1930 and 1940 of persons who were sixty-five years old or over in 1940 amounted to 25.1 per cent of all persons in that age group on the census date. California, the state in which migrants constituted the next highest share, had gained 10.3 per cent of its elderly residents during the preceeding decade. Migration between 1940 and 1950 accounted for 28.0 per cent of the older inhabitants of Florida and for 14.6 per cent of those living in California on the census day in the latter year.

It is well established that large numbers of white persons have migrated to Florida subsequent to retirement. It is usually assumed, on the other hand, that Negroes have not shared in this movement in appreciable numbers. This notion is based in part on the existence in the state of the tradition majority-minority social structure of the South, which is believed to make it unattractive to members of nonwhite races, and it is reinforced by the absence of noticeable facilities for nonwhite retired persons. The state census conducted in 1945 demonstrated that only one non-southern state, New York, was the birthplace of as many as 1,000 of the 28,096 Negroes then residing in the state. In the light of the state census data, it seems likely that most of the older Negro migrants who arrived in the state during the decade under consideration originated in nearby states, notably Georgia, Alabama, and South Carolina.

It should be observed also that the procedure followed in gauging the amount of migration combines intercounty and interstate movements. It is possible that intercounty, especially rural-urban migration is of particular significance in the case of older Negroes.

The results presented above indicate that with respect to numbers of white persons the largest increments went during the decade in question to areas located in the peninsular section of Florida; all except one (Orange) of the counties involved are situated on the Gulf of Mexico or the Atlantic Ocean. The five counties which gained 3,000 or more migrants are found in central and southern Florida. Only one county in northern Florida, Duval, gained as many as 1,000 new elderly residents. Moreover, all counties whose increases were over 1,000 older white persons were areas of rapid growth, none having gained less than 33.0 per cent of its population during the decade.

Both of the counties (Pinellas and Sarasota) which more than doubled their expected aged white populations are located on the Gulf in the west-central part of the peninsula and both experienced extremely rapid growth of their total populations during the decade being reviewed. Pinellas' and Sarasota's over-all increases of 73.4 and 79.0 per cent, respectively, were far above the state's gain of a 46.1 per cent. All counties for which the ratio of enumerated to expected elderly population ranged between 150 and 199 lie in the peninsula, only one (Clay) located in the northern part of the area. Eleven of the thirteen counties with highest proportional increases of older people experienced substantial rates of increase for their total populations, ranging from 33.0 to 121.4 per cent during the decade. The two exceptions were Charlotte County and Osceola County, in which the gains in population were 17.0 and 12.7 per cent respectively. Charlotte is notable for having had 14.7 per cent of its people in the sixty-five and over category at the time of the 1950 census. Osceola County, in which 21.6 per cent of the residents were aged at that time, includes the small city of St. Cloud, which had 41.6 per cent of its people in the older classification.

Gains in population as a result of migration of aged Negroes were much smaller in numbers and affected few counties. Three of the four counties which received from 200 to 450 elderly Negroes—Pinellas, Hillsborough, and Polk—are contiguous, lying in the west-central part of the peninsula. Duval County, which registered the greatest increase of nonwhites through migration (444), is found in the extreme northeast portion of the state and is well known as the mecca of many migrants of both races from nearby areas in Florida and from contiguous states. None of these four counties increased its total population less than 38.7 per cent during the decade. The nine counties in which increases of aged Negroes ranged between 100 and 199 are found in what is usually known as West Florida as well as in the central and southern parts of the state. Each grew rapidly (from 20.5 per cent to 110.9 per cent) during the year period.

The relative increase of elderly Negroes through population movement was much less striking than that of the white population. In no county was the ratio of actual aged population to expected aged population as high as 150. For Bay, in the panhandle of the state, the ratio was 147.9; for Polk, near the center of the peninsula, it was 130.3. Bay County, situated on the Gulf, grew at the rate of 106.4 per cent between 1940 and 1950; Polk, an inland county, increased 43.1 per cent. Migration in the eleven other counties which received 100 or more elderly persons during the decade was in no case of large proportions.

If the technique used in measuring migration of the elderly produces valid results, the volume of the movement into Florida between 1940 and 1950 was nearly double that of the immediately preceding decade. Various evidence which cannot be detailed here suggests that this movement has proceeded at an increasing rate since 1950. It would seem, therefore, that certain parts of the state which are favored by retired people because of mild climate, accessibility to coasts, housing, and recreation facilities, and the institutionalization of the status of retired person will continue to realize larger increases, absolutely and relatively, in the aged part of their population.

## SUMMARY

Census data have been analyzed for the purpose of ascertaining the number of elderly persons who migrated to and from Florida counties during the decade ending in 1950 and the relative importance of these migrants in terms of the numbers of aged persons expected to survive on the basis of the national mortality experience. A large proportion (96.0 per cent) of the 66,500 aged migrants to the state were white. Counties which gained the largest numbers of older white persons are found in the central and southeastern parts of the peninsula. Those which had the largest proportional increases are located in the west-central portion of the peninsula. In general, counties in the panhandle and in the northernmost part of the peninsula did not experience large absolute or relative gains of older white persons. Migration of aged Negroes to Florida counties was relatively small in volume and affected few counties to the extent of gains of 100 or more persons. With minor exceptions those counties which received the largest volume of migrants, absolutely and relatively, of either or both races, had high rates of growth for the total population during the decade and were located on seacoasts. No county lost as many as 100 aged persons—total, white, or Negro—due to migration during the ten year period.

## SEX ROLE AS FACTORS IN LONGEVITY*

### Frederick A. Conrad

The greater longevity of women in our society has been explained by some as an aspect of sex, as a difference in genetic factors which determine constitutional differences and the relative life chances of the male and female. Thus, it is assumed that the male is inherently more active, consumes more energy, is physically stronger, but dies at an earlier age than the female who is less active, consumes less food but conserves more energy and consequently lives longer. Accordingly, a theory of "the natural superiority of women" has been given as a scientific explanation of their greater longevity.

This hypothesis seems plausible in view of certain data on death rates. Deaths due to congenital malformations, birth injuries, and certain diseases of early infancy are significantly higher for males than females.

*Reprinted by courtesy of *Sociology and Social Research,* Volume *46,* January, 1962.

In every age group, with few exceptions, male death rates are regularly higher than those of females. Thus, in spite of the fact that the number of males exceeds females at birth and that immigration has added to our male population, the number of males reaching the age of seventy five years and over is significantly lower than the number of females.

Such terms as "weaker" and "superior" are, however, qualitative terms applied to data that are not strictly comparable. By what objective standards can we measure the natural superiority of women? At this point the fact that women outlive men is used as evidence. This in turn is explained by assuming that a mysterious factor in the sex chromosome of females determines constitutional differences which are the basis of sex mortality differences. This is a closed biological argument that over-simplifies the problem.

Differences in life expectancy between white males and white females increased from 2.85 in 1900 to 6.4 years in 1957. This increasing gap in life expectancy has been attributed by Madigan and others to constitutional differences which give females greater resistance to the degenerative diseases than males. This assumes that degenerative diseases can be isolated as a distinct category and measured "under conditions of equal stress."

Unfortunately, vital statistics, from which mortality rates are determined, report only specific causes of death as medically determined. They do not reveal the combination of factors which may be involved indirectly in the death rates from particular diseases. The lethal potentials of epidemics of influenza, of pneumonia and other infectious diseases in relation to the degenerative diseases are matters of record in a patient's medical history that do not appear on the death certificate signed by the attending physician.

A recent study by the Metropolitan Life Insurance Company of mortality from pneumonia and influenza for the period 1954-1960 shows some significant variables according to sex, age, and color. An appreciable increase in death rates occurred during two epidemics of Asiatic influenza in 1957 and 1958. During these years death rates were uniformly higher among nonwhites than among whites. Percentage increases in mortality for the period 1954-1958 show, however, that the greatest increases occurred among white females at ages fifteen to thirty-four years. These increases were approximately double those of white males and much greater than those of nonwhite males.

These outbreaks of influenza not only raised death rates from respiratory diseases but there were also excessive deaths from other diseases, particularly cardiovascular-renal conditions. Deaths from those conditions were estimated to be greater than deaths from pneumonia and influenza. This correlation between epidemics of influenza and excessive deaths from cardiovascular-renal conditions indicates the difficulty of isolating degenerative diseases with any certainty that mortality differentials in such diseases are strictly due to constitutional differences.

Enterline concludes there is little to support a biological explanation of recent increases in sex mortality differentials when consideration is given to advances in medicine and public health which have reduced female death rates in child bearing and in certain infectious diseases which have been unfavorable to young adult females in the past. On the other hand, the excessive deaths of young adult males have been due primarily to automobile accidents rather than degenerative diseases.

Sex differences in longevity show divergent trends in rural and urban populations. A study of the age group seventy-five and over in cities of 100,000 and over shows sex ratios of 73.8, 72.9, and 68.8 males per 100 females for the years 1930, 1940, and 1950, respectively. The comparable sex ratios for rural farm population were 122.5, 120.3, and 120.6. That these differences are due to such factors as a surplus of farm laborers who remain on farms in their retirement or to a selective migration from farms to cities is not indicated by the data.

It seems plausible to assume that there are differences in the roles of males and females in rural and urban environments which explain these divergent trends. High birth rates, long hours of toil with little leisure, inferior housing and sanitation, inadequate medical facilities and care have been the common lot of millions of farm women. Mechanization, which has relieved the farmer of much hard labor, has not been equally shared by the farmer's wife. On the other hand, urban women have been relieved of drudgery in housekeeping by mechanical and electrical appliances. The transfer of many economic and social functions of the urban family to various community agencies gives urban housewives a measure of leisure and freedom from toil which rural women cannot achieve.

Farmers and industrial workers also have been affected differently by mechanization. The farmer now sits on his machines while he works and engages in multiple operations during the day. The substitution of mechanical for human power has relieved him of most of his back breaking labor. The industrial worker, who stands in the assembly line all day, engages in a single operation which is subject to time and motion studies designed to secure maximum production. When he cannot keep up the pace with younger men he faces early retirement. Automation goes a step farther and eliminates his job entirely. This is the plight of millions of industrial workers whose unemployment and insecurity make the fulfillment of their roles and expectations as breadwinners and heads of families doubtful.

That such changes and transitions in our society as industrialization, urbanization, mechanization, and automation have a bearing on the longevity of different groups in widely different environments seems fairly obvious. The effect of these occupational changes and differences needs more study, but they should be considered in their relation to the general social roles of the sexes. Occupational roles and sex roles have a cultural context which defines them differently in different cultures and also at different periods within a given culture.

Sex differences have, no doubt, been an important factor in the development of a division of labor which was at first based upon physical needs in the struggle for survival. In time, this division of labor became subject to a complex set of regulations which assigned different social roles and statuses to each sex. By definition, being a male or a female thus came to have a social as well as an organic reference. Social roles in many details have no necessary basis in organic differences and could be interchanged without impairing physiological functions. Women who bear children may have careers outside of the home but the sphere of their activities has been greatly restricted by folkways which define their social roles in society.

The roles assigned to the male in the folkways, mores, and laws are those of the fighter, provider, and protector of the female and her offspring. The male child is expected to become manly which, by definition, implies such qualities as being brave, resolute, noble, and, by contrast, not effeminate, cowardly, or womanish. Punishment, ostracism, and loss of status await the men who fails in his function as the protector and provider. Our sense of chivalry says "women and children first." A man is regarded as cowardly who struggles with women to get on a lifeboat when the ship is sinking. Thus, chances of survival as between the sexes are no longer strictly physical tests of skill and endurance.

In the etiology of particular diseases it is being belatedly recognized that social as well as physiological factors are involved. We should, for example, know what physical and emotional strain the breadwinner is under to maintain a satisfactory status in industry, to fulfill the expectations of his family and friends as a generous provider, a good husband and father, a good neighbor, and a good risk for creditors who have sold him insurance, automobiles, real estate, furniture, et cetera. We should also know what his conception is of his roles and how he evaluates his success in achieving his personal goals and those of his family. A woman's ambition to keep up with the Joneses may become a factor in differential death rates as well as differences in metabolism. Although we have no data on how much male energy is consumed in such competitive struggles to maintain high standards of living and to achieve a higher social status, we cannot ignore such considerations in our analysis. Data exist, however, which indicate the relation of prolonged unemployment and financial failure to suicides and the personal demoralization of males who fail to fulfill the expectations of success as breadwinners and heads of families.

How sex roles may become important factors in differential death rates is suggested in data on accidental deaths. Under the age of five, male death rates from accidents are considerably higher than those of females and rise rapidly during childhood and adolescence. Deaths by firearms, drowning, and traffic accidents, for example, have no basis in sex except for the social roles assigned to each sex. Little girls are protected and restricted in their activities whereas boys have more freedom to be on the streets, join gangs, play with mechanical toys and guns, go swimming, and be out later at night. Boys assume more risks, encounter more hazards, are more daring, and are encouraged to fight and not to be sissy. Girls playing with dolls assume relatively few risks. Boys playing with toy weapons in such roles as soldiers, cops and robbers, soon begin to toy with real weapons. Deaths due to firearms are more frequent among boys than girls and such deaths among girls are frequently due to the careless handling of weapons by boys rather than by their own carelessness.

Deaths due to motor vehicle accidents occur in each age group but rise sharply and reach their greatest number in the age group fifteen to twenty-four. Male deaths in this age group were 4.4 and 4.3 times the number of female deaths for the years 1950 to 1958 respectively. The inference drawn from such data that women are naturally better drivers is not warranted when the different conditions and uses of motor vehicles are considered. The use of different types of motor vehicles such as motor scooters, motorcycles, trucks, and automobiles; the different uses of automobiles, such as driving to and from work, business and social uses; the amount of time spent daily in driving; the annual mileage covered; the conditions under which motor vehicles are operated; and the relative risks and hazards encountered—these suggest variable responses to motor vehicles which have become a basic factor in changing the patterns of living since the turn of the century.

Women for example do not encounter as many risks as men for several reasons: (1) relatively few women operate motor scooters, motorcycles and trucks; (2) the business and work uses of automobiles by women are relatively less because they represent a minority in the labor force; (3) the social uses of automobiles by women do not involve the same risks which men encounter in their business and work uses. The urban housewife, who plays bridge in the afternoon and stops at a nearby grocery for supplies, assumes less risks in her daily routine than the bread winner who drives variable and often considerable distances to work and returns in the rush hours of the evening after a fatiguing day's toil.

Sex mortality differences due to automobile accidents in the age group fifteen to twenty-four may be reasonably explained by differences in sex roles in their relation to the uses made of automobiles. Young married couples living in the city or its suburbs can usually afford only one car. The preoccupation of the female with child bearing and child rearing confines her to the home more hours of the day and limits her uses of the family car. The role of the male as the bread winner and head of the family gives him priority in the use of the car and exposes him to risks not encountered by his wife.

Likewise, the preoccupation of adolescent males with motor scooters, motorcycles, hot rods, and cars implies more driving under variable conditions and more risks of accidents than those encountered by the female. In his roles as a suitor, as a new recruit in the labor force, as an aggressor seeking recognition and status as an adult, and as a prospective head of a family, the automobile becomes the *modus operandi* for the young male which is not equally true of the young female.

The age of retirement presents quite different problems to the sexes. For the typical housewife no change in her habits and work is required. Her financial security is generally provided through insurance, inheritances, widow's tax exemptions, and social security. To the bread winner, however, retirement usually involves drastic changes in his life organization. Unless he has been prepared for this, he may suffer serious personal disorganization. Being pushed aside by younger men, suffering a loss of status and income, and feeling that he is no longer wanted, may be heart-breaking. A life of inactivity soon becomes boresome and deadly. The fact that his chances of being killed by an automobile as a pedestrian are twice those of his wife, suggests that he spends relatively much more time on the streets.

Industrial accidents and fatalities also fall heavily on male workers for several reasons: (1) approximately one-third as many women are gainfully employed as men; (2) women are employed in less hazardous occupations; (3) protective legislation provides standards for women's work which do not apply to men even when they engage in the same occupations.

Each of the states has laws covering such subjects as maximum daily and weekly hours, day of rest, meal and rest periods, night work, hazardous or unhealthful conditions of work, plant facilities, etc. Such laws are limited, with few exceptions, to women and minors. Not every state has laws on each of the subjects and standards vary somewhat from state to state.

Twenty-four states, for example, have one or more limitations on the employment of adult women. These prohibit employment in dangerous or injurious occupations such as work in mines, bar rooms, foundries, or in handling dangerous substances or machinery. Even where laws do not prohibit such work, custom prescribes that women should not be employed in dangerous occupations. Thus, in lumbering, construction, iron and steel, machinery, and other heavy industries the number of women in the production lines is relatively small.

In such occupations as nursing, teaching, clerical work, domestic and other service work, which largely employ women, and in such fields as finance, insurance, real estate, and detailing, which employ many women, the hazards are relatively small. More than one-half of the women factory operatives are concentrated in apparel, textile, and food industries. These are the less hazardous industries. In each of these industries where men and women work, the standards of work designed to protect women do not apply to men. Thus, in no sense are the risks to life and health of male and female workers shared equally.

Data on the frequency and severity rates of injuries in manufacturing show relatively high rates in industries employing men exclusively or predominantly. A study of work injuries in 1949, estimates a total 1,870,000 injuries. Of these, 15,000 were fatal, 1860 resulted in permanent total disabilities, 79,400 in permanent partial disabilities and 1,774,000 in temporary disabilities. The sex distribution of these injuries is not given but it may be assumed from the industries in which they occur, that the total number of injuries to women was relatively small. An estimate of less than fifty deaths a year occur among women in industrial places despite the millions so employed. A comparative study of industries employing men and women compiled by the Women's Bureau concludes that "in general the frequency of injuries is considerably lower for women than for men." This conclusion was based upon the per cent women were all workers and the per cent of injuries to women were of all injuries.

In this connection we should also consider the relative risks of occupational diseases, unemployment, work stoppages, technological changes and loss of craftsmanship, job insecurity and premature retirement, job placement, and various other sources of grievances and dissatisfaction with the conditions of work. What the direct and indirect effects of these conditions are upon the health and longevity of males and females is difficult to estimate. That there is such a relation is suggested by the fact that death rates for males are higher in urban than rural areas and that the most significant decline in sex ratios occurs in the age groups fifty-five and over and in the highly industrialized cities of 100,000 population and over.

The comparative study of occupational data suggests the importance of diseases, as well as accidents, which occur in the hazardous occupations. Silicosis, for example, is directly attributable to conditions of work to which women are not exposed. The indirect and cumulative effects of exposure to extremes of temperature, humidity, dust, and poisonous gases are not indicated in a death certificate which gives pneumonia or other respiratory diseases as the cause of death. The debility and unemployability which may result from accidents and occupational diseases in hazardous industries may be indirectly related to mortality differences which are attributed to the degenerative diseases. Obviously, the combined effects of accidents, injuries, and occupational hazards to life and health have quite different implications for the 40 million males who were reported in the labor force in 1950 compared with an equal number of adult women who were not reported in the labor force.

The following conclusions are suggested by this study.

1. Inadequate consideration has been given to sex roles in studies of sex mortality differentials and of recent increases in such differences. That sex roles are relevant is assumed but conclusions on their significance are not warranted on the basis of present data.

2. Studies of age, income, class, and occupational groups are necessary to determine variable adjustments to social and tech-

nological changes. Data on accidental deaths and injuries suggest the importance of sex roles as factors in mortality rates. The divergent trends in sex ratios in the higher age groups of farm and urban population indicate multiple factors in longevity which need further investigation.

The study of sex differences in longevity should be made under comparable conditions. Differences in the physiological functions and social roles of the sexes introduce variables which are difficult to measure under conditions of rapid change. Experimental studies must find ways of equating these differences before reliable conclusions can be drawn on the reasons for the greater longevity of women.

# Chapter 4

## ECONOMIC ASPECTS OF THE AGED
### INCOME AND ASSETS OF THE AGED*
#### MONEY INCOME AMOUNTS

D IFFERENT STUDIES use different definitions of the income unit, and so come up with somewhat different distributions of income. However, no matter what the income series cited, it is likely to show some 50 to 60 per cent of the persons aged sixty-five and older have less than $1,000 total case income for the year.

### Census Studies

Data from the Bureau of the Census for aged persons, and for families with aged head, are the most comprehensive. They show for the year 1959, the latest available:

Of 15.3 million *persons* 65 and over  (not in institutions) —
55 per cent had less than  $1,000
23 per cent had $1,000 to $2,000
9 per cent had $2,000 to $3,000
13 per cent had $3,000 or more

Data for individuals have the limitation that they don't indicate how many persons depend on the income. In the case of married couples, some of the income attributed to the husband must go for support of his wife, who may be under sixty-five. Similarly, some wives dependent on their husbands will be shown as having little or no income. However, less than one-fifth of all persons sixty-five and over are married women, and many married couples have less than $2,000 between them. Therefore, even if the reported income data were adjusted to reflect an equal sharing by husband

*Reprinted by courtesy of Special Committee on Aging, U.S. Senate, June 2, 1961, U.S. Government Printing Office, 87th Congress, 1st Session.

and wife, the per cent of persons sixty-five and over having less than $1,000 would be very little less than shown.

Of 6.2 million *families* with head 65 and over—
Half had less than $2,830
One fourth had less than $1,620

These incomes were for the support of 2.6 members, on the average, totaling about 9.3 million aged and about 6.7 million younger persons. Often, the younger relative contributes a substantial share of the family's income.

Of 3.6 million aged persons living alone or with nonrelatives—
Half had less than $1,010
Four-fifths had less than $2,000

There were in addition 2.3 million aged persons living in the home of a younger relative who are counted in the figures for "persons," but who are not included in this family income analysis. Such aged persons in the main are not financially independent, and usually have lower incomes than those who live in their own household as the head or spouse of the head.

The low income of the aged stems from the fact that most are no longer employed, and retirement benefits or other sources of income in retirement are usually lower than earnings. Thus the one in five aged men who were employed full time the year round in 1959 had a median total income of $3,980, two and one-half times that of all other aged men. Aged women working full time all year averaged income three and three-fourths times that of all aged women, but such workers represented only one in twenty-five women sixty-five and over.

## BOASI Survey

The BOASI survey of aged beneficiaries in 1957 indicated a median income for retired couples of $2,250, and for nonmarried men and women of about $1,170 and $990, respectively. A survey today would show higher incomes—first, because of the general increase in benefit levels put into effect in 1959 and, second, because the pattern of steadily rising earnings results in a higher benefit award to aged beneficiaries newly coming on the OASI rolls.

A rough calculation of the effect of these changes on the income of retired couples in current payment status at the end of 1959 suggests that the median would be about 10 per cent higher than in the 1957 survey. OASI beneficiaries as a group exclude those at the top of the income range, i.e., the relatively few still working full time, and those at the bottom, i.e., those with no income at all from earnings or any public programs.

## MONEY INCOME SOURCES

### Where the Aged, as a Group, Get Their Income

Of the estimated 17 million persons sixty-five and over at the beginning of 1961, almost 11 million or well over three-fifths were receiving benefits from the OASDI program. A total of 2.3 million were on old-age assistance, of whom close to three-fourths of a million received assistance to supplement their OASDI benefit. Relatively few of the aged are employed and, of those still at work, most receive OASDI benefits as well as earnings.

The extensive overlap among the various income sources of the aged is shown by the following figures for December 1960:

Of these aged persons in December 1960—

4.1 million had earnings (3.2 million earners and 0.9 million nonworking wives of earners) .

    3 million were simultaneously receiving public benefits or assistance;

    1.5 million were not yet receiving OASDI, but could have drawn benefits were it not for these earnings.

10.8 million received OASDI benefits.

    2.2 million had earnings as well as benefits;

    0.7 million received assistance to supplement their benefits;

    1.3 million had payments from another public retirement or veterans' program;

    6.6 million had no earnings or payments under other public programs.

1.7 million had veterans payments; 1.0 million had benefits

from public employee retirement systems and 0.6 million had railroad retirement benefits.

1.3 million of those under these programs also received OASDI;

0.6 million had earnings.

2.4 million received public assistance.

1.7 million were primarily dependent on this source;

0.7 million received assistance to supplement OASDI.

1.5 million had no income from employment or public programs.

## State Differences

OASDI, while a major source of income in all States, is received by a somewhat smaller proportion of the aged in the South and Midwest than in the more industrialized States. These variations among States, shown in Table 1 as of March 1960, should continue to decrease as the extensions of coverage in recent years have their full effect.

## LIQUID ASSETS

Older persons are more likely than younger persons to have some savings, but in general those with the smallest incomes are the least likely to have other resources to fall back on. Moreover, most of the savings of the aged are tied up in their homes or in life insurance, rather than in a form readily convertible to cash.

## All Aged Spending Units

*Liquid Asset Holdings*—According to the Federal Reserve Board Survey of Consumer Finances, of some 8 million "spending units" with head aged sixty-five or more in early 1959:

29 per cent had no liquid assets, i.e., bank accounts or savings bonds

17 per cent had $1 to $500

21 per cent had $500 to $2,000

33 per cent had $2,000 or more

*Liquid Assets in Relation to Income*—Among spending units with head sixty-five or over, the 1959 survey found:

# TABLE 1
PERSONS AGED SIXTY-FIVE AND OVER: TOTAL AND NUMBER RECEIVING OASDI, OAA, OR BOTH, PER 1,000 AGED POPULATION BY STATE, MARCH 1960
[In Thousands]

| State | Total Population Aged 65 and over (Apr. 1, 1960) | No. per 1,000 Persons Aged 65 and over Receiving— | | | |
| --- | --- | --- | --- | --- | --- |
| | | OASDI, OAA, or both | OASDI[1] | OAA | Both OASDI and OAA[2] |
| United States[3] | 16,559.6 | 716 | 616 | 141 | 41 |
| Alabama | 261.1 | 807 | 511 | 378 | 82 |
| Alaska | 5.4 | 749 | 574 | 268 | 93 |
| Arizona | 90.2 | 666 | 558 | 155 | 47 |
| Arkansas | 194.4 | 773 | 533 | 284 | 44 |
| California | 1,376.2 | 695 | 598 | 186 | 89 |
| Colorado | 158.2 | 727 | 545 | 299 | 117 |
| Connecticut | 242.6 | 727 | 693 | 60 | 26 |
| Delaware | 35.7 | 686 | 661 | 36 | 11 |
| Dist. of Columbia | 69.1 | 521 | 489 | 45 | 13 |
| Florida | 553.1 | 686 | 601 | 126 | 41 |
| Georgia | 290.7 | 758 | 480 | 333 | 55 |
| Hawaii | 29.2 | 675 | 634 | 51 | 10 |
| Idaho | 58.3 | 738 | 650 | 127 | 39 |
| Illinois | 974.9 | 690 | 634 | 76 | 20 |
| Indiana | 445.5 | 731 | 684 | 63 | 16 |
| Iowa | 327.7 | 691 | 613 | 106 | 28 |
| Kansas | 240.3 | 688 | 598 | 119 | 29 |
| Kentucky | 292.0 | 746 | 589 | 193 | 36 |
| Louisiana | 241.6 | 797 | 429 | 517 | 149 |
| Maine | 106.5 | 761 | 693 | 110 | 42 |
| Maryland | 226.5 | 616 | 584 | 42 | 10 |
| Massachusetts | 571.6 | 738 | 667 | 139 | 68 |
| Michigan | 638.2 | 761 | 696 | 97 | 32 |
| Minnesota | 354.4 | 706 | 608 | 134 | 36 |
| Mississippi | 190.0 | 813 | 497 | 421 | 105 |
| Missouri | 503.4 | 747 | 583 | 232 | 68 |
| Montana | 65.4 | 700 | 627 | 107 | 34 |
| Nebraska | 164.2 | 677 | 606 | 92 | 21 |
| Nevada | 18.2 | 632 | 566 | 143 | 77 |
| New Hampshire | 67.7 | 742 | 697 | 72 | 27 |
| New Jersey | 560.4 | 711 | 688 | 34 | 11 |
| New Mexico | 51.3 | 652 | 480 | 209 | 37 |
| New York | 1,687.6 | 697 | 665 | 49 | 17 |
| North Carolina | 312.2 | 726 | 594 | 156 | 24 |
| North Dakota | 58.6 | 695 | 596 | 125 | 26 |
| Ohio | 897.1 | 715 | 644 | 100 | 29 |
| Oklahoma | 248.8 | 761 | 486 | 362 | 87 |
| Oregon | 183.7 | 752 | 692 | 93 | 33 |
| Pennsylvania | 1,128.5 | 700 | 668 | 44 | 12 |
| Rhode Island | 89.5 | 765 | 722 | 75 | 32 |
| South Carolina | 150.6 | 763 | 531 | 217 | 15 |
| South Dakota | 71.5 | 715 | 617 | 126 | 28 |
| Tennessee | 308.9 | 697 | 538 | 179 | 20 |
| Texas | 745.4 | 725 | 498 | 297 | 70 |
| Utah | 60.0 | 714 | 615 | 132 | 33 |
| Vermont | 43.7 | 741 | 657 | 130 | 46 |
| Virginia | 289.0 | 631 | 585 | 51 | 5 |
| Washington | 279.0 | 760 | 654 | 178 | 72 |
| West Virginia | 172.5 | 745 | 642 | 114 | 11 |
| Wisconsin | 402.7 | 739 | 677 | 89 | 27 |
| Wyoming | 25.9 | 676 | 595 | 127 | 46 |

Footnotes to the table ————————→

*When income was less than $3,000* (70 per cent of the total)
    47 per cent had less than $200 in liquid assets
    44 per cent had assets of $500 or more
*When income was $3,000 to $5,000*
    21 per cent had less than $200 in liquid assets
    70 per cent had assets of $500 or more

*Marketable Securities*—Only 11 per cent of the aged spending units owned corporate stocks and bonds or marketable government securities in early 1957 when this question was last studied by the Federal Reserve Board, and virtually all of these stockholders were among the group that already had over $2,000 in other liquid assets as defined above.

## Aged OASDI Beneficiaries

Data from BOASI Beneficiary Survey in 1957 show even more clearly than the Federal Reserve Board statistics that relatively few of the elderly have accumulated substantial savings they can draw on readily, and these few are more often the ones with already high incomes than those with the low.

The beneficiary Survey data are more inclusive than the Federal Reserve Board data in two respects: (1) They include aged persons living in the home of a younger relative—who are not identified as aged in the data for spending units; (2) they also count in with liquid assets any corporate stocks and bonds and mortgage notes as well as the cash in the bank and savings bonds in the Federal Reserve Board surveys.

Thus, in 1957 among aged OASDI beneficiary couples:
    28 per cent had no liquid assets at all; an additional 12
    per cent had less than $500.

Among "nonmarried" (widowed, divorced, never married) beneficiaries:
    43 per cent had no liquid assets; an additional 13 per
    cent had less than $500.

Aside from their own utility as a resource to fall back on, assets

---

[1]State data estimated from distributions for December 1959 and June 1960.

[2]Data for February or March 1960.

[3]Excludes data for aged beneficiaries living in Guam, Puerto Rico, Virgin Islands, and foreign countries.

can be income producing and thus in themselves raise total money income.

When beneficiary couples were classified by the amount of their OASDI benefit—

Among those at the minimum, only 1 in 4 had as much as $75 in income from assets for the year;

Among those near the maximum, more than 1 in 2 had as much as $75 in income from assets for the year.

### LIFE INSURANCE

Life insurance is a fairly common form of asset or saving, although less so among the aged than among younger families. The policies of the aged have a relatively low face value, however, and some of them have no cash surrender value, so that the proceeds could be used more to finance burial costs or pay some of the bills outstanding after a terminal illness than to meet costs of current medical care.

### Holdings of Aged Spending Units

Fifty-six per cent of the spending units with aged head owned a life insurance policy in early 1957, compared to 79 per cent of all spending units. (The value was not obtained.)

### Holdings of Aged OASDI Beneficiaries

Among OASDI beneficiaries studied in the fall of 1957, 71 per cent of the married couples and half of the other aged beneficiaries carried some life insurance. The median face value was $1,850 for the policies carried by couples and less than half as much for non-married beneficiaries.

Following are the proportions holding policies with a face value of $5,000 or more, on the one hand, and less than $1,000 per person ($2,000 for a couple) or no insurance at all:

| *Aged Beneficiaries* | *None or Under $1,000 per Person Percent* | *$5,000 or More Percent* |
|---|---|---|
| Married couples | 68 | 2 |
| Single retired workers | 77 | 9 |
| Aged widows | 85 | 1 |

## HOMEOWNERSHIP

Equity in a home is the most common "saving" of the aged and represents the major portion of their net worth. Like other forms of saving, homeownership is more common among those with higher incomes.

### Aged Spending Units

In early 1959, 66 per cent of the nonfarm "spending units" headed by a person sixty-five and over owned their homes. Of these homes, 83 per cent were clear of mortgage debt.

Among aged spending units with liquid assets of less than $200, half lived in rented quarters or with relatives. Among aged spending units with liquid assets of $200 or more, more than two-thirds owned their home.

### Aged OASDI Beneficiaries

Just about two out of three married OASDI beneficiaries and one out of three of the nonmarried studied in 1957 owned a nonfarm home. Most of these homes were mortgage free, but the equity was relatively modest:

Among OASDI beneficiaries owning nonfarm homes late in 1957, the median equity was about $8,000 for couples and widows, about $6,000 for single retired workers.

Nearly eight out of ten of the beneficiary couples with income of $5,000 or more, but fewer than two out of three with less than $1,200, owned their homes.

*While homeownership can mean lower out-of-pocket costs, it does not mean living rent free.* Data from the 1957 beneficiary survey indicate that urban couples keeping house alone in a paid-up home averaged about 30 per cent less for taxes, upkeep, and utilities than the average outlay for rent, heat, and other utilities by couples renting their living quarters. The BLS, using similar data, estimates the saving at one-third.

## NONCASH INCOME

Many aged persons have noncash resources and income, usually an owned home. Such "nonmoney" income enables those who have it to enjoy better living than their money resources alone could make possible, but it does not necessarily release an equivalent number of dollars for purchasing goods and services, such as health care.

The 1957 BOASI beneficiary survey gives some indication of the number of aged who have noncash incomes but not of its dollar value.

In 1957, four out of five OASDI couples and three out of five nonmarried beneficiaries had some form of nonmoney income—an owned home or rent-free housing, food home grown or obtained without cost, or medical care for which no one in the household paid. Some with no noncash income received some support from the children or relatives with whom they lived.

### Homeownership as Noncash Income

Assuming homeownership is always profitable, some two-thirds of all beneficiary couples and one-third of the nonmarried beneficiaries derived income from their home. Actually, about 20 per cent of the homeowners reported current housing expenses for the year that exceeded the estimated rental value of the home.

Roughly every third homeowner reported noncash income from another source as well, usually food. Homeowners, as would be expected, are more likely to have a garden and other opportunities to raise food. Such food makes for a better and more interesting diet, but the net saving in food costs is likely to be something less than dollar for dollar.

### Other Sources of Noncash Income

For one-eighth of all couples and about one-fourth of the other aged beneficiaries, the noncash income was solely from sources other than homeownership.

A fourth of the couples in all and a tenth of all other aged beneficiaries had some home-produced food.

Clothing gifts were negligible, but one in nine couples and one in six nonmarried beneficiaries received some medical care at no cost to them.

## MEASURES OF NEED—BUDGET COSTS

### The Revised Budget for a Retired Couple

Budget costs of a "modest but adequate" level for a retired elderly couple in twenty large cities in autumn 1959 have been estimated by the Bureau of Labor Statistics for a retired man and wife in reasonably good health for their age, requiring no unusual medical or other services, and keeping house by themselves in a small rented unit. This budget is a revised and updated version—to take account not only of rising prices, but of changing consumption patterns—of the Budget for an Elderly Couple developed by the Social Security Administration in 1948.

BUDGET COSTS IN LATE 1959

In terms comparable to the original Social Security Administration budget, the total cost of goods and services ranges from $2,390 in Houston to $3,110 in Chicago, as shown by the following figures:

In terms comparable to the current budget for a city worker's family of 4, costs are somewhat higher because that standard includes a small allowance for auto expense and a more expensive list of food items:

| | | |
|---|---|---|
| Atlanta | $2,467 | $2,720 |
| Baltimore | 2,571 | 2,840 |
| Boston | 3,067 | 3,304 |
| Chicago | 3,112 | 3,366 |
| Cincinnati | 2,698 | 2,925 |
| Cleveland | 3,011 | 3,244 |
| Detroit | 2,865 | 3.096 |
| Houston | 2,390 | 2,641 |
| Kansas City | 2,802 | 3,034 |
| Los Angeles | 2,851 | 3,111 |
| Minneapolis | 2,906 | 3,135 |
| New York | 2,812 | 3,044 |
| Philadelphia | 2,684 | 2,909 |
| Pittsburgh | 2,842 | 3,102 |
| Portland, Oregon | 2,792 | 3,049 |
| St. Louis | 2,858 | 3,099 |
| San Francisco | 2,949 | 3,223 |
| Scranton | 2,492 | 2,681 |
| Seattle | 2,990 | 3,252 |
| Washington, D.C. | 2,770 | 3,047 |

*Situations in Which the Budget Does Not Apply*—The living arrangements assumed for the budget describe the situation of only a minority of elderly people today. The more typical couple lives

in a home they own rather than rent. How the cost range should be
adapted for those in small cities and towns, and for the large number of widowed, divorced, or single older people who live alone or
share the home of a relative, is still an open question. All the
estimates are derived from averages. Thus they cannot be used for
the "unusual" family, and even a "usual" family can have an unusual year. A family with more than average sickness or a long
hospital stay would be "unusual" in terms of this budget.

*Budget as a Measure of Income Adequacy*—On the whole, the
budget costs appear relatively high compared with the actual income of the elderly even when allowance is made for the estimated
savings in housing costs that many have as homeowners.

Relatively few couples with incomes less than the cost of the
budget standard would have sufficient savings and other assets
readily convertible into cash to make up the difference. On the
other hand, how much families need and how they spend their
money are highly individual matters of balancing resources and
preferences. For a retired couple, how well they are able to live
before and the inventory of goods now on hand play an important
role.

Current income data from the Bureau of the Census are not
available for aged couples living alone. However, on the basis of a
special analysis for 1956 of income data for aged couples living
alone for those living with relatives, and for other families with
aged head, the median income in 1959 of all elderly couples living
alone in urban areas may be estimated at roughly $2,600–$2,800
in 1959.

Thus, the cost of maintaining an elderly couple, in reasonably
good health for their age and living alone in a rented dwelling in
a large city may have been beyond the reach of more than half of
them. Lowering the budget to a range of $2,100-$2,700 to allow
for the estimated amount of housing costs that many of the couples
would save as homeowners would reduce the number for whom the
budget standard would be more than income could provide, but
this number would still be considerable.

*Budgets for One*— Many of the aged, particularly older women,
live by themselves, not with a spouse. There is currently no refer-

ence standard for an elderly person living alone comparable to the budget for a couple.

Pending further research, the relationship of the cost of living for a single individual to that for a couple must remain uncertain. For some categories of the couple's budget determined separately for each member—such as clothing, recreation, or medical care—there is already a built-in divider. For food it is possible to use the adjustments suggested by the Department of Agriculture for its food plan which forms the basis for the food component of the budget.

For other components, as indeed for the total budget cost, there is no readily accepted adjustment factor. There is likely to be general agreement, however, that the least suitable approach is a simple division by two. For some items, such as housing, it is probably necessary to assume that the cost for a single individual will be but little less than for two.

The Bureau of Labor Statistics has developed a scale, based on the relation between food expenditures and income, according to which the income required for an elderly person living alone would be 59 per cent of that for an elderly couple living at the same standard. This factor represents an averaging of income-expenditure patterns for families throughout the entire range of income.

Further study will most likely show that the higher the income, the greater the differential for shared living that should be presumed in estimating costs for an individual from those for a couple. When incomes are low and consumption is already close to the marginal level, it may cost only a little less for an aged person alone than it does for two.

But accepting as a workable estimate the BLS-suggested 59 per cent ratio would bring estimated costs for an elderly person considerably above average means:

On this basis a "modest but adequate" standard for an elderly person living alone would take from $1,410 to $1,835 in the twenty cities studied. But median income for unrelated individuals aged sixty-five or over living in cities was $1,140 in 1959.

## TAX PROVISIONS FAVORING THE AGED

The Treasury's tax policies recognize the special problems encountered by older persons. It is apparent, however, that as with savings, homeownership, and similar resources of the aged, one usually must be in a relatively favorable income situation to begin with in order to have the advantage.

No overall appraisal is available of the extent to which State and local taxes effect the aged. Of the thirty-five States that levy personal income taxes, seventeen allow additional deductions for the aged.

### Tax Relief for Older Persons

Federal income tax laws grant substantial relief to older people or to members of their family who are responsible for their support:

The filing requirement for persons sixty-five and over is $1,200 compared with $600 for other persons.

Older people who are blind may get in addition the extra exemption of $600 allowed blind people.

Social security and railroad retirement benefits are exempt from tax, as are modest amounts in other pensions, annuities, dividends, etc., under the special retirement income credit provision of 1954.

Thus, with the 10 per cent standard deduction, a husband and wife both sixty-five can have up to $2,675 income, in addition to their OASDI or railroad retirement benefit and any other retirement income credit, tax free.

Furthermore, for medical expenses other than drugs, older people in computing their tax may deduct full costs, unlike the younger persons who are limited to expenses in excess of 3 per cent. A provision enacted in 1960 will afford this same right to children with respect to medical expenses incurred in behalf of aged dependent parents.

### Federal Tax Savings for Older Taxpayers

It is estimated that, in 1960, more than $0.5 billion in taxes was saved by the 7 million older persons claiming the double personal exemption.

Over $100 million in taxes was saved by the retirement income credit.

About $100 million of taxes was saved by the more than 1.5 million older persons who benefit from the more liberal treatment of medical expenses for older persons. (In 1958, aged taxpayers itemizing their medical expenses were able to deduct 97 per cent of these expenses compared with 64 per cent for taxpayers under sixty-five.

### Aged Persons Subject to Federal Tax

Further liberalization of income tax laws could have relatively little benefit for the large majority of elderly persons since so few are at present subject to tax. It would be possible, of course, to ease the burden for such younger persons as now are responsible for the support of dependent parents and other aged relatives who do not themselves file a return.

Of the approximately 15 million persons sixty-five and over in 1957, only 6.5 million filed a return (or had one filed for them), and only 3.2 million of these returns were taxable. This means that fewer than one in five persons sixty-five or over is now having to pay a Federal tax on his income.

## PRE-RETIREMENT ANTICIPATION AND ADJUSTMENT IN RETIREMENT[1]

### Wayne E. Thompson

In an important sense, retirement is what one makes of it. Unlike most changes in status, a correlative institutionalized role does not typically await the retiree. Instead, he must create for himself a pattern of activities which serves as an effective substitute for his job. Thus adjustment in retirement involves a considerable personal input, over and above that required to assimilate new activi-

---

[1]This paper is a part of a larger analysis which seeks not only to relate anticipatory factors to adjustment but also to analyze the antecedents to positive anticipation and to analyze the way in which situational factors in retirement diminish, counteract, or supplement anticipatory orientation. Reprinted by courtesy of *Journal of Social Issues, Volume 14* (2) :35-45, 1958.

ties and patterns of interaction which stand ready-made and waiting as a part of a well-defined institutional structure.

It follows that pre-retirement anticipation of the status of retiree may play a crucial part in the adjustment process; for if the creation of a retirement role is largely incumbent upon the retiree, it would seem to be particularly important that he does not enter retirement totally unprepared. Stated more formally, it may be hypothesized that *adjustment in retirement is conditioned by pre-retirement anticipation of the retired status.*

This proposition is accepted as a basic premise by advocates of pre-retirement counseling programs.[2] Moreover, it would seem to be held implicitly by those who seek to evaluate pre-retirement counseling; for insofar as such studies go beyond measuring extent of participation and expressed enthusiasm for a given program, they are concerned with the manner in which such factors as pre-retirement attitude toward retirement, knowledge of retirement, and planning have been affected by participation in a program. Studies of this sort have made important contributions in answer to the question of how pre-retirement orientations may best be altered. Interestingly enough, however, the basic assumption is rarely questioned, even though systematic evidence as to the relationship between preretirement anticipation and adjustment as measured *after* retirement is largely lacking.

This is the analytical problem to which the present paper is directed. Although we predict that adjustment in retirement is conditioned by pre-retirement anticipation, we take the proposition not as given, but as problemmatical. Even more important, if the

---

[2]The premise of the effectiveness of retirement conditioning evidently is accepted by some to such an extent that they think in terms of the following syllogism: retirement conditioning facilitates adjustment; XYZ company has a pre-retirement counseling program; therefore, XYZ retirees will likely be "happily retired." Clearly, given this sort of reasoning, a troubled "industrial conscience" is soothed by establishing some kind of pre-retirement counseling program. But such reasoning is questionable, not only because of the dearth of evidence in support of the major premise, but also because it begs the prior question of the extent of participation in programs of retirement conditioning. In our research we find that among the respondents who we know *from company report* are covered by some form of pre-retirement counseling, only 10 per cent indicate that their company tries to do anything to help them prepare for retirement, outside of pensions.

several aspects of anticipation can be shown to be significant, analysis may demonstrate their relative importance and the inter-dependence or independence of each. Thus, by taking a step back-ward in carving out our research problem, perhaps we will be better able to understand, on a general level, the dynamics of anticipatory activities.

### THE ANALYTICAL DESIGN

In general, the analytical design involves attempting to relate differences in adjustment as indexed *after* retirement to differences in anticipation which were indexed *before* retirement occurred. This is made possible by the panel design of the Cornell Study of Occupational Retirement, for all of the participating retirees have been contacted not only after they stopped working, but also at least once while they were still gainfully employed. The analysis which follows includes all of the currently active male participants who had retired by the time of the third follow-up in 1957.

Three different anticipatory factors are considered in the analysis: pre-conception of retirement; pre-retirement attitude to-ward retirement; and having plans for retirement[3] (Fig. 1) . Among

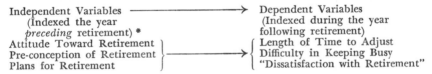

Independent Variables ——————————→ Dependent Variables
  (Indexed the year                                  (Indexed during the year
  *preceding* retirement) *                    following retirement)
Attitude Toward Retirement ⎫                Length of Time to Adjust
Pre-conception of Retirement ⎬————→ Difficulty in Keeping Busy
Plans for Retirement ⎭                          "Dissatisfaction with Retirement"

*Excepting pre-conception of retirement. See the text regarding this item.

Fig. 1. The Analytical Design: Anticipation as a Factor in Adjustment.

---

[3]Having plans for retirement is determined by a positive response to the question, "Have you made plans for anything you would like to do after you stop working?" Attitude toward retirement is a measure developed through the use of the Gutt-man scaling technique and includes the following three items:
1) Some people say that retirement is good for a person, some say it is bad. In general, what do you think? [Positive response: it is good for a person]
2) Do you mostly look forward to the time when you will stop working and retire or in general do you dislike the idea? [Positive response: I look forward to it]
3) If it were up to you alone, would you continue working for your present com-pany? [Positive response: I would stop working]
Reproducibility, 1952: .96; Error Ratio, 1952:    .32

these, attitude and planning were indexed during the year immediately preceding retirement. The third, pre-conception of retirement, is indexed by the response elicited in 1957 to the following statement: Agree-Disagree: "I had a pretty good idea of what my life would be like in retirement even before I stopped working." Those who agree with the statement are taken to have had accurate knowledge of what their retirement would be like; those who disagree obviously include not only persons who simply had no idea of what their retirement would be like, but also those who had an idea which was found to be incorrect once retirement occurred. Of the indices of anticipation, only this one relies on the memory of the respondents, and in a sense, even *it* does not; for only retirement would it be possible for the retiree certainly to discover whether his pre-conception of retirement was correct.

The indices of adjustment in retirement are in each case based upon responses given during the first year of retirement.[4] The first of these, length of time to get used to not working, serves as an index of the facility with which adjustment has taken place. Broadly speaking, getting used to not working is precisely the problem of adjusting to the changed status; and the length of time in which this is accomplished reflects the ease with which adjustment occurred.

---

[4]The indices of adjustment in retirement used in the analysis are the following:
1) Length of time to get used to retirement, indexed by the answers to the question, "It takes some people a little while to get used to not working. About how long would you say it took you to become used to not working?" "Negative" responses are: "It took me more than three months," or "I am still not used to it."
2) Difficulty in keeping busy, indexed by the responses, "often" or "sometimes" to the question: "How often do you have times when you just don't know what to do to keep occupied?"
3) Dissatisfaction with Retirement," a measure developed through the use of the Guttman scaling technique. This measure includes the following items:
How often do you miss the feeling of doing a good job?
[Negative response: often]
How often do you feel that you want to go back to work?
[Negative response: often]
How often do you worry about not having a job?
[Negative response: often, or sometimes]
How often do you miss being with other people at work?
[Negative response: often, or sometimes]
Coefficient of Reproducibility, 1954:   .97;   Error Ratio, 1954:   .40

The second, difficulty in keeping busy, in an index of a specific aspect of successful adjustment in retirement. That is to say, those who have no trouble finding things to do may generally be assumed to have successfully created a retirement role for themselves. And as we suggested in our introductory remarks, this may be an aspect of adjustment in which anticipatory factors play a particularly important part.

The third index of adjustment in retirement is a general index of satisfaction with retirement. Insofar as becoming disaccustomed to gainful employment is a mark of good adjustment in the new status, those who express satisfaction in this sense may be regarded as well-adjusted retirees. Presumably satisfaction with retirement reflects success in meeting a whole range of specific adjustment problems, but it may directly reflect favorable anticipation as well.

## THE FINDINGS

### Facility in Adjusting

When considered separately, it would appear that having plans for retirement, an accurate pre-conception of retirement, and a favorable pre-retirement attitude toward retirement each are important factors which facilitate adjustment once retirement occurs. In every case, those who anticipated their retirement in a positive fashion were the less likely to have taken more than three months to become used to not working: 39 per cent of those whose pre-retirement attitude was favorable as compared with 63 per cent of those whose attitude was unfavorable; 43 per cent of those with an accurate pre-conception of retirement as compared with 65 per cent of those without; and 45 per cent of those with plans as compared with 53 per cent of those who had not made plans for retirement.

But this may be an oversimplified view of the relationship, for as one would expect, the three anticipatory factors are themselves interrelated. Those who have plans for retirement are more likely also to have an accurate idea of what retirement will be like, perhaps reflecting a greater systematic expenditure of effort to find out about the circumstances of retirement. Also, having plans for retirement and an accurate idea of retirement are associated independently and cumulatively with a favorable pre-retirement attitude. It is important, therefore, to determine the way in which the three factors *in combination* relate to facility in adjusting, for their interrelationship may qualify certain of the relationships which seem to be significant when each factor is considered separately.

Analysis shows this to be the case. Although a favorable pre-retirement attitude toward retirement and an accurate pre-conception of retirement serve independently to facilitate adjustment, having plans for retirement evidently does not (Table 1). Among those who held an accurate pre-conception of retirement, planners are more likely than non-planners to take less time to adjust; *but among those who did not have an accurate idea of what retirement would be like, those* without *plans actually are more likely than those* with *plans to take less time to get used to not working!* In other words, there is a relationship between planning and facility in adjusting among those who did not have "a pretty good idea of what retirement would be like even before I stopped working"; but the relationship is the reverse of what one might expect.

TABLE 1

LENGTH OF TIME TO GET USED TO NOT WORKING AS RELATED TO PRE-CONCEPTION OF RETIREMENT, PRE-RETIREMENT ATTITUDE TOWARD RETIREMENT AND HAVING PLANS

| | Percentages Who Took Less than Three Months to Become Used to Not Working* | | | |
| | Had An Idea of What Retirement Would be Like | | Did Not Have An Idea of What Retirement Would be Like | |
| | Favorable Attitude | Unfavorable Attitude | Favorable Attitude | Unfavorable Attitude |
| --- | --- | --- | --- | --- |
| Had Plans | 71% (200) | 47% (81) | 37% (52) | 15% (34) |
| Did Not Have Plans | 64% (180) | 41% (176) | 47% (72) | 32% (122) |

*The figures in parentheses indicate the number of cases on which each percentage is based.

It would appear that when one lacks an accurate pre-conception of retirement, the process of adjustment is *more* difficult if one has plans for something he would like to do in retirement. In a sense, having plans, but an inaccurate view of retirement, may create a double problem of adjustment: not only must the retiree cope with the inevitable problems of a changed status, but also he must cope with the disappointment of thwarted plans and must readjust his own thinking and planning in terms of reality as he finds it. The situation of the planner is analagous to that of a traveller who not only must deal with the hazards of the highway, but also must revise his incorrect maps as he proceeds toward his goal. The goal may remain the same, but it is made more difficult of attainment because of false starts and wrong turnings. By way of contrast, the non-planner is headed for no especial place at no particular time and relatively more readily comes to feel at home in his jaunt through new territory.

## Success in Adjusting

But perhaps the payoff is success: while facility in adjusting is important in its own right, perhaps an even more important measure of the way in which anticipation affects adjustment is relative satisfaction with the retired status, achieved with whatever difficulty.

We have hypothesized that one of the key factors which contributes to satisfaction with retirement is the successful creation of a pattern of activities which effectively substitutes for one's job. As one highly literate, albeit disgruntled, respondent expressed the need:

> Once you retire you simply must find some kind of rewarding activity, or you're sunk. You researchers refer to the "retirement vacuum"; I think "retirement vacuousness" is more apt, for according to my Webster this carries fuller connotations of a dull, witless, and pointless idleness. I can speak for no one but myself, but I wish to God I were back on the job.

In point of fact, the respondent might well have considered himself the spokesman for many others, for statistical analysis shows dissatisfaction with retirement generally to be much more likely among those who find it difficult to keep busy; 43 per cent were "dissatisfied" among those who had difficulty keeping busy, while only 12 per cent were "dissatisfied" among those who had no such difficulty.

In turn, differences in difficulty in keeping busy (which we assume reflects relative success or failure in creating a retirement role) is highly related to pre-retirement anticipation of the retired status (Table 2). At the one extreme—among those who hold a favorable pre-retirement attitude toward retirement, and an accurate pre-conception, and who had plans for retirement—fully 80 per cent seldom or never had "times when [they] just [didn't] know what to do to keep occupied"; at the other extreme—among the "non-anticipators"—only 39 per cent seldom or never had such difficulty.

TABLE 2

DIFFICULTY IN KEEPING BUSY AS RELATED TO PRE-CONCEPTION OF RETIREMENT,
PRE-RETIREMENT ATTITUDE TOWARD RETIREMENT AND HAVING PLANS

| | *Percentages Who Had No Difficulty in Keeping Busy* | | | |
|---|---|---|---|---|
| | *Had An Idea of What Retirement Would be Like* | | *Did Not Have An Idea of What Retirement Would be Like* | |
| | *Favorable Attitude* | *Unfavorable Attitude* | *Favorable Attitude* | *Unfavorable Attitude* |
| Had Plans | 80% (200) | 60% (81) | 65% (52) | 47% (34) |
| Did Not Have Plans | 66% (180) | 57% (176) | 49% (72) | 39% (122) |

But between these extremes, a somewhat more complicated picture emerges. First of all, it would appear that planning for retirement is largely unimportant except among those who hold a favorable pre-retirement attitude toward retirement. The implication is that planning in conjunction with a favorable attitude is a mark of determination, a matter of a concrete objective willingly sought. By way of contrast, among those who hold an unfavorable attitude, planning is not enough; those people may have concrete objectives proposed for their retirement, but objectives which are less desired than continued employment. The point made by a retired semi-skilled worker is well taken:

They kept telling me at [his former company] that I ought to make some plans for my retirement, and they worried me about it until I did some thinking about it and decided I'd have me a shop down in the basement to putter around in and maybe make some money here and there on the side. Well, I'm retired now, and, you know, I don't suppose I've been down there more than a half a dozen times in the last year and a half. I guess the truth of the matter is that if I'm going to do woodwork, I'd rather be doing it on a regular job.

As it happens, this particular retiree had worked out a satisfactory routine which he apparently enjoyed following, but his pre-retirement planning was largely irrelevant as a contributing factor. Evidently, so it is with many whose plans for retirement are not enthusiastically and willingly pursued.

Beyond this, pre-retirement attitude toward retirement and preconception of retirement are roughly equivalent factors which contribute to success in establishing a satisfactory retirement role. Again, determination is suggested by the fact that attitude toward retirement is slightly more important than pre-conception among those who had plans for retirement, whereas it is apparently somewhat more important to have an accurate notion of what lies ahead than it is to hold a favorable attitude, among those who lack pre-retirement plans. But the magnitude of these differences is small; and one might legitimately weigh pre-retirement attitude and pre-conception of retirement equally as determinants of successful role development. In fact, the essential anticipatory ingredients in the process of creating a new role might be held to be these two factors: a favorable pre-retirement attitude toward retirement and an accurate preconception of retirement.

This assertion is further supported when one considers the relationship between anticipatory factors and the more general index of success in adjustment, "dissatisfaction with retirement" (Table 3). Of the three, planning for retirement is of relatively little im-

TABLE 3

"DISSATISFACTION WITH RETIREMENT" AS RELATED TO PRE-CONCEPTION OF RETIREMENT, PRE-RETIREMENT ATTITUDE TOWARD RETIREMENT, AND HAVING PLANS

| | Percentages Who Were Not "Dissatisfied with Retirement" | | | |
|---|---|---|---|---|
| | Did Not Have An Idea of What Retirement Would be Like | | Had An Idea of What Retirement Would be Like | |
| | Favorable Attitude | Unfavorable Attitude | Favorable Attitude | Unfavorable Attitude |
| Had Plans | 77% (52) | 62% (34) | 91% (200) | 69% (81) |
| Did Not Have Plans | 68% (72) | 54% (122) | 88% (180) | 72% (176) |

portance; but both a favorable pre-retirement attitude toward retirement and an accurate pre-conception of retirement make an
important contribution to general satisfaction with retirement as
it is expressed by the retiree.

The importance of these two anticipatory factors is even more
fully supported in further analysis which seeks to determine whether the anticipatory factors relate to general satisfaction independently of the specific factor, i.e. difficulty in keeping busy.
In such analysis, one finds a prototypic instance of an independent
and cumulative relationship, in this case between difficulty in
keeping busy, pre-retirement attitude toward retirement, and pre-
conception of retirement on the one hand and general satisfaction
with retirement on the other. The proportion who are relatively
satisfied with retirement shows a steady progression from the least
satisfaction among the "non-anticipators" who have a problem of
keeping occupied (42 per cent) to the most satisfaction among
those who anticipate retirement favorably and have no problem
finding enough to do (94 per cent).

As one might predict, of the factors considered, the one most
highly related to general satisfaction is our index of success in
meeting the specific problem of finding a retirement role, that is,
difficulty in keeping busy. But, as we have seen, this is itself related
to anticipatory factors; and in addition, both pre-retirement attitude toward retirement and preconception of retirement are independently important. Overall, we conclude that *as far as anticipatory factors are concerned, the prescription for successfully meeting
the challenges of retirement includes a favorable pre-retirement
attitude and an accurate pre-conception of retirement.*

In part, the picture is one of the way in which an anticipatory
attitude serves as a basis for systematic bias in experience. Since no
situation is wholly pleasant or wholly unpleasant, selectivity of
perception and evaluation of one's life situation inevitably partially
reflects one's orientations. In the present context, this means that
subjective evaluation of retirement by the retiree is made partly in
terms of an attitude which he held *before* retirement took place.

It is evident also that adjustment to a new status, including the creation of a correlative role, is facilitated and success made more probable if one holds an accurate anticipatory "cognitive map." Knowing what to expect, the retiree can more quickly and more successfully program a pattern of living which he can satisfactorily accept.

To be sure, anticipation is not everything. There remain the cold, hard facts of the retirement situation with which each individual must cope. But having a psychological bias which emphasizes the good over the bad, and a sound idea of what to expect, the retiree is much better equipped to face and meet the problems which arise.

# CHANGING PATTERNS OF RETIREMENT*

### MARGARET S. GORDON

Among the meaningful activities in which elderly persons might engage, work for pay or profit is declining in relative importance. In 1900, out of a population of slightly more than three million persons aged sixty-five and over, approximately two out of five were gainful workers. By 1959, the population in this age group had expanded to nearly 15 million, of whom only about one in five was in the labor force. Thus, as the number of elderly persons in the population has increased, the number of nonworkers has risen much more rapidly than the number of workers.

*This paper was presented at the annual meeting of the Gerontological Society, Inc., Detroit, Michigan, November 12-14, 1959. It is a brief summary of a chapter on work and patterns of retirement for a volume to be entitled *Aging and leisure: research perspectives on the meaningful use of leisure time* (Robert W. Kleemeier and others, Eds.), to be published by the Oxford University Press. Preparation of the volume was sponsored by the Research Subcommittee of the Section on Psychology and the Social Sciences. Gerontological Society, Inc., with the assistance of a grant from the Ford Foundation.

The investigator wishes to express her appreciation for the assistance of Malcolm Gutter, Research Assistant, Institute of Industrial Relations, University of California (Berkeley) in the preparation of data for the present paper. Reprinted by courtesy of *Journal of Gerontology*, Volume *15*:300-304, July, 1960.

The demographic changes that are responsible for the marked increase in the number of older people in the population are by now thoroughly familiar. There is also general awareness of the fact that the decline in the percentage of workers in the aged population is entirely attributable to a fall in the proportion of elderly men in the labor force. The percentage of elderly women in the labor force has been very small throughout the present century but has risen slightly in recent years.

The striking increase in the number of non-workers in the aged population, with its parallels in all industrialized nations, has been responsible for a marked upsurge of interest in the issue of work versus retirement for elderly people. Much of the discussion of this issue has revolved around the question of compulsory versus flexible retirement policies. This is part of the problem, and a growing part, but there are many other aspects of the issue of work versus retirement for elderly people that require study and debate.

In a broader sense, the issue of work versus retirement for older persons involves all those aspects of management, union, and government policy that affect the decisions of older persons to work or retire. Policies affecting the hiring and retention of the older worker, the adequacy of public and private pension benefits, the availability of disability and health insurance, the retirement age and retirement test under the Social Security Act, and retirement programs for government employees are all closely related to the problem. And in a less direct but even more important sense, all those aspects of social policy that affect the general level of employment are highly relevant.

If intelligent decisions are to be made on these questions, a great deal of information bearing on the circumstances and conditions under which people actually retire is needed. There has been a substantial amount of research on attitudes toward work and retirement, chiefly among the employees or retirees of sizable corporations, and some significant research on reasons for retirement. But there has been surprisingly little study of the actual process of retirement as it is experienced by large groups of elderly persons who have not been employed by large corporations. Even so, it is possible to piece together a somewhat impressionistic picture of various patterns of retirement on the basis of scattered sources of information, and to draw certain inferences that are highly relevant to issues of retirement policy.

## THE LIFE CYCLE IN WORK PATTERNS

By no means do all persons work steadily to age sixty-five and then abruptly retire. An understanding of patterns of retirement requires, first of all, an accurate picture of the life cycle in patterns of work. The proportion of men in the labor force rises to a peak at ages thirty-five to forty-four and then declines steadily with advancing age. However, the decline is quite gradual up to about age fifty-five and then begins to accelerate. At ages sixty-five to sixty-nine, only about half of all men are in the labor force, while among men aged seventy and over approximately a fourth are working or seeking work.

Equally significant is the fact that among the men who work, middle-aged men are more likely to work full time the year round than either younger or older men. The older male population includes not only a large percentage of men who have left the labor force, but also a substantial proportion who are working part time or intermittently. Among those aged 65 and over who are in the labor force, only about four out of ten work at full-time jobs the year round.

The life cycle in labor force participation of women has undergone a striking change since 1900. Whereas formerly the proportion of women in the labor force reached a peak in the age group from twenty to twenty-four and then descended sharply, it now rises to a second peak at ages forty-five to fifty-four. If recent trends continue, this second peak is likely before long to be substantially higher than the peak in the early twenties. However, the proportion of women aged sixty-five and over in the labor force is very small, amounting only to about 10 per cent.

Full-time work plays a relatively less important role in the lives of female workers of all ages than in the case of men, and among women aged sixty-five and over full-time work is rare indeed. Even within the relatively small group of these elderly women in the labor force, less than a third work full time the year round. Most of the others work on a part-time basis.

## THE PROBLEM OF RETIREMENT

If patterns of work vary greatly with changing age, so do attitudes toward retirement. For the young man who is primarily concerned with his current and future job status, retirement is a distant prospect. But increasing age tends to be accompanied by increasing apprehension over the prospect of retirement. Indeed, there are indications that, the closer the worker comes to retirement age the more likely he is to repress the whole idea. And there is growing evidence that once this critical stage is behind him and he is actually retired, his attitude may become less negative.

Attitudes toward retirement also differ greatly among occupation groups. Friedmann and Havighurst (1954) found that the proportions of men who wanted to continue working fell sharply between the top and the bottom of the occupational scale. However, the Cornell retirement study suggests that, except for professional workers, persons at higher occupational levels tend to look more favorably on retirement than those in the lower occupation groups. The study also indicates that the more favorable attitudes of workers in the high occupation groups appear to be closely associated with the fact that they can look forward to a higher retirement income.

Although professional and managerial workers are particularly likely to find their work intrinsically interesting, they likewise have a greater tendency to make careful preparations for retirement and are more likely to have in mind a number of leisure-time activities which they expect to enjoy in retirement. As one writer has put it, the whole idea of planning for retirement may well be a middle-class concept.

Contrary to a widespread impression, involuntary retirement provisions are not the most prevalent reason for retirement, except perhaps in relatively large corporations. Several nationwide studies conducted in the early 1950's indicated that only a small proportion of retired workers had been forced to retire because of involuntary retirement provisions. Most of the retired workers had quit their jobs voluntarily, and in the great majority of these cases failing physical capacity and ill health were the reasons cited for quitting. In addition, an appreciable percentage of retired workers had left the labor force because their jobs had been discontinued, or because they had become involuntarily unemployed for other reasons.

It is likely, however, that the proportion of workers retiring because of involuntary retirement provisions is higher now than in the early 1950's, a point to be elaborated below.

## PATTERNS OF RETIREMENT

It is apparent that retirement is a process which occurs in many different ways. Probably the most important patterns are: 1) retirement at the normal retirement age, or a later age, under the provisions of a formal retirement system; 2) early retirement under a formal system, sometimes followed by a shift to other employment; 3) retirement from a stable job in a firm without a formal retirement system; 4) an unstable pattern of retirement in which an older worker (a) loses a stable job and is subsequently forced to rely on unsteady or part-time employment until he finally leaves the labor force or (b) has been engaged in casual or short-term employment and finds it increasingly difficult to get work as he grows older.

Although only a minority of workers retire under the provisions of formal retirement systems, there is ample evidence to suggest that the proportion is growing. Since few firms have formal retirement systems in the absence of a pension plan, data on the growth of pension plans may be relied on to provide an indication of the spread of formal retirement systems. The number of workers covered by private pension plans increased from 2.7 million in 1930 to 19.0 million in 1958, or from 5.4 per cent to 28.8 per cent of the civilian labor force. In addition, more than four million government employees were members of retirement systems in the latter year. Thus, nearly a third of the civilian labor force was covered by a pension plan or a government retirement system.

Pension plans are more likely to be found in large firms than in smaller companies. Coverage also varies widely by occupation and industry.

Pension experts are inclined to think that the rapid growth in pension coverage which has characterized the 1940's and 1950's is not likely to continue, and that growth will proceed at a slower rate in the years to come. As Holland has put it, the "more likely situations for the introduction of pension plans have already been tapped, and only the harder cases remain." Yet it must be kept in mind that the most rapid gains in employment are occurring chiefly in white collar occupations and in such sections of employment as finance and government, in which pension plan coverage is comparatively high. Thus, the percentage of the civilian labor force under pension systems may continue to increase at a fairly rapid rate because of shifts in the structure of employment.

Most of the available evidence suggests that, among workers covered by pension plans, the proportion subject to some type of involuntary retirement policy is very high indeed. However, involuntary retirement provisions are somewhat less prevalent under negotiated pension plans than under unilateral plans. The relatively rapid growth of negotiated plans during the 1950's has apparently resulted in a slight decline in the relative importance of involuntary retirement provisions, and in some tendency to stipulate age sixty-eight or seventy, rather than age sixty-five, as the required retirement age where involuntary retirement prevails. Age sixty-five continues, however, to be the involuntary retirement age in the great majority of unilateral plans. Nevertheless, since the proportion of workers covered by pension plans has been increasing rapidly, the percentage of all workers affected by involuntary retirement provisions has undoubtedly been rising substantially, despite a slight decline in the proportion of pension plans with involuntary retirement provisions.

Just recently, as a result of the sluggishness of the recovery of employment in the wake of the 1957-58 recession, there have been indications of a rise of sentiment within union circles, reminiscent of the 1930's, in favor of involuntary retirement, or of lowering the retirement age in order to get older workers off the labor market and improve job opportunities for younger workers.

Only scanty data are available on the percentage of workers who retire with pension benefits before the normal retirement age, but such studies as have been made on the age of retirement from private employment suggest that the proportion may be as high as 20 to 30 per cent. However, little is known about the extent to which these workers later take other types of jobs. Under retirement plans for federal government employees, early retirement is much more prevalent than in private industry, approximating 60 per cent of all annuitants under the civil service retirement system.

Probably the most typical pattern of retirement is from a steady job in a firm without a pension plan. Ill health is clearly the most prevalent reason for retirement for this group, and inadequacy of retirement income tends to be a critical problem. Only those relatively few who have received comparatively high incomes are likely to have accumulated enough savings to provide any appreciable supplement to social security benefits. And despite the succession of increases in OASDI benefit levels adopted during the 1950's, the average benefit received by a single retired worker is only about $73 a month.

This is not to suggest that workers retiring from firms with pension plans always receive adequate benefits. But the combination of a private pension and OASDI benefits is more likely to approach adequacy than is the latter alone. Nor does the answer to the problem necessarily lie in the direction of extending private pension plan coverage to all workers not now included under such plans. An alternative approach would be a very substantial increase in the average level of OASDI benefits.

Although there is little direct information bearing in the point, a reasonable inference can be drawn from scattered data that workers retiring from firms without pension systems would, on the average, retire earlier if they could look forward to an adequate retirement income.

Unstable patterns of retirement are experienced by substantial numbers of elderly workers who undergo prolonged spells of unemployment and never again succeed in getting steady jobs. Unstable patterns are also to be expected in certain occupations (e.g., farm labor, lumber work, and building trades) in which work is typically seasonal or short-term in character. Workers in these industries are likely to find it increasingly difficult to achieve steady employment in the later years of working life.

In many respects the retirement problems of these groups resemble those of workers retiring from steady jobs without private pensions. But the personal financial assets of the former as they approach retirement are likely to be even less adequate because of the drain imposed by periods of unemployment. Further, the OASDI benefits for which they are eligible are likely to be lower because of the impact of these same spells of unemployment on their average monthly earnings under the system.

## CONCLUSIONS

There is little doubt that the ratio of workers to nonworkers in the aged population will continue to diminish. But how rapidly the decline will occur in the next decade or two will depend primarily on conditions in the labor market. If the rate of expansion of employment opportunities—in a period when the supply of youthful workers will be rising sharply—is not high enough to absorb the increase in the labor force, the decline in the proportion of workers in the older population is likely to be accelerated.

Even if a satisfactory rate of employment expansion is achieved for the economy as a whole, the gains are likely to occur chiefly in white collar employment. In an age of automation and rapid technological change, expansion of employment in many blue collar sectors has come to a halt in recent years, and in a growing number of industries employment of manual workers is declining. In this type of environment, there is likely to be pressure from the younger members of a good many unions for more restrictive retirement policies to hasten the retirement of older members.

If this happens, it is to be hoped that the alternatives will be carefully weighed and examined. Apart from broad national policies designed to stimulate the expansion of employment, what is needed, above all, is a flexible approach by both management and labor to the problems of technological change and declining employment in particular industries. Examples of imaginative approaches to these problems are represented by the mechanization fund recently established for West Coast longshoremen and by the automation fund set up by the Armour Company.

In the first instance, West Coast longshoremen are referred to jobs through a union dispatching service aimed, in general, at sharing the work equitably among members of the "fully registered work force." In its 1959 agreement with the union, the Pacific Maritime Association accepted the principle that union members were entitled to a share in the savings resulting from mechanization and undertook to accumulate out of such savings a special "mechanization" fund, to be distributed among members of the fully registered work force. The basis of distribution was to be left for later determination, but it was anticipated that the fund would be used to compensate workers for reduced employment resulting from mechanization.

The 1959 agreement between Armour and Company and the United Packinghouse Workers established an "automation" fund, to be administered by a special management-labor committee with an impartial chairman. The committee was to conduct special studies and make recommendations with respect to use of the fund, "including training employees to perform new and changed jobs and promoting employment opportunities within the Company for those affected" by technological changes.

Even if it is agreed in some industries that the retirement of older workers should be speeded up, alternative methods of achieving this result should be carefully considered. Is it more desirable, for example, to facilitate voluntary retirement through more adequate retirement benefits or to hasten retirement through introducing or lowering a compulsory retirement age? What are the differential effects of these two alternatives on the types of workers who retire at given ages, and what are the relative costs involved if one takes into account the probability that involuntary retirement provisions have a greater tendency to bring about the retirement of workers who are still highly productive?

In considering the various alternatives available, moreover, there is a need to give more thought to the implications of the increase in life expectancy. Age sixty-five has been selected as the compulsory retirement age under many retirement programs since the latter part of the nineteenth century. Yet life expectancy, even for those who have already reached age sixty-five, has been gradually increasing. A major break-through in the battle against either heart disease or cancer could greatly accelerate this trend. Even if the rate of expansion of employment opportunities should slow down, would it be wise to consider forcing retirement at earlier ages in spite of increased life expectancy? And in those employment situations in which a compulsory retirement age is considered essential, should some thought be given to a gradual increase in the required retirement age?

If the increase in the ratio of white collar to blue collar workers is creating apprehension in union circles concerned about sluggish employment opportunities for manual workers, it also has many other important implications in relation to the retirement picture. Along with this change there is likely to be a decline in the proportion of workers retiring because of ill health, and there may also tend to be a decrease in the proportion retiring as a result of a prolonged spell of unemployment, since these reasons for retirement are relatively less important for white collar workers. But, for reasons already suggested, there is also likely to be a substantial increase in the proportion of workers retiring under the provisions of formal retirement systems. Hence the question of compulsory versus flexible retirement, although it is only one among many issues of retirement policy, is likely to be a matter of vital concern to a growing proportion of workers.

## OLDER WORKERS AND THEIR JOB EFFECTIVENESS*
### Robert L. Peterson

About 65 per cent of America's working population is engaged in industrial, retailing, office, and managerial tasks. While everyone is aware that these millions of workers are growing older each day, there has long been a question in the minds of business administrators and others as to how older employees in these tasks

*Reprinted by courtesy of *Geriatrics*, Volume *10*, January, 1955.

compare in work efficiency with average younger employees. Because there has been so much talk about the effectiveness of older workers, and so few facts offered in support, several well-known midwestern organizations were asked to cooperate with the Bureau of Business Management of the University of Illinois in a survey on the effectiveness of older industrial, retailing, office, and managerial personnel.

This is a composite report which describes findings elicited through three separate studies, covering a total of 3,077 personnel sixty years of age and older (78 per cent male, 22 per cent female) in eighty-one organizations. The first study was undertaken when a group of retailers raised a question concerning the possible use of older people to meet personnel shortages in retail stores. To obtain information a rating form was developed and supervisors in twenty-two retail stores evaluated 527 older personnel. The findings were so revealing that a second study was conducted, covering 1,525 older industrial personnel in thirty-nine industries. Later, a third study was conducted covering 1,025 older office and managerial workers in twenty organizations. Incidentally, there is a great similarity in the findings of each of these three studies, indicating that the performance of older personnel is not greatly affected by the kind of work in which employees are engaged.

## SURVEY PROCEDURE

The studies were initiated by asking top executives in cooperating organizations to determine how many employees they had on their payrolls who were sixty years of age and older. It was found that older workers constituted approximately 5 per cent of the total employees in these organizations. An appropriate number of employee rating forms was then sent to each organization for distribution to supervisors. Supervisors in these organizations were then asked to rate each of their workers who was sixty and older. In addition, they were admonished to "Answer all questions honestly and realistically," and were informed that "Ratings are entirely confidential." After supervisors had completed their evaluations the rating forms were sent to the University of Illinois where the results were tabulated on IBM machines.

It will be observed that in obtaining data concerning older worker effectiveness complete reliance was placed on supervisory opinion. This was because it appears that fully objective, laboratory-controlled answers cannot be obtained with reference to the effectiveness of large groups of older personnel in different types of work. It is believed that confidential evaluations prepared of older personnel by their immediate supervisors are the best indices obtainable of their competence and performance.

The average age of personnel in the survey group was approximately sixty-four. The group was distributed into age categories as follows:

| Age Groups | 60-64 | 65-69 | 70-74 | 75 and over |
|---|---|---|---|---|
| Number of employees | 1,940 | 821 | 225 | 91 |
| Per cent of total | 63 | 27 | 7 | 3 |

The high percentage of employees in the sixty to sixty-four age group is doubtless due to the fact that in approximately one-half of the cooperating organizations there were policies in effect requiring all employees to retire at sixty-five or soon thereafter.

There were several employees in the survey group who were eighty years of age. One was a tool worker who had been with his present firm for fifty-nine years. He was given an over-all rating of "Good" and was reported by his supervisor to be capable of rendering at least two more years of satisfactory service. His weaknesses were reported to be "Declining eyesight and a tendency to fatigue more easily." Nevertheless, he was reported to have a lower record of absenteeism and to be more dependable than average younger workers.

Another employee of eighty was a man employed in an insurance company whose work consisted of checking insurance applications. He had been employed by his company for less than a year and was rated by his supervisor as "Good." It was reported that he had fewer absences than the average younger worker, and was as good as average younger workers in such qualities as dependability, judgment, work quality, work volume, and getting along with others. It was reported that he had no apparent age-connected weaknesses, and that it appeared he would be able to continue working for an indefinite period.

It might be expected that most of the older workers in the survey group had been with their present organizations for most of their working careers. However, it was disclosed that only 24 per cent had spent thirty or more years with their present organization. Surprisingly, 38 per cent of these older workers had been with their present organizations *less than ten years.*

These figures suggest that postwar shortages in the supply of available workers have been instrumental in encouraging employing organizations to raise their age limits in employment and to seek recruits from among the older age groups. That employers were not unwise in pursuing this course is reflected in the specific findings of the survey which follow.

## SURVEY RATINGS

All employees in the survey group were given one of the following ratings by supervisors on their over-all performance: excellent, very good, good, fair, or poor. The ratings assigned by supervisors to the 3,077 older personnel in the survey group were distributed as follows: excellent, 14 per cent; very good, 28 per cent; good, 38 per cent; fair, 18 per cent; and poor, 2 per cent. No important differences were noted in the ratings assigned to employees in the four age categories; while one might expect the favorableness of the ratings to decline sharply as age increased, the figures do not support such an expectation:

|  | 60-64 (Per Cent) | 65-69 (Per Cent) | 70-74 (Per Cent) | 75 and Older (Per Cent) |
|---|---|---|---|---|
| Excellent | 14 | 15 | 12 | 14 |
| Very good | 28 | 27 | 37 | 22 |
| Good | 39 | 35 | 33 | 43 |
| Fair | 17 | 20 | 15 | 20 |
| Poor | 2 | 3 | 3 | 1 |

There is, of course, a question as to how younger workers in these organizations would have fared in a similar evaluation of over-all performance. While no ratings of younger personnel were prepared, it seems unlikely that employees under sixty years of age would, as a group, have received ratings more favorable than those given older personnel. This is indicated by the following data in which supervisors have specifically compared the performance of older workers with that of *average younger workers.*

## Absenteeism

Older personnel were rated by their supervisors as being much less prone to absenteeism than average younger personnel, with distribution as follows: less absenteeism, 66 per cent; about the same absenteeism, 25 per cent; and more absenteeism, 9 per cent. There were no important differences in the ratings assigned to employees in the four age categories. Actually, the survey results show a very slight decrease in absenteeism paralleling advancing age.

## Dependability

Older personnel were rated by their supervisors as having a high level of dependability. Note the following data reporting that fully one-half of these senior workers were regarded by their supervisors as being more dependable than average younger workers: more dependable, 51 per cent; as dependable, 43 per cent; and less dependable, 6 per cent. No important differences were found in the dependability ratings assigned to employees in the four age categories. Those in the far-advanced age groups were given ratings on dependability which compared favorably with those assigned to employees in less-advanced age groups.

## Judgment

Only the office and managerial group (about one-third of the total) was rated on the element of judgment. Supervisors rated older workers, in comparison with younger workers, as follows: better judgment, 33 per cent; about the same, 57 per cent, and poorer judgment, 10 per cent. Again, no important differences were noted in the ratings assigned to employees in the four age categories. Good judgment appears to be an enduring quality which may persist into far-advanced years.

## Work Quality

All older workers except those in the retailing group were rated by supervisors on the quality of their work, in comparison with average younger workers: better work quality, 34 per cent; about the same, 59 per cent; and poorer work quality, 7 per cent. A check of ratings assigned to employees in the four age groups reveals no evidence of a decline in work quality paralleling advancing years.

## Work Volume

A major criterion in the evaluation of an employee is productivity. In this survey the various supervisors were asked to compare the work volume of older personnel with that of average younger workers, with the following distribution: higher work volume, 24 per cent; about the same, 56 per cent; and lower work volume, 20 per cent. There was a slight decline in work volume paralleling advancing years. Nevertheless, in the oldest age category (employees 75 and over), 10 per cent were reported to have a higher work volume, 59 per cent were reported to have a volume about the same, and 31 per cent were reported to have a lower volume of work than average younger personnel. In other words, more than two-thirds of the oldest personnel in the survey group were rated as having a work volume as good as, if not better than, average younger personnel.

## Getting Along With Others

Supervisors rated each older worker on his human relationships, in comparison with average younger workers, with the following findings: get along better with others, 32 per cent; get along about the same, 59 per cent; and get along less well with others, 9 per cent. No important differences were found in the ratings assigned to employees in the four age categories, thus providing no support for the traditional belief that workers present problems in human relations the older they become.

## Remaining Years of Service

One of the most important questions asked in the study related to the number of additional years of productive service which supervisors believed older personnel would be able to give their present jobs. As shown on the rating form, supervisors were asked to write "indefinite" if an employee showed no signs of weakness or decline which suggested a specific limit on the number of years he would be able to continue working. The survey results showed that 26 per cent of the group were rated as "indefinite." Of the remainder, the average individual was estimated to have before him approximately five and a half years of additional service.

## Age-connected Weaknesses

Supervisors were asked to list any weaknesses in employees which they regarded as age-connected. They were not to list unfavorable qualities, such as inaccurate work or stubbornness, unless they considered these characteristics to be the result of advancing age. It was startling to find that 69 per cent of these employees were rated "none"—indicating that they had no apparent age-connected weaknesses. Of the remainder, the weaknesses noted in order of number were *general slowing down, poor health, psychological difficulties (such as forgetfulness), impaired eyesight,* and *impaired hearing.* While the enumerated weaknesses are those commonly associated with older people in general, it is noteworthy that supervisors attributed these weaknesses to less than one-third of the older employees in this survey group.

## Influence of Supervisor's Age

To investigate the possibility of an age bias, the age of rating supervisors was compared with the ratings on over-all performance which supervisors assigned to their older workers. Contrary to the long-standing belief that older supervisors may tend to think more charitably of older workers than do younger supervisors, the survey results show a startling absence of any relationship between age of supervisor and ratings. It was found that supervisors in each age group rated their older employees with remarkable similarity.

## CONCLUSIONS

The findings of this study are highly favorable to older personnel. However, the reader is cautioned to infer no more than is actually indicated. There is a suggestion, for example, that older people tend to become more efficient by virtue of their age alone. This inference, of course, is not sound because it fails to consider that the older personnel in this survey group represent a highly selective group in several senses—only those with the best apparent capabilities were selected for employment, only those with high motivation have continued to work, and only the fittest have survived dismissal.

The survey results also suggest that people sixty years of age and over should be selected for employment in preference to younger people, However, this inference is also unsound because it overlooks the necessity in business organizations of employing younger persons who will be able to give long years of experienced service to the organization and who will be available to replace senior workers who must ultimately leave the organization.

The findings of the survey do, however, support the following conclusions:

1. Supervisors in business and industry consider *a majority* of their workers sixty years of age and older to be as good as, or superior to, average younger workers with reference to absenteeism, dependability, judgment, work quality, work volume, and human relations.
2. There is no specific point of age at which employees become unproductive. Supervisors indicate by their ratings that satisfactory work performance may continue into the eighth decade.
3. Supervisors indicate by their ratings that organizations which require employees to retire at a certain age, such as sixty-five, are losing a great deal of valuable productivity.
4. Supervisors believe that about one-quarter of their workers sixty years of age and older will be able to continue working indefinitely.
5. Supervisors believe that *a majority* of their workers sixty years of age and older have no apparent and specific age-connected weaknesses.
6. Supervisors have had generally favorable results with new employees recruited from the ranks of the middle-aged. The fact that 38 per cent of the employees in this survey group have been with their present organizations less than ten years means that these persons must have been hired when past fifty years of age.
7. There is no indication that the age of the supervisor has anything to do with the favorableness of ratings assigned to older workers.

# SOCIOLOGICAL IMPLICATIONS OF RETIREMENT*

### Clifford Kirkpatrick

Retirement may begin in anticipation years before a name is stricken from a payroll and a gold watch presented. Retirement is not merely the transition from work to play, for there can be many anticipatory retirements in terms of both dread and pleasant yearning.

Although there is increased employment of women, retirement may not have the same meaning for them as for men. It may also involve a distinction between the rich and the poor and the healthy and the ailing. It is not easy to isolate retirement from the more general process of aging or to single out a more subtle retirement from an aspect of living, such as parenthood. There can be subjective retirement from life without change in labor force status. Retirement is difficult to define, and it is not easy to say when and how it takes place.

## PERSPECTIVE ON RETIREMENT

Retirement can be viewed as affected by social change. Urbanization, industrialization, and large-scale business enterprise give distinctively modern aspects to retirement experiences. Basically, retirement from work is now controlled by others rather than by the one who is retiring. Compulsory retirement is an aspect of bureaucratic social organization. It is interesting to note that statistics for 1957, showing that 53 per cent of the men between the ages of sixty-five and sixty-nine were still in the labor force, are qualified by overrepresentation of older men in the diminishing agricultural pursuits. The corresponding figure of 18.6 per cent for women may mean that they have not yet been drawn into bureaucratic organization to the same degree as men.

A new dimension is also given to retirement by the extension of life expectancy at birth since 1900 by some twenty years to 69.6 in 1956. Other data for 1956 show that the life expectancy at birth of

*Reprinted by courtesy of *Geriatrics*, Volume *14*, May, 1959.

white women is 6.4 years beyond that of white men, which suggests greater frustration for women in both work and family life, and that white women now retire early from motherhood but have a life expectancy at sixty-five of fifteen and one-half years as compared with thirteen years for white men of the same age.

Retirement can also be looked upon as one of the life transitions accompanied by varied rites throughout the world. It is not dissimilar to a puberty transition, a marriage accompanied by fertility rites, motherhood accompanied by isolation and purification, or death associated with ritualized mourning. Retirement resembles divorce both in view of variable circumstances and the absence of a fully developed ritual functionally appropriate to ease the strain of transition. Certainly, in all human societies there are changes of status of which retirement is only one.

Retirement can also be thought of in terms of roles and images; almost by definition it is a loss of role. Havighurst and Albrecht very usefully describe the older persons of Prairie City, a small community in the midwest, in terms of numbers and types of roles they must play. A role implies a concept of one's place and an image of oneself in a matrix of activities and expectations. To the question, "Who are you?," a person must answer, "I am a retired such and such" and qualify his answer in terms of how he sees himself. As the sociologist Cooley showed long ago, a self-image is not to be dissociated from the social mirror held up by others. The retired person must come to terms with images which other people have of his retirement.

Again, retirement is related to the universal process of classification according to age and sex. Every culture provides containers for the amorphous potentialities of a particular age and sex. There may be rigid, dichotomous, coercive containers for the male and female or for the old and young. On the other hand, there may be flexible, permissive, cultural containers with provision for intermediate age-sex potentialities. Certainly some people in our culture are pushed prematurely into cultural containers with categorical expectations as to age and retirement. The category of "femininity" in our culture does not fit all women, and the category "over sixty-five and retired" does not fit all Americans. The proposition "over sixty-five and hence retired" illustrates a cultural container pressing painfully upon employees who are healthy, vigorous and creative.

## RETIREMENT AS A DILEMMA

A policy dilemma might be defined as a social situation in which there are two somewhat incompatible goals, each associated with a penalty or price, the price of one choice standing in contrast to the price of another.

One illustration might be a policy-dilemma involving optimism and realism. It is good to cheer the aged by tagging them with such pleasant labels as "senior citizen," assuring them of happy retirement years, exaggerating their work capacity, promising them worthy status, and minimizing biological senescene. However, adopting a more realistic attitude toward their health, income, social relations, housing, and personal adjustment makes for more effective personal planning. The price of unrealistic optimism is frustration, disillusionment, and neglect. A retired person living on an old age pension of fifty dollars a month may feel that he is being treated like a child, beguiled by myths and fairy tales. He could say, "Senior Citizen, O.K., but don't forget that my arthritis hurts." On the other hand, the price of a realistic approach may be a dread of aging and a puncturing of wishful fantasies which, for a given individual, may actually ease the transition into the category of "aged and retired." Aldous Huxley in his "Brave New World" contributes to the thought that realism means denial of the soothing benefits of myth and Miltown.

Another abstract policy-dilemma involves social integration as compared with social segregation. To illustrate, the aged and retired can be regarded as just people grown older or as a large minority group differing biologically from others because of their aged bodies. There is virtue in a policy which makes an aged person feel part of the family, the work force, and the community. The price, however, for such a policy is continued straining and striving, frustration of incomplete acceptance, and ignoring of special needs. On the other hand, the segregation of the aged in special classes, in special clubs, in special housing arrangements in special jobs, in special forms of leisure activity, and in roles defined by age means that a contrasting price might be paid by some. This price may involve inferiority feelings, a sense of isolation, or the painful breaking of old habits.

A third somewhat more specific illustration of a dilemma is a "flexible" versus a "rigid" retirement policy. A flexible policy recognizes individual differences and thus yields many benefits to society and to the still youthful older person. The price involves lack of preparation in view of the hope that retirement may be deferred or gradual, with an additional component being invidious comparison and suspicion of injustice. Perhaps one characteristic of senility is obtuseness as to the appropriateness of retirement. The other horn of the dilemma involves a price which is better recognized. A rigid, inexorable, sudden retirement at sixty-five means loss of work achievement to youthful individuals and to society and, furthermore, fosters a sense of injustice all the more acute because of realistic self-estimates of continued competence.

A dilemma framework guards against wishful thinking and prompts a rational comparison of contrasting types of benefit and price. It stimulates a search for a middle ground between the horns of a dilemma but with recognition that a middle choice generally means that some compromise price must be paid.

### ROLE CHANGES WITH AGE

Retirement may also be considered as a time of role transition or role change, such as takes place in adolescence, upon entrance into the labor force, and in the transition period from single to married status, childless to parent of first born offspring, well to sick, sick to well, married to divorced, married to widowed, and civilian to soldier.

Generalizations derived from such role transitions could help in understanding the transition from employed to retired status. Probably in every case there is anticipation of this transition by both self and others. Emotional ambivalence is also characteristic of role transition, as illustrated, for example, by the marriage license which is not used, the mixed feelings of parents about launching children into adult life, and a generalized and selective nostalgia for the pleasant aspects of a prior role.

One aspect of adjustment to role transition is judicious assessment of a new pattern of obligations and privileges. Some newly retired persons may seek a double quota of privilege, privileges of the prior role plus those of the new role. To illustrate, a newly retired businessman may still want to boss the business and yet enjoy the leisure of retirement. Some people may want to work as hard as ever at making a living and yet feel duty bound to make the most of retirement by devoting part of their time to providing new services for others.

There is also a timing aspect to the changing role in view of the fact that social roles are transmissible, with other persons taking an abandoned role. Although one person may be pushed prematurely by others into a retirement role or may push himself into that role with undue haste, others may delay and resist an appropriate role transition. For example, overly dependent adult offspring or incompetent subordinates may delay retirement, or a person may himself frantically resist his retirement beyond his own good and the good of others.

### LIFE CYCLE AND RETIREMENT

The life cycle concept provides still another approach to aging and retirement. One implication of this viewpoint is awareness that the population moves through the stages of educational preparation, work and reproduction, and, then, retirement. Questions can be raised concerning the distribution of social burdens carried by the young, middle-aged, and the aged. Does education, because of the time needed for its acquisition, preclude contributions to the total national income especially in view of the need for early work experience for later work experience? Does the labor force carry too great a burden in supporting both the old and the young? Could a fairer distribution of burdens throughout the life cycle be achieved by new forms of insurance, pensions, wage structure, taxation, and social security provisions of the federal government? More equitable distribution of burdens throughout the life cycle would provide more balanced experience in work and reproduction, effort and leisure, and achievement and enjoyment.

The cycle of family life might also be altered to provide a happier answer to the question of what happens after retirement. In our culture, the family consisting of parents and children only is now favored over the extended family which includes other relatives, such as grandparents or aunts and uncles. This new family group tends to be child-centered in that children are given no clear role to play with respect to retired parents. With greater educational and cultural homogeneity, adult offspring might render more service to retired parents and retired parents to adult offspring. Perhaps grandparents need not be so undervalued as baby sitters or as assistants when mothers return to employment after their children are in school.

From a financial point of view, adequate earnings prior to retirement could subsidize offspring who are young parents in exchange for help with annuities when the burden of child rearing is past in the younger generation. For example, 50-year-old fathers could help twenty-five year old sons and be helped at seventy by forty-five year old sons now at their peak of earnings, with offspring well launched. There is no implication that trends in family life will be abruptly revised, but, before consigning protection of the aged to the state, the ancient tradition of mutual aid throughout the different stages of family life might be re-examined.

## CHANGED DISTRIBUTION OF POWER

Distribution of power changes throughout life and, in general, retirement brings with it a relative decrease of power in its various aspects. The power struggle is reflected in such terms as "Old Hag," "Old Meanie," and "Old Grouch," which are occasionally countered by such epithets as "Young Pup" or "Smarty Pants."

In their recent book, *The Academic Marketplace,* Caplow and McGee note that resignation of an academic position brings little departmental regret and is rarely associated with a ritual of farewell. Retirement means increased power to successors, and anticipated retirement probably means a loss of power prior to retirement. A subordinate can murmur: "I can talk back to him now for he won't be around to vote against me." As reported by Caplow, the professors who resigned on very short notice probably saved themselves the strain of an anticipatory power shift.

## RESEARCH AREAS

Further study of retirement in relation to the family pattern seems highly desirable. There is some evidence that family life has great influence on job satisfaction before retirement. If William Whyte's account of *The Organization Man* be accepted, there is a growing integration of job and family. Certainly work needs to be done on a comparative study of the retirement-adjustment pattern of married, widowed, and never-married persons. In a study of unknown authorship in which retired married university professors were sampled, a marked relationship was found between the creativity of these professors after retirement and the educational characteristics of their wives.

In regard to parent-child patterns, early studies showed that aged persons often have rather unhappy relations with their grown offspring. Such interview studies of different generations need to be repeated with varying and recent samples. It would be fruitful to explore the possibility that the vestigial sense of duty toward their retired parents would be felt differently by adult offspring, depending upon sex, birth order, and experience in childhood. Perhaps there is a relatively important sense of duty felt by daughters as compared with sons. This sense of duty is often closely related to whether an aged adult is taken care of at home under doctor's orders or sent to a medical care facility, such as a nursing home.

It may also be noted that, with the increased employment of married women, the traditional picture of retirement by a male family head is no longer realistic. Although women are far less likely than men to be in the labor force after the age of sixty-five, in the future the more durable and younger employed wife may often retire after her husband. His earlier retirement might bring special frustration with a loss of male dominance based upon a traditional role as breadwinner. Changing husband-wife relationships give new facets to the retirement problem.

In addition, we need to know more about the impact of retirement upon personality. Drastic reorientation upon retirement may occur more often in fantasy than in reality. Degrees of freedom are reduced by age, but general orientations may remain rather constant throughout life. Future research may show that a prior orientation remains distinctive after retirement, a plausible hypothesis being that people after retirement remain what they were before, only less so because of diminished life energy. Perhaps William Whyte will write a book entitled "The Organization Man Grows Older." It may also be true that persons who are retiring seek especially to continue satisfying experiences of the past and to avoid or to compensate for unpleasant experiences. For example, cherished scientific creativity may be continued without a laboratory, or the work monotony experienced in the past may be replaced by an overzealous drive for adventure.

It would also be interesting to probe further the possibility that certain people have a built-in toughness and adaptability which endures throughout their lives. Longitudinal studies of identical and fraternal twins could be made with reference to retirement. Identical twins might show a differential similarity in adjustment which extends to the retirement period.

It is also possible that retired persons could accept and understand the needs of younger persons better than the reverse. It may be that, throughout the stages of family life, a mature and experienced person can show more understanding of a younger person now playing a role which the older person once had. The retired grandfather has been an adolescent, but the adolescent has never been a retired grandfather. It is doubtful that the sympathy and insight of children would support an extensive program seeking to establish older people as "Foster Grandparents," although there might be some modest success in this type of undertaking.

## RETIREMENT ASPIRATIONS

The retirement period is characterized by deprivation of youth, meaningful friends, and relatives and, in general, by fewer and lower aspirations, with less conflict and frustration. The study made of older people in Prairie City showed that about 40 per cent seemed happy and only 18 per cent seemed unhappy and that good health, fair income, social activity, and success in handling stress situations of the past were associated with happiness and adjustment after retirement.

A very simple aspiration after retirement, when there is less danger of disapproval, is to live by principle rather than expediency, in moral freedom rather than in bondage to the opinion of others. Since future generations have become more meaningful to them because they have lost many friends and relatives, retired persons could provide invaluable moral leadership. It is granted that after retirement people may just watch television and be concerned about a good meal, but some find, in their freedom from work, time to care about the future of mankind.

# Chapter 5

## HEALTH PROBLEMS OF THE AGED
### BASIC FACTS ON THE HEALTH AND ECONOMIC STATUS OF OLDER AMERICANS*

#### THE SPECIAL HEALTH CONDITIONS OF THE AGED

#### National Health Survey

T HE FINDINGS of the U.S. Public Health Service's National Health Survey, published in the *Health Statistics* series, reveal clearly the differences in health conditions between the population aged sixty-five and over, and the under-65 population. For example:

1. The proportion of aged persons with chronic illness (such as heart disease, cancer, diabetes, arthritis, etc.) is about twice the proportion of persons under the age of sixty-five with chronic illness—seventy-seven per cent versus thirty-eight per cent.

2. While the aged constitute about 9 per cent of the total population, they make up more than 55 per cent of all persons with limitations due to chronic illness.

3. The lower income aged in particular have a high proportion of limitation of activity due to chronic illness: 82 per cent of the over-65 population with family incomes under $2,000 have such limitations in activity, as against 75 per cent of the aged with family incomes $4,000 or more—and less than 40 per cent for the total younger population.

4. The proportions of the aged with one or more chronic conditions range from a low of 74.7 per cent in the Middle Atlantic States to a high of 82.0 per cent in the South Atlantic States.

#### University of Michigan Study

The Study of Character and Effectiveness of Hospital Use conducted by the University of Michigan, while confined to the an-

---

*A staff report to the Special Committee on Aging, United States Senate. Printed for the use of the Special Committee on Aging. U.S. Government Printing Office, Washington, June 2, 1961.

TABLE 1

PERCENT DISTRIBUTION OF PERSONS SIXTY-FIVE AND OLDER WITH ONE OR MORE CHRONIC
CONDITIONS BY GEOGRAPHIC DIVISION, JULY 1957-JUNE 1959

| *Regions* | *Percent with one or more chronic conditions* | *Regions* | *Percent with one or more chronic conditions* |
|---|---|---|---|
| All regions | 77.3 | South Atlantic | 82.0 |
| New England | 75.5 | East South Central | 80.4 |
| Middle Atlantic | 74.7 | West South Central | 79.2 |
| East North Central | 74.9 | Mountain | 80.3 |
| West North Central | 79.4 | Pacific | 76.4 |

Source: U. S. National Health Survey, Series C, No. 6.

alysis of hospital inpatients in that State alone, nevertheless reliably portrays the general differences between the older and younger patients in types of ailments leading to hospital admission, as Table 2 indicates.

TABLE 2

PERCENTAGES OF PATIENTS IN EACH AGE GROUP AND BY DIAGNOSTIC CATEGORIES
[General and Special Hospitals Combined, Excluding Newborn]

| *Diagnosis* | *Age of Patient* | |
|---|---|---|
| | *Under 65* | *65 and older* |
| Diseases of circulatory system | 5.7 | 18.5 |
| Nervous system and sense organs | 3.1 | 10.9 |
| Malignant neoplasms | 2.1 | 9.4 |
| Diseases of digestive system | 6.3 | 8.9 |
| Accidents, poisonings, etc. | 6.4 | 6.3 |
| Diseases of genitourinary system | 6.2 | 5.9 |
| Acute myocardial infarction | .7 | 3.9 |
| Fracture of neck of femur | .2 | 3.6 |
| Bones and organs of movement | 2.5 | 2.9 |
| Diabetes mellitus | .9 | 2.8 |
| All other diagnoses | 65.9 | 26.9 |
| Number of cases | (9,252) | (1,444) |

Source: Hospital Use Study, University of Michigan, 1958.

This table shows only the ten most frequent diagnostic categories among aged hospital patients. *These ten most frequent diagnoses account for nearly three-fourths of all the aged patients,* in contrast to only one-third of the under-65 group. Indeed the first five diagnoses—circulatory diseases, nervous system, malignant neoplasms, digestive system ailments, and accidents—account for more than one-half of all the aged patients in the Michigan study.

Six of the diagnoses quite clearly set off the aged from the under-65 hospital population:

*Diseases of the circulatory system:* the rate among the aged is more than three times that for the under-65 hospital population.

*Nervous system and sense organs:* rate among the aged more than three times that for the other ages.

*Malignant neoplasms:* more than four times the rate among the under-65 hospital population.

*Acute myocardial infarction:* more than five times the rate among the younger inpatients.

*Fracture of neck of femur:* more than eighteen times the rate among the under-65 hospital patients.

*Diabetes mellitus:* more than three times the rate among the younger patients.

TABLE 3

AVERAGE LENGTH OF STAY IN EACH TEN MOST FREQUENT DIAGNOSTIC CATEGORIES AMONG THE GENERAL POPULATION AND THE AGED (MICHIGAN, 1958)

| Diagnostic Category | [Days] All Ages | 65 to 69 | 70 and Older |
|---|---|---|---|
| All diagnoses | 7.5 | 13.2 | 14.1 |
| Diseases of circulatory system | 10.6 | 12.6 | 15.0 |
| Nervous system and sense organs | 10.1 | 12.5 | 17.6 |
| Malignant neoplasms | [1] 16.5 | 17.5 | 15.4 |
| Diseases of digestive system | 9.0 | 14.6 | 9.5 |
| Accidents, etc. | 6.6 | 8.4 | 10.7 |
| Diseases of genitourinary system | 7.1 | 17.0 | 10.6 |
| Acute myocardial infarction | 19.7 | 18.9 | 14.7 |
| Fracture of neck of femur | 27.5 | 30.7 | 53.0 |
| Bones and organs of movement | 9.0 | 14.3 | 9.6 |
| Diabetes mellitus | 12.9 | 12.5 | 14.0 |

[1]Distributed mostly in 45-64 age group, with 18.8 average days.

Source: Hospital Use Study, University of Michigan.

## MEDICAL SERVICES UTILIZATION AND COSTS OF THE AGED

### GENERAL HOSPITALS

Aged people go to the hospital more often and stay longer than those at younger ages. As a result, the number of days per year spent in a general hospital is two to three times as large, on the average, for persons sixty-five and over as for younger persons.

## National Health Survey

*General Utilization Rates*—The National Health Survey found the following differences for persons over and under sixty-five discharged from short-stay general hospitals in 1957-58:

|                                   | Persons Under 65 | Persons 65 and Over |
|-----------------------------------|:----------------:|:-------------------:|
| Discharge per 1,000 persons       | 97               | 121                 |
| Average length of stay in days    | 7.8              | 14.7                |
| Aggregate days per 1,000 persons  | 764              | 1,778               |

*Utilization in Last Year of Life*—This survey considerably understates the hospital utilization of aged persons because it excluded the hospitalization experience during the survey year of persons who had died prior to the interview. The hospitalization of decedents is of considerable significance in total hospital utilization by the sixty-five and over group with its relatively high mortality rate.

A special report of the National Health Survey ("Hospital Utilization in the Last Year of Life") based on data from surveys in the Middle Atlantic States, shows that the inclusion of hospitalization received by decedents during the survey year results in an increase of 14 per cent in the volume of hospitalization among persons of all ages, and an increase of 42 per cent for persons sixty-five and over.

## Survey of OASDI Beneficiaries

*General Utilization Rates*—The 1957 survey of OASDI beneficiaries found somewhat more days of general hospital care for persons sixty-five and over during a year—2,360 per 1,000 aged persons. The difference results in large part from the fact that the National Health Survey includes the aged persons still in the labor force, who are less likely to be hospitalized. The beneficiary survey figure, moreover, includes time spent in a general hospital by persons who were otherwise in an institution, whereas the National Health Survey is restricted to the noninstitutional population.

Following is the distribution of hospitalized aged beneficiaries

(11.1 per cent of the total) by total number of days in hospital, regardless of number of stays within the year:

| Number of days in hospital during year: | Percentage Distribution |
|---|---|
| All aged persons hospitalized | 100.0 |
| 1-30 days | 81.9 |
| 31-60 days | 12.4 |
| 61-90 days | 3.2 |
| 91 and over | 2.5 |
| 120 days and over | 1.7 |
| Average days of care per year | 21.2 |

The survey showed that every fourth or fifth beneficiary who spent any time in a general hospital during the year had more than one admission.

*Terminal Illness Costs*—The BOASI 1957 beneficiary survey also gives some indication of the heavy volume of hospitalization which may characterize a person's last illness. Although no data were obtained for nonmarried beneficiaries dying during the survey year, data were obtained for the small number of persons who died leaving a spouse drawing a retired worker's benefit. Among the couples were a spouse (usually the wife) had died, three times as many had one or both members hospitalized during the year as among those where both partners survived the entire year. The average known medical cost for the year was two and one-third times as high for the couples with one member dying as when both lived through the entire year.

### LONG-STAY INSTITUTIONS

In addition to their high rate of general hospital use, aged persons are heavy users of nursing homes and other long-stay institutions. Much of this care is publicly financed.

Relatively little is known about admission rates and length of stay in the chronic-care facilities because most population surveys exclude persons in institutions, as did the National Health Survey.

### Aged OASDI Beneficiaries

The 1957 BOASI survey, however, did obtain information on the length of time spent by aged beneficiaries in an institution during the survey year.

For every five beneficiaries in a general hospital, there was one who was in a long-stay institution for chronic care.

The average stay in such chronic-care facilities was much longer than in a general hospital, however. In the aggregate there were close to two days in a long-stay institution for every one day in a general hospital.

| Kind of Institution | Number in Institution per 1,000 Beneficiaries | Aggregate Days per 1,000 Beneficiaries |
|---------------------|-----------------------------------------------|----------------------------------------|
| General Hospital | 111 | 2,360 |
| Long-stay institution | 23 | 4,480 |
| Nursing home | 13 | 2,760 |
| Other | 10 | 1,720 |

It is not known for how many of the beneficiaries in nursing homes the care was primarily residential and custodial, and for how many it was skilled nursing and medical care. But it is known that nearly a third of those reporting nursing home care also spent some time in a general hospital—outside the home—during the year.

### PHYSICIANS' VISITS

### Frequency of Visits

Information on the rate at which older persons consult a physician, compared with those younger, is available from the National Health Survey for the two year period July 1957—June 1959.

On the average, the aged person saw a doctor at the rate of 6.8 visits a year as against 4.8 visits per person for the rest of the population.

### Income and Visits

The rate of visits for older persons would probably be greater if all sought and received as much medical care as they need.

One of the limiting factors in persons getting all the care they need is ability to pay:

At family incomes of less than $2,000 (including income of any relatives in the household as well as that of the aged person himself), aged persons averaged 6.5 visits per year.

At family incomes of $7,000 or more, aged persons averaged 8.7 visits per year.

This means that at the higher income an aged person had four visits to a doctor for every three by a person in the lower income group, a differential greater than that prevaling among the rest of the population.

This differential exists even though the aged with lower family income were considerably more likely to suffer chronic and disabling conditions, and hence need more physician care, than the aged with higher incomes:

At family incomes of less than $2,000, 48 per cent had a chronic condition limiting activity; the average number of bed-disability days was 16.5 per year.

At family incomes of $7,000 or more, 37 per cent had a chronic condition limiting activity; the average number of bed-disability days was 10.8 per year.

These factual data suggest a serious questioning of the frequent assertion that all the aged obtain all the medical attention they may need.

## Place of Visit

Doctors' visits, as defined in the National Health Survey, included consultation by telephone or in person, at the office, hospital clinic, or other health facility as in the patient's home.

Possibly because some older persons requiring a physician's services find transportation a problem—

Twenty-two per cent of doctors' visits for older persons took place in the home compared with only 8 per cent for persons under sixty-five.

Usually a doctor's regular fee is higher for a house call than for an office visit. This is perhaps a partial explanation of why a recent study by the Health Information Foundation found:

Private outlays for physicians in behalf of persons sixty-five and over averaged almost twice as much per person per year (in 1957-58) as for persons under sixty-five—$55 and $29, respectively.

### Per Capita Expenditures

Although opinions differ as to the standard against which to measure resources of the aged, it is generally agreed in the case of medical care that their lower than average income is accompanied by higher than average need—the more so since they are less likely than younger persons to have health insurance.

## Health Information Foundation Report

According to Health Information Foundation's survey, persons aged sixty-five and over spent over twice as much per person for medical care in a year as do persons under sixty-five. This includes only private expenditures of the noninstitutional population—leaving out the heavy costs for terminal illness among aged persons living alone, the cost of care in nursing homes, mental or tuberculosis hospitals, and other institutions (much of which is publicly financed). Left out also is the value of care provided at no charge to those individuals who cannot pay.

| ANNUAL PRIVATE EXPENDITURES FOR MEDICAL CARE PER PERSON, BY AGE, 1957-58 | | |
|---|---|---|
| | *Under 65* | *Age 65 and Over* |
| Total | $86 | $177 |
| Physicians | 29 | 55 |
| Hospitals | 19 | 49 |
| Drugs | 18 | 42 |
| Dentists | 14 | 10 |
| Other | 6 | 21 |

Source: Health Information Foundation.

# THE PHYSIOLOGY OF AGING*

## NATHAN W. SHOCK

With the virtual conquest of want and infectious disease in technologically advanced countries, men and women in increasing numbers are living out the promised Biblical life span of three score years and ten. The diseases of age and the fundamental process of aging are moving to the center of interest in the practice of medicine and in medical research. Few people die of old age. Mortality increases rapidly with age—in precise logarithmic ratio to age in the population as a whole—because the elderly become more susceptible to diseases that kill, such as cancer and cardiovascular disease. The diseases of old age are the province of the rela-

*Reprinted by courtesy of *Scientific American*, Volume *206*:100-110, January, 1962.

tively new medical specialty known as geriatrics. A still younger discipline called gerontology deals with the process of aging itself. This is a process that continues throughout adult life. It goes on in health as well as in sickness and constitutes the primary biological factor underlying the increase in susceptibility to the diseases that are the concern of geriatrics.

Gerontology is still in the descriptive stage. Investigators have only recently developed objective standards for measurement of the decline in the performance and capacity of the body and its organ systems, and they have just begun to make such measurements on statistically significant samples of the population. The first general finding in gerontology is that the body dies a little every day. Decline in capacity and function over the years correlates directly with a progressive loss of body tissue. The loss of tissue has been shown to be associated in turn with the disappearance of cells from the muscles, the nervous system and many vital organs. To get at the causes of death in the cell gerontology has entered the realm of cellular physiology and chemistry.

The ideal way to study the aging of the human body would be to apply the same battery of tests to a large group of people at repeated intervals throughout their lives. Such a program would require dedicated subjects and a scientific staff organized for continuity of operation over a period of perhaps fifty years. Obviously some compromise must be made. Instead of starting observations on a group of subjects at age thirty and following them for fifty years, it is possible to begin with subjects of various ages and follow them for twenty years. At our laboratories in the Gerontology Branch of the Baltimore City Hospitals we started such a study on 400 men in 1958. Until this and similar undertakings have had time to yield results, gerontologists must rely on data accumulated from one-time tests of rather large numbers of different individuals ranging in age from twenty or thirty up to eighty or ninety. Although subjects of any specific age differ widely, the average values for many physiological characteristics show a gradual but definite reduction between the ages of thirty and ninety. Individual differences become quite apparent, for example, in studies of the amount of blood flowing through the kidneys. Whereas this function generally declines markedly with age, it is the same in some eighty year old men as it is in the average fifty year old man.

One of the most obvious manifestations of aging is the decline in the ability to exercise and do work. In order to measure the extent of the change it is necessary to set up laboratory experiments in which the rate of output and the amount of work done can be precisely determined along with the responses of various organ systems. Subjects may be put to walking a treadmill or climbing a certain number of steps at a specified rate. In our laboratory the subject lies on his back and turns the crank of an ergometer, an apparatus for measuring the work done. When our purpose is to measure the subject's maximum output in a given time, the crank can be adjusted to turn more stiffly or more easily. With the subject lying supine it is easier to make the necessary measurements of blood pressure, heart rate and heart output (blood pumped) and to collect the respiratory gases through a face mask for the measurement of oxygen consumption and carbon dioxide production. These measurements are customarily made before, during and after exertion in order to establish the subject's norms, his capacity and the rate at which vital functions recover their normal or resting rates.

As a common denominator of capacity we seek to determine the maximum amount of work a subject can do and have his heart return to normal within two minutes after he stops working. Men thirty years old achieve an output of 500 kilogram-meters per minute (the equivalent of lifting 500 kilograms one meter in one minute), whereas seventy year old men on the average reach only 350 kilogram-meters per minute. Thus at age seventy a man's physical capacity as defined by this test has declined by 30 per cent. Over the years from thirty-five to eighty the maximum work rate for short bursts of crank-turning falls almost 60 per cent, from about 1,850 kilogram-meters per minute for young men to 750 kilogram-meters for the eighty year old.

Physical performance, of course, reflects the combined capacity of the different organ systems of the body working together. The ability to do work depends on the strength of the muscles, the coordination of movement by the nervous system, the effectiveness of the heart in propelling blood from the lungs to the working muscles, the rate at which air moves in and out of the lungs, the efficiency of the lung in its gas-exchange function, the response of the kidneys to the task of removing excess waste materials from the blood, the synchronization of metabolic processes by the endocrine glands and, finally, the constancy with which the buffer systems in the blood maintain the chemical environment of the body. In order to determine the causes of the decline in over-all capacity, it is necessary to assess the effects of aging on each of the organ systems.

Tests of the strength of the hand serve in our laboratory to isolate one aspect of muscle function. The subject simply squeezes a grip-measuring device as hard as he can for a moment. In a group of 604 men the strength of the dominant hand dropped from about 44 kilograms of pressure at age 35 to 23 kilograms at age ninety. Although the dominant hand is stronger at all ages, it loses more of its strength over the years than the subordinate hand. Endurance, measured by the average grip pressure exerted for one minute, drops from 28 kilograms at age 20 to 20 kilograms at age seventy-five. That muscle performance is not the only factor involved in maximum work rates is indicated by the fact that the decrease in muscular strength over the years is less than the decline in work rates.

The nerve fibers that connect directly with the muscles show little decline in function with age. The speed of nerve impulses along single fibers in elderly people is only 10 to 15 per cent less than it is in young people. Simple neurological functions involving only a few connections in the spinal cord also remain virtually unimpaired. It is in the central nervous system, where complex connections are made, that aging takes its toll. Memory loss, particularly for recent events, often plagues the elderly. The older person requires substantially more time for choosing between a number of possible responses to a situation, although with enough time he arrives at the correct decision. Certain routine mental activities, on the other hand, hardly change with age. Vocabulary comprehension, for example, remains strong in most people. Experienced proofreaders maintain a high degree of accuracy even at advanced ages.

Because muscles engaged in sustained exercise require extra

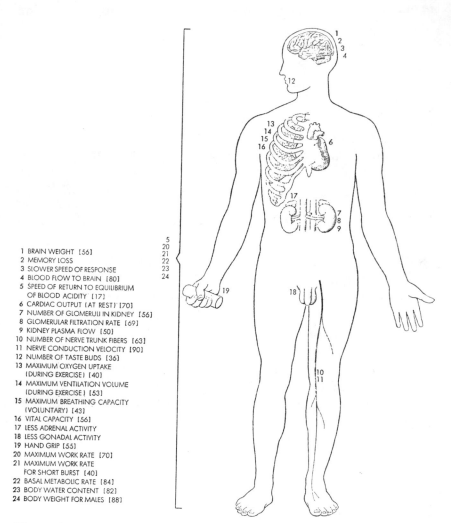

1  BRAIN WEIGHT  [56]
2  MEMORY LOSS
3  SLOWER SPEED OF RESPONSE
4  BLOOD FLOW TO BRAIN  [80]
5  SPEED OF RETURN TO EQUILIBRIUM
   OF BLOOD ACIDITY  [17]
6  CARDIAC OUTPUT (AT REST)' [70]
7  NUMBER OF GLOMERULI IN KIDNEY  [56]
8  GLOMERULAR FILTRATION RATE  [69]
9  KIDNEY PLASMA FLOW  [50]
10 NUMBER OF NERVE TRUNK FIBERS  [63]
11 NERVE CONDUCTION VELOCITY  [90]
12 NUMBER OF TASTE BUDS  [36]
13 MAXIMUM OXYGEN UPTAKE
   (DURING EXERCISE)  [40]
14 MAXIMUM VENTILATION VOLUME
   (DURING EXERCISE)  [53]
15 MAXIMUM BREATHING CAPACITY
   (VOLUNTARY)  [43]
16 VITAL CAPACITY  [56]
17 LESS ADRENAL ACTIVITY
18 LESS GONADAL ACTIVITY
19 HAND GRIP  [55]
20 MAXIMUM WORK RATE  [70]
21 MAXIMUM WORK RATE
   FOR SHORT BURST  [40]
22 BASAL METABOLIC RATE  [84]
23 BODY WATER CONTENT  [82]
24 BODY WEIGHT FOR MALES  [88]

**Fig. 1.** Physiological decline accompanying age appears in many measurements throughout the body. Changes are great in some cases, small in others. The figures in brackets following most of the labels in the key at left are the approximate percentages of functions of tissues remaining to the average seventy-five year old man, taking the value found for the average thirty year old as 100 per cent.

oxygen and other nutrients and produce more waste to be carried away, the heart must work harder to move more blood through the system. During exercise the heart pumps more blood at each stroke, at a faster rate and at higher pressure. Although the resting blood pressure in healthy individuals increases only slightly with age, a given amount of exercise will raise the heart rate and blood pressure in old people more than it will in young. And when subjects exert themselves to the maximum, the heart of the older person cannot achieve as great an increase in rate as that of the younger. During exercise, therefore, the cardiac output, or amount of blood pumped per minute, is less in the old than it is in the young. This, of course, imposes limits on the amount of work the elderly can do.

Cardiac output can be measured directly and, in subjects at rest, quite easily. (The measurements are difficult during exercise.) In one procedure a known amount of blue dye is injected into a vein of one arm and blood samples are taken periodically from a small catheter in the large artery of the opposite leg. The dilution of the dye provides a measure of heart output. The amount of blood pumped falls from an average of 3.75 liters per minute (a liter is slightly more than a quart) per square meter of body surface in twenty year olds to two liters per minute in ninety year olds.

The lung plays as important a role in exercise as the heart. We have studied the two aspects of lung function—the maximum amount of oxygen that can be taken up from inspired air during exercise and the ability of the lung to move air in and out. The amount of oxygen that the blood takes up from the lung and transports to the tissues during exercise falls substantially with age. The blood of twenty year old men takes up, on the average, almost four liters of oxygen per minute, whereas at age seventy-five the rate is only 1.5 liters per minute. This function has been tested in several individuals over many years. D. Bruce Dill, a physiologist now at Indiana University, found that his own maximum oxygen uptake declined from 3.28 liters at age thirty-seven to 2.80 liters at age sixty-six.

Another measurement reveals that in order to double the level of oxygen uptake during exercise the older individual must move about 50 per cent more air in and out of his lungs. No doubt the

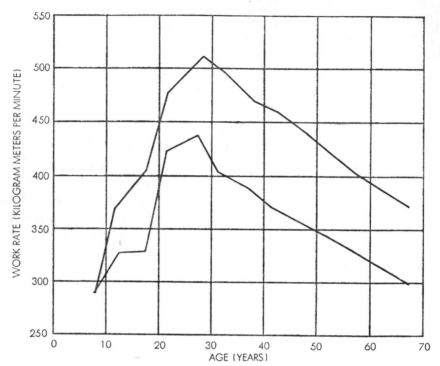

Fig. 2. Changes in work rate with age are striking. The function reaches a peak at age twenty-eight and declines steadily thereafter. Rate for miles shown in upper line, for females in lower line.

decline in oxygen absorption reflects in part the reduced heart output, for less blood flows through the lungs of the older person in a given time. But the great difference in oxygen uptake between young and old shows that the lung tissue too has changed.

The decline in respiratory function also reflects a loss in simple mechanical efficiency. In normal respiration less air turns over and the amount of dead air space in the lungs increases, although total lung volume remains almost unchanged. Even the "vital capacity" (the amount of air that can be forcibly expired from the lung) diminishes with age. The nature of this impairment becomes clear when one measures the subject's maximum breathing capacity—the amount of air can move through his lungs in fifteen seconds. The chart for this test shows a decline of about 40 per cent between

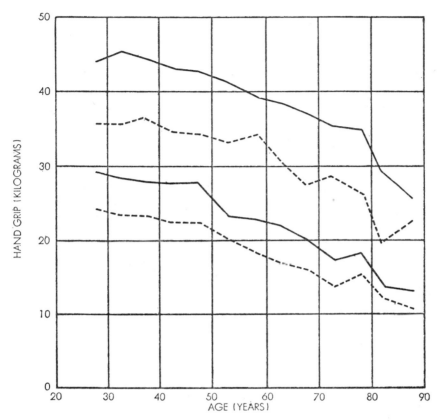

Fig. 3. Hand grip grows weaker with age. Rate for men is shown in upper lines, for women in lower lines. Solid lines represent dominant hand; broken lines represent subordinate hand.

the ages of twenty and eighty. Since the older person expels about as much air at each breath as the younger person does, it is clear that his capacity is less because he cannot maintain as fast a rate of breathing. The impairment is an expression of the general decline in neuro-muscular capacity.

Exercise produces acids and other metabolic waste products that are excreted primarily by the kidney. Because the heart pumps less blood with advancing age, less blood flows through the kidney in a given time. Changes within the kidney itself further reduce the flow of blood as well as the efficiency with which the kidney processes the wastes. The kidney puts the blood through a delicate, multistaged process. First it filters the blood, flushing the waste products out of the bloodstream in a filtrate from which it withholds the red cells and larger molecules; then it processes this filtrate, recovering the smaller useful molecules, such as those of glucose, that get through the filter; and finally the kidney actively excretes waste molecules, some of them too large to pass through the filter. The active functions take place in the tubular lining of the nephrons, the functional units of the kidney. A full test of kidney performance involves measurement of the amount of filtrate formed per minute, the quantity of blood plasma (the liquid portion of the blood) passing through the kidney per minute and the maximum excretory capacity of the nephrons. The measurements are made by infusing the blood with substances that the kidney removes in different ways; one substance, the metabolically inert -polysaccharide inulin, goes out through the filter, whereas paraaminohippuric acid must be actively excreted. Analysis of blood samples and urine during the infusion shows how efficiently the kidney is working. Such tests show that between the ages of thirty-five and eighty the flow of blood plasma through the kidney declines by 55 per cent. The filtration rate and the maximum excretory capacity, as well as glucose reabsorption, decline to the same extent.

Intravenous administration of the substance pyrogen increases the flow of blood through the kidney in young and old. Apparently reduction in blood flow through the kidney is an adaptive mechanism of the aging body. It seems to result from constriction of kidney blood vessels, which makes more blood available to other organs. Because the kidney of the older person has less blood to work on it cleanses the blood of waste more slowly; giving enough time, however, it will do the job.

The endocrine glands regulate a wide variety of physiological processes, ranging from cellular metabolism to regulation of the diameter of small blood vessels and consequently the amount of blood reaching various tissues. At the center of the endocrine system is the pituitary gland, which secretes hormones that stimulate the adrenal glands, the thyroid, the ovaries, the testes and other glands to release their hormones. There is no way to test the performance of the master gland in human subjects, but the responsiveness of other endocrine glands can be tested by administering the appropriate pituitary hormone. Sometimes the level of activity of a given gland can be estimated from the amount of its hormone or of the breakdown products of the hormone that appear in the urine. Adrenal activity is customarily measured by this means and shows a decline with age. Administration of the pituitary hormone that stimulates the cortex of the adrenals produces a smaller elevation of adrenal activity in older people. Since the adrenal hormones are the "stress" hormones, this indicates a reduction in the capacity to respond to stress. On the other hand, the pituitary hormone that stimulates the thyroid gland produces the same result in the old as it does in the young. Even at advanced ages the thyroid retains its ability to manufacture and release thyroxine, which regulates the basal metabolism, or the rate at which the resulting subject consumes oxygen.

Normal function in the cells of the body requires that the chemical composition of the fluids surrounding them be closely regulated. Because the intercellular fluids cannot be sampled directly, estimates of the internal environment must come from analyses of the blood. Such factors as total blood volume, acidity, osmotic pressure, protein content and sugar content remain constant in both young and old subjects at rest. But when these variables are deliberately altered, the older person needs a much longer time to recover internal chemical equilibrium. The acidity of the blood, for example, can be increased by oral administration of ammonium chloride; a younger subject recovers normal acidity within six to eight hours, whereas the seventy year old requires thirty-six to forty-eight hours to recover.

Although the average blood-sugar level remains quite constant even into advanced age, the rate at which the system removes extra glucose drops significantly in older people. Insulin, normally secreted by glands in the pancreas, greatly accelerates the removal of sugar from the blood. When we administer insulin intravenously along with extra glucose, the glucose disappears from the blood of the young person at a much higher rate than it does from the old.

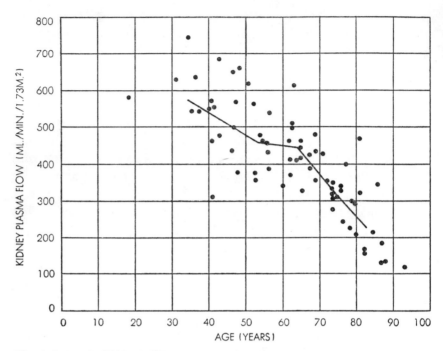

Fig. 4. Large individual differences in aging show up when, for example, the
rate of flow of blood plasma through the kidney is plotted against age for
some seventy men. The plasma flow is measured in milliliters per minute per
1.73 square meters of body-surface area.

It may well be that subtle changes in the chemical composition
of the blood and other body fluids account for certain physiological
changes in the elderly. So far as the gross chemical characteristics
go however, the old animal or human easily maintains a constant,
normal internal environment when completely at rest. But increasing age is accompanied by a definite reduction in the capacity
to readjust to changes that accompany the stresses even of daily living. In other words, a key characteristic of aging is a reduction in
the reserve capacities of the body—the capacities to return to
normal quickly after disturbance in the equilibrium.

Another important element in the aging process shows up in
those functions and activities that involve a high degree of co-

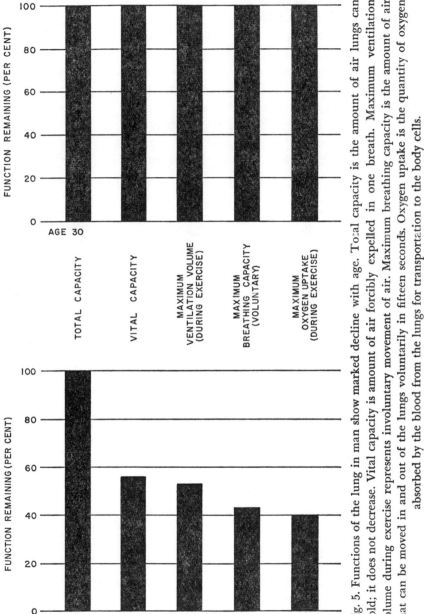

Fig. 5. Functions of the lung in man show marked decline with age. Total capacity is the amount of air lungs can hold; it does not decrease. Vital capacity is amount of air forcibly expelled in one breath. Maximum ventilation volume during exercise represents involuntary movement of air. Maximum breathing capacity is the amount of air that can be moved in and out of the lungs voluntarily in fifteen seconds. Oxygen uptake is the quantity of oxygen absorbed by the blood from the lungs for transportation to the body cells.

ordination among organ systems. Co-ordination breaks down, in the first place, because the different organ systems age at different rates. Conduction of the nerve impulse, for instance, hardly slows with age, whereas cardiac output and breathing capacity decline considerably. Thus in those functions that involve the simultaneous output of several organ systems—sustained physical exercise, for example—the performance of the body shows marked impairment. Most of the debilities of age apparently result from a loss of tissue, particularly through the death and disappearance of cells from the tissues. The wrinkled and flabby skin so apparent in elderly people offers mute testimony to this loss. Body weight declines, especially after middle age. In a large sample of the male population of Canada average weight showed a decline from 167 pounds at ages thirty-five to forty-four to an average of 155 pounds for men sixty-five and over. A sample of men in the U.S., all of them seventy inches tall, averaged 168 pounds in weight at ages sixty-five to sixty-nine and 148 pounds at ages 90 to 94. Women sixty-five inches tall weighed, on the average, 148 pounds at ages sixty-five to sixty-nine and 129 pounds at ages 90 to 94.

Individual organs also lose weight after middle age. For example, the average weight of the brain at autopsy falls from 1,375 grams (3.03 pounds) to 1,232 grams (2.72 pounds) between ages 30 and 90. The same striking loss in total weight and in the weight of specific organs shows up also in the senile rat: the total weight of certain muscle groups drops 30 per cent.

————————————————————————————→

Fig. 6. Percentage changes with age for nine different physiological functions are shown in these two diagrams. The average value for each function at age thirty is taken as 100 per cent. Small drop in basal metabolism (1) is probably due simply to loss of cells.

1 BASAL METABOLIC RATE
2 WORK RATE
3 CARDIAC OUTPUT (AT REST)
4 VITAL CAPACITY OF LUNGS
5 MAXIMUM BREATHING CAPACITY (VOLUNTARY)
6 NERVE CONDUCTION VELOCITY
7 BODY WATER CONTENT
8 FILTRATION RATE OF KIDNEY
9 KIDNEY PLASMA FLOW

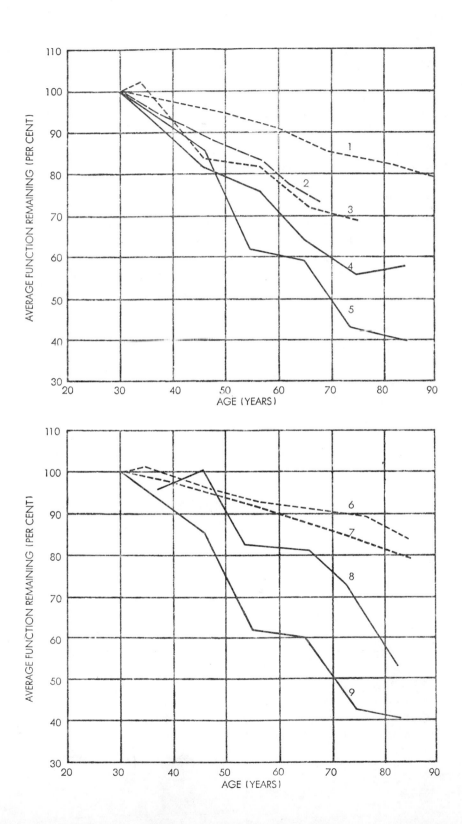

The microscope shows that in many tissues a decrease in the number of cells accompanies the weight loss. Connective tissue replaces the lost cells in some cases, so that the loss of cells is even greater than the reduction in weight would indicate. In the senile rat the muscle fibers show degenerative changes with replacement by connective tissue and an increase in the spaces between fibers. Such loss of muscle fibers no doubt accounts in large measure for the lower muscular strength of elderly humans as well.

The nervous system shows a similar decline. The number of nerve fibers in a nerve trunk decreases by 27 per cent at advanced ages. In the kidney the disappearance of cells is accompanied by a reduction in the number of nephrons. According to counts made by Robert A. Moore of the State University of New York Downstate Medical Center, the number drops over the life span from 800,000 to 450,000. A final example: The number or taste buds per papilla of the tongue falls from an average of 245 in young adults to eighty-eight in subjects aged seventy to eighty-five years.

In early life the body is endowed with tremendous reserve capacities. The loss of a few hundred or a few thousand cells hardly affects the performance of an organ. As age advances the losses accumulate, however, impairments develop; eventually the stress of daily living or disease imposes demands beyond the reserve capacity of the organism.

Understanding of the process of aging will ultimately require discovery of the factors that cause the death and disappearance of individual cells. It may be that the death of individual cells is merely a chance event that occurs on a statistical basis in most tissues. It is more likely that changes in the internal metabolism of a cell damage its capacity for self-repair and reproduction. Biochemical study of the life processes in tissue cells is in its infancy. Within the past few years investigation of tissues from the rat and lower organisms such as the hydra have begun to reveal the effects of age on enzyme activity in body cells.

One key to understanding aging and particularly to taking action that might extend the human life span can be found in the differences in the rate of aging observed in different individuals. These differences indicate that many factors play a role in aging.

When we know why some people age less rapidly than others, we may be able to create conditions that will minimize the loss of functioning cells and tissues, thereby enabling many more people to live as long as those who live longest today.

# THE FORSAKEN ELDERLY
## PROBLEMS IN THE PROVISION OF ADEQUATE MEDICAL CARE FOR THE AGED*

### Louis Carp

"I am seventy-three years old and a very sick old man only looking forward for a quick death. I will my body to any institution that wants. Here is a list of my sicknesses—a sacroiliac, diabetes, double hernia. The 26 April got a heart attack, the 28 of April, a stroke. Cannot hold my water. Would like to enter any chronic disease hospital that would want to take me. Is there anything you can do for me? I will pray for you. My reference, I worked in one place fifty-one years, have no hospitalization. Please do something for me and may God bless you."

The man who wrote these words was one of a surprisingly large number of aged, desperate people—clutching at straws of hope—who responded to one of three letters I recently wrote to the *New York Times*. As a physician particularly interested in the care of old people, I was recommending systems of hospitals in New York State for a bedridden aged with chronic and prolonged illnesses who can't get the proper treatment at home. The "very sick old man," like many others, incorrectly assumed that my name signed to these letters meant that I might have the power to help him.

Had this man been fortunate enough to have financial resources, most of his pitiful troubles could have been handled. I know of one rich woman of ninety-two who for four years has spent $24,000 annually for care at home, exclusive of rent. But so few families can give from their pocketbooks humanly decent care

*Reprinted by courtesy of *American Journal of Economics and Sociology*, Volume *18*:No. 1, 15-24, October, 1958.

to a chronically ill, bedridden old person. The high cost of hospitalization, physicians' fees, laboratory tests, medication, nursing, physiotherapy and all other treatments add up to figures which are prohibitive for those in middle or low-income groups.

What do those sixty-five years and over live on? The Twentieth Century Fund reports that early in 1953, 33 per cent were on OASI or related public and private retirement programs, 30 per cent were at work or were the wives of wage earners, and 20 per cent were receiving public assistance. Twelve per cent had income from personal savings, insurance, investments, relations or veterans benefits. Those in public or private homes, hospitals and other institutions comprised 5 per cent. When these figures are broken down, 36 per cent have no income of their own, 38 per cent have incomes up to $999.00, 11 per cent up to $1999.99 and 15 per cent $2000.00 or more.

Often families go broke after an illness of twenty days—let alone an illness that may last twenty years. Even doctors can't always predict the duration of long-term illness. What frequently looks like the beginning of the end may suddenly reverse itself. The medical—and financial—problem cycle is then re-established.

# I

How widespread, then, is the plight of very sick old people "only looking forward to a quick death?" According to the Census Bureau, the population in this country is 174,000,000. There are some 14,500,000 people over sixty-five years and over. Of these it is estimated that 870,000 with chronic illness, excluding those who can be admitted to mental or tuberculosis hospitals, *need* hospitalization with its mobilization of professional skills. But there are only 72,000 non-federal beds available for prolonged illnesses in all age groups. Since most federal beds are occupied by veterans, it is reasonable to assume that there is no adequate care for most of the remaining 798,000.

The whole problem of hospitalization for the aged with prolonged illnesses is far more complex than that of hospitalization for other groups. Thus, the number of non-federal beds is in striking contrast to the regulations governing the Federal Hospital

Survey and Construction Act of 1946. This Act recommends chronic disease hospital beds on a basis of two beds per 1000 population, making a total of 348,000. Actually, appropriations have not been made to carry out this recommendation. It is further significant that there are three times more of the forsaken elderly than younger people with long-term illnesses and that their illnesses last three times as long. For administrative, budgetary, medical and family reasons, the problem of their care has not been solved by methods that have been applied to other sick people. We seem to be stymied. In the wealthiest nation in all history and in its most prosperous period, we have not yet found a way to provide for the health needs of the forsaken elderly.

To be sure, some constructive steps have been taken. Thus, in Veterans Administration Hospitals, 10 per cent of the patient load is elderly. Some other hospitals have allocated a small percentage of their total bed capacities to those with prolonged illnesses. New York State has established a small Regional Chronic Disease Hospital in Buffalo, Maryland, Massachusetts and Connecticut have taken similar steps. As of May 1, 1950, Illinois converted thirty outlawed almshouses into modern institutions with approved standards for care for the chronically ill.

The medical and social concept, especially in the elderly, that certain prolonged illnesses should be treated in hospitals is nothing new. Voluntary St. Barnabas and Montefiore Hospitals in New York City did just that from the times they were founded in 1866 and 1884. Translating this concept into beds, doctors, nurses and laboratories has been tragically slow.

But in July, 1939, the late Dr. S. S. Goldwater, Commissioner of Hospitals in New York City and a world-famous and far-seeing hospital administrator, in his late sixties was able to see one of his long cherished dreams come true. On Welfare Island (formerly Blackwells Island) in the East River, there once stood a penal institution known as The Work-house. It was demolished to make way for the opening of the new, modern, completely equipped 1,500-bed Welfare Hospital for Chronic Diseases. It has since been renamed the Goldwater Memorial Hospital and expanded to an 1800-bed capacity.

Patients with mental illness and pulmonary tuberculosis are not admitted. Quite naturally, the major portion of its patients fall into the older age groups. They suffer from the degenerative diseases of advancing years: heart, circulatory, lung, liver, genitourinary, gastrointestinal, joint, neoplastic, neurological and metabolic disorders. Others have the permanent disabling effects of physical injury or infection. Here, at last, is a municipal hospital which recruited a dedicated personnel for research in the causes and prevention of degenerative disease; its diagnosis and treatment in all specialties; rehabilitation, recreation, occupational therapy, medical social service, library service, and contact with ministers in the several faiths. Patients and their families don't have to worry about the high cost of hospital care, the specter of interruption of hospitalization or the fear of shuttling from pillar to post. There is no time limit for such hospitalization for prolonged illness.

An impecunious pharmacist of seventy-three, who lived alone and had all sorts of difficulty getting hospital care for a chronic heart and kidney ailment over a prolonged period, had finally found adjustment and total care at the Goldwater Memorial Hospital. "You've no idea what this all means to me," he said "I'm too thankful." He has also been plagued by a large hernia in the groin for twenty years. "I'm tired of the truss which doesn't hold the rupture back anyway," he said. Surgery under local anesthesia took care of that defect.

A pleasant, neat-appearing widow of 80 has been in the hospital for seventeen years after transfer from another municipal hospital where it was difficult to keep her any longer. She has heart and gallbladder disease, an intestinal ailment, chronic rheumatoid arthritis, and part of her stomach is in the chest cavity (upside-down stomach). She has repeated heart attacks and is confined mostly in bed and in a wheel chair. There are insufficient family financial resources. Her children could not take care of her at home even with community help. The hospital has referred her to the Welfare Department for care in a nursing home. It has turned out that this move would be impractical because the patient has recurring episodes of acute heart failure.

Encouraged by the success of Goldwater Memorial Hospital, New York City has further expanded its needed hospital facilities for long-term patients. In 1952, the Bird S. Coler Memorial Hospital was opened with a bed capacity of 1920. In the fall of 1956, the old Coney Island Hospital was converted into a 300-bed facility for the treatment of the chronically ill aged. It is integrated with a large, new "acute" hospital on the same grounds.

Recent Hospital Commissioner Basil C. MacLean also had a plan afoot for "homestead" units which would utilize existing buildings adjacent to municipal hospitals for discharged patients who have no place to go, but who could receive hospital care quickly as it became necessary. Early in 1958, this plan was implemented at the Goldwater Memorial Hospital. One of its wings was reconverted into a 360-bed facility for the chronically disabled but not really sick patients. A bright, homelike atmosphere is projected by colorful walls, drapes and other furnishings. Millions of dollars will be saved annually when similar projects go into operation in other municipal hospitals for those who are chronically disabled but don't require regular, continuous, around-the-clock medical services. Homestead care will cost about $8.50 a day, as against $14.00 in chronic disease and $25.00 in general hospitals.

## II

There is, however, an additional method for the care of prolonged illness, sponsored enthusiastically by many well-known authorities in the field. It is the very helpful, formalized and well-integrated home care program, admittedly one-fourth the expense of hospitalization. It embodies the pooling of community resources for medical care, social service and domestic service for household chores. The community hospital is the central administrative focus with government and/or private subsidy when necessary. Dr. E. M. Bluestone, hospital consultant in New York City, pioneered in January, 1947, a full scale home care program as an extramural project of Montefiore Hospital when he was its executive director. Others have followed in his footsteps both here and abroad. Fourteen New York City municipal hospitals and the Department of Welfare are included in the home care project. But the program needs expansion and has been effective only in selected cases, particularly those discharged from a hospital after partial medical rehabilitation, those classed as custodial cases or those who cannot attend clinics. The Department of Welfare accepts only Old Age Assistance recipients.

In October, 1956, the Hospital Council of Greater New York released a voluminous, factual and objective study of patients in home care. Many advantages are highlighted for the 93 per cent considered successful. Also many disadvantages! At Montefiore Hospital, for example, "patients whose requirements for nursing visits will exceed three times per week over a prolonged period are usually not eligible (for home care), unless the family can be taught to assume the nursing tasks." Other reasons for rejection by the municipal hospitals are a patient who is too ill, financially ineligible, living alone or with inadequate housing, or rejection by the family of the home care plan. There is no provision for emergency visits by physicians after 5 P.M. According to interviewers and case workers, who are essentially sympathetic to the home care program, only 40 per cent of families can make a financial and emotional adjustment.

How often is formalized home care the expedient for lack of facilities for institutional care? Does home care generally meet its exacting specifications across the country, especially for twenty-four hour service? What can be the administrative, financial, family, housing and environmental difficulties? Dr. Bluestone has written "When the destiny of the patient is governed by financial economies or by the need for conserving intramural hospital beds, the extramural service runs the risk of incompleteness, mediocrity and neglect. Does the home care program function within a reasonable radius of the hospital to make adequate care and supervision possible? Medical neglect or hospital neglect of a patient suffering from prolonged illness is a subtle form of euthanasia of which neither should be guilty."

Quoting again from the Hospital Council report: "Home care is not— and cannot be—a substitute for hospital care. It is impossible to provide adequate medical care in the home to a patient who requires hospital care. Rather home care should be considered an additional dimension that broadens the general scope of medical care available to the long-term patient."

### III

Those who have seen the agonizing and fruitless attempts of families and the medically indigent to give good care to their chronically ill, bedridden elderly, know the hard and unrewarding roads they have to travel. There just aren't enough facilities. There are few places for such patients to go and their waiting lists are too long. Voluntary, municipal and county hospitals shy away from patients who potentially will have a long-term illness. They "take up a bed" and prevent patient turnover for acute illness. Proprietary nursing and old age homes can be expensive and generally they don't have the staffing or equipment for standard medical care. These facilities usually refuse to admit those who are too sick or who are likely to disturb others. And in New York State, for example, half the nursing and convalescent homes and homes for the aged are in non-fire-resistive and hazardous structures, and only 25 per cent offer suitable twenty-four hour professional care.

The last time a statistical study was made in the early part of 1953, the New York State Joint Legislative Committee on Problems of the Aging reports that this progressive state had 113,950 Old Age Assistance recipients, of whom 4.1 per cent were bedridden. Among the remainder, 15.4 per cent required the kind of care that would justify hospitalization. Albert J. Abrams, director of that committee, has said, "The indigent aged on Old Age Assistance rolls have a better chance to obtain preventive medical care in nursing homes, public infirmaries and hospitals, than do the middle-income and those below middle-income who are not on Old Age Assistance." A survey in the same state in 1957 indicated that the existing number of suitable beds for the chronically ill was approximately 6,972 (this has been increased slightly since), whereas the total requirement was 32,280.

The frantic appeals of families for help fall on sympathetic ears. But executives and boards of directors, for want of beds, find themselves in a vise, powerless and helpless. Responsibility finally stays with the well-intentioned family. For years I have seen family disruption and quarrels, tears, threats of complete rejection of a sick old person, nervous breakdowns, inroads on already impoverished purses, and lowered living and educational standards. There's many a daughter or son whose chances for marriage have been ruined by the responsibilities of sick parent care.

One member of the family usually carries the load, with double duty at home and business, absenteeism, or the complete sacrifice of a job. Around the clock care is a necessity. Sleep is interrupted. Turned practical nurse, that member of the family becomes immobilized with the jobs of lifting the patient in and out of bed, sheet changing, bathing, bedpan service, the care of incontinence, physical support for ambulation, and the administration of several medications at specific times. Chronic fatigue ensues, with the added homemaker's responsibility of marketing, cooking, dietetics, feeding, cleaning, laundry and mending. Patient care falls short. Filial duty, heroic self-sacrifice and patience become exhausted. The burden is too great. And meantime, gigantic social and economic problems are created by immobilization in homes of one or more members of thousands and thousands of families who don't want to duck responsibility. Despite the continued advance in automation, the nation is weakened by a shortage of workers, by lowered creative and productive power and by family incomes which become choked off.

A widow in her late seventies lived with a single daughter in her late forties from whom the mother got her sole support. She just about made a living at a desk job. She was a commuter. For nine years her mother had been afflicted with severe heart attacks, diabetes, colitis, gall bladder trouble and failing vision. "I loved my mother dearly," said the daughter, "and I cared for her with all I could give. I'd return from work, tired and under nervous tension. Then I had to nurse her. I lost sleep. I was exhausted. At one time fourteen tanks of oxygen were used to help her breathing."

Her eyes became misty and her voice broke as she continued. "Doctors' bills, laboratory tests, cardiograms—it was all too much for me financially. My mother had always been an extremely active woman when well. When she became sick, she resented her incapacities and without knowing it, took it out on me. The whole thing took a terrible toll on me emotionally." She stopped for a moment and swallowed a lump in her throat. "Things kept getting worse and finally she began to suffer mentally. 'I'm praying to God that he will take me,' she used to say. I gradually began to pray that her wish would be granted."

A patient who was interviewed through the Hospital Council study "was an elderly woman with heart disease and the residual of a cerebrovascular accident (a stroke) who was regularly incontinent of urine and occasionally involuntary of feces. All the housework was done by the patient's daughter, who also cared for her own three children, aged five to fourteen. She reported: 'I can't lift her to change the bed unless I call a neighbor to help me. Then we lay her on the floor. . . . There's an awful lot of laundry and she has to be fed. It's too much for me.' " And this was home care under the supervision of a hospital!

If the patient develops abnormal personality traits and eccentricities, memory defects, lack of cooperation and resistiveness, the whole situation becomes charged with emotional tension and almost impossible to solve. Many times such patients wind up in mental institutions where some of them do *not* belong, so that administrators are forced to send them home.

Taking highly representative New York State as an example again, we find that it has well-organized and efficient systems of institutions for mental illness (with about 95,000 resident patients), for the criminally insane, epileptics, mental defectives, physically handicapped, and for those afflicted with cancer or tuberculosis. *But the aged with prolonged illnesses have no comparable care. They still remain stepchildren.* If an oldster can walk and attend to his daily routine, government and private agencies have programs to help him—economic, recreational, and occupationally therapeutic. If he can't walk, he may find himself consigned to the scrap heap.

Many legislators, organized medicine, social agencies and citizens have at last become aware that there is an elderly *lost generation.* Sincere hospital planning for long-term illness has been initiated by such agencies as the U. S. Department of Health, Education and Welfare, the Commission of Chronic Illness, the New

York State Joint Hospital Survey and Planning Commission, and by the provisions of the amended Federal Hospital and Survey Act of July, 1954. Nineteen states have set up machinery to help solve the major health problem. It's been slow going and so far there have been few palpable results.

## IV

A program for giving *needed adequate* hospitalization to our senior citizens with prolonged and chronic disease might begin with the following measures:

1. A nation-wide study of the costs of adequate medical care of the aged by an organization such as the National Science Foundation to give reliable information on the financial problem for better planning to meet it.

2. With government subsidy, university medical centers and other approved hospitals should make their highly professional skills and research facilities available to connected hospitals for the chronically ill. Such organization would be similar to that existing at the Columbia Presbyterian Medical Center, to which is attached Delafield Hospital for cancer and allied diseases, financed by New York City, and the Psychiatric Institute, subsidized by New York State. According to Dr. Marcus D. Kogel, a recent Commissioner of Hospitals in New York City, hospitals for the chronically ill should be specially designed to include "familiar, pleasant and homelike environment with more than the usual comforts, protection from accidents and special psychological and emotional support." Their function would be in-patient and out-patient service, research in the causes and prevention of degenerative disease, teaching on the professional level, consultation service for practicing physicians and a statistical staff for fact-finding.

3. Voluntary, municipal and county hospitals, approved nursing and old age homes, should allocate with government and/or private subsidy, wings, floors, wards and (where permissible) moderately priced private or semi-private rooms for those with prolonged illnesses.

4. Government should construct needed hospitals in strategic geographical areas lacking medical centers or other large hospitals.

5. Formalized home care programs under hospital supervision for those who no longer need hospital care should be expanded to free hospital beds for those who need them.

6. Custodial facilities should be established for patients who can be discharged after sufficient rehabilitation but who have no place to go.

7. Insurance against illness is provided in most welfare and pension funds, which now apply to some 75,000,000. If they keep growing, practically all the elderly will be covered to some degree within a decade. These funds, as applied to individuals, are not earmarked for medical projects for the care of the incapacitated aged. This needs to be done. According to the September 1956 survey of the U. S. Public Health Service, only 36.5 per cent of persons aged sixty-five and over have some form of health insurance, much of it limited in extent. Most health insurance companies incorporate a clause in their policies whereby these are cancellable at age sixty-five or they continue in force only at the option of the company and then at open rates. It is urgent that insurance companies make equitable provisions for post-65 coverage.

8. At this writing, the Forand bill (H.R. 9467) proposes an additional 1 per cent social security payroll tax shared equally by employer and employee. This fund would be earmarked for insurance against the cost of hospital, nursing home and surgical services to all those eligible for old-age and survivors benefits or who would be eligible if they applied. Patients would have free choice of hospitals, physicians and other personnel. Nothing in the bill is construed to give administering agencies authority over the internal management of participating institutions or over the practice of medicine or the manner in which medical services are provided. This is *not* socialized medicine.

By 1975, there will be about 20,000,000 people in the United States who will be sixty-five years and over. They will comprise about 10.8 per cent of the population. Many readers of this article will be in this group. Therefore, we have the special responsibility of influencing our federal, state and local governments in joining to provide long overdue hospital facilities for this age group which needs them but cannot be provided for. Dr. Bluestone has said,

"When the blessing of a full quota of years is mixed with the curse of prolonged illness, the hospital must help to find a way of disentangling the combination." There's more than economy involved. The problem must not be swept under the rug. If it is, statistics show that we run a great risk of finding *ourselves* the victims of prolonged illness without proper care—and our families besieged by merciless responsibilities.

> CAST ME NOT OFF IN THE TIME OF OLD AGE;
> WHEN MY STRENGTH FAILETH, FORSAKE ME NOT.
> *Psalm 71:9*

# ADVANCES IN REHABILITATION*
## HOWARD A. RUSK

The greatest advance that has been made in the rehabilitation of the physically handicapped is the new acceptance of a third dimension of medical responsibility.

## THE 'THIRD PHASE OF MEDICINE'

Rehabilitation has often been termed the 'third phase of medicine,' following 'preventive medicine' and 'curative medicine and surgery.' It is that period when the 'fever is down and the stitches are out,' the period 'between the bed and the job.' In contrast to 'convalescence,' in which the patient is left alone to let nature and time take their course, rehabilitation is a dynamic concept in which the skills of the rehabilitation team, consisting of the physician, physical therapists, occupational therapists, nurses, social workers, counsellors and other trained personnel, are integrated as a single force to assist the patient in reaching the maximum of his physical, emotional and social and vocational potentials.

The first objective of rehabilitation is to eliminate the physical disability if that is possible; the second, to reduce or alleviate the disability to the greatest extent possible; and the third, to retrain

---

*Reprinted by courtesy of *The Practitioner*, Volume *183*:505-512, October, 1959.

the person with a residual physical disability 'to live and to work within the limits of his disability but to the hilt of his capabilities.'

## PRESENT-DAY PROBLEMS

Until the last fifty years, the saving of human life as the traditional and cherished goal of medicine was largely a matter of saving individual patients. With the first half of the Twentieth Century, the whole character of medicine's traditional goal was changed. The expansion of research into the etiology and therapy of communicable and infectious diseases 'struck specifics.' The establishment of new and effective public health measures and the rich findings in the basic fields reported elsewhere in this Special Number of *The Practitioner* gave the life-saving functions of medicine mass proportions. These, combined with similar advances in greater availability of medical and hospital care, improved nutrition, increased education, better housing and all the contributing factors to our unprecedented current standard of living, mean that hundreds of thousands of persons are alive today who at the turn of the century would have died with the same medical problems. Yet many of them have not come out unscathed. They have survived only to find themselves confronted with residual disability. The paraplegic whose back is broken in a fall does not die today as he would have done fifty years ago. He has strong arms, an active mind and a burning desire to live the best life he can with what he has left. Antibiotics control the upper respiratory and urinary infections of the severely involved cerebral palsied youngster who would have succumbed before their development. He seeks his place in society. The survivors of infection get their share of the degenerative diseases. These are present-day problems which must be solved.

The day-to-day experience of all practising physicians shows that not only has there been a substantial increase in the gross number of disabled persons, but that a growing percentage of our population suffer from long-term illnesses and substantial physical impairments. Two thousand years ago the average length of life was but twenty-five years; at the turn of the century, it was forty-nine; by 1950 it had reached sixty-seven; and we are now on the threshold of the legendary three-score and ten, contrary to opinions expressed by some, the growing incidence of chronic disability is a tribute to medicine rather than an indictment. But as the physician has been largely responsible for this development, he must assume leadership in its solution.

## EXPANDING OPPORTUNITIES

One of the most significant medical and social advances of the past decade is the growing interest, both professional and among the public, throughout the world of the development of rehabilitation services for the physically handicapped. Undoubtedly, much of this interest in expanding rehabilitation opportunities and services for the handicapped has resulted both directly and indirectly from the 1939-45 War, when attention was focused on the problems of disabled servicemen. Such advances, however, are not entirely due to this impetus, as the growth of rehabilitation services for the handicapped is a part of a total pattern of an expanding community, national and global consciousness of social welfare, which is reflected in similar advances in all educational, health, and social services. As in all great social movements, this increased interest in rehabilitation has been a result of the impact and recognition of increased needs: in this instance, the rapid increase in the developed parts of the world of the incidence of chronic disability as a result of the increasing age of the population.

Although some nations of the world still have pressing problems of communicable disease, and life expectancy rates vary from nation to nation, depending upon the availability of medical care, public health measures, food supply, and the general standard of living, the trend in all nations is towards a greatly increased life expectancy, with the result that throughout the world the population is gradually becoming older. At the same time that the average age is advancing in the developed parts of the world, a new concept of the dignity of man and the value of the worth of the individual is beginning to emerge in those nations of the world which do not have the benefits as yet of modern programmes of public health and medical care. This new concept of the worth of the individual has been symbolized, and is finding its expression in many instances in the desire of these nations to institute program-mes of services for their physically handicapped.

Rehabilitation has been defined as the ultimate restoration of the disabled person to his maximum capacity—physical, emotional, social and vocational. Implicit in this definition is the need for a team whose members can bring together a wide variety of skills and understandings. No one profession can furnish all the services needed. Rather is rehabilitation an area of specialized activity with-in a number of professional disciplines.

## THE PHYSICIAN'S RESPONSIBILITY

Until recent years, the great majority of the medical profession looked upon rehabilitation as an extra-curricular activity of medi-cine: something dealing with social work and vocational training, but something which had little concern, and which held but few implications, for medicine. Today, however, that trend is being reversed and, although there are still many physicians who are unfamiliar with the aims and procedures of rehabilitation, more and more is medicine beginning to recognize that medical care cannot be considered complete until the patient with a residual physical disability has been trained 'to live and work with what he has left.' Except in a few isolated instances, the physically handi-capped person must be retrained to walk and travel, to care for his daily needs to use normal methods of transportation, to use ordinary toilet facilities, to apply and remove his own prosthetic devices and to communicate either orally or in writing. These are such simple things that they are often overlooked, but the personal, vocational, and social success of the handicapped person is de-pendent upon them.

The practice of rehabilitation for the general practitioner, or for any doctor, begins with the belief in the basic philosophy that the doctor's responsibility does not end when the acute illness is ended or surgery is completed; it ends only when the individual is retrained to live and work with what is left. This basic concept of the doctor's responsibility can be achieved only if rehabilitation is considered an integral part of medical services. Any programme of rehabilitation is only as sound as the basic medical service of which it is a part. The diagnosis and prognosis must be accurate, for it is upon them that the feasibility of retraining is determined.

## REHABILITATION SERVICES IN HOSPITALS

Although some outstanding rehabilitation programmes in various parts of the world have demonstrated that rehabilitation to the point of self-care and even to full or limited employment is possible for many of the chronically ill who have been hospitalized for long periods, patients in few hospitals receive comprehensive rehabilitation service. Hospitals complain that the chronically ill are responsible for their overcrowding, but few of them provide the third phase of medical care which will permit many of these patients to leave the hospital.

Just as certain specialized centres for the care of particular diseases requiring specialized personnel and facilities have developed, there has been a trend in the United States, particularly since the last war, to develop 'rehabilitation centres.' In some instances, these 'centres' have been distinct public or non-profit institutions designed to serve all physicians and all hospitals, but have had no direct affiliations with hospitals. Others have been integral parts of hospitals or medical centres. As compared with but a small handful of such facilities before the 1939-45 War, the total now numbers well over a hundred. Although these independent 'rehabilitation centres' provide a valuable and needed service within a community, if any major attack is to be made on the problems of disability there must be an expansion of rehabilitation services in general hospitals, for it is to the general hospitals that the practising physicians turn for the care of their patients. It is also within the general hospital that such services can be brought to the patient at the earliest possible time, and costly and damaging physical, emotional, social and vocational sequelae of the acute disease process or trauma be alleviated or minimized. To ignore the development of rehabilitation services within general hospitals is to guarantee the continued deterioration of many less severely disabled persons until they, too, reach the severely disabled and totally dependent category. The neglect of disability is far more costly than an early aggressive programme of rehabilitation which restores the individual to the highest possible level of physical, economic, social and emotional self-sufficiency.

Twelve years of experience in the first comprehensive rehabilitation service in a general civilian hospital—Bellevue Hospital, New York City—together with extended observation and study of other general hospitals, indicate that rehabilitation services within the hospital can best be provided by the organization of a 'bed service' which has a relationship to the other hospital services similar to that of the x-ray and laboratory divisions. For example, in Bellevue Hospital the rehabilitation service provides consultants for each of the other major services such as fractures, paediatrics, surgery, and neurology. Its resident and visiting staff regularly makes rounds with the resident and visiting staff of these services. Its staff may, for example, see a patient in consultation before his leg is removed, indoctrinating him as to what he must expect, why he cannot keep his stump on a pillow, why he has to lie on his abdomen. Medical responsibility during the period of definitive care, of course, rests with the initial or admitting service. As soon as the stitches are removed, the patient is transferred to a rehabilitation ward. At this time, the rehabilitation service assumes the major responsibility for his care, fitting of the prosthesis, and training in its uses. The roles are now reversed; the surgical service has become the consulting service.

Before the actual transfer of the patient to a rehabilitation ward, however, he attends one of the rehabilitation service's semi-weekly evaluation clinics, where his problem is analysed and discussed by all members of the staff—physical therapists, occupational therapists, nurses, vocational counsellors, speech therapists, social workers and psychologists—as well as resident and visiting medical staff. The decision as to the feasibility of transferring the patient to the rehabilitation service is then made on the basis of the service's ability to contribute to his over-all physical, emotional, social and vocational rehabilitation.

## PLANNING FOR THE CHRONICALLY DISABLED

One of the major problems now confronting medicine, which will be further accentuated in the next twenty years by the growing incidence of chronic disease and chronic disability, is how these services can be brought most effectively and most economically to those patients needing them.

Physicians, hospitals, social workers, community agencies and families err constantly in the loose interpretation of the term 'chronic illness.' A recent government publication in the United States reports that: 'in 1950, 17 in every 100 persons aged sixty-five and over were estimated to have a long-term disabling chronic illness, as compared to 3 or 4 per cent. per 100 among the general population.' Among these seventeen in every 100 persons aged sixty-five and over, there are many who are 'chronically ill' in that they require continuing medical services of the type which can be provided only or best within a hospital. Among them, however, are others who are 'chronically disabled' in that although they have static physical impairments (such as hemiplegia following a stroke), they are not in need of continuing hospital care. But since there is nowhere else for them to go, they are forced to live for months or years in an environment where pain and death are a part of the daily routine.

This situation was brought into the professional spotlight recently by a study conducted under the auspices of the New York Foundation at Goldwater Memorial Hospital, a municipal hospital of the City of New York. In this study of ninety-five unselected cases (average age, 68.5 years), it was found after intensive medical, social, psychological and economic evaluation, that only seven were felt to be in need of continuing hospitalization; and there was considerable doubt about this in two of them. Using the customary rehabilitation standards, eleven patients were considered suitable for rehabilitation with a better than 50:50 prospect of success. The remaining eighty-four of the original ninety-five patients were considered to be in no need of either rehabilitation or definitive medical care. An analysis of but three of these patients showed they alone had been cared for in municipal facilities for a total of nearly 19,000 days. Calculating arbitrarily and conservatively at $12 per day as cost for their care, the total cost of these three patients alone to that point was $228,000 and the end was not in sight. This is a sizeable sum, but it is only money. What about the cost to these three individuals in boredom, anxiety, frustration and resignation?

### 'HOMESTEADS'

Following this initial study, a subsequent study was made in which it was found that one out of every five patients in New York City's huge municipal hospital system was there not because he needed hospital services, but simply because he had no place to go. Currently the City of New York is engaged in remedying this situation by the creation of a new type of institution known as a 'homestead.' These new institutions created through the modification of existing, unneeded buildings, are adjacent to municipal hospitals so that the residents of the 'homesteads' may be immediately transferred into hospitals should they need medical care from time to time.

With this new approach, New York City will save substantial sums and at the same time the residents of the new 'homesteads' will have much richer and fuller lives than in hospitals where they are surrounded by illness and must conform to hospital régimes which are unrelated to their needs.

### PLANNING FOR THE AGED

Like other national and community problems, the very size and complexity of development of services for our aged makes over-all planning for such services difficult. Even though we have failed at both the national and community levels to make adequate preparations to meet the complex and multiple needs of our increasing number of aged, this does not prevent action programmes designed to solve or alleviate at least one aspect of the problem. This is what New York City is doing with its 'homesteads.' These will not solve the problems of the city's aged, but they will at least alleviate one aspect of the problem.

Although it is generally agreed that there are no diseases exclusively characteristic of aging, experience strongly supports the statistical findings that elderly people take a disproportionate share in the chronic and disabling diseases. This does not necessarily indicate a need for separation of medical and health services for the aged from those for the young, but rather an adaptation and extension of existing resources to suit their special needs. The ageing patients constitute perhaps the largest single group which could benefit from an extension of home-care services to provide them with the necessary medical and nursing help after their discharge from the hospital. The addition of medical rehabilitation to the conventional clinical services has enabled many an elderly man and woman, previously considered hopelessly crippled, to regain his or her functional independence and continue to live without burden to themselves or their environment. While clinical medicine continually strives to free the elderly from the distressing physical and mental illnesses, the basic biological sciences endeavour to explain the many enigmatic questions connected with ageing.

## CONCLUSION

Rehabilitation during the first quarter of the century was characterized by the development of orthopaedic surgery, physical therapy, occupational therapy, and the State-Federal vocational rehabilitation programmes, all outgrowths of the 1914-18 War. Under the stimulus of the 1939-45 War, the second quarter of the century has seen a recognition that the problems medicine faces in meeting the growing incidence of chronic disease and disability extend far beyond any medical specialty; they are problems which must be faced and solved by medicine as a whole. The concept of rehabilitation and the basic techniques must be made a part of the armamentarium of all physicians, for regardless of the type of disability the responsibility of the physician to his patient cannot end when the acute injury or illness has been cared for. Medical care is not complete until the patient has been trained to live and to work with what he has left.

If any major attack is to be made on the problems of chronic disability, the general hospital and the individual practising physician must be the focal points of that attack. It is only in doctors' surgeries and in general hospitals that such services can be brought to the patient at the earliest possible time and that the costly and damaging physical, emotional, social and vocational sequelae of the acute disease process or trauma may be alleviated or minimized.

Rehabilitation of the chronically ill and the chronically disabled is not just a series of restorative techniques: it is a philosophy of medical responsibility. Failure to assume this responsibility means to guarantee the continued deterioration of many less severely disabled persons until they, too, reach the severely disabled and totally dependent category. The neglect of disability in its early stages is far more costly than an early aggressive programme of rehabilitation which restores the individual to the highest possible level of physical, economic, social and emotional self-sufficiency.

## GERIATRIC SERVICES FROM THE PRACTITIONER'S VIEWPOINT*

### T. ERIC REYNOLDS

Much of what I am about to say may seem somewhat heretical. In fact, the theme of this presentation is a belief that I do not think is commonly held and one that may seem startling to you; but it is one that I have found to be true in my own office practice and that I am sure is supported by other practitioners. This is the belief that the problems, even the medical problems, of the older aged patient are as much the concern of the community and family as they are of the physician.

When we use the term "aged" by definition we mean those sixty-five or older. Actually, no such arbitrary dividing line is sensible from a clinical point of view; for, as we all know, chronologic and physiologic age differ widely in different people. However, for statistical and actuarial purposes, we have to accept some birthday as an end point—or should I say beginning point?—so it may as well be the sixty-fifth birthday.

### REASONS FOR CONSULTING DOCTORS

There are few statistics as to why people of any age consult doctors. There are even fewer figures on the motivation of those over sixty-five to see physicians. Comparing my own records with a study made at the University of Washington and published in 1955, and drawing on my memory and opinions, I have come up

*Reprinted by courtesy of *Geriatrics*, Volume *15*, December, 1960. Read before the Western Branch, American Public Health Association, San Francisco, June 1, 1959.

with a few ideas of what brings the elderly group into the physician's office or causes him to see them at their home. Leading the list in frequency is cardiovascular disease, including, of course, coronary artery disease, hypertension, angina pectoris, cerebral hemorrhage and thrombosis, valvular heart disease and venous conditions, especially varicosities, thrombosis, hypostatic skin disease, and leg ulcers.

Arthritis and all the related musculo-skeletal diseases, including low back strains and neurologic symptoms such as sciatic neuralgia and muscular headaches, bursitis, and tenosynovitis, come a close second. Next, perhaps, in the order of frequency, would come the respiratory diseases, not only the viral and microbial infections but asthma, emphysema, fibrosis, bronchiectasis, and the various manifestations of cardiopulmonary insufficiency. Somewhere below this in frequency come neoplasms, hernias (especially direct ones, abdominal and diaphragmatic), fractures, anemias, and prostatic disease. It is interesting that hip fractures, especially in female patients, and prostatic obstruction in males, are two of the largest hospital expense items for conditions of the older age group. All of the above diagnoses account for considerably less than one half of the visits to the physician's office. One large category of the remainder is psychoneurosis, especially with conversion symptoms referable to the digestive tract. Dietary fads and inadequate food habits are common among this group.

Management of geriatric disease is often made more difficult because so many old people do not have a clear understanding of their medical problems for various reasons, such as education, insight, forgetfulness, childishness, and general lack of a realistic approach to the symptoms of disease. Many simply do not accept their age and its implications. So one finds them "shopping around"—often to quacks and soothsayers—with symptoms that have been explained by their physicians as irremediable, except for palliation. This may account for the fact that far too many doctors are unhappy with older patients and seem to protest the various insurance systems which may lead them to doctors' offices. This is indeed unfortunate, but I fear it is true.

## HIGH MORBIDITY—LOW INCOME

This age group has a high incidence of morbidity at a time when economic resources, or at least income, is the lowest. As time goes on, more and more older people should come under arrangements for paid-up insurance, extended benefits, and such devices; but in the meantime, some form of subsidy may have to fill part of the gap.

It is to be hoped that this can be done without the need for a colossal, self-perpetuating bureau to be formed where administrative red tape tends to become "the tail that wags the dog." Perhaps the quality of medical care is high in some of our veterans facilities and "old soldiers' homes," and so on, but time and efficiency certainly mean nothing. Neither, it seems, does expense to the taxpayer.

The employment and extension of visiting nursing services, better nursing homes, convalescent hospitals, homemaker services, "meals on wheels" and such things, need to be fostered and extended. Rehabilitation, as far as it can apply to the older age group, is highly desirable.

One thing is certain, almost every case has to be individualized and managed according to circumstances of (1) family situation, (2) economic status, (3) temperament, (4) vigor, and (5) mentality. Certainly just putting people under custodial care with many others, often worse off, tends to undermine the mental and emotional stamina of many old people to the point where they become hopelessly passive and dependent. Whereas such a simple expedient as an arm for an older person to lean on during a short walk, a call on a friend or relative, or a visit to a day-home or an occupational center, might keep this same individual active and alert.

## MORES AND MEDICAL PROBLEMS

To a great degree the medical problems of the aged are rooted in the mores of our culture. Also, to a great extent our medical problems after the age of sixty-five are determined by such things as (1) the care of the individual before that time, (2) his or her attention to infections, (3) mental cultivation and relaxation, (4) physical fitness and exercise, (5) smoking habits, (6) the use of alcohol, (7) weight control and, (8) food habits. Perhaps vitamins and hormones, both natural and otherwise, play some part, and certainly part of it is pure caprice, such as the factor of injury or exposure and stress and strain beyond the control of the individual. Heredity is definitely a factor in the medical problems of older people. Indeed, barring accidents, the choice of ancestors often determines whether an individual will qualify to reach that category.

It is my opinion that the two most prevalent difficulties of old age are (1) boredom and (2) loneliness and that much of the medical attention sought by them is based on these two underlying conditions.

Our society has moved from a relatively simple agrarian economy with handicraft production to a vast complex of industrial capitalism. Technology and automation have made employment less meaningful to most workers, except in terms of earnings and working conditions. For instance, the button-pusher in a great shoe factory simply does not have the pride and interest in good shoes that a handicraft cobbler formerly had. Hours of labor are shorter and inevitably will be still shorter and hence chances for leisure will be greater. But what is done with leisure? Or rather we should ask what is *not* done with it.

Fewer and fewer people are self-employed. Everything is bigger —factories, farms, banks and stores—and so the emphasis of necessity has shifted from individual initiative to security. The standard of living is higher, life is easier and in most respects better, and the sweatshops have all but disappeared. How does all this prepare one for leisure and retirement? Or does it? Now the man or the woman off work, or retired, can sit in front of a TV screen and be spoon-fed on a cultural diet which, to say the best for it, leaves something to be desired. Its purpose is to sell deodorants, detergents, patent medicines, beer and cigarets, and programs are beamed accordingly. That in itself is not so bad but what is bad is that this occupation is so completely passive. We all recognize that some aspects of patient loneliness have been relieved by this medium, but the total cultural effect on the developing community may not lead to the kind of inner resourcefulness that should be the greatest asset of the declining years. Let us ask ourselves to what extent the radio and television supply the sitter who has gone from eight hours on the assembly line or at the necktie counter with resources with which to enjoy twenty years of social security benefits, after mandatory retirement at the age of sixty-five. Not too much, I am afraid.

These I know are extreme examples but they illustrate a point. Perhaps we need to approach these problems by education for leisure as well as by providing paid-up insurance. Perhaps Aunt Emma darning socks or granddad weeding a small cabbage patch has some merit after all. In case you think I am just saying these things by way of cracker-barrel philosophizing—I am not. Time and time again in my own clinical experience men approaching retirement age have answered my questions as to "What preparation have you made for retirement?" by the statement "Oh, this is no problem, doctor, I will go fishing" or "Oh, I just want not to have to catch that early bus each morning" or "I will read more" or "just sit around." And what happens, after the novelty wears off? Boredom sets in, little pains become bigger ones, anxieties mount, father begins to look for dust on picture frames around the house, mother's friends don't drop around to call because hubby's home all the time, and tempers flare. What was once a healthy wholesome household atmosphere becomes strained, and psychoneurotic manifestations appear in both members.

These are actually observed cases of my own experience, many times multiplied. So perhaps busy hands and minds are also happy hands and minds. This is what I meant by stating that much of this is rooted in our society and in our culture. Somehow or other the idea has come about that work is degrading, but it is my opinion that merely sitting and watching entertainment, fishing, hunting, bowling, or even golfing are not enough and may lead to frustration. The mind requires a challenge to keep it flexible, just as muscles need exercise.

Changes in our family living have reduced both the ability and the willingness of children to provide for older relatives. Smaller houses, the migration to the suburbs, the tax structure, inflation and installment buying of mass produced goods have conspired to make this virtually impossible. The younger relatives themselves are mostly living on next week's paycheck. Here is a real opportunity for the physician to practice preventive medicine by preparing his younger and middle-aged patients of today for tomorrow's older age. A serious talk to younger patients about the development of habits of mind as well as hobbies and games may be even more important than a perfunctory glance through a fluoroscopic screen, on a periodic examination. Preparation, while still young, for the stresses and strains of leisure, is possibly the greatest need.

## A CULTURAL RESPONSIBILITY

Now all this may sound as if I am angry at somebody or even angry at the world. Forgive me if it does sound that way, for I really am not. But I would like to drive home the point to physicians, as well as to the other disciplines, that there is a lot more to all this than the passing of a law, the creating of a bureau and the spending of public money. As was said before, the medical problems of the aged are manifold and a large part of this is a family and cultural responsibility. Physicians, I believe, have a social responsibility here because, in a large sense, medical science created the problem, largely reducing infant mortality and making it possible for so many to live into this later period of life. When the keys to malignancy and vascular degeneration have been found, there will probably be much more of this problem. But is it enough merely to stay alive and not to "live?" Most of us, if we could have our choice, would not think so. Here, I think, are some of the most urgent needs in the medical care of the aging population. By thought, study, and effort, many of them can be resolved.

# PSYCHOTHERAPY WITH GERIATRIC PATIENTS: A REVIEW OF THE LITERATURE*

### ALLAN RECHTSCHAFFEN

This review is written with a view toward evaluating the current status of geriatric psychotherapy and outlining some of the

*Reprinted by courtesy of *Journal of Gerontology,* Volume *14*:73-83, January, 1959.

major questions and problems that require research. The nature of geriatric problems will be discussed only insofar as such discussion is necessary in considering the rationale underlying particular therapeutic techniques; for more comprehensive reviews of geriatric pathology, the reader is referred to Shock's excellent bibliographies. Neither shall the scope of the geriatric mental health problem be discussed. The results of a recent study at a Minnesota state hospital may be sufficient to indicate the magnitude of the problem. This study showed that while the percentage of the people in the state over sixty-five years of age increased from 4.7 per cent to 9.0 per cent between 1920 and 1950, the percentage of patients admitted to the hospital for the first time who were over sixty-five increased from 12.4 per cent to 33.9 per cent during a comparable period. The emphasis in the present paper will be on therapeutic rationale and technique rather than on an evaluation of results, for well-controlled studies of the effectiveness of psychotherapy are few. Psychotherapy will be dealt with in a somewhat limited sense and excluded from consideration are such works as Lawton's effort toward defining a geriatric mental hygiene; the planning of social programs discussed by Donahue and Tibbitts; the social group work programs for the normal aged, typified in the work of Kaplan and Tarrel; the more medically oriented treatment programs of Clow and Allen. While the above programs are psychotherapeutic in the broad sense, they may be differentiated from the face to face patient-therapist relationship which is here implied by the term psychotherapy.

## A PIONEER SPIRIT

The first highly organized psychotherapeutic program for the aged was spearheaded by the energetic and apparently infectious enthusiasm of D. Lillien J. Martin, a psychologist who, after her own retirement, founded the San Francisco Old Age Counseling Center in 1929 and directed its activities until her death at the age of ninety-two. The "Martin Method" of rehabilitation is described in three of her books. The approach was as essentially directive, inspirational one. It consisted of a series of planned interviews, five of which, according to Dr. Martin, were usually sufficient in 87 per cent of successful cases.

The first interview was aimed at personality evaluation and psychotherapy. It included the following procedures:

1. The client was asked to relate his life history in detail from his earliest memory up to the present. In so doing, the client was also asked to report any irrelevant side thoughts or images which might come to his mind in order to get at "subconscious complexes." The interpretation of dreams was not stressed because, ". . . in general, these are less enlightening to the counselor, since they tend to be recalled confusedly, unless they recur frequently and regularly."

2. A brief twenty minute series of tests was given, and the results were integrated with the life history and clinical observations to arrive at what Dr. Martin believed to be a comprehensive picture of the client's assets and liabilities.

3. The client was then prepared for psychotherapy by convincing him how ". . . imperative it is for him to banish all physical and mental resistance and adopt the 'will-to-do' attitude."

4. The counselor proceeded to analyze the results of his observations, the life history, and the tests with the patient in an effort to have him realistically appraise what had been maladjustive in his reaction patterns.

5. At the close of the first session, the client was provided with corrective slogans, e.g., "Each immoral act makes reformation more difficult," and "Sweep the cob-webs out of your mind." Psychological setting up exercises were also provided, e.g., "Have I today banished the purposeless activity called 'nervousness'?" and "Have I tried to solve rather than to forget my problems?" The client was finally sent home from the first interview with the strong assurance that ". . . he can and will make the effort for self-improvement necessary to gain for him a full and growing life functioning to replace the unsuccessful and unhappy existence that led him to seek counsel at the Old Age Center." Subsequent interviews were largely devoted to filling out charts by which the client could regulate his daily activities, budget, recreation, and future goals. Of her therapeutic approach, Dr. Martin said, ". . . troublesome states of mind and the complexes that underlie them are more quickly discovered by the Martin Method than by psychoanalysis. . . . When

the core of these ideas is found the client must be helped to recognize its existence, to understand its implications in daily life, and to banish it from his mind."

In her own enthusiasm, Dr. Martin was perhaps overly optimistic. By current standards one interview that accomplished the taking of a life history, diagnostic testing, personality analysis, and the administration of corrective slogans must have been superficial. Nevertheless, by virtue of its vigor and optimism, the Martin Method may have had the therapeutic effects of overcoming pessimistic inertia and of convincing the client that he had his maladjustments corrected. Aside from whatever results she might have achieved, Dr. Martin was a pioneer by virtue of her readiness to administer psychotherapy to the aged.

In spite of her efforts, Dr. Martin has had small influence on the development of geriatric psychotherapy, and she is very rarely quoted today. Perhaps a major reason for her lack of influence is that she seemed to proceed without an articulate theoretical framework, and hence there was little apart from her enthusiasm and devotion upon which others could build. Since her work was moved more by inspiration and faith than by psychiatric concepts or curiosity, no explicit systematic issues or research problems arose from her approach.

## THE PSYCHOANALYTIC APPROACH

The early thinking about the extension of psycho-analysis to the treatment of the aged was marked with the skepticism of Freud, who listed at least three reasons why old people, as a rule, were not accessible to his therapeutic methods.

One reason involved the limitations of the aged ego or intellect. In this regard Freud ventured that, ". . . near or above the fifties the elasticity of the mental processes, on which the treatment depends, is as a rule lacking—old people are no longer educable. . . ." While, as will be seen in the discussion to follow, many writers continue to take note of such intellectual limitations, various modifications of psychoanalytic theory and practice have militated for diminished skepticism on this point.

Another caution raised by Freud was that ". . . the mass of

material to be dealt with would prolong the duration of the treatment indefinitely." This objection appears to rest on an assumption that successful analysis requires a more or less complete anamnesis of the life history and a resolution of most, if not all, major conflicts experienced during a lifetime. In one sense, such an assumption appears unworkable, for it seems to depend upon a further assumption that there is little generality of personality pattern from life episode to life episode and that there is little generalization of therapeutic effect from one conflict resolution to another. Such a view would render all psychotherapies relatively ineffectual in the long run. In view of the over-all character of his theories, it is doubtful that Freud would today seriously subscribe to the assumptions of specificity which underlie the view that the elderly have too much life history behind them for successful analysis. In this regard, it is of interest that the argument of over-abundant life history has not been seriously considered by writers subsequent to Freud.

In an earlier paper, Freud had cited the "accumulation" argument discussed above, but had added: "With persons who are too far advanced in years it [psychoanalysis] fails because, owing to the accumulation of material, so much time would be required that the end of the cure would be reached at a period of life in which much importance is no longer attached to nervous health." The questioning of the importance of "nervous health" in the later years seems to constitute a third contraindication on Freud's part to initiating psychoanalysis with the aged, though the exact implication of the statement quoted is not apparent. Perhaps Freud meant that the mental health of the aged was not so highly valued as that of the young—a view which would imply a fundamental devaluation of old age. Without entering into the discussion of values which the issue implies, it might suffice to mention the title of Eissler's recent book, *The Psychiatrist and the Dying Patient,* as an indication that mental comfort, at least to some therapists, assumes great value as long as there is *any* mental life. On the other hand, this statement of Freud suggests an extremely cogent argument. In young persons, where there is anticipation of thirty or forty years of happier living, the investment of time, money, and effort, and the partial delay of gratification may be as justifiable as the expenditure of resources for education. In older people the total economics of therapeutic investment is opened for review. Except for those exceptionally adventurous old people who can accept therapy as an exciting new experience, the trials of therapy are more heavily weighed. There may be an inclination on the part of both patient and therapist toward greater tolerance of pathology, which in turn is probably related to acceptance of the geriatric patient's dependency. Hollender has stressed this factor, venturing that, "Perhaps the best explanation for the fact that analysis is not a procedure for people in their fifties and over is that there is not enough to hope for in the future to provide the motivation needed to endure the tensions mobilized by analysis."

Also to be seriously considered in this regard is the emotional price paid when a patient reviews the failures of his past. It must be exceedingly difficult for a person nearing death to look back upon the bulk of his life as having been neurotic or maladjusted. It is this consideration that led Grotjahn to suggest that it was important for the aged person to integrate his past life experiences as they have been lived, not as they might have been lived.

Abraham offered the first note of optimism regarding the analysis of the aged. He described the successful analysis of four neurotic patients about fifty years of age and concluded that ". . . the age of the neurosis is more important than the age of the patient."

Another of the early analysts to deal extensively with geriatric problems was Jelliffee, who echoed Abraham's thinking with the statement that "chronological, physiological, and psychological age do not go hand in hand." Armed with this dictum, Jelliffee proceeded with seemingly orthodox analyses of several older patients, and he published a description of several remarkably successful cases. But along with the successes, Jelliffee frankly related that in many cases ". . . the neurosis or psychosis was a better solution of their life difficulties than any that I, as an agent of reality, could offer." Fenichel has more recently re-emphasized this caution as an important consideration in deciding upon the feasibility of psychoanalysis for aged patients. In contrast to more contemporary analysts like Alexander and French, to be discussed shortly, Jelliffee seemed most concerned with the suitability of the patient for the existing treatment, i.e., orthodox psychoanalysis, rather than considering modifications of his method. In this regard, he stressed the emotional fiber of the patient. "At one time I was even as brave as a lion in the belief that 'some acquaintance with the patient's unconscious would be of benefit to him in the treatment of his annoying symptoms.' Now I am much more inclined to tell my older patients that disease symptoms, physical often as well as psychical, are for the most part intuitively found compensations for inner character defects; that if psychoanalytic principles be rigorously applied their most cherished beliefs and fundamental philosophies, and their consequent emotional valuations will be quite profoundly stirred and they will not like it; that they will probably curse me out and call me a quack or a shyster, but if they have real guts and can look themselves fairly and firmly in the face then much can be done for them."

In contrast to the criteria of analyzable patients suggested by the above writers, Kaufman has more recently described a fairly successful outcome for two patients who, according to more traditional thinking, were relatively inaccessible on two counts; both patients were not only over fifty-five years of age, but were also in psychotic depressions when treatment was initiated. While Kaufman was quite cautious about making extensive generalizations on the basis of these two cases, he did venture that neither analysis was in any way complicated, and he felt that the relatively rapid change he observed in short periods did not sustain the contention that in older patients long periods of treatment are necessary before any changes take place. In a later paper dealing mainly with psychoanalytic theories of the aging process, Kaufman further questioned Freud's early views concerning the rigid ego of the aged. Kaufman observed that rather than being an immutable constant, "The rigidity seems to be a type of dissociation and the lack of elasticity really expresses a deeper repression of the anxieties with an increasing fixity of the reaction formations originally laid down as character traits." In a discussion appended to Kaufman's last-mentioned paper, Atkin expounded on this theme. Accepting Kaufman's suggestion that the rigidity is an ego defense, Atkin further ventured that it might be psychoanalytically treated as one might treat other defensive operations, rather than accepting it as an irreversible physiological impairment.

While earlier writers had called attention to the fact that their successes with geriatric patients were often in the nature of "transference cures," Grotjahn, in his discussion of the pychoanalytic investigation of a seventy-one year old man with senile dementia, was the first to give strong emphasis to the real immediate needs the analyst was called upon to fill in the life of the geriatric patient. He wrote: "Not only is the senile person's relationship to reality changed by his psychotic withdrawal, but the reality situation itself is fundamentally changed by the biological and social dependence and helplessness of an old man. This fact and the genital impotence of old age make the analytic situation similar to the child analysis. In both, the analyst is not a more or less unreal image, but a vivid active part of reality engaged in the management of the patient's hospital life." With these remarks, Grotjahn seems to have anticipated the development of modified analytic techniques in the treatment of the aged.

## MODIFIED PSYCHOANALYTIC TECHNIQUES

Alexander dealt with the problem of the treatability of the aged within the scope of the general problem of treatability. In his discussion of modern modified, analytic techniques he delineated two broad types of treatment—insight therapy and supportive therapy. He spelled out the essence of insight therapy as the extension of ego control over previously repressed impulses which are released in the course of therapy. But where, for a variety of reasons, the ego is weak, then it is unreasonable to encourage release of impulses, since the ego will not be able to control them. In these cases the patient is given supportive therapy, where the patient's need for assistance is answered by actual guidance; where inferiority feelings are met with reassurance; where anxiety is relieved by the therapist's assuming a protective role; and where guilt is relieved by permissive attitudes. It is within the context of the above information that Alexander discussed the management of aged patients. While he did not state it explicitly, the implications of his approach clearly suggest that a primary consideration in treatment of the aged should be the degree of ego strength available. For example, he discussed the cases of two men, one sixty years and the other sixty-six, who came to him shortly after their retirement from business careers. In the case of the younger man, the patient's handling of trial interpretations indicated a weakened ego-integrative capacity which, combined with other factors in the case, prompted a decision not to treat the patient. In contrast, the older client showed a more constructive handling of trial interpretations, and therapy was undertaken and successfully pursued.

In another work, Alexander and French emphasized another important factor. They suggested that therapy usually implies some change in the life situation, and where no such change is possible, therapy may be contraindicated. While the authors were careful to point out that advanced age is not an absolute contraindication, they suggested that "prognosis is better for the young who have a far greater opportunity for change and who, therefore, usually respond more readily to treatment." (It is not clear from this formulation whether the possibility of change is important because external change helps the therapy along, or because therapy is to little avail without the possibility of external change.)

Fenichel has been more explicit on this point. He suggested that in difficult living situations or where the patient was physically ill or crippled, the neurosis itself still may provide the best type of adjustment. Hollender has also elaborated on this theme with the following caution: "When a person has turned to the past or developed fixed ways of doing things to derive narcissistic gratifications or to protect against injuries to self-esteem, we should *not* tamper with these defenses unless we are sure that we can provide adequate substitutes for them."

With the path opened by Alexander and French for a frankly supportive type of analytic therapy, it remained for new workers in the area to give special attention to an elaboration of modified analytic techniques with the aged. Wayne has written on this topic and has offered the following suggestions: 1) Enough historical material is gained to permit a psychodynamic formulation and an understanding of transference behavior. "In the early interviews the patient's productions are guided by appropriate but unobtrusive questions in order to limit tangential material." 2) "Goal limitation is decided upon from the outset, as soon as an appraisal of the patient and his difficulties is made." 3) A crucial current problem may be used as the mainstream of therapy and can serve to keep the patient from feeling that therapy is becoming tangential by keeping in focus the problems he consciously recognizes. While material is not deliberately avoided, no attempts are made to rekindle old conflicts even though they may not have been handled in an entirely healthy manner. 4) The therapist's role relatively active, not only in directing the course of therapy, but also in providing reassuring discussion, guidance, and even environmental manipulations where indicated. 5) The vis-a-vis position is used to decrease anxiety, promote a feeling of being understood, minimize overdependence, and lessen the quantity of repressive material. 6) "The patient must be given a readily perceivable part in solving his own problems." Some direct educational techniques may be used, such as realistic discussions of the cultural attitude toward the elderly and the physiology of the aging process. 8) Scheduling is flexible, and the general plan is to progressively decrease the number of weekly sessions. Therapy need not be finally terminated. "Tranquility—the goal of old age living, and the actual biologically quieter tempo of life can be accepted and expressed tacitly in the flexibility and wide spacing of interviews, as well as in the therapeutic atmosphere."

Meerloo is another contemporary writer whose comments reflect the changed outlook of psychoanalysts toward the aged. Meerloo has displayed a persistent optimism on the subject and has offered several suggestions to the therapist treating the elderly. Like Wayne, he has emphasized the need for education, environmental modification (which he views as being largely the role of the home-visiting social worker), indeterminate termination, and a gentle handling of resistance. Like Grotjahn, he has called attention to the real, immediate way in which the therapist has to fill a need for interpersonal relationships which are otherwise missing in the patient's life. In contrast to Freud, who saw geriatric rigidity as precluding successful analysis of the elderly; and in contrast to Kaufman and Atkin, who saw the rigidity as a defense to be dealt with therapeutically, Meerloo spoke of a decreased resistiveness in the aged. He explained that there is less resistance, ". . . because approaching death presses them unconsciously to a reviewing of life and a comparison between early goals and actual achievements. My impression is that because of the weakening defenses, there is a better and more direct contact with the unconscious. Older patients react more easily to interpretations and feel more easily relieved by relating the actual conflicts with those of the past." Grotjahn has taken a similar view, observing that ". . . resistance against unpleasant insight is frequently lessened in old age. Demands of reality which in younger people are considered narcissistic threats may finally become acceptable. . . . It seems as if more or less suddenly resistance is weakened and insight occurs, just because it is 'high time.' "

Meerloo has offered an explanation for a supportive approach with geriatric patients which is not inconsistent with his observation of decreased resistance in these same patients. He reasoned that the very weakness of the defenses which made it possible to reach the patient's unconscious also made it more difficult to diminish ties with the therapist. This is a challenging thought—that the older person is *too* open to self-examination. It seems to stand in fundamental disagreement with the experience of the majority of therapists who have spoken of the excessive needs of the aged patients to cling to a self-concept developed over a lifetime. The two points of view can, of course, be partly reconciled by viewing the rigidity as a defense against the excessive contact with the unconscious. Such a reconciliation, however, seems to obscure essential differences in the two points of view. For example, the overt behavior of geriatric patients is seen by one group of therapists as stubborn failure to consider oneself differently; and by the other group, as excessive self-examination. There is little doubt that some older patients are more open to self-inspection than some younger patients, and that some older patients are less open to self-inspection. However, it is not possible for older persons taken as a group to be at the same time both more and less open to self-inspection than younger persons, unless one is willing to hypothesize two distinctly different types of self-inspection. Therefore, the relative accessibility of insight to older people remains a major issue for geriatric psychotherapy.

Before leaving this point, it is of interest to note that in a more recent article Meerloo has observed that old people often show lessened suggestibility. He interpreted this positively, commenting that "Old age may represent a mental stability and continuity correcting the innate ambivalence and vacillation of man." To draw a composite, then, of the traits of elderly patients as Meerloo has described them, the picture is one of an individual who is ready to examine himself honestly and who has an inner stability that makes him resistant to suggestion. While these traits are by no means incompatible, the question arises whether Meerloo was more interested in picturing the most positive attributes of some geriatric patients or an overview of what is most characteristic.

With regard to transference dynamics in geriatric psychotherapy, Meerloo has, along with several other therapists, noted the frequent formulations of the reverse-transference, i.e., the patient views the therapist as his child. Meerloo has described one case in which such a reverse-transference was not discouraged but utilized to further the therapy.

Although he stands as another of the contemporary analytic writers who propose the use of modified techniques and goals in the treatment of the aged, Hollender seems to hold a much more reserved point of view than Meerloo. In fact, except for the advocacy of supportive techniques, Hollender seems to have taken a fairly traditional psychoanalytic view of the problem. For example, on the topic of rigidity, Hollender has written of the increased resistance to change and the increased difficulty in new learning with advancing age. Unlike Kaufman and Atkin, who have stressed its defensive aspect, Hollender has tended to view the rigidity as a more normal change—as both a physical and mental entrenchment which should be accepted by therapists as appropriate regearing, in much the same way as a move to a warmer climate might be considered beneficial. "Only when it [the entrenchment] is out of keeping with the real situation should it be regarded as an expression of an emotional difficulty." Except for the advocacy of supportive techniques, Hollender has remained in essential agreement with Freud. This is revealed in Hollender's concluding remarks on the topic, which express a view fairly representative of many contemporary practitioners toward geriatric psychotherapy: "In summary, it may be stated that while uncovering types of therapy can seldom, if ever, be used with older people, supportive forms of treatment selected on the basis of a sound evaluation can accomplish much by helping to re-establish an emotional balance that has been shaken by the stresses of the latter years of life."

It is of interest to note that although Hollender and Meerloo appear to differ in their view of older patients and in their theoretical formulations, both advocate seemingly similar treatment techniques, i.e., support and a gentle handling of resistance. Hollender differs with Meerloo with regard to the interpretation of the reverse-transference. Hollender has ventured that, "The aged individual feels toward the therapist as he feels toward an adult son or daughter—but a son or daughter who would be like a parent to him."

Weinberg is still another of the contemporary psychoanalysts who have proposed modified techniques in the treatment of the aged. He has advised that allowances be made for the possibility of unduly disturbing those patients who have severe psychosomatic conditions; and that allowances be made also for the reduced vigor, agility, and learning capacity of the aged. Like Wayne, he has also suggested that the therapist be relatively active and direct in the treatment of older people.

Lawton has proposed that psychotherapy with older persons "differs only in degree, not kind, from that employed with younger age groups. No new principles or techniques of therapy need to be involved, though old ones need to be modified." This generality has frequently been made about geriatric psychotherapy, but it appears to have little communicative value in itself, i.e., it depends largely on where one is willing to draw the line between what is a "modification" and what is "new." Lawton has also proposed that prognostic indicators for older persons are the same as for younger persons, but that fewer older persons "will qualify as suitable candidates for thorough-going psychological help as they get older." He has estimated that successful psychotherapy is possible with about 25 per cent of those older persons applying for therapeutic help, but he has not elaborated upon the kind of patients, type of therapy, criteria of success, or control observations which may or may not have entered into his estimation. While Lawton believes that psychoanalysis may be indicated for some older people, he stands with those who believe that more "superficial" approaches are generally indicated with the aged.

Lawton has contributed some clarification of the "rigidity" issue in geriatric psychotherapy by classifying the rigidity of older people into the following four types: 1) the diminished capacity for new learning which is based upon largely irreversible physiological changes; 2) the "rut formation" which develops through the continued practice of old habits; 3) the "protective" rigidity against change which is involved as a defense against fear; 4) the compulsive rigidity of perfectionistic persons. He has sketched out what must be accomplished to combat the various types of rigidity, although the explicit means of doing so was not always made apparent. In a discussion of attitudes toward geriatric psychotherapy, Lawton has pointed out that one of the reasons why older persons are reluctant to enter this kind of treatment is that they grew up at a time when psychotherapy was not widely accepted by laymen.

Lawton has also discussed the need for training in geriatric psychotherapy. While he has not gone so far as to propose specific training programs or procedures, he has noted some of the skills which need to be developed in geriatric psychotherapy; e.g., learning to differentiate between irreversible and reversible reactions, between true depressions and reactive depressions, and between repeated neurotic patterns and reactions to reality situations. Lawton's writings leave the impression that he fights as an ally at the side of the geriatric patient against the vicissitudes of reality, the unrelenting biological forces of decline, and the depreciating attitudes of society. In contrast to therapy with younger patients where one senses a pattern of continuing reaction and counter-reaction between patient and therapist, therapy with older patients often involves a sense of patient and therapist struggling together against forces hostile to both of them. Thus Lawton says, "Those who wish to aid older persons with their adjustments need the greatest amount of training and experience in learning how to help the older individual outwit and circumvent adverse community regulations and attitudes."

In contrast to those who have tended to minimize the importance of psychotherapy for the elderly, Lawton pointed out that the aged are often in highest positions of leadership, and as such, the consequences of their mental health are important for the rest of society.

Cutner has provided an extremely interesting account of a sixty-three year old neurotic woman who was treated by Jungian methods. Of special interest were Cutner's introductory remarks concerning the psychoanalysis of the aged. Following the teachings of Jungian psychology, she proposed that whereas the normal concerns of the first half of life are entrenchment in the outer world and the propagation and care of children, the task of the second half of life is individuation—the introversion of libido in the service of discovering and integrating the heretofore unconscious parts of the psyche. Of particular significance here is the contrast with the apparent goals of Freudian therapy. By comparison, the Freudians appear much more oriented toward youth, i.e., the emphasis is on contact with reality, affectual contact with other people, and productivity. Thus, for example, many Freudians see therapy with the aged pessimistically because of the decreased opportunity for libidinal gratification for these patients. For the Jungian psychologist, the task for the aged person has a merit of its own. Old age is the time of life for a person to come to know himself, rather than merely to attempt a reconciliation with an environment in which he has difficulty achieving the most desired forms of productivity and emotional fulfillment. While contact with the unconscious is a most important method for the Freudian, the method is directed largely toward the goals of youth. For the Jungian, contact with the unconscious becomes the goal itself.

Thus, while contemporary psychoanalysts have tended to think in terms of limited goals, Cutner's paper raises the question of *different* goals. This point has been most recently raised by Grotjahn who, although himself a Freudian, said, "The task of integrating one's life as it has been lived and the final acceptance of one's own death are problems of existence. To deal with them is the great task of old age. They are essentially different from the tasks of infancy, childhood, adolescence, and maturity."

To summarize thus far, the history of the psychoanalytic movement in regard to treating geriatric patients may be seen as having started with Freud's pessimism, a pessimism which was shortly thereafter mitigated by the initial attempts and successes of analysts like Abraham and Jelliffe. Through these early years, the keynote of analytic treatment of the aged was that chronological age did not of necessity involve a deterioration of those intellectual and emotional capacities required for analysis, and hence *some* older persons could successfully undergo orthodox treatment. Later, the general evolution of modified analytic techniques under the guidance of Alexander and French prompted explorations of new approaches which would be applicable to a wide variety of geriatric problems. Therapists like Grotjahn, Wayne, Meerloo, Hollender, Weinberg, and Lawton used modified analytic approaches to the treatment of the aged, approaches which stress support and the active participation of the therapist. Still, as Hollender has suggested, there is no intrinsic contradiction between the early pessimism of Freud and the active efforts of contemporary psychoanalysts toward treating older patients. Freud was pessimistic in regard to treatment by orthodox methods toward a psychoanalytically ideal goal of bringing repressed material to conscious awareness and control, in order to attain greater libidinal satisfaction in reality. Whenever modified approaches have been attempted, they have generally been modified either in accord with more limited goals, or with the support of defenses, or they have relied upon direct intervention and environmental modification by the therapist. To the extent that these modifications are brought to bear, the pessimism of Freud concerning more ideal goals still obtains. A Jungian approach, on the other hand, has raised some new considerations regarding the goals of geriatric psychotherapy.

Several unresolved issues still pervade psychoanalytic thinking, then, many of which may be amenable to research. To restate some of them briefly, there are questions regarding intellectual efficiency, capacity for insight, motivation for and resistance to change, opportunity for libidinal gratification, and the choice of goals. Since these are questions which, in the main, confront the whole field of geriatric psychotherapy, these questions will be raised again in the last part of this paper.

## GOLDFARB'S BRIEF THERAPY

While the approach of Goldfarb is based largely on psycho-analytic thinking, it is, more than any other approach, specifically oriented to the aged; and it has evolved in such organized form that it is deserving of separate attention. It is a therapy, furthermore, used with the brain-damaged aged who, in Goldfarb's view, present a most important and most difficult problem in the area of geriatric psychotherapy. Working in a home for the aged, Goldfarb and his associates have devoted themselves to the development of a practicable individual psychotherapy for their clients, so that, judging from the literature, they stand among the most experienced workers in the area. In comparison to the one or two therapy cases discussed by most of the previously-mentioned writers, Goldfarb and his associates speak from experience with over 100 cases, more than two dozen of which are individually reviewed among their several published articles.

While it is true the very nature of brief therapy allows for an easier accumulation of case material, the very accumulation reflects the fact that geriatric psychotherapy has reached a certain level of maturity—for not more than a decade ago therapy with a person over sixty-five was generally viewed as a somewhat novel experiment. Now, in the "Brief Therapy" of Goldfarb, there is at least one approach that is something more than an extension of an old technique to a new population. It stands as a landmark in geriatric psychotherapy, for it has developed from a formulation of the crucial problems of the aged, from a consideration of the resources older people are likely to bring to a therapeutic relationship, and from an appraisal of the practical problems involved in the geriatric treatment situation.

The major point of departure for Goldfarb is the dependency of the aged, dependency which in much the same way as earlier writers, he attributes to somatic changes, intellectual impairment, and socio-economic and personal losses. However, whereas previous writers have generally responded in one of three ways, i.e., either with discouragement as to what few resources remain for therapeutic work, by promoting acceptance of the dependency, or by providing real gratification for dependency needs, Goldfarb has deliberately attempted to use the increased dependency of the aged as a therapeutic resource.

Reasoning that the increased dependency makes the older person especially prone to view the therapist as a parent-figure, Goldfarb attempts to encourage this misperception to the extent that the patient develops the illusion that he is actually dealing with a very powerful parental authority who is capable of wielding great influence in his life. Once the illusion is firmly established, it is then used to provide gratification of emotional needs for punishment, affection, respect, and protection. Goldfarb claims substantial success with his techniques even though contacts are usually extremely brief, i.e., five- to fifteen-minute interviews once a week or less.

In his brief interviews, Goldfarb attempts to give the patient the feeling that a protective parent has been found. While little in the way of explicit, concrete aid is given in these sessions (Goldfarb at the same time emphasizes that in a wide variety of disorders, other types of therapy must accompany the psychotherapy) the therapist apparently behaves in such a manner as to leave the implication that such help can be forthcoming. With the patient who had never been able passively to enjoy a dependent position and who characteristically had to fight with others to gain gratification, Goldfarb attempts (partly by granting him small concessions) to create in him the feeling of having triumphed over the parent and therefore of having won control of the resources of gratification.

Several positive aspects of Goldfarb's approach immediately appear: 1) The therapy takes into account the increased dependency of the aged and hence, unlike some other approaches, it makes little demand for creative emotional resources within the patient.

2) The therapy is carried out almost entirely on the level of relationship, so that there is little demand for the intellectual resources which are required by insight and introspective therapies. Thus, the intellectual intactness of the patient becomes of relatively minor concern as compared to most other therapies. 3) The therapy is not structured in terms of self-reappraisal, so that many of the defensive resistances ordinarily stirred by psychiatric attention are circumvented. 4) The therapeutic regime is practical in terms of the amount of the therapist's time involved with each patient. 5) According to Goldfarb, the brevity also makes the therapy more practical from the point of view of the patient with shortened life expectancy.

On the other hand, there are objections to Goldfarb's approach. In a discussion appended to a paper by Goldfarb and Sheps, Stieglitz has commented, "Notably lacking was any voluntary effort and any encouragement toward a *mastery of self*. The patient's self-esteem was bolstered by deliberately cultivating the illusion of victorious mastery over the parent-surrogate therapist and others. So far as I can detect, the therapist did not transmit any of his interest and desire to be helpful to the patients so that they might wish to help others in their intimate community and thereby enrich their sterile lives with purposefulness. True and constructive satisfactions can be developed, though perhaps not as quickly or easily as illusions can be fostered."

Certain of Stieglitz's objections seem of secondary importance. His objection to the lack of encouragement toward "mastery of self," might be countered with the argument that while therapists tend to agree that there is a quality, or faculty, of self-directedness in people, there is no widespread agreement as to how self-directedness is achieved. It does not seem unreasonable that even though Goldfarb's approach begins with the encouragement of an illusion, the resulting relief from tension and unhappiness might serve to liberate self-mastery in the patient. Certainly this argument seems as plausible as the suggestion that self-mastery can be attained by a therapist's "encouraging it." If anything, modern therapeutic practice has evolved as a reaction against the apparent unproductivity of the "pull yourself together" approach to emotional disorders.

Stieglitz objected that Goldfarb's approach does not make patients socially productive. Yet patients who have the illusion of being well protected, or the illusion of being in control of the sources of gratification, may feel well enough endowed themselves to be able to turn their attention to helping others. Goldfarb has reported instances where patients become more helpful in the institution following brief therapy.

There nevertheless remain certain potential weaknesses in Goldfarb's approach. While no data are available for comparing the results of brief therapy with those of other approaches, it would appear on rational grounds alone that:

1. Since the therapist becomes such a potent productive figure in the mind of the patient, it is possible that the patient may interpret the occurrence of difficulties in his everyday life as a sign of a waning of the therapist's interest or power. This could serve to magnify distress or to send the patient scurrying back repeatedly to the therapist for reassurance. Goldfarb, while pointing out that "success breeds success," and while reporting averages of only five to nine treatment sessions for various groups of patients, does go on to report: "However, when the defects of resources are so great as in the brain-damaged aged person, it cannot be expected that realistic mastery can continuously take place and the cycle cannot be self-perpetuating. Then the psychotherapeutic effort must be a continuous or recurrent reinforcing technique." Thus it would appear that in Goldfarb's own experience, continuous reinforcement has been necessary only with the patients who have minimal resources.

2. The efficacy of brief therapy may be somewhat limited to institutional settings where the psychiatrist's position on the staff gives him real power with which to enhance and perpetuate the illusion to be fostered; where the therapist can be on hand whenever reinforcement of the illusion is necessary; where problems of referral, motivation for treatment, and accumulation of diagnostic information are minimal; and where reports from institutional personnel can substitute for the extended periods of appraisal of therapeutic progress which would be required in out-patient treatment.

3. The solution that is based upon illusion is nonreactive to

the original source of difficulty, difficulty which may continue to stand as a potential threat to the patient or those around him. The facility with which it can be administered threatens to seduce therapists into using this approach, even where the potential for realistic solution by the patient, therapist, or societal forces is still substantial.

It is difficult to assess the present status of Goldfarb's approach among geriatric psychotherapies. There has been little discussion of it in the literature by those outside Goldfarb's immediate group. While many therapists may use similar methods, it is doubtful that many of them do so with Goldfarb's conceptual framework clearly in mind. In comparison with other approaches, it must be said that Goldfarb's concept of geriatric treatment is relatively straightforward. Two major issues need resolution. First is the question of the efficacy of the treatment; and while Goldfarb has presented figures describing the relative percentage of successful and unsuccessful cases, his methods of evaluation lack certain controls that would lead to undisputed acceptance of his conclusions. Second, there is the question of the long-term wisdom, irrespective of immediate gains, of using an approach based upon the creation of an illusion.

## OTHER APPROACHES

There are several therapists whose work with aged patients does not seem to fit clearly into one or another "school" of therapy, or whose reports have been more in the nature of comments on geriatric psychotherapy rather than developments of systematic approaches.

Noting that old people are often confused, failing in memory, and suffering from sensory impairments, Stieglitz campaigned for clarity and simplicity in giving the patient instructions "on how to live." While Stieglitz appeared to take a paternal or "expert" role in instructing his patients, the stated rationale of his approach seems very different from that of Goldfarb. For example, Stieglitz emphasized, ". . . let us be honest. Mature individuals accept reality far better than the young. They are entitled to honesty, and they are entitled to be told that there are limitations on what can be accomplished. We should not promise more than what we have a right to expect." In general, Stieglitz's was a teacher-student relationship to patients, with the therapist providing the patient with clear, concise, "honest," information on how to live a healthy life. While his intent and stated methods appear to be very different from those of Goldfarb, similar factors may be involved in both approaches. For example, beyond the specific information given them, Stieglitz's patients must have derived considerable comfort from the feeling that an authoritative father-figure was interested in them.

Offenkrantz has made some points similar to those of Goldfarb. He has suggested that the geriatric patient needs the same things from the therapist that a child needs from his parent, i.e., a dependent relationship and the feeling of being appreciated, cared for, and important. In similar fashion to Goldfarb, Offenkrantz has ventured that the therapist could allow those old people who have never learned consciously to enjoy dependent relationships to be quarrelsome, demanding, contentious, and unconsciously dependent.

The approach of Rockwell was based largely on the technique of distributive analysis and synthesis advocated by Adolph Meyer. Rockwell explained the approach as follows: "This consists of an analysis of all the factors involved, starting from the complaint, and taking into consideration the psychodynamic and somatic features, the situational conditions, and the constitutional make-up. Each interview is terminated with a constructive formulation synthesizing the material covered. The analysis is distributed along the lines suggested by a careful anamnesis and by the subjective needs of the patient as they become apparent during treatment. The physician assumes full obligation for the twenty-four hour day of the patient and utilizes data collected currently by nurses or other observers." While Rockwell placed great emphasis on understanding the total life situation of the patient, he gave little explanation of how such understanding is to be utilized. Much use was made of manipulation of the situational setting, drugs, and diet, but Rockwell gave no description of a general rationale underlying the management of the psychotherapy itself.

If there is any general characteristic of Rockwell's approach which distinguishes it from others, it is that it seems to rest heavily on the repression of disturbing material. For example, in discussing the hostile patient, Rockwell proposed that ". . . it is helpful to discuss neutral topics and to avoid contradictions and arguments." In proposing occupational therapy for apathetic patients, Rockwell noted that one of the beneficial effects of reviving an old interest of the patient's was that it provided "a good neutral topic for discussion." With regard to sexuality, the comment was made, "The analysis of sexual dynamic factors in the more sweeping types of personality disorders, if indicated at all, is carried out cautiously during the period of convalescence." This last quote reflects another prominent, although implicit feature of Rockwell's approach, i.e., the tendency to avoid direct psychotherapeutic attack upon severe pathology. It is as though acute symptoms were viewed as storms to be weathered, rather than to be treated. Thus, "Any attempt to study the dynamic factors involved in the attitude of aversion should be delayed until the psychosis in which it occurs has disappeared."

Mittleman has discussed psychotherapy with geriatric patients who suffer from psychosomatic disorders. He delineated two types of psychosomatic disorders: 1) Those which are not related to the aging process as such, and are therefore similar to psychosomatic disorders which might occur at any age; and 2) those which represent aggravations of and reactions to functional and structural disturbances connected with aging. With the first group, Mittelman suggested that psychoanalytic treatment could proceed in much the same fashion as with similar disorders in any age group. He held that prognosis was generally as favorable here as with younger patients, especially with those older patients who came for consultation and who agreed to treatment. Where the psychological disorder was related to organic malfunction associated with aging, e.g., coronary disease and hypertension, Mittelman advised that psychotherapy should proceed concomitantly with medical treatment, or, if the patient had had a severe organic attack, then psychotherapy should proceed as soon as convalescence sets in. In this latter group of patients, Mittleman has advised more caution in dealing with any topic likely to cause an emotional crisis lest the physical condition be aggravated. Within the limits of this caution,

Mittelman expressed optimism with regard to reducing the functional features of the disorder. He was much more pessimistic when organic brain damage was involved. In this regard he ventured that the most that could be done was to decrease the patient's irritability and moodiness through use of the transference relationship, and that a major reliance would have to be placed upon environmental modifications, drugs, and institutionalization.

Cameron presented what are perhaps the most convincing arguments regarding the presence and etiology of rigidity and intellectual impairment of the aged. In contrast to writers who have spoken of instances of flexibility and unimpaired intelligence in individual geriatric patients, Cameron has cited evidence from experimental research to show that old people, as a group, show inflexibility and intellectual impairment. While granting that personal defensiveness and adjustive factors are involved in the old person's resistance to change. Cameron has emphasized that ". . . quite apart from personal and emotional involvement, there are certain inevitable deficiencies in performance with age which are dependent upon cellular and humoral changes. These have been shown to affect impersonal as well as personal activities, unemotional attitudes as well as emotional. Older persons often place greater reliance upon already fixed habitual attitudes and routines for the simple reason that they are incapable of learning, retaining, and utilizing new ones without considerable effort, and even then only to a limited degree."

Cameron has proceeded to spell out the implications of this view for therapy as follows: "If a large proportion of older persons are biologically incapable of adapting successfully to certain kinds of novelty, and this can be determined for the individual case, it is of little use to attack the problem as primarily one of anxiety and inadequate repression. More of the attention and effort of the patient, the relatives, the social worker, and the therapist can then be focused upon the development of greater tolerance toward such incapacity on all sides and particularly on the part of the patient himself, and upon exploring the possibilities of ameliorating its effects through introducing more flexibility into the environmental arrangements."

There are other authors whose contributions to the literature on geriatric psychotherapy, while more limited in scope, are of interest here. Gitelson and Aldrich have discussed the role of medical practitioners in the management of emotional problems of old people. Lokshin, Herkimer, and Ryder have discussed social casework approaches to geriatric problems, pointing out advantages of counseling with several family members, especially the geriatric patient's grown children. Some general comments on the increase of optimism in the psychotherapeutic treatment of the aged were made by Ross. Brenman and Knight have given an especially interesting report of the successful treatment by hypnotherapy of a seventy-one year old woman suffering from hysterical psychosis.

Stern discussed work with the aged in an old age counseling center. Ginzberg stressed the use of environmental modification in psychological approaches to the aged. In this regard, he urged that, "If with younger individuals the main task is to help them adapt to environmental difficulties, it is the other way around with elderly patients—we must try to adapt the environment to them." One of the measures advocated by Ginzberg was that in cases where underlying factors were not clearly understood, the therapist should always side with the elderly person in any conflict with relatives or supervisors. Ginzberg has also written several articles discussing the maintenance of therapeutic attitudes in psychiatric geriatric wards. Aronson has discussed the same problem with reference to homes for the aged.

## GROUP APPROACHES

Group therapy with the aged will be dealt with only very briefly. Smith, Bryant, and Twitchell-Allen reported on a four week program of intensive resocializing activities for forty-three elderly psychotic women, and Silver reported on group psychotherapy with senile psychotic patients. Both studies claimed success in improving the behavior of patients.

Linden has provided the most extensive reports of group therapy procedures with the aged. Working with female patients in a state hospital, Linden provided data indicating that his procedures had been successful in improving behavior and in increasing rates of discharge from the hospital, although he was quick to point out the lack of control measures in his evaluations. There seems to be no single systematic approach in Linden's work. He himself has explained that, "Since it was found expedient to use almost every method of group approach at one time or another, the process came to be known as 'opportunistic group therapy.'" Of note was the use of the group sessions to provide real, immediate social satisfaction. For example, "Contrasting with traditional individual and group psychotherapy, an aura of serious effort was not regarded as a *sine qua non*. Every opportunity for light-hearted fun and laughter was exploited to the fullest." Linden's experience showed that usual group therapy methods of allowing topics of discussion to come from the patients were relatively ineffective with his aged female patients. Among the methods he used to stimulate the group were giving more or less didactic talks, calling on individual group members and questioning them about biographical items, chiding patients with good-humored sarcasm, and using a female co-therapist. In one of his papers Linden has presented an extensive discussion of the various transference reactions encountered in geriatric patients.

Rechtschaffen, Atkinson, and Freeman have described an intensive treatment program for geriatric patients in a state hospital where group and supportive individual therapy were utilized along with an organized ward program which included occupational, recreational, and work therapy approaches. The rate at which these patients were discharged from the hospital was increased by over 300 per cent following the initiation of the program, although it is difficult to determine how much of the increase in discharge rate resulted from the therapy *per se* and how much from the intensive effort to place patients out of the hospital whenever this was considered advisable. The results of a follow-up study, which showed no improvement on a behavior rating scale after treatment, would tend to support the hypothesis that the latter factor was the more important.

It is of some interest that more attention has been given to the systematic evaluation of therapeutic outcome among the group approaches as compared to the individual approaches, probably because group approaches lend themselves more readily to the accumulation of large samples and the establishment of control groups or base rates. This is true at least in institutional settings.

## COUNTERTRANSFERENCE PATTERNS

Various writers have discussed countertransference phenomena in geriatric psychotherapy, i.e., the emotional reactions of the therapist to the patient, and the topic appears important enough to warrant separate discussion.

Stern, Smith, and Frank called special attention to the anxiety aroused in the therapist by the unconscious identification with the helplessness of some older clients. Along with Meerloo, they spoke of the wounds to a therapist's narcissism that are involved in dealing with irreversible situations, e.g., the approaching death of a client. Stern, Smith, and Frank have also referred to countertransference attitudes of hostility and guilt, but they were less explicit in outlining the dynamic structure of these reactions.

Meerloo and Grotjahn discussed the anxiety that is aroused in dealing with the sexual problems of the aged. Meerloo observed that the same kind of resistance that Freud met in calling attention to sexuality in children is now being met with regard to the aged. Meerloo has elaborated on the confusion and shame that sexuality produces in the aged and has lamented that, "Even today medical countertransference often denies sexual gratification to the old." Grotjahn has written, "A therapist who wishes to be older than he is may hide unresolved sexual conflicts behind such a wish. He hopes in an unrealistic way that the old persons will live beyond sin and sex, like little angels. Such a therapist may not be tolerant and realistic enough to understand his elderly patients in one of their most important sources of conflict, guilt, and depression."

Much of countertransference in geriatric psychotherapy has to be understood in terms of the "reversed transference" constellation, i.e., the tendency of the older patient to view the therapist as his son. Since many of the therapist's reactions will undoubtedly be in response to such a perception of himself by the patient, some additional remarks on the reversed transference itself may be in order at this point.

Grotjahn has provided the most extensive discussion of the reversed transference. He sees it as the Oedipus complex, from the father's point of view; and he advises that it be allowed to develop, and that it be interpreted and integrated into the entire experience of the patient, in much the same way that Meerloo has proposed. Grotjahn's remarks on this topic are of such theoretical significance as to warrant the following extensive quotations:

"The patient is allowed to see in the therapist the younger person. He may later accept in his therapist the representative of the younger generation and perhaps of the future. It was once the task of the son to work out his conscious and unconscious relations to his parents. It is now time for the father to go once more through his unconscious relation to another man in reversed order. In relation to the therapist, he has once more the chance and task to analyze in the transference relationship the Oedipus complex, but this time in reverse. The father should not submit to the son, nor should he kill him like the father of Oedipus tried to do. The father should realize that his life may be continued in his son."

Important in the context of the present discussion are the countertransference reactions to the reversed transference. Once again, to quote Grotjahn:

"The good son-therapist should not feel guilty for being younger. If necessary, he may develop an almost paternal attitude. He must be secure enough to withstand the onslaught of the older patient's hostility and [the patient's] attempt to make the younger man feel guilty and defensive for being younger."

Wayne is another who has discussed the countertransference patterns of avoidance and irritation that may result when unresolved hostility toward parental figures is projected onto the elderly patient.

Grotjahn has also written about countertransference attitudes which may be based upon earlier relationships with grandparents.

This discussion of countertransference leads to the question of the extent to which theorizing about geriatric psychotherapy may be influenced by such countertransference attitudes. For example, some of the resistance to working with the aged may stem from anxiety aroused in therapists by dependency needs of aged patients.

Giving help to an aged patient may be avoided because it symbolizes the relinquishment of dependency claims by the therapist himself. If we are caring for the parent, who remains to care for us? It is also possible that the anxiety aroused by hostility toward parent figures may lead to a watering down of the therapeutic process and to an exaggerated emphasis on supportive and covering-over procedures. Defending against his own anxiety, a therapist may propose only the most benign interpretations, and may assume an attitude of reverence toward an older patient that is out of keeping with the patient's actual readiness to examine himself. The question might even be asked, does the emphasis on supportive measures for older patients in part represent a tendency to provide a less valued form of therapy for a less valued segment of the population?

## SUMMARY AND DISCUSSION

From a historical perspective, psychotherapy with the aged had a slow, pessimistic beginning. Then, as interest in the area developed, there was a wave of optimism about how accessible older people are to psychotherapy and about how much can be accomplished. In retrospect, much of this optimism seems to have been exaggerated, perhaps largely as a reaction to the previous neglect of mental health in older people. At present a more considered attitude seems to prevail, with several investigators attempting to develop concepts of geriatric psychotherapy consistent with clinical and experimental observations of the resources and limitations of the aged. The actual practice of geriatric psychotherapy is not as extensive as psychotherapy with younger patients, but considering population trends, the prevalence of maladjustment in the aged, and current attempts to change cultural attitudes toward the elderly, it would not be surprising if, before long, psychotherapy might be as widely applied to old people as it is today to children.

As we have observed, there are divergent conceptions of geriatric psychotherapy; yet there appears to be a general trend developing in actual practice. Although there are exceptions, current thinking seems weighted toward the belief that most older persons, as compared with younger, profit most from supportive approaches in which the therapist plays a more active role. Therapeutic approaches might be arranged along a continuum of the degree of patient participation, as follows: 1) insight approaches, 2) supportive approaches, 3) direct gratification and environmental modification, 4) illusion-of-mastery therapy.

In general, the trend has been to use approaches toward the last-named end of the continuum with the following characteristics of the aged being offered as reasons: the increased dependency which arises from realistically difficult circumstances; the immodifiability of external circumstances to which a neurosis may be an optimal adjustive mechanism; irreversible impairments of intellectual and learning ability; resistance (or lack of resistance) to critical self-examination; the economics of therapeutic investment when life expectancy is shortened. There is considerable disagreement as to what weight the various factors actually carry.

It will be readily agreed that older people vary greatly with regard to the strength of their internal and external resources. Some are intellectually alert and emotionally adventurous; others are obviously impaired. Some older persons have a number of choices open to them; others, for varying economic, physical, and social factors, are relatively frozen in a given situation. In view of such wide individual differences, it would be well for therapists to remain open to a variety of possible approaches to older patients. As a concomitant, it would be well to emphasize the potential contribution of diagnostic appraisals, including psychometric and social service evaluations, in deciding which approach it most feasible for which patient.

In a sense, the emphasis on individual differences begs important issues regarding what is most general or most characteristic of older people and what is usually the most effective treatment for them. There is no reason to discuss geriatric psychotherapy as distinct from any other psychotherapy, unless there is some assumption that there are, or should be, some distinctive features about it. Still the central issues and problems regarding those distinctive features remain unresolved. These unresolved issues may be enumerated as follows:

1. As is true for psychotherapy as a whole, systematic, con-

trolled studies of the effectiveness of various treatments of older people are still lacking. Ultimately, there must be empirical grounds for predicting which type of treatment will work best for which type of patient.

2. There is still debate as to the extent to which the impairments of intellect and learning ability in old people are determined by dynamic or by physiologic factors. As Cameron has noted, research evidence favors the latter. Some question remains as to whether the kind of intelligence and learning thus far studied experimentally is sufficiently similar to that involved in achieving self-insights to permit generalizations from the research to the therapy situation, but it would appear probable that a certain amount of generalizing from the test to the therapy situation is warranted.

3. There is a very active disagreement regarding the extent to which old people are open to self-examination. This problem should be amenable to research. It might be found that there is more variability among older than among younger persons, with impending death causing the frankest soul-searching in some aged patients, but causing massive denial in others.

4. Finally, there is the question of the goals of geriatric psychotherapy. The attainment of certain goals may be limited in very real and immediate ways by cultural attitudes. We refer now to the limitation that negative attitudes toward the aged in our society place upon the amount and kinds of happiness that can be achieved by old people. If, at best, social reality is cruel, what can therapy hope to accomplish? There is genuine despair when the therapist himself cannot visualize a happier life for the geriatric patient who is physically ill, mentally clouded, socially ostracized, and approaching death. When the values of our culture are largely those of productivity and vigor, what satisfactions can psychotherapy produce for the old person? This is more than a rhetorical question, for it may be the principal obligation of geriatric psychotherapy to investigate the gratifications that can be evolved for older persons. We are reminded of Eissler's pioneering explorations into the possible sources of libidinal gratification for the dying patient, a problem even more difficult than the one posed here. Per-

haps the greatest benefits to come from geriatric psychotherapy will be in its influence on the goals for the aged, rather than in the attempts to squeeze some happiness for old people out of the currently rejecting milieu.

## Chapter 6

# RELIGION, RECREATION, POLITICS, AND CRIME

## THE PERSONAL ADJUSTMENT OF THE OLDER PERSON IN THE CHURCH*

### Robert M. Gray

THE PURPOSE of this paper is to present the results of an investigation of the personal adjustment of older persons who are members of a church.[1] The study was directed toward determining the role of church experience with respect to personal adjustment of older persons and is an analysis of the aged members of two church groups in the Chicago area. The study is concerned with six pertinent questions: (1) Do older members in the church have less favorable personal adjustment than the younger members have? (2) Does the religious activity of the church member increase with age? (3) Do persons who are closely affiliated with the church have more favorable personal characteristics and engage in more activities than the nonclose members? (4) Is an aged person closely affiliated with the church better adjusted than a comparable individual less closely affiliated with the church? (5) What is the role of the older person in the church institution and how does he conceive of this role? (6) What is the value of the church experience to personal adjustment in old age?

*Revised version of a paper read at the joint annual meeting of the American Sociological Society and the Society for the Study of Social Problems, September 1955. The material for this article has been taken from the writer's unpublished doctoral dissertation, "A Study of the Personal Adjustment of the Older Person in the Church," University of Chicago, 1954. Reprinted by courtesy of *Sociology and Social Research*, Volume *41*:175-180, January, 1957.

1This study and the problems it investigates were in general suggested by the conceptual scheme on old age as developed by the Social Science Research Council as reported by Otto Pollak in *Social Adjustment in Old Age—A Research Planning Report* (New York: Social Science Research Council, 1948).

## SAMPLE AND FINDINGS

The study group was comprised of 565 members of the two church groups in the Chicago area. Two hundred and ninety-six members, fifty years of age and over, eventually took part in the study.

The present study employed a questionnaire, "Your Activities and Attitudes," which was developed and standardized by the Committee for the Study of Later Maturity of the University of Chicago and is used to measure personal adjustment of persons in later life. The schedule is comprised of two main sections called the Attitude and Activities Inventories. The validity of each section has been thoroughly tested and the schedule accepted as a satisfactory and reliable measure of personal adjustment in old age.[2] Forty-eight extensive personal interviews supplemented the questionnaire data.

*Age in Relation to Characteristics and Activities of Church Members.* The first major inquiry was directed toward determining if younger church members had more favorable personal characteristics and engaged in more activities than the older members, this being one reliable measure of personal adjustment.[3] We proceeded to develop information regarding this inquiry through an analysis of the data concerning both church groups, utilizing these thirty-one items. Our analysis of the church members with regard to this factor revealed that there were no important differences between the younger and older church members with respect to the proportion of each group having favorable personal characteristics and the percentage of members engaging in activities associated with good personal adjustment.

*Activity and Attitude Toward the Church in the Later Years.* The second section of the study had as its objective the analysis of the hypothesis that the religious activity of the church member increased and attitudes toward religion became more favorable

---

[2] R. S. Cavan, E. W. Burgess, R. J. Havighurst, and H. Boldhamer, *Personal Adjustment in Old Age* (Chicago: Science Research Associates, 1949).

[3] E. W. Burgess, "The Aged and Society in Industrial Relations," Champaign, Illinois (Research Association, Editor, Milton Derber, Twin City Publishing Company).

with age. This proposition was tested through an examination of several factors, contained in the Activities and Attitudes Schedule, which relate to the religious experience and church activities. Our analysis revealed approximately the same findings for both church groups for males and females. There were no differences between the younger and older men in either church group with respect to church activities and attitude toward religion. The women in both groups, except for two items, did not significantly differ. (They did differ in that older women read their Bibles more, in both church groups. The younger women in one group also tended to listen to church radio services more frequently than did the older females.) Other than these minor variations there were no noteworthy differences between the younger and older members.

*Closeness to the Church in Relation to Characteristics and Activities of Church Members.* The third phase of the study was to find out if members closely affiliated with the church have more favorable characteristics and engage in more activities than persons not so close to the church. The analysis reveals that there were minor differences between the close and nonclose members of Church A. The women differed in that the closely affiliated members tended to be more regular church attenders than did the nonclose persons. The close males also were more regular church attenders and more frequently reported having a feeling of economic security than did the nonclose males. These differences are relatively insignificant in that even if there were no personality differences in the two groups we should expect the close group to be better church attenders due to the inherent nature of the process by which the study group was subdivided into close and nonclose groups. One of the criteria used to divide the group was the church attendance factor. Therefore, this difference would exist, though there were no differences in personal adjustment. The only other difference was the feeling of economic security factor in which the males differed.

The investigation of the relation between degree of church affiliation and characteristics and activities in the Church B group revealed important differences concerning eleven of the thirty-one factors subjected to investigation. The data disclosed that the closely affiliated members reported significantly more favorable to these eleven inquiries than did the nonclose group.

We were able to conclude from the analysis of the thirty-one subsidiary propositions that the hypothesis, aged persons closely affiliated with the church will have more favorable personable characteristics and be more active than comparable individuals less closely affiliated with the church, is not true for the Church A study-group. There appears to be a positive relationship between favorable personable characteristics and activities and church affiliation in the Church B group in that persons maintaining close ties with churches tend to be more active and have more favorable characteristics than do nonclose members.

***Closeness to the Church and Personal Adjustment.*** The fourth section of the study was concerned with whether or not there was any relationship between personal adjustment and closeness to the church. The study had up to this point indicated the importance of the church experience to the lives of older persons, and the next step was to develop further information regarding the association between the degree of church affiliation and personal adjustment.

The analysis of the data disclosed that out of a total of 296 church members there were only five persons with "poor" adjustment, with the other 291 members reporting "good or average" adjustment for the two church groups. These developments, along with the disclosure that in one of our church groups members close to the church are better adjusted than nonclose members, would tend to give added evidence to the importance of the church experience in personal adjustment in old age.

One significant point merits mention, and that is that the same findings developed for both of our church groups when we used the Activity section and later the Attitude Scale, which gives added relevance to the reliability of our findings that reveal the importance of church membership to personal adjustment in old age.

***The Adjustment Value of the Church Experience.*** The fifth section of the study concerned the nature of the circumstances in the church that contribute to good adjustment in old age. Extensive use was made of materials acquired in personal interviews with forty-eight persons who had been selected to represent various age, sex, and closeness of church affiliation categories. The analysis of the interview materials disclosed that the church performs a valuable function in alleviating problems of old age and does contribute to good personal adjustment. First, it was found that the church experience tends to alleviate anxieties and fears concerning death through a provision of comfort and reassurance, since it was found that the church member's fear of death was diminished through a belief in an after-life which is fostered by the church teachings.

The analysis further revealed that the church offers to the individual an opportunity to participate in an atmosphere that is conducive to finding companionship and in continuing friendships that are sometimes ended in other spheres because of circumstances brought about by old age. A significant finding was that the church provides activities and an opportunity for its members to participate in a social environment in which the older person is welcomed, which is not necessarily the case in other social institutions in the community. The inquiry demonstrated that the church helps in adjustment to the death of one's spouse, which is one of the major problems of old age because it presents a crisis to which the individual must adjust. It was further found that the church offers support and encouragement in times of crisis and in dark days of life which are experienced at one time or another by most persons. Another finding was that an aged person's relationships continue in the church after the time of retirement, physical disability, or old age, even though associations with friends, co-workers, and relatives sometimes do not. A final contribution was that the church experience tends to satisfy some of the basic needs of its members, such as the need to be loved, to belong, to be useful, and tends to minimize feelings of loneliness which are so common among older persons.

The significant conclusion which developed in this section was that the church does perform a valuable function in alleviating problems of the older person and does contribute to good adjustment in old age.

**The Role of the Older Person in the Church.** In introducing the final phase of the study the analyses revealed that many older persons were experiencing dissatisfactions in their relationships with the younger members in the church. It was further found that this, together with other factors having their origin in old age, prevented the older person's relationship with the church from being as helpful to his adjustment to old age as it would if these conditions were not present.

The investigation revealed that many oldsters feel that they are being neglected in favor of the younger members. Some reported being pushed out of church jobs because of their age and being replaced by younger members. Others reported dissatisfactions and embarrassment encountered because they were unable to contribute financially to the church, due to reduced incomes typical of old age. It was found that not a few oldsters were discontent and staying away from the church because they couldn't afford to dress properly. Others were staying home because of the lack of suitable transportation and because in some cases they could not afford the fare on the streetcar or bus. As would be expected, one of the major reasons the subjects gave for slowing up in their church activities was because of the extent and severity of physical illness among older people.

It was further disclosed that many oldsters were unsatisfied with changes that have taken place in the church to which they had not been able to adapt. This led to dissatisfactions in many cases according to the interview materials. Finally, it was disclosed that older persons sometimes experience dissatisfaction because they believe younger members imagine them to be "old fogies" and "has beens" and are trying to take over their jobs in the church. The oldsters not only resent this, but they feel that they, because of their wisdom and experience, should supply much of the leadership for the church. This conflict was so severe that in some cases members quit participating in church activities and others stopped going to church entirely. The significant conclusion that developed in this phase of the study was that the role of the older persons in the church is not entirely satisfactory, because they experience dissatisfactions in their relationships with the younger members and because of other factors associated with old age.

## SUMMARY AND CONCLUSION

The evidence provided from an analysis of aged members of two church groups indicated the following findings:

1. There were no significant differences between the younger and older church members with respect to personal adjustment.

2. Outside of the fact that older women in both church groups read their Bibles more frequently and younger females listen to radio religious programs more often than older women, the analysis revealed no significant differences between the younger and older church members with respect to church activities and attitudes toward religion.

3. The investigation of the relationship between closeness of church affiliation and favorable personal characteristics and activities which is one measure of personal adjustment, revealed no significant differences in the Church A study-group. There appears to be a positive relationship in the Church B group in that persons maintaining close ties with the church tend to be more active and have more favorable characteristics than do the nonclose members.

4. With respect to the relationship between personal adjustment and closeness of church affiliation, our data revealed that nearly all of our older church members had good or average personal adjustment as compared with poor adjustment. There were no significant differences found between the close and nonclose member in Church A with respect to personal adjustment in old age. The analysis revealed that the closely affiliated Church B members were better adjusted than the nonclose members.

5. The church does perform a valuable function in alleviating problems of the older person and does contribute to good personal adjustment in old age.

6. Finally, the role of the older persons in the church is not entirely satisfactory, because they experience dissatisfactions in their relationships with the younger members and because of other factors associated with old age.

# RELIGIOUS PRACTICE AND PERSONAL ADJUSTMENT OF OLDER PEOPLE*

### Charles T. O'Reilly

Religious practices are not, of course, limited to churchgoers. Attendance at church, however, is an objective, measurable religious activity and may be assumed to be related to the acceptance of religious beliefs. For some older people religion, as expressed in religious activity or practice, may be a crutch or an escape mechanism as it probably is for many insecure and unhappy people. In an attempt to study some of the relationships between religious practice and personal adjustment, people over sixty-five in a working-class Chicago community were asked a number of questions about their religious practice and personal adjustment. Cluster sampling was used in an area containing seventy enumeration districts. Dwelling units in chosen districts were visited, and only one person over sixty-five was interviewed in any one dwelling unit. Interviewees numbered 6.5 per cent of the 4,511 older persons in the area and corresponded closely to the population of older persons in terms of distribution by sex, age, marital status, citizenship, and national origin. The findings reported here are based upon the answers of the 108 men and 102 women in the sample who were Catholics and physically able to attend church. The religious behavior and the adjustment of the Catholics were studied because the criteria of their religious practice were more objective than those obtainable for the other subjects in the study.

The religious activity of the Catholic includes two practices considered essential by the Catholic Church. One is the obligation to attend Mass on Sunday; the other is the requirement to receive Holy Communion at least once a year, but preferably as often as possible. While there are other requirements for remaining in good standing in the Catholic Church, these basic ones are readily meas-

*I wish to thank the members of the Research Seminar, School of Social Work, especially Mr. Thomas Brown and Mrs. Elizabeth Detrick for their contributions to this paper. Reprinted by courtesy of *Sociology and Social Research*, Volume 42:119-121, November, 1957.

urable and can be used as a limited but workable index of the Catholic's religious practice. The index rated Catholics who attended Mass daily or weekly high in church attendance, and those who attended Mass less than weekly were rated low. Daily to monthly reception of communion was rated high, and less frequent reception of communion was rated low. The very few subjects who did not answer either or both of these questions were rated low in either or both practices. The subjects were then divided into three groups: the "more active" in religious practice, those rated high in both Mass attendance and the reception of communion; the "medium," those rated high in one practice and low in the other; and the "less active," those rated low in both practices. Half of the subjects were "more active," 34 per cent were "medium," and 16 per cent were "less active." Among the women 62.7 per cent were "more active" in the practice of their religion, compared with 37.9 per cent of the men. Also, fewer women were less active than would have been the case if only chance had governed their distribution. Religious practice was significantly related to sex at better than the 1 per cent level.[1]

Did age effect religious practice? Subjects between sixty-five and seventy-five were compared with those over seventy-five. While 45.5 per cent of those under seventy-five were more active in the practice of their religion, 67.4 per cent of those over seventy-five were more active. Thus among those physically able to participate in religious activities, there was a tendency for religious practice to be related in increased age.

Were those who claimed that religion had become more helpful to them in the last ten years more active in practicing their religion? Religion had become more helpful to 49 per cent of these older people, remained the same for 6.6 per cent, and had not become more helpful for 35.2 per cent. Practice was most active among those for whom the helpfulness of religion had been relatively constant. Of those for whom religion became more helpful, 61.2 per cent were in the religiously more active category, compared with 28.4 per cent of those for whom it had not become more helpful.

---

[1]Tables showing the distribution of subjects may be obtained by writing to the author.

Religion could easily serve as an escape for lonely older people who have lost family and friends and keenly feel the impact of loneliness. In fact, however, did more of the lonely older people turn to religion? Forty-eight per cent of the religiously more active people reported that they felt lonely, as did 55 per cent of those who were less active. The slight tendency for less active subjects to be lonely was not significant. Since 44 per cent of the lonely people were more active in the practice of their religion compared with 55.7 per cent of those who were not lonely, the lonely apparently did not use religion as an escape.

One might also ask whether unhappiness has anything to do with the practice of religion. The subjects had reported whether they felt very happy, moderately happy, or less happy. More than half of the very happy were more active in the practice of their religion compared with 34 per cent of those in the medium and 11 per cent in the low activity group. The moderately and less happy showed a somewhat similar pattern with 47 and 44 per cent more active, 32 and 38 per cent medium, and 21 and 18 per cent less active. Although happier people were somewhat more active in the practice of religion, the less happy and moderately happy were not too different from them. The less happy obviously had not plunged into religious activity as an escape.

It is often assumed that those who identify themselves with a church are churchgoers and practitioners of the religion with which they identify themselves. Data on church identification are not necessarily meaningless in studies of religious, political, or other behavior, but must be used with caution. Individuals may reflect the attitudes of a cultural subgroup to which they have belonged, especially if they still choose to be identified with it, but identification with a church cannot be equated with adherence to its tenets and used as a basis to talk about "Catholic" or "Jewish" political behavior, for example, as if political behavior in some way stemmed from religious belief. Although all the subjects in this study had identified themselves with a church, they differed considerably in terms of church attendance and the meaning they ascribed to religion. Based upon an examination of answers to questions about the meaning of religion, subjects' attitudes toward religion were classified as positive, negative, or neutral. Of those with a positive attitude toward religion, 71 per cent attended church weekly, while at the other extreme 80.8 per cent of those with a negative attitude attended church seldom or never. The tendency for attitude toward religion and church attendance to be related was significant at better than the 1 per cent level. Mere identification with a church or a statement of religious preference would not have provided an adequate criterion for separating churchgoers from nonchurchgoers, practitioners of a religion from nonpractitioners.

This study revealed some interesting facts about the religious practices of some older people. It showed that women were significantly more active in the practice of their religion than men and that religious activity tended to increase as people grew older. However, older people who were lonely or unhappy did not turn to religion more than other older people. Furthermore, although all subjects identified themselves with one church, their religious practice and attitude toward religion varied greatly. This illustrates the real limitations of questions about church membership in studies of attitudes and behavior. In view of the increasing number of older people in our society, the role religion plays in their lives and its relation to personal adjustment merit further and more deeper investigation.

# A STUDY OF FREE-TIME ACTIVITIES
# OF 200 AGED PERSONS*

## JERE HOAR

Although not gainfully employed, aged persons are unlikely to think of themselves as having much "free time." They busy themselves with self-appointed or obligatory home tasks—women to a greater extent than men. However, with increasing age there is a narrowing of interests, reflected in utilization of free time, organizational membership, attendance at meetings, voting practices, and

*Reprinted by courtesy of *Sociology and Social Research,* Volume 45:157-162, January, 1961.

the use of the telephone for social calls. These are among facts revealed in a study of mass communications' consumption and preferences of 200 aged persons in a town in Mississippi.

***Procedure.*** On the basis of census data, white persons in the community sixty years of age and more were calculated, in the summer of 1957, as numbering not more than 388. Limitations involving time and financing made the interviewing of every person impracticable. A sample of 200 was decided upon.

A private census resulted in a file card of 350 addresses and the names of aged persons believed to reside at those addresses. A primary sample of twenty-five cards was drawn from the file, and one aged person at each address was interviewed. After a review of the results, it was thought unnecessary to revise the questionnaire or procedure, the usable interviews were retained, and drawing of the continuous sample from the card file was resumed. The questionnaire, four legal-sized pages long, called for eighty-three responses. It was administered by nine interviewers, including the author. All proper respondents were interviewed. Interviews were timed at from forty-five minutes to three hours.

***The Respondents.*** The composite aged woman of the sample was unemployed and in her sixties or seventies. A widow, she was graduated from high school, but attended no business, trade, or other specialized school. She had an income of not more than $2,000 (but modal response indicated it would most likely be less than $500). She owned her own home and did not work at a paid job. She had access to daily and weekly newspapers, her favorite magazines, a radio set, and a television set. She described her health as "good" and her hearing and vision as adequate.

Although also unemployed, the composite aged man was almost surely younger (in his sixties), married, and not so well educated as the composite aged woman. He had eight years of formal schooling, had not attended a trade or specialized school, and probably had been a farmer during his active life. By modal response his income was from $1,000 to $1,999, but more than half the men interviewed said they had incomes in excess of $3,000. He owned his own home, and had access to all the agencies of mass communication. He said his hearing and vision were adequate, but was more likely to complain of failing vision than hearing. He said his health was "good," but was somewhat more likely to describe it as "fair" or "poor" than was the composite aged woman.

*Amount of Free Time.* Forty-one per cent of the respondents said they had only a few hours free each day, 38.5 per cent said they had all day free, and 20.0 per cent said they were free about half a day. Higher percentages of men than women said they had half or all of each day free.

The percentage of males who said they had all of each day free increased as age increased; having all of each day free were 31.7 per cent of those in their sixties, 57.8 per cent of those in their seventies, and 83.3 per cent of those in their eighties. Nineteen and five-tenths per cent of men in their sixties said they had half of each day free as did 16.6 per cent of those in their eighties. "A few hours free" was the response made by 48.7 per cent of men in their sixties and 42.1 per cent of men in their seventies. No man in his eighties said he had a few hours free. No man in his seventies said he had half of each day free.

Increase in leisure time as age increased did not seem to be so characteristic of women as of men. Even women in extreme old age kept busy. They cooked, sewed, baby sat with grandchildren, cared for sick relatives (frequently their husbands), and busied themselves in other ways. Only 55.5 per cent of women in their eighties and nineties said they had all day free in comparison with 83.3 per cent of the males. Thirty-nine and two-tenths per cent of those in their seventies and 23.2 per cent of those in their sixties said they had all day free. Having half of each day free were 21.4 per cent of those in their sixties, 27.4 per cent of those in their seventies, and 18.5 per cent of those in their eighties. More than half of the women in their sixties had only a few hours free. This response was also made by a third of the women in their seventies and 25.9 per cent of those in their eighties.

*Use of Free Time.* With increasing age there seemed to be a corresponding narrowing of interests and a change in the nature of the activities listed. Activities of older respondents as a rule required less exertion.

Most popular activities among males in their sixties were gardening (including related activities, such as cutting grass and light repairs), watching television, and fishing or hunting. Males in their seventies mentioned most frequently resting, watching TV, gardening, and reading. Males in their eighties indicated preferences for loafing, reading, and gardening. They mentioned only five types of spare-time activities in comparision with fourteen by men in their sixties and eleven by men in their seventies.

Among women, the pattern of diminishing spare-time activities was also evident. Respondents in their sixties mentioned eighteen different things they did in their spare time. Respondents in their seventies mentioned fifteen activities, and those in their eighties, nine. Women who refused to reveal their ages listed fourteen spare-time activities. In order of frequency of mention, the three most popular spare-time activities among women in their sixties and seventies were reading, visiting, and watching television. Among women in their eighties, reading, resting, gardening, and sewing were most frequently listed. Women who refused to reveal their ages mentioned most often reading, visiting, keeping house, and playing cards.

Of twenty-four activities mentioned, eleven accounted for less than 2.0 per cent of each of the responses. Approximately one third of all comments made by respondents had to do with mass communications. Reading accounted for 19.9 per cent of responses, watching television for 11.2 per cent, listening to the radio for 2.0 per cent, and going to the picture show for 0.2 per cent. Of course, no limit was placed on the number of things respondents could say they did in their spare time. This means that the percentages used here represent proportions of total responses.

*Connectedness and Meetings Attended.* More than half of the persons interviewed said they held membership in one or more organizations. But more than half of them also said they had attended no meetings in the previous thirty days. Forty-five per cent of the respondents had membership in no organizations, 37.0 per cent had membership in one or two organizations, 13.0 per cent in three or four, and 5.0 per cent in five or more.

Among men, membership in organizations was less characteristic of those in their eighties than of those in the sixties and seventies. The percentage holding membership declined as age increased. It declined from a high of 58.5 per cent of those in their sixties to 52.6 per cent of those in their seventies to 33.3 per cent of those in their eighties. Only men in their sixties and seventies belonged to three or more organizations. And the percentage having membership in one or two organizations was highest among men in their sixties, lowest among those in their eighties.

To that group of women holding memberships in organizations, those who refused to reveal their ages contributed nearly 86 per cent of their number. Nearly 36 per cent of women in their sixties, 58.8 per cent of those in their seventies, and 45.0 per cent of those in their eighties were *not* members of organizations. The differences observed between men and women in the matter of organizational membership did not appear to be great. Approximately the same percentage of women in their sixties, 33.7 per cent, and seventies, 33.3 per cent, held membership in one or two organizations. Similarly, 40.2 per cent of those in their eighties and 42.8 per cent of those who refused to reveal their ages held membership in one or two organizations. By far the highest percentage of women holding membership in three or more organizations (nearly 43 per cent) came from those who refused to reveal their ages. For other age groups from the youngest to the oldest, percentages were 28.5 for the sixties, 7.8 for the seventies, and 15.0 for those in their eighties.

*Attendance at Organizations and Meetings.* Highest attendance was claimed by "ageless" women. Nearly forty-three per cent of all women interviewed (not just those who claimed organizational membership) had attended half or more of the meetings of their clubs in the previous thirty days. An additional 14.2 per cent had attended all of them. There was a decline in attendance at meetings as age increased. Attendance at all meetings dropped among women as age increased through the three age categories from 25.0 per cent to 13.7 per cent to 10.0 per cent. There was a similar drop in those attending half or more of the meetings, from 16.0 per cent to 11.7 per cent to 10.0 per cent. Women in their eighties were more likely than those of other ages to say they had attended fewer than half of the meetings.

Two-thirds of the men in their eighties had attended no meetings; 63.1 per cent of those in their seventies and 58.5 per cent of those in their sixties had attended no meetings. Of males in their eighties who had attended meetings, all were present at more than half of those held. Ten and two-tenths per cent of those in their seventies had attended fewer than half, and 14.6 per cent of those in their sixties had attended fewer than half. Of males in their seventies, 10.5 per cent had attended half or more of the meetings held, and 15.7 per cent all of them. Of males in their sixties, 12.1 per cent had attended half or more of the meetings held, and 14.6 per cent all of them. Little difference was observed in the attendance record of men in their sixties and seventies.

*Voting Participation.* Old people are enthusiastic voters. Nearly 83 per cent of them said they had voted in the most recent national election, and 78.5 per cent said they had voted in the most recent local election. One nonvoter said, "They wouldn't bring the ballot box over this time." Another said she had tried unsuccessfully to have her daughter vote for her.

Males eighty and more seemed to keep up their interests in voting somewhat better than women of that age. While 60 per cent of women in extreme old age said they had voted in the most recent national election and 50 per cent had voted in the most recent local election, 83.3 per cent of men had voted in both elections.

There was a drop in voting participation by males at age moved from the sixties to the seventies, but climbed again in the eighties. Nearly 93 per cent of men in their sixties said they had voted in the most recent national election and 90.2 per cent said they had voted in the most recent local election. Among those in their seventies, the percentages voting were 78.9 per cent and 73.4 per cent. In the eighties, the percentages climbed to 83.3 per cent for both elections.

Among females, voting participation was highest among those in their seventies (90.1 per cent and 86.2 per cent). "Ageless" women were second in participation (85.7 per cent and 85.7 per cent), those in their sixties third (76.7 per cent and 73.2 per cent). Voting participation among women in their eighties and nineties totaled 60.0 per cent in the previous national election and 50.0 per cent in the local election.

In view of the unusually high percentages of persons who claimed voting participation, perhaps some examination should be made of their claims. There are several facts which lead one to believe that voting participation is high. For one thing, in a Southern rural town aged persons are likely to know the family of or be personally acquainted with candidates. For another, aged persons in Mississippi are exempt from the payment of poll tax. The onerous necessity of producing tax receipts for two years previous to the voting period does not apply to these respondents. Finally, an examination of county poll books showed that a sufficiently large number are registered voters to justify the replies.

***Telephone Access and Use.*** It appeared that the telephone was a major way in which aged persons kept in contact with friends and relatives. Ninety-three per cent had access, and when asked about the number of social calls they made or received on the telephone on the average day, 35.0 per cent said they received or made three or more calls, 37.0 per cent made or received one or two calls, and 26.5 per cent said they did not use the telephone for social calls often enough to record.

The percentage of men who did not use the telephone for social calls ranged from 16.6 per cent of those in their eighties to 47.3 per cent of those in their seventies; 41.4 per cent of those in the sixties also replied negatively.

As might have been expected, women were more often found to be users of the telephone for social calls than were men. The percentages of women who did not use the telephone ranged from 14.2 per cent of those who refused to reveal their ages to 35.0 per cent of those in their eighties. Of those in their sixties, 16.0 per cent said they did not use the telephone for social calls on the average day. Among those in their seventies, the percentage not using the telephone was 17.6 per cent. Eighty-five and seven-tenths per cent of women who refused to reveal their age said they used the telephone once or twice a day for social calls; 42.8 per cent of those in their sixties, 31.3 per cent of those in their seventies, and 35.0 per cent of those in their eighties made the same reply. The percentages of women who used the telephone three or more times a day for social calls were as follows: in their sixties, 41.0 per cent; in their seventies, 48.9 per cent; eighty and more, 30.0; "ageless," 00.0 per cent.

*Summary*. Forty-one per cent of the respondents said they had only a few hours free each day, but 38.5 per cent said they had all of each day free. Spare-time activities diminished in number and changed in nature as age increased.

More than half of the respondents had membership in one or more organizations, but more than half also said they had not attended a meeting in the thirty days previous to the interview. Membership in organizations dropped off, in general, as age increased. Attendance at meetings also decreased as age increased.

The respondents seemed to be enthusiastic voters. More than four in five said they had voted in the most recent national election and three in four in the most recent local election.

Almost all respondents had access to the telephone, and nearly three in four used it daily for social calls. Women most often said they read when asked what they did in their free time. Men most frequently said they engaged in gardening.

Differences in age seemed to be related in respondents' patterns of activity in many areas.

# ANALYSIS OF OLD AGE POLITICS IN THE UNITED STATES*

ABRAHAM HOLTZMAN

Political behavior on the part of our aged citizens, as such, and the nature of its impact upon our social security system have remained neglected subjects in the field of gerontology. The most recent studies which refer to old age politics, those of Fisher and Pollak, point to a startling paucity of knowledge, although old age movements exploded upon the American scene as early as 1933 and can be expected to agitate politics for years to come. At the same time the increasing proportion of aged people among eligible voters has caused serious alarm in many quarters. It is the purpose of this

*Reprinted by courtesy of *Journal of Gerontology*, Volume 9:56-65, January, 1954.

article to explore two major questions in the hope of contributing to a better understanding of the problem of old age politics: 1) Why have the aged in the United States undertaken independent political action in contrast to a conspicuous absence of such behavior elsewhere? 2) To what extent will old age pension movements play a role in the social security politics of tomorrow?

## THE ROLE OF OLDER CITIZENS IN SOCIAL SECURITY POLITICS

Faced with grave problems of old age insecurity, governments everywhere have been called upon to assume an increasingly greater role in providing for the older citizen. Only in the United States, however, have older citizens acted as a separate political force, banding together to impose their special demands upon society. The significance of this behavioral pattern has been largely overlooked. With the exception of an abortive attempt to organize a Townsend Movement in Canada, political movements among the aged failed to emerge in other countries. In the United States, the very nature of the Social Security Act has from its inception been intimately affected by the politics of the aged. Elsewhere the enactment of social legislation for the aged has been disassociated from any special efforts by old people as a group.

## THE ABSENCE OF A SEPARATE POLITICAL ROLE OUTSIDE THE UNITED STATES

A combination of factors foreclosed the possibility for separate political consciousness and action on the part of old people in countries of European culture. Protection for the old was provided in varying degrees by most of the major countries of the world long before our Congress was compelled to deal with this problem in the depression decade of the 1930's. Toward the end of the 19th Century other governments had already begun to deal with old age insecurity on a systematic national scale. What characterized other countries so as to explain the absence of old age pension movements? It might be surmised that an earlier concern with the problem of old age insecurity antedated the full development of popular democratic government. The reverse is true, however, for national protection of the aged coincided with and benefited from the expansion of democratization.

The existence of old age security systems may have helped prevent the formulation of specific demands on the part of the old people. Therein, however, lay no explanation why the aged failed to participate in the very inception and extension of these programs. *Independent old age politics failed to develop because citizens reaching advanced years were accommodated within major institutions, precluding any autonomous role for the aged in politics.*

The emergence of powerful labor movements and the leadership furnished by influential Socialist parties preempted the role which old age pension movements fulfilled in the United States. It is evident that the labor movements in the late 19th and early 20th Centuries and the Socialists were largely responsible for modern national plans protecting the aged.

In Germany a system of national compulsory old age insurance, the first of its kind, was initiated as one of Chancellor Bismarck's measures to defeat a rising Socialist movement. In some countries Socialists and labor enacted the initial legislation themselves. Hohman credits the Social Democrats as being largely responsible for shaping social policy in Sweden, including old age protection.

In another set of circumstances, the nascent power of organized labor and the Socialists in alliance with political liberalism secured pension legislation. The Old Age Pension Law enacted in Great Britain, in 1908, its first great reform since the Poor Laws of 1601, arose primarily from the massive defeat suffered by the Conservative Party in 1906 at the hands of a coalition of labor and the middle class. True, the previous propaganda efforts of Canon William Blackley, the careful reports of Charles Booth, and Joseph Chamberlain's espousal of pension legislation contributed to a growing political concern with the problem. But it was the support provided by the Cooperative Unions, the Trade Union Congress, and the Fabians which furnished the political stimulus that made old age pensions necessary legislation for such radical Liberals as Lloyd George.

Across the world in New Zealand the Old Age Pension Law of

1896 was enacted under the auspices of a radical Liberal Party blending together a politically conscious trade union movement with land-hungry farmer groups. Lipson points to the Old Age Pension Law as a successful political maneuver to regain for the Liberals the votes lost in the urban districts in previous elections. To cite one example in South America, the general compulsory old age and sickness insurance act passed in Argentina in 1923 is attributed by Epstein to agitation on the part of organized workers.

To credit the role of labor and Socialism in the development of old age pension and insurance programs is to espouse the obvious. What must be emphasized is that these forces eliminated any grounds for a self-conscious political effort on the part of the aged. Aggressive, social security minded, and politically potent organizations advanced the interests of old people as an integral part of a general program of reform. Ideologically, moreover, the programs of Socialism and of labor left no place for the concept of an independent aged pressing separate demands upon society. In addition the serious divisions, social, economic, political, and even religious at times, into which the populations of most countries are so antagonistically split, precluded any new division on the basis of age alone.

The existing political environment was not conducive to separate pension action. An acceptance of a positive role for the state in many of these countries facilitated a national approach to old age protection. Secondly the major political parties, not only the labor-socialist left, undertook to promote old age pensions. In one of the few countries where pension legislation was not directly related to fear of Socialism or to labor agitation. Denmark, it was the progressive Left Party of the farmers which passed the first national noncontributory pension law. It is noteworthy that conservative as well as liberal parties have advanced the cause of social reform. Aside from an espousal by the parties, the parliamentary system helped prevent the emergence of independent pension groups. The non-party pressure group is at a disadvantage in attempting to maneuver between voter and candidate, between party leadership and legislator, and between executive and legislature in a parliamentary system.

The nature of the family and the general status of old people in European cultures further inhibited independent old age politics. Greater respect and social status are granted the aged in European cultures than in our own. Sociologists have stressed the exceptional emphasis upon youth in contemporary American culture and the isolated position of the aged from "participation in the most important social structures and interests." The extreme conjugal type of family and the isolated role it forces upon old people failed to develop as extensively in Europe as in the United States. The European aged retained vital social and psychologic ties with basic institutions from which they derived status and respect.

## FACTORS LEADING TO OLD AGE POLITICS IN THE UNITED STATES

The forces creating old age insecurity in the United States were similar in many respects to those characterizing other countries. Industrial progress precipitated a devaluation in the status and situation of older people. In contrast to conditions of 1880 when the vast majority of our population was a rural one centering primarily around agriculture, by 1920 the majority was engaged in industrial and non-agricultural occupations, and over 50 per cent of the population resided in urban centers. The aged, too, were encompassed in this trend; by 1930, over 50 per cent of those sixty-five years of age and over were living in urban communities.

Under the impact of these altered conditions the former security of old people was shattered and any possible future security seriously impaired. The rural family in contrast to the urban one, as Smith has shown, is a more cohesive unit with firm ties and one wherein aged parents and grandparents can contribute to its solvency. In the transition from a land economy to a money industrial economy the work of the older people lost its former value. The average city family no longer lived in dwellings adequate for the sheltering of aging parents and relatives. Nor were there large families, gardens, or kitchens in which the aged could be of assistance. The smaller size of the family contributed to the precariousness of old age. There were fewer children to provide for their parents, and the burden upon the younger people was consequently a greater one. Home ties and family solidarity were also weakened by the high mobility which has characterized the population in the United States. Under the impact of industrialization and urbanization, the sustaining and conforting support for the aged found in the rural community and the strong family disappeared for many.

At the same time the ability of the average worker to provide for old age and that of the older worker to retain his self-sufficiency were severely restricted. Changes in technology and a lowering of the hiring age weakened the position of old people within the labor force. A long term decline in farm employment and the expansion of occupations wherein older people were less relied upon greatly limited employment opportunities. In 1890, about two-thirds of all men sixty-five years of age and over were in the labor force; by 1930 this rate had declined to slightly over one-half.

As the American economy began to affect adversely the position of the aged, the proportion of older people within the population was increasing. Those sixty-five and over had constituted approximately 3 per cent of the total population in 1870, numbering 1,153,649; in 1930 this group comprised 5.4 per cent, or 6,633,805. The total population by 1930 had increased three-fold since 1870, but the number of those sixty-five and over was nearly six times as great as before. On the average men and women reaching sixty-five in 1930 could anticipate more than eleven additional years of life.

Another factor, the maldistribution of income, played a role in equating old age with insecurity. According to a study of family income and savings by the Brookings Institution for the year 1929, three-fifths of the families in the United States earned $2000 or less and could save little or nothing. Not only were families of industrial and agricultural workers unable to save, but many in the so-called middle class found themselves in a similar predicament. As late as 1940 the Director of the Bureau of Employment Security, Social Security Board, characterized as fairly liberal estimates of 10 or 20 per cent for the number of persons reaching an independent old age through savings.

In spite of many similarities, socio-political conditions in the

United States were radically different from those of other countries dealing with the problem of old age insecurity. As has been pointed out with reference to the aged in European cultures, the emphasis upon youth in our culture and the predominance of the extreme type of conjugal family robbed many older people of a vital stabilizing force. Parsons has suggested that this structural isolation from "kinship, occupational, and community ties is the fundamental basis of . . . political agitation" on the part of aged in America. The aged also remained isolated from any meaningful representation in the political or economical arena. With little if any political response emerging to minister to their needs during the depression, the aged became susceptible to appeals by new messiahs. Given a political environment in which pressure politics is an intrinsic part, they resorted to independent political action.

The movement for old age security up to the time of the depression was almost completely divorced from economic or political expression; conversely the efforts that were made stemmed from forces which were politically impotent. The relationship of economic and social problems to political results is generally only a function of the legislators' cognizance of what is considered potent in politics: organization, pressure, votes, and money.

Only in the 1920's did organized groups begin a concerted drive to secure pension legislation. It is a revealing commentary on the nature of this endeavor that the Fraternal Order of Eagles is given primary credit for the few state pension laws that were in existence. For years the leaders of the American trade union movement opposed any form of social insurance legislation, and it was not until 1922 that a national convention of the American Federation of Labor endorsed the principle of a federal old age pension. The A. F. of L. was primarily concerned with wages, hours, and working conditions. It did not compare in size, influence, or political maturity with the extensive labor movement in Europe nor did it incorporate their basic political approach or possess a similar link with Socialism. The American Association for Labor Legislation has become active in this field only since 1922. It was as late as 1927 that the American Association for Old Age Security, under the leadership of Abraham Epstein, was organized to unite community leaders and social workers in a campaign for the protection of the aged.

An abrupt deterioration in the condition of the aged brought about by the depression of the 1930's and the inadequacies of ameliorative measures helped create the potential from which old age pension movements arose. Evidence points to a continued isolation of the aged at the very time when their crisis had reached its zenith. In 1928 Epstein estimated that 30 per cent of the aged sixty-five years and over were dependent upon others for support, the majority being assisted by relatives and children. In view of known statistics on the low incomes and the inability of three-fifths of the nation's families to save, the strain on family resources must have been great.

Only six of the forty-eight states provided old age assistance, less than 1000 persons being cared for. A few private pension plans and governmental retirement plans were in operation, but the number of persons covered was extremely limited, and many of the plans were poorly constructed and badly financed. The remainder of the dependent aged was compelled to seek the meager aid offered by private charity or that furnished by local communities through outdoor relief or almshouse confinement.

Estimates for 1930 placed the dependent aged at 40 per cent of those sixty-five and over, or about 2.7 million, and by 1935, 50 per cent. With unemployment well over the 10 million mark in the depths of the depression, the burden of supporting aged relatives became impossible for many families. Private charity and pension plans proved useless before the magnitude of the task; many of the latter collapsed entirely. The decline in employment was more severely felt by the aged than by any other adult group; labor force participation among men sixty-five and over dropped sharply from 54 per cent in 1930 to 42.2 per cent by 1940. At the same time, the number of aged sixty-five and over increased from 6.6 million and 5.4 per cent of the population in 1930 to an estimated 7.5 million and 6 per cent in 1935.

During the five gravest years of the depression, when the plight of aged citizens had become extremely critical, the national government failed to meet their particular problem. It was not until late

1934 that a presidential committee was appointed to study problems of economic security. In this failure to act lay a major responsibility for the rise of independent action by the aged. From 1910 when the first national old age pension bill was introduced until 1930, Congress refused to consider such legislation. Committee hearings were held for the first time in 1930 and 1931, but no bill was reported to the floor of Congress. Favorable recommendations were granted pension bills in the next Congress, but none were submitted to a vote. In 1934, the fifth year of the depression, a national old age pension bill (S. 493) was approved by the Senate, which immediately rescinded its action in deference to the President's call for a special study on economic security.

State governments proved unable to cope with a problem that was national in scope. By the end of 1934 only 180,00 persons were receiving old age assistance; twenty-eight states had enacted pension laws but three of these were inoperative. The population in twenty-three states was not protected by old age assistance.

A significant change occurred, meanwhile, in the composition and character of the dependent aged. Jobs having disappeared, businesses ruined and savings wiped out, an influx of despoiled professional men, retired farmers, skilled workers, and independent businessmen entered the ranks of the aged. There were the people who had attained a high degree of independence and economic security. The *laissez faire* philosophy. which had predominated during their lifetime, taught that the virtues of hard work and steady thrift were rewarded by an old age of comfort and security. The fact that the vast majority of Americans could not save placed these groups in a special position—for they had exemplified the rewards and beliefs in the prevailing system; they had proved it and, therefore, trusted and believed in it. Yet they too were as helplessly broken on the economic wheel as were their less fortunate brethren. These new accretions to the ranks of dependent aged represented a sensitive force receptive to protest thinking.

In the economic arena the aged possessed no bargaining position whatsoever. And in politics, the one sphere of action in which the influence of their numbers and votes could be felt, they were voiceless. The principal organizations advocating pension legislation remained isolated from the aged themselves; their efforts lacked the political dynamics of mass movements to whose symbols politicians must respond.

Certainly the political leaders and parties were aware of the existence of this socio-economical problem; the 1932 Democratic platform called for old age pension legislation through state action. Up to 1934, however, they were unaware of its political extent; they were not confronted with a threat to themselves. In light of the intrinsic nature of the American political system, it was only natural that the pressure group should occupy this political vacuum.

The American constitutional framework places a premium upon political action by groups independent of the major political parties. Its viability stems primarily from the separation of power principle incorporated in our governmental organization and from the nature of our major parties, each of which is a loose coalition of state parties and groups with divergent interests. Party leadership and responsibility, both within our bicameral legislatures and between executive and legislature, are extremely fragmentalized and party discipline negligible. Legislatures are characterized by fluid majorities, constantly changing and cutting across party and sectional lines. Individual legislators may with impunity defy party or Administration leadership without fear of undermining either or of incurring disciplinary action. Their party nomination and generally their election to office are autonomous local affairs from which the national party organization and frequently the national platform are excluded.

Under such circumstances well organized, vociferous, special interest groups, entrenched in local communities, may intervene advantageously in both the electoral and legislative process. Major parties generally avoid the championship of new or unorthodox causes until the political viability of the latter has been assured. If dissatisfied or ignored in representation by parties, special interest groups may initiate independent action at all levels of the political process and in the local, state, or national arenas. If the major parties would not or could not incorporate within their politics protection for the aged, it was inevitable that such a large, unstable political element would find its expression in the pressure group or in the third party. Moreover, a separate division on the basis of old age alone was possible in the United States in the absence of fixed antagonistic divisions within our population.

A number of the new depression messiahs, principally Upton Sinclair and Huey Long, sought to make political capital out of old age discontent. Not only were they limited to restricted areas in their political operations, but their appeal to the aged, promises of $30 and $50 a month pensions to all over sixty years of age, was merely an incidental political tactic.

One minor pension promoter, Dr. J. E. Pope, tapped for a brief time the rich potential that lay in a specialized appeal to the aged. In proportion to the small size of his organization and the limited locale of operations, the response he evoked among the aged in the Southwest was astonishing. His program, however, offered nothing of particular attraction to capture the imagination of vast numbers of aged or of a large segment of the population, and Dr. Pope was early exposed as a fraudulent promoter with a criminal record. The aged were ripe for organization and politics, and as inadequate as his organization and efforts were, they could not but draw a response.

The full articulation of the aged came about through the efforts of Dr. Francis E. Townsend and the Townsend Movement which brought their interests into the highest political refinement and expressed them in typically indigeneous American fashion: money radicalism (a reliance upon monetary panaceas—cheap money, enforced spending—as the principal solvent for economic crises), the pressure group, and the third party. Only when despair of the aged assumed a threatening political form did the parties and political leaders weigh its strength and future in conjunction with their own.

Although somewhat peripheral, an additional factor might be cited as contributing to the inception of old age politics. The concentration of a large and extremely sensitive group of older people in a state characterized by weak political parties and a tradition of independent political action provided a fertile environment. In 1930, California, the nation's fifth most populous state, contained the fifth largest group of aged sixty-five years and over in the United States, 366,125. While it ranked eighth among the states with the highest proportion of aged, 6.4 per cent, none of these states contained more than a fifth the number of aged living in California, except Washington with less than a third.

The situation of these aged was one of recent migration to California, a high concentration within one area of the state, and a drastic deterioration in economic position. From 1920 to 1930 the population of the state increased over 65 per cent. At the same time its aged population, sixty-five and over, increased over eighty per cent. In this decade the number of aged in the nation had increased by about 14 per cent. Not a single state approximated the rate of growth evidenced in California. These figures indicate an extremely high influx into California of older people from the rest of the nation. An even greater concentration occurred within the state, principally in Southern California; the number of people sixty-five and over increased by 100 per cent or more in Los Angeles and Long Beach and by over 90 per cent in San Diego and Pasadena.

Consequently, very few of the older people in the state had resided there for any great length of time, most of them having arrived in the decade prior to the depression. For many important primary group ties had been severed, and for an abrupt transition had occurred at a stage in life when readjustment is most difficult. At this unstable transitional period the depression caught the aged of California in a particularly exposed position. Many of the elderly had sought semi-retirement and easy living, bringing incomes with them rather than appearing as job seekers. During the depression pensions and savings were wiped out or frozen through the mass of bank failures, small marginal businesses failed, and the collapse of the stock market and the California real estate boom carried away the economic security of thousands of these new Californians. A large number of aged, recently concentrated in a small segment of a state, found themselves in extremely dire straits, bereft of their incomes and beyond the employable age.

The state itself provided a political atmosphere conductive to the rise of old age reform movements. In California, Crouch and McHenry have shown that political parties are relegated to a meager and normal role—impotent, ill-organized, and dishonored.

Well organized and well financed pressure groups, as a consequence, have occupied an influential position, benefiting greatly from the availability of the initiative, referendum, and the recall. In terms of new political and economic revivals, Utopianism, Technocracy, E.P.I.C., this state became a western "burned-over" area.

The Townsend Plan, which appealed directly to the aged, started in Long Beach, within the solid Southern California community of aged. It promised to provide economic security for old people as well as to restore their former usefulness to society by making them the instruments for the economic recovery of the nation. Rapid initial expansion of the Townsend Movement was facilitated by the very large number of elderly people residing in this area. Aged Townsendities and their brethren were able to see immediate, concrete results in terms of increasing membership, financial contributions, publicity, *and* political recognition.

Without this concentration of a particularly unstable group of aged in a politically atomized community, the Townsend Movement might never have attained that initial impetus which fired it across California and into the other states of the nation. This is not to suggest that independent old age politics could not have been promoted elsewhere; Dr. Pope's Old Age Pension Association had been active when the Townsend Plan was initiated. However, special conditions in California launched a pension movement which succeeded in covering the entire country, one whose features and success stimulated the organization of additional pension movements throughout the nation.

Old age discontent and organization crystalized at a time propitious for social reform. The country had reached a stage of crisis wherein the *laissez faire* social philosophy had proved bankrupt; almost all groups within the population sought immediate aid from the national government which alone possessed the requisite powers and resources. National political leadership, moreover, had been transferred to a dynamic individual sympathetic toward social reform, whose operational philosophy incorporated a belief in the desirability for strong executive leadership, the need for immediate national action, the need for bold imagination and improvisation.

Certain reforms were more imperative than others and received top priority. As Francis Perkins has pointed out, the political threat raised by the Townsend Movement forced the hand of the President—he had not intended originally to include old age protection within his program of social security in 1934-1935. However, the President believed it politically expedient at this time to recommend a reasonable alternative to the Townsend Plan.

## PROSPECTS FOR FUTURE OLD AGE POLITICS IN THE UNITED STATES

Does America face the prospect of a war of generations old, *vs.* young, as was recently suggested by the economist for the American Medical Association? Certainly many forces which have aggravated old age insecurity remain active today. In 1950, among persons sixty-five and over, 64.7 per cent resided in urban centers, a ratio higher than that for the general population. The proportion receiving earnings had declined to 30 per cent, representing in part a further reduction in employment opportunities for older people. At the same time, the aged sixty-five and over increased by 86 per cent since 1930, numbering 12.3 million or 8.2 per cent of the population.

Since the aged comprise an ever increasing proportion of the eligible voters in the United States, what does this portend for social security politics? Will the aged again resort in large numbers to independent political action? Havighurst has warned that if the aged group should ever form a solid political bloc, it could secure almost anything it might demand from the government. Old age movements of the depression decade, Clague has contended, were in their political infancy in comparison to the pension movements of the future.

On the basis of a study of the Townsend Movement from 1933 to the present and some of the corollary pension movements, I believe that such pessimistic hypotheses are largely unfounded. They reflect a lack of awareness that socio-political conditions have been so altered as to inhibit old age politics comparable to that of the depression decade.

The major political parties have adopted, as an integral part of their politics, favorable attitudes toward the social security system. One need only refer to the party platforms or to actions of Republican and Democratic leaders to comprehend the popularity of social security as a political issue. On the same day that the President of the United States labelled the Tennessee Valley Authority as an example of "creeping socialism" he praised the social security system and called for its expansion.

The American people have enthusiastically accepted the socialization of risk for old age, unemployment, and death. A political party would seriously penalize itself if it failed to reflect this sentiment. It can be expected, therefore, that the extension and liberalization of the present old age insurance and assistance programs will be championed by the major parties. Their leadership in the extension of protection for the aged will preempt that position which special pension movements have sought to monopolize.

An aggressive, influential labor movement now concerns itself with politics. Its leaders have committed themselves to a campaign, political as well as economic, to insure the future security of their members. Adequate pensions for the aged constitute a primary objective in their program of social reform. It was the economic espousal of organized labor and not independent political action by the aged which compelled a reconsideration of social security legislation in 1950. The brief success of George McLain's pension group in the California election of 1948 may be attributed in part to a favorable climate of public opinion generated by labor's agitation for old age security.

In contrast with the depression period when no national pension legislation existed, the social security system today protects millions of workers and their families. The latest extensions have included many of the self-employed and other groups, previously excluded. Old age assistance, a joint federal-state project, is operative in all the states. Consequently, an ever improving system of protection removes much of the economic incentive that agitated old people to participate in pension movements. Their predicament can never again approximate the desperation and hopelessness which prevailed in the 1930's. A growing concern today with the socio-psychologic needs of older people promises to reduce the isolation in which many find themselves. Governmental, university, and private agencies are devoting themselves to research on all aspects of this problem.

To imply, however, that independent political action on the part of the aged may henceforth be ignored is as foolish as to suggest that it will increase in gravity. Old age pension movements will continue to agitate American politics. Viewed in proper perspective, their political significance can be evaluated as minor.

National and state pension organizations remain active today. In many of these organizations clubs furnish a warm social environment for the old—opportunities for friendship, marriage, and a sense of belonging, avenues for leadership and respect. Participation provides meaningful activity enabling elderly people to feel that they retain a voice in society. Some pension organizations assist old people in obtaining their benefits under our complicated social security system. A major part of the appeal of the California Institute of Social Welfare has been its successful efforts to mediate between the aged and the complexities and impersonal qualities inhering in the administration of this system.

Certain states will continue to be active areas of pension politics. Revival of old age politics can be expected where a high concentration of aged is accompained by a tradition of political unorthodoxy, an easy availability of the initiative for independent action, and a state of disorganization within the major parties. Such conditions are particularly characteristic of some of our western states; Florida, parts of New England and of the Middle West, which have had strong concentrations of Townsend Clubs as well as local pension movements, can also anticipate such activity.

Our social security system lends itself to continued pension politics as old age assistance focuses pressure upon state parties and legislatures. As long as needs tests, relative responsibility clauses, and other restrictions are imposed by state legislatures, they will generate discontent among our aged, many of whom consider pensions a matter of right, not need. In addition pension movements should find an attractive appeal in an espousal of medical benefits for the aged. The problem of maintaining health is a particularly acute one for old people as has been shown by the President's Commission on the Health Needs of the Nation.

In the event of an economic recession, it is unlikely that old age insurance benefits will be reduced, as major party leaders are well aware of the popular support behind social security. Old age assistance programs are more amenable to restriction; such action would presage a resurgence of independent politics in certain states. If inflation is again permitted to cut sharply into the real income of the aged, aggressive pension politics can be expected on the part of pension groups and unions. On the whole, however, alarming prospects for extensive old age politics envisioned by Clague, Dickinson, and Havighurst remain negligible.

## SUMMARY

This article attempts to deal with the following questions: 1) Why have the aged in the United States resorted to independent political action in contrast to an absence of such behavior elsewhere? 2) To what extent will the aged in our country continue to assume an independent role in politics? In countries of European culture, powerful labor and Socialist movements included old age pensions within their general programs of social reform, making special old age organizations unnecessary. The political environment, as well as culture patterns in which the aged retained status and respect in society, further inhibited such action.

Although urbanization and industrialization in the United States destroyed the security formerly found by the aged in a rural society, political and social institutions failed the old people. The proportion of aged people increased at a time when the economic system was restricting their opportunities to provide for themselves. A conjugal type of family, characteristic of our population, and an emphases upon youth in our culture contributed to their isolation. On the political and economic scene the plight of the old people failed to secure any meaningful representation.

Under the impact of the depression the condition of the aged deteriorated radically with little if any compensatory social adjustment. Private and local governmental efforts proved useless. During the gravest period, no particular action was undertaken by the national government to aid the older citizen, and nearly one-half of the states offered no old age assistance whatsoever. Under such circumstances many aged became susceptible to the appeals of new messiahs arising from the discontent of the times.

The American political system places a premium upon independent political action by special interest groups. In the absence of leadership from our major parties, the aged resorted to separate pressure politics. The Townsend Plan promised to restore them to a valued position in society, utilizing old age pensions to conquer the depression. Profiting from its inception in Southern California, where large and particularly unstable groups of aged were concentrated, the Townsend Movement gained sufficient organizational impetus to carry it across the nation. Under conditions propitious to the enactment of social reform, the threat of the pension movement compelled an immediate consideration and adoption of national old age pension legislation.

Are the aged to assume a more aggressive, independent political role in the future? It has been suggested by some authorities that we are threatened by such danger. In my opinion these conclusions are unwarranted; they ignore important socio-political changes which now constitute barriers to such action.

Our major political parties deem it imperative to espouse an expansion and liberalization of the old age security system. In addition, the present labor movement is committed to an aggressive pursual of such goals. Championship by such powerful and respectable proponents has considerably weakened the appeal of special interest groups to the aged. Moreover social security protection already covers a major portion of our population. The state of insecurity which characterized the aged during the depression decade and in which pension movements flourished can never reoccur. Governmental and private organizations, concerned with the socio-psychologic problems of the aged, are attempting to reverse the isolated position in which many find themselves.

Many old people will continue to be attracted to organizations advocating independent pension politics. Participation in pension organizations provides old people with opportunities for social activity and leadership roles. The social security system retains a number of features which expose it to pressure politics, especially upon the state level. States in which a high concentration of aged coincide with a weak party system and available instruments for independent action will be prone to pension politics. Especially is this to be expected if social security benefits are reduced or inflation is allowed to depress the real income of old people. Independent pension politics comparable to the 1930's, however, is highly unlikely on the national level or in most states.

# THE AGED INMATE*

## George F. Baier, III

The California Men's Colony, established as a specialized institution by the California Department of Corrections in July, 1954, is uniquely dedicated to provide a program especially designed for the training, rehabilitation, and replacement in civilian life of the elderly and infirm offender in a setting apart from the more secure and expensive restraint necessary for younger offenders.

Mr. John H. Klinger, the institution's Superintendent, in an address before the research-minded Western Gerontological Society at San Francisco in May, 1957, emphasized that this objective could be met only through a compulsive recognition by all staff employees of the need to provide facilities and atmosphere that meet the physical, emotional, intellectual, and spiritual needs of the elderly. Mr. Klinger's ideals have put into action: much of the matter presented herein points out how this has been accomplished.

Wisely, the selection of the physical site for this unusual departure in penology was a former hospital (the U. S. Army's Camp San Luis Obispo) in a geographical area of low altitude and a mild and equable climate.

Of the men in the California Men's Colony, nearly all are ill at one time or another; many are remittently ill; a majority of them are constantly sick. With an average age of about fifty-five, in an inmate population of approximately 1,360, there is found every

*Reprinted by courtesy of *American Journal of Correction*, Volume 23:4-6, March-April, 1961.

type of disease. There are, for example, 150 heart cases, 125 arthritic inmates, sixty-five diabetics, just under 300 luetics, 250 tuberculosis cases, and more than 100 asthma-allergy subjects at this writing. In a population such as this, it is inevitable that many rare disease conditions be encountered. However, the majority of the conditions found at the California Men's Colony are those that are concomitant with age and the attending deterioration that accompanies it.

As age advances, individuals develop arteriosclerosis and senility. However, the amount of arteriosclerosis and/or senility in any one individual varies extremely, in relation to the age. In other words, some people become old while young, and some people remain young while old.

People who develop arteriosclerosis are subject to and, indeed, frequently become afflicted with chronic debilitating diseases such as those of the kidneys and heart. Also, as a result of sclerosis of the arteries of the brain such people are subject to strokes. Also, as a result of arteriosclerosis of the peripheral arteries, people are subject to high blood pressure and peripheral vascular disease. Of course, all these conditions result in disability to a lesser or greater degree, depending upon the type, duration, and extent of the disease developed as a result of the arterial changes. It is to be realized, then, that any inmate who looks or seems old may be suffering from any one of the diseases or any combination (and usually it is a combination) of the diseases mentioned above. These individuals may have accumulation of waste products in their system, which adversely affects their health in general. They may have shortness of breath. They may have pain in the chest. They may have poor nourishment to the brain, which interferes with memory and other mental functions. They may have headaches from high blood pressure. And they are subject to an attack of heart failure, or stroke, or terminal kidney failure, spoken of as uremia. Because of their physical condition, therefore, it is obvious that such inmates require considerably different treatment from those inmates who are younger and free of senility and arteriosclerosis.

The diet of older people should not contain an excess of protein, and should contain very little fat unless, of course, they are undernourished and underweight. A high carbohydrate diet is excellent for elderly pepole. Foods containing cholesterol may hasten arteriosclerosis and, therefore, shorten life. Foods high in cholesterol are egg yolks, butter, the fat part of milk, and animal fats. Elderly people should masticate their foods thoroughly to facilitate digestion and overeating is strictly to be avoided.

In old people, so-called indigestion is quite commonly due to heart disease rather than to intestinal, gall bladder, or stomach trouble. An attack of acute indigestion in an elderly person quite often turns out to be a heart attack, called coronary thrombosis. Also pain in the calves precipitated by walking is a symptom of arteriosclerosis and is, therefore, not uncommon in elderly people. Dizziness and headache also are common symptoms of aging arteries.

It has often been said that individuals are as old as their arteries. This is quite true. Old age, however, does not necessarily imply chronic illness; yet most of the disabilities that come about in old age, and the misery that they bring and the uselessness that results, are consequences of chronic degenerative diseases and not of age *per se.*

In addition to the physical change, inmates who are arteriosclerotic and senile undergo characteristic mental and personality changes. In older people, there is a greater difference between individuals; two old people are much more unlike than two young people. This is true because people change as a result of their experiences, and older people have had more experiences. They have had more injuries, more physical insults, more diseases, more emotional trauma, more social encounters, more successes, more failures. Hence, successful dealing with older people absolutely necessitates individualization.

Another important point in dealing with older inmates is recognizing that their tolerance for stress and strain of all types is diminished. Their ability to maintain equilibrium is slow and imperfect. In other words, older people cannot adjust as well as younger people to anything—to changes of temperature, changes in food, changes of habit, changes in living quarters, or changes of environment. This impaired adaptation must be recognized by correctional officers and the medical staff. It must be recognized that the margin of safety for older people is decreased by their impaired adaptability and that minor things can readily disturb their balance of both physical and mental health.

Symptoms and signs of disease in the aged are much less conspicuous than in younger people. In a similar disease of a similar extent and severity, an older person will have less fever, less pain, less rapid pulse, less swelling, less diarrhea, etc. So, manifestations of various diseases are much easily recognized. Appendicitis can be readily overlooked, and the same is particularly true for intestinal obstruction, septicemia, pneumonia, diabetes, and tuberculosis. By the same token, minor deviations and subtle suggestions of dysfunction take on a much greater significance. And, therefore, severity of symptoms is wholly unreliable in evaluating the severity of disease in the elderly.

Correctional officers as well as the medical staff should realize also that repair and healing in the aged are very slow. Wound healing is retarded. A much longer time is required to recover from an infection. Convalescence must be prolonged, and patience on the part of all concerned is therefore necessary. Exercise, for example, can be increased only very slightly each day in the process of rehabilitating an elderly person who has been immobilized temporarily as a result of disease or injury. Just a trifle more each day can be tolerated: yet this trifle more must be insisted upon in order to progress with the rehabilitation of such individuals who have, of necessity, been at bed rest.

It should also be mentioned that elderly people require and must be given much smaller dosages of drugs. The drugs are absorbed more slowly, though sometimes less completely. Their elimination is also diminished, and because of this drugs are likely to accumulate in the system, especially if there is circulatory impairment or kidney dysfunction, both of which are common in the elderly. Sedative drugs, particularly barbituates, are poorly tolerated by the elderly; they produce toxic effects in relatively small doses, they readily produce disorientation, forgetfulness, apprehension, and unsteadiness.

In elderly individuals there is an even wider variation psychologically and emotionally than physically. The alterations of personality that occur are more quantitative than qualitative.

The miser becomes more miserly, the egotist becomes more egotistical, the complainer becomes more of a complainer, the helpless becomes more helpless, the tolerant becomes more tolerant, the generous becomes more generous, the childish becomes more childish. Emotional immaturity in the aged merely means that they were emotionally immature before they became aged. Youth feels the need for hard confirmation and acceptance, which leads to partial repression of their true character. The elderly no longer feel a strong necessity for acceptance, conventionally, or conformity; their true traits, therefore, become clear and outspoken. Normal personality changes that occur do so insidiously: personality changes that occur rapidly or abruptly suggest mental illness rather than normal senile changes.

Normally, elderly individuals no not change; they lose their flexibility. As a result of loss of flexibility there is a fixation of their habits. If early in their life their habits and interests had been broad, this feature of fixation is little noted. But a life of limited scope and interests leads, in old age, to further narrowing of interests and ideas and, therefore, to rigidity.

It probably does not need to be mentioned that memory, especially for recent events, becomes very unreliable with age. There is loss of acuity of the special senses that assist in memory. And if the will to remember is less, so is the motivation to remember. Details become much less significant, impressions become less brilliant, and attention becomes less intent. Regardless of the factors that result in poor memory, the correctional officers and medical staff members must remember that elderly inmates cannot be expected to remember what they are told. Patience, thoroughness, simplicity, and repetition are essential in instructing or assisting the elderly inmate. All instructions must be precisely specific, and if they are at all important they must be written out clearly and unmistakably.

It might also be mentioned that the truly aged frequently feel extremely insecure. Prison frightens them, illness frightens them, new faces frighten them, correctional officers frighten them, authority frightens them, other inmates frighten them, financial insecurity frightens them, the future frightens them, a fear of having no place to live when they are released from prison frightens them, the realization of their loss of strength and vigor frightens them, the fear of death in prison frightens them. It is surprising that we do not see more panic-stricken cases in the senile penal institution. No doubt we would if every opportunity were not taken to overcome this fear that we realize is created within them. Every opportunity is taken to improve their morale and to give them encouragement. Effort is made to improve their family relations as this is a very important element affecting their emotional tranquility. Aggressive incorrigibles are not permitted to be housed with them, for probably nothing can be more panic provoking to an aged or infirm inmate.

Elderly inmates are extremely grateful for assistance, kindness, and patience. They are as helpless as children, but not unappreciative like children. On the other hand, we must not do too much for them, for it is important that they continue to maintain a maximum degree of self-sufficiency.

The supreme tragedy of senility is the awareness of uselessness. They may realize that they are not needed by their family, society, or by anyone. They feel the rejection. A purposeless existence predisposes to psychological imbalance and mental breakdown. Elderly inmates must be given hope, and one of the greatest hopes they can be given is a hope that they will have something purposeful to do in life, a place in life. In order to accomplish this they must be given a job, a place, a thing to do in prison. If this is not accomplished, the elderly inmate is likely to feel that people who are closest to him no longer want him and are merely waiting for him to die. When such an attitude, or idea, is engendered in their minds, it can rightfully be expected that paranoid antagonism will be created and may, indeed, be acted upon violently. There is a greater hazard for the aged in being too restricted in their activities, than there is in their overdoing. Consequently, elderly people must be allowed to continue their occupation, even if it may mean the danger of a tragedy occurring as a result of physical disease. In other words, at all costs, their life should be made as happy and contented as possible. The correctional officers should encourage physical and mental activities and general interests, realizing that the patient is more important than his illness. At the California Men's Colony, there are many inmates who can get about only in wheelchairs. These cases present special problems and considerations. In the first place, an attendant, another inmate, is assigned on a successfully volunteer basis to each such inmate to help him in and out of his wheelchair, in and out of bed, etc. They often also need help to get to and from the commode, and to assist in this and to help them support themselves while on the commode, rails made of one-inch plumbing pipe have been placed on each side of each commode.

It is also necessary to have special tables in the mess hall for the wheelchair cases so that they can wheel themselves up to the tables and eat comfortably without getting out of their wheelchairs. The height of the tables is regulated to the average height for a man eating comfortably while seated in a wheelchair.

Arrangements should also be made whereby wheelchair cases can handily use the handicraft and hobby shops. It is, of course, important that these inmates engage in the occupational therapy program; it is perhaps even more important for these inmates than for those who are less disabled.

Mr. Richard A. McGee, Director of the Department of Corrections, has said that the purpose of the Department of Corrections is "prevention of delinquency and crime, and protection of society through rehabilitation of offenders, and the restoration of inmates as productive citizens." To accomplish this aim, there are numerous programs in the Department of Corrections of the State of California. There are guidance programs, social living programs, recreation programs, work programs, educational programs, psychiatric programs, occupational therapy, and others. In connection with the above, there are two important points that should be emphasized.

The physically debilitated require the assistance of all the programs of an institution, not just as much as other inmates, but more so. Idleness and unemployment in this group are naturally difficult to avoid but can be prevented through concerted efforts of a coordinated institutional staff. Part-time work should be undertaken in every possible case. Some will require planned programs in addition to those mentioned above, such as physiotherapy programs, geriatric programs, and special programs for certain classes of inmates such as the blind and the wheelchair cases.

The second point is that programs in themselves are not as important a factor in their success as is the attitude of the individuals who conduct them. For instance, medical care is excellent, but if the attitude of the physicians, medical technical assistants, or nurses is poor, the entire medical program is unsatisfactory. And, the Department of Corrections is far better off without an individual, no matter how scientifically capable he may be, if he curses, or if he ignores the inmates. The attitudes of correctional and medical personnel make the geriatric penal institution what it is, a prison or a home. Perhaps the most important part of the over-all rehabilitation program is carried out in the halls, dormitories, hospital wards, and other places where the correctional officers, medical staff, and others come in daily contact with the inmates.

Success in treating patients must start with establishing rapport. This requires, first and foremost, that inmates be confronted with an attitude and atmosphere of sympathetic understanding. Following this, there must be politeness, and, finally, there must be a genuine show of interest in the disabled inmate. Many of the inmates, such as the sex offenders, have rejected themselves; hence, if they are rejected by the institution's personnel also, nothing can happen but to make the inmate and the situation worse. It is true that inmates, even though they are physically disabled, may at times need to be punished, just as a child, but they do not need to be rejected any more than a child in a home should be outcast. The physically incapacitated may be severely punished successfully if rejection is clearly avoided; this includes even the blind. On the other hand, even very little punishment is detrimental to the institution, the Department's program, and all concerned, if it is associated with, or implies, any amount of rejection.

The physically disabled inmate must be allowed to do everything that he can except, of course, violation of regulations. Rehabilitated inmates invariably recognize that what they do for themselves towards their rehabilitation is more than half, and far more important qualitatively, than that which is accomplished by authoritative groups or individuals. It is important for correctional officers and others to warn the inmates that, even though they are physically disabled, they must adhere to the rules and regulations, and they should warn such inmates of the consequences of violation. On the other hand, they must give to inmates assurance, reassurance, and assured assistance. Rejection is incompatible with treatment. In prisons where rejection of inmates is evident, treatment and rehabilitation programs will invariably be difficult and probably ultimately completely unsuccessful.

It has been said that some prisons in the country are becoming hospitals. If this is so, it is because the officials and employees, especially the custodial officers, have made it so, through a benevolent and aspiring attitude. Undoubtedly inmates receive adequate punishment by the loss of freedom, and nothing further is gained by a rejecting and/or an unsympathetic attitude prevailing. The attitude towards disabled inmates, and not the name of the institution, opens or obstructs the inmates' road to higher virtues. Inmates don't act, they react. If we have them realize that we believe they are good, kind, just, and fair, they will be at their best.

It is true that certain drugs, the tranquilizing drugs, have been a boon to prison medicine, but it is to be recognized that the pacifying they produce is but transitory and in no way permanently curative. Psychotherapy (and all that has been stated above is psychotherapy) is of much more lasting duration. Reserpine and the like may make inmates weep: but may they not then cry aloud for more when they are released from the institution?

Individuals like individuality, but those who have become physically incapacitated are likely to lose a great deal of their ability for individuality. Thus, they are more likely to feel inadequate. And, it is well to recognize that inadequacies are often the hidden force behind aggressive behavior. In such cases, it is important that correctional officers control their temper. "Hold in your arms the child" when it is agitated. Indeed, imperturbability is probably the greatest virtue that a correctional officer, or others who work in a penal institution, can possess. They must restrain their indignation when elderly inmate patients do what they are told not to do; expect them not to heed their advice; expect them to be disinterested in the programs and the treatments that are for their benefit. Elderly inmates are curious creatures, and the staff is at their mercy, just as much as they are at the mercy of the staff. They are full of fads and eccentricities; they are full of whims and fancies; but the more closely we study them, the more surely will be our conviction that their weaknesses are not unlike our own. The staff needs to have infinite patience; and realize that these inmates will perhaps have to exercise the same toward the staff. Sanford Bates recently said: "Correctional work is challenging and difficult; so only people who *want* to accept the challenge and who have the courage to go into this type of work can be considered acceptable personnel." Probably one of the most distressing features in dealing with disabled and debilitated inmates is the uncertainty which pertains to the results the staff, as individuals, will obtain. In absolute truth, the aim is the unattainable, and correctional workers must be content with finding few successes and many failures in striving toward complete rehabilitation.

The problem is much more difficult than when dealing with those who do *not* suffer infirmities and physical disabilities in addition to their derelict behavior. In any case, the best advice that can be heeded is that such inmates will exert great pressure upon our finer spirit; yet we must never let their indifference or misbehavior ruffle our equanimity. Patience and cheerfulness will be our best tools; and if we will combine persistence with these, we will have at least, a memory of a well-spent life in helping others who depend upon us.

*Chapter 7*

## COMMUNITY RESPONSIBILITY AND RESEARCH

### RETIREMENT HOUSING AND SOCIAL INTEGRATION*1

Irving Rosow

A MAJOR CHANGE in people's later years is the contraction of their social world, a process hastened by failing health and income. There is an atrophy of social roles and a shrinkage of primary groups. This attrition of membership groups reduces their customary support and may result in an old person's social alienation. Spouses, relatives, and friends retire or get sick and die. Children, friends, and neighbors migrate and move away. As people age, they simply spend more and more time at funerals and saying goodbye to those who were once close to them. As the most meaningful people in the lives of older people disappear, the social integration of the old person is undermined, and the risk of his alienation, isolation, and demoralization is increased.

Such effects, however, are not uniform. Only a minority of old people is lonely, varying up to 1/3 of different groups, depending on the particular sample and how the loneliness figure is derived. But it is a sizable minority. Significantly, Townsend found the most loneliness among those with the most disrupted lives—the widowed, the infirm, and those living alone. In the same vein, he also found that people with moderate social isolation were lonelier than the most isolated, who presumably included the recluse and the volun-

*Reprinted by courtesy of *The Gerontologist, Volume 1*:85–91, June, 1961.
1Presented at the Fifth Congress of the International Association of Gerontology, San Francisco, Calif., August 7-12, 1960. This paper will also be published in Aging around the world, Vol. III, Social and psychological aspects of aging. Proceedings of the Fifth Congress of the International Association of Gerontology (in press). The work on which this paper is based is supported by a grant from the Ford Foundation, whose aid is gratefully acknowledged.

tarily withdrawn. Hence, shrinking primary groups apparently intensify alienation and produce old people who are vulnerable to growing dependency and frustrated social needs.

## THE PROBLEM

The problem this presents is 2-fold. For those who may become alienated: (1) What substitutes exist for their shrinking primary groups? (2) How can retirement housing figure in their social re-integration?

Clearly, only a minority of older people have a housing problem, even though it may be acute when it does occur. Seldom do even 5 per cent spontaneously mention housing as a problem in various surveys, and only up to 15 per cent say they are not satisfied with their living arrangements when asked about this directly. There-fore, we are not here considering the bulk of the aged.

But the problem of housing old people who need it is typically seen in a narrow architectural perspective, mainly as a problem of physical design for safety, comfort, and convenience. This archi-tectural bias may be a serious error, because the physical aspects of housing seem strictly secondary. The Yonkers Housing Authority finds that its old tenants generally manage in ordinary apartments without special provision about as well as the young. Some investi-gators point out that many so-called housing standards for old peo-ple are simply good housing standards as such for all age groups. Further, while special design features are desirable, most of these are quite simple and straight-forward and pose no problem beyond that of additional cost. Thus, if no sub-standard housing is in-volved, the physical aspects of housing are important, but are certainly not the problematic issue.

For the alienated aged, the crucial issue is the social conse-quences of different living arrangements, the social patterns which they breed or sustain, and the social networks which they engender.

Housing experts tend to regard housing as a direct physical means to given social ends and to assume that changes in housing produce specified social changes, but research clearly shows that housing as such seldom structures social life directly. It may modify the physical environment. The physical setting is merely a stage, however, on which the normal social forces which affect individual integration, family life, generational relationships, and community structure play themselves out. While certain social changes may follow new housing arrangements, their causes lie in the familiar social forces which have free play in the new physical setting. In other words, in housing we may manipulate the *conditions,* but not the *determinates* of social life.

In this sense, the most problematic variable in housing the alienated aged is their immediate social environment—specifically, the age composition of the local neighborhood.

## ALTERNATIVE AGE STRUCTURES

The age structure of old people's neighborhoods is one of three basic types: (1) normal or integrated; (2) isolated; and (3) segregated. The normal is the typical urban area of all age groups, with old people scattered through it almost randomly in numbers proportional to their part of the total population. The isolated, exemplified by institutions in the country or true retirement villages, are self-contained, completely separate settlements exclusively of older people. The segregated is the intermediate type, with disproportionate concentrations of older people in enclaves embedded in a larger community. Thus, the isolated pattern concentrates old people together and physically separates them from any surrounding social life. The segregated pattern also concentrates old people, but insulates rather than separates them from a larger community environment.[2]

## HOUSING IDEOLOGY

Gerontologists have firm ideological convictions about the relative merits of normal, segregated, and isolated neighborhoods. They dislike segregated and isolated patterns because these seem undemocratic, invidious, and demoralizing. Presumably these pattern intensify the alienation process without mobilizing any counter-forces. On the other hand, gerontologists like age-integrated

---

[2]These 3 types can be abstracted from the patterned variation of 2 variables: (1) concentration or dispersion of older people, and (2) their physical separation or non-separation from younger people and/or a surrounding community.

neighborhoods and want to keep people in their normal, familiar surroundings as long as possible because this maintains continuity in their lives. Gerontologists also like age-integration for the alienated aged with disrupted lives. It is assumed that different age groups in normal neighborhoods will develop social intercourse and mutual support. More formally stated, gerontologists believe that residential integration will maximize social integration.

However, after this orthodox ideology is stated, we then confront a paradox. Usually ensuing discussions of model retirement housing are almost invariably based on age-segregated examples. These models embrace a familiar catalog—the retirement villages of Ryderwood, Wash.; Youngtown, Ariz.; and Salhaven, Moosehaven, or Kissimee, Fla.; Tompkins Square House in New York City; Cobb's Hill Village in Rochester, N.Y.; the Omaha Teachers cooperative apartment; Senior Center in Santa Barbara, Calif.; Carmel Hall or Presbyterian Village in Detroit; Cedar Apartment in Cleveland; the trailer courts or the various Lavin Hotels in Florida.

This implies that our uncritical ideological position may not be appropriate to the alienated aged. Therefore, we propose to examine here the social effects of these neighborhood types in the light of existing information and research.

## SOCIAL CONSEQUENCES OF NEIGHBORHOOD AGE COMPOSITION

*Isolation*—Residents of neighborhoods which are isolated in terms of their age structure show varied patterns of satisfaction. Presumably, true retirement villages, such as Ryderwood, Moosehaven, or Youngtown, arouse the enthusiasm of their sponsors, residents, and visitors alike. Studies in Moosehaven, for example, show that residents have a high sense of security and morale. But other places which are virtually isolated Homes or relatively inaccessible institutions, often in the country, give a picture of lower morale and other correlates of adjustment.

The critical factor in morale is apparently whether an isolated setting is a full-fledged, self-contained community. To the extent that it approximates a community with all a community's facilities, then it seems to support a thriving social life and to integrate its members.

*Segregation*—Life in segregated arrangements seems to have few of the unfortunate consequences for older people feared by detractors. Reports about such places as Tompkins Square House, Senior Center, Carmel Hall, and the Lavin Hotels, portray their members as involved and engaged in an active social process. The same kinds of reports have been made of residents in Florida trailer courts.

Further, where special facilities are provided in segregated settings, the local aged use them disproportionately for the total age group. For example, only very small proportions of the 65+ age group patronize Golden Age Centers or their local equivalents anywhere. In New York City, the figure is about 1.3 per cent; in a Syracuse sample, less than 5 per cent; and the highest proportion reported anywhere in the literature for normal areas is 12 per cent in a borough of East London. Seldom do as many as 5 per cent of the age group participate. However, in Cleveland, in a public housing retirement apartment with a substantial Golden Age facility, 1/3 of the residents are members, and fully 1/2 of all members are drawn from the retirement apartment project or its adjacent public housing units. Similar results are reported for a Chicago public housing project with a somewhat smaller proportion of elderly. Such findings indicate that segregation favors the use of services which would otherwise be uneconomic and perhaps unsupportable.

Furthermore, Hoyt shows that a high order of mutual aid appears in a trailer park during illnesses which leave isolated old people in normal neighborhoods vulnerable. Informal groups in other segregated settings similarly become mutual aid groups.

We have very little evidence about older people's prior attitudes toward segregated neighborhoods. In Washington state, Stone and Slocum found that only 10 per cent of a rural and small town sample were even tentatively interested in segregated living arrangements, possibly reflecting a low level of housing need. But, when we turn to needier groups, the proportions rise significantly. In two samples of aged public housing applicants in New York

City, about 1/3 of each group preferred segregated arrangements. A survey of older clients of five social agencies in Schenectady showed that of those in need of re-housing, 60 per cent did not want to live in a neighborhood with young children. Experience indicates that, regardless of original preferences, when either public or private segregated housing promises to solve old people's housing problems economically, there is no dearth of applicants for such housing. People apparently accept and adapt to improved housing of whatever type, even though they may have preferred alternatives. This is seen in a recent British housing study in which most people did not get their preferred choice of several different housing types:

> As time went on, tenants tended to become identified with the [dwelling unit] type that they were occupying, and the majority of them came to claim that theirs was the best type in the scheme.

This principle is reflected in the only available data on reactions to segregated living. Hoyt reports that 88 per cent of his trailer park sample preferred ". . . to live in a community such as this where everyone is retired" rather than in one of employed people. In another study of 125 people in four segregated facilities and 175 in several normal public housing projects, Steinle found that roughly 65 per cent of each group preferred the type of neighborhood that is was currently occupying.

For those in sub-standard quarters or with any housing problem, any new housing as such seems more determinate of their reaction than the particular type of facility they are offered. Thus, after they had experienced it, 62 per cent of the residents preferred a segregated neighborhood to one of normal age composition. Furthermore, the segregated residents in good health made this choice almost as often as those in poor health (57 per cent vs. 69 per cent). But this difference in preference according to health was much sharper in the normal, integrated projects where the sick preferred segregated settings three time as frequently as the healthy (65 per cent vs. 22 per cent).

Residents of some retirement communities, like the Florida trailer parks, may be self-selected, but those of other segregated settings, as in Steinle's samples, are not. Self-selection might account for the high level of approval of segregation in the trailer parks, but it would not account for almost two-thirds of Steinle's segregated group preferring this neighborhood type. If some variables of self-selection may affect social integration, this still must be specified in terms of types of people who can adapt to this environment.

The limited data available indicate that for people with housing problems, re-housing itself is the primary determinate of their reaction. Old people respond favorably to segregated settings regardless of their health, and, as the health of those in normal neighborhoods declines, their choice approximates that of segregated residents of comparable health.

However, although the evidence is fairly clear that segregated neighborhoods may effectively integrate their members, few gerontologists have even questioned the assumption that segregation is inimical to old people.

*Integration*—Clearly, the over-riding consideration to be remembered about normal neighborhoods is that they have produced the bulk of our problematic group, the alienated aged, and, therefore, they offer old people no assurance of effective social contact with others.

We can postulate perhaps four conditions under which the aged may be socially integrated into normal neighborhoods. Old people may be integrated to the extent that: (1) they are long-term residents. (2) in a relatively stable, unchanging neighborhood which is (3) socially homogeneous, especially for social class and racial, religious, and ethnic minorities, and (4) the person's local primary groups of family, relatives, friends, and neighbors are still reasonably intact. But to the extent that these conditions are not met—and people are recent arrivals, the neighborhood changes or is socially heterogeneous, and their primary group supports melt away—then their chances of becoming alienated from the social environment increase. It is clear that the alienating forces of residential mobility and neighborhood change are accelerating in urban areas.

If the effect of these independent trends is to alienate, then the crucial problem is the social integration that may result from the residential mixture of different age groups. Specifically, what kinds of social relationships develop between them? We will shortly review some compelling, if provisional and unpleasant evidence, especially for people living alone—about 24 per cent of those over sixty-five in 1950 in the U.S.A.

It has been argued that the urban residential community is not a viable basis of social integration, and this might be peculiarly applicable to the aged, especially after retirement. It is certainly axiomatic among gerontologists that older people have more difficulty in making friends than when they were younger. This is probably intensified by the social distance and negative attitudes toward the aged maintained by other age groups.

It is consistent with this that the aged have been trenchantly analyzed as a quasi-minority group in America, one viewed in stereotypes by others, suffering from discrimination and from their own defensive reactions in the fashion of other minority groups. And, like other minority groups, they accept many of the stereotypes about themselves of those around them. Indeed, for all practical purposes, young and old people have the same images of the aged.

But where residential integration can destroy the social distance and negative images held by dominant groups about racial, religious, or other minorities, this apparently does not apply to old people. A study by Drake shows that younger people's attitudes do not vary by their experience with or exposure to the aged, as measured by their living with older people at any time, or their frequency and intimacy of contact with them. In other words, stereotypes about the aged seem resistant to change by exposure.

Such inflexible images fit in with the patterns of association between generations. Aukes reports that the relations of younger adults and children to old people in a Chicago housing project ". . . was fraught with the usual prejudices and lack of mutual interest and understanding." Similarly, in a Florida retirement community, which was also occupied by young and middle-aged people, friendships and informal groups developed almost exclusively within age groups. This echoes the findings of an unpublished study in a retirement public housing apartment in which one-third of the units were specifically reserved for younger families in order to stimulate their association with the old. Out of the eighty-eight friendships reported by a sample of both age groups, only one crossed the age barrier. A more recent pilot study with a 50 per cent sample of the aged in this same apartment checked this point again and showed that of all the old people's friendships with neighbors, only 4 per cent were with young neighbors. By the same token, Terreberry found that old people living alone in an integrated Detroit housing project were socially isolated and had almost no significant contact with their young and middle-aged neighbors.

Such evidence is fragmentary, but pending further research, it is clear and consistent. Except under conditions previously noted, in modern urban settings, viable friendships do not spontaneously develop between age groups, but are confined almost exclusively within them. There is apparently an effective social barrier between the old and the young or middle-aged.

As unpleasant as this may be, it is not surprising, since it reflects the age-grading of the larger social order. In a mass, industrial society, friendship groups are peer groups—people with basically similar social status, occupational rank, education, stage in the family cycle, values, problems, and life styles. These guides to selective social groups also become the mechanisms of age-grading. The symbols and stigmata of age ranks are increasingly externalized, formalized, and shared through numerous institutions: the educational system, adolescent or youth culture, career stages, suburbia, forced retirement, and the like. In a mass society, informal age-grading reduces the social bonds between age groups which may still survive where mobility and bureaucratization have not seriously weakened local community identification. There is probably a growing trend of age-grading which links and binds people by characteristics which are highly correlated with age and which reduces the common problems and shared experience of people of different generations.

Both the life cycle and societal trends weaken inter-generational relations. The attrition of occupational and familial roles, of health and income, and the development of technology, science, and general social change all combine to intensify the differences between generations, to limit the reciprocity of their relations to each other, and to weaken the basis of their association. The result is that a common social frame of reference exists primarily with one's own age peers.

In the U.S.A. where the larger portion of society is youth-oriented and rejects old age, to accept old age is to document one's social obsolescence and marginality—unless effective social insulation is established.

We have been concerned with the current situation of the aged. Here some major social class differences also enter the picture. Bell's studies show that the major differences in anomie occur between social classes rather than between age groups per se. In his samples, the old were not significantly more anomic than the young within the same social class. The relative importance of determinates of anomie proved to be: social class factors, social isolation, and finally, age. Significant for the alienated aged, social isolation was inversely related to family activity, although highly intensive contact with children has been reported as depressing morale, especially of the middle class aged. In addition, the working class is much more dependent on neighbors as a source of friends than the middle class. Indeed, the middle-class aged may actively avoid the formation of friendships and entangling ties with neighbors. Further, residential isolation is tantamount to social isolation and anomic for the working class, but not for the middle class. Thus, the middle classes apparently have more personal resources or interest which make them considerably more self-sufficient than the working class and less dependent on the immediate social environment for their support, morale, and social integration.

If this is the case, if our society remains informally age-graded, and if the working class, to which the bulk of the aged belong, is strongly dependent on neighbors for its associates, then normal neighborhoods may be excellent instruments for insuring the isolation and demoralization of alienated old people. With the attrition of family, friends, and other former ties, the dispersal of their age peers in a normal neighborhood reduces the number of potential new associates around them. The field of eligible new friends is thin and scattered, and the effects of this are intensified by any decline in health or mobility, Except under special conditions, then, normal neighborhoods may attenuate the possible axes of social integration of older people.

This may be the basic reason for the success of segregated retirement communities—they concentrate rather than diffuse the field of potential friends and support, thereby maximizing the conditions of social integration. This is not to suggest that new friendships necessarily attain the meaning, intensity, or intimacy of the old. As people age, affect becomes less important in life and they consequently reduce their emotional investments. In other words, their emotional relations become more superficial. But, under these conditions, even superficial friendships may be adequate to sustain the alienated.

Thus, there are grounds for re-appraising the suitability of age-integrated and segregated environments for alienated old people. We hypothesize that the segregated neighborhood will more effectively integrate old people socially than the integrated neighborhood.

## POSSIBLE FUNCTIONS OF AGE-SEGREGATION

What, then, are some possible consequences of a heavy residential concentration of older people?

First, significant economic gains are feasible in the volume of both housing and special services which might be provided. It is much cheaper to build a large number of dwelling units in one place than an equal number of scattered units. Similarly, one can provide various services more economically and effectively to a concentrated than to a dispersed market.

Second, major social gains may be realized from new groups memberships. The concentration of people with common status and problems and with similar life experience and perspectives maximizes the opportunity for new friendships. By the same token, the high exposure to a field of eligibles maximizes the opportunity for re-marriage. In Moosehaven, for example, almost 30 per cent of the couples got married after meeting each other there (Kleemeier, 1954), and the evidence is conclusive that married older people are better adjusted than the widowed. Further, new group memberships afford new identifications and psychological support, as well as mutual aid. The sheer undermining of isolation may be an important barrier to demoralization, especially in the working class.

The re-integration of older people into new groups may facilitate their transition to a new aged role, especially when there has been confusion about this. Age peers provide role models on which a person may pattern himself. The older group can also generate new activities which crystallize new role dimensions. By clarifying expectations and appropriate behavior, especially in dealing with the leisure of retirement, old people provide each other with new norms. In legitimizing these norms, age peers may aid the acceptance of older self-conceptions and hedge this in with supports which are presently lacking, to the apparent detriment of adjustment. Indeed, if older people can accept their age peers as a new reference group, as a source of standards for themselves, then their chances of developing clear, acceptable, new roles to which they can make some satisfactory adjustment may decidedly improve. They may no longer need to cling to youthful standards which they cannot meet and for which the necessary life conditions have withered away.

Two conditions will favor these effects of residential segregation. The most important is that residents will be of basically homogeneous social composition, of broadly similar backgrounds, social class, and life experience, whether the mechanism of selection be the market, self-selection, or tenant-selection policy. Sharing similar values, interests, and problems can preserve a basic continuity in their lives and simulate social intercourse. The second condition is that the context of segregation be insulating rather than invidious or stigmatizing. Segregation must impinge on residents in socially acceptable terms rather than in terms of de-valuation, marginality and loss of status.

## SOCIAL WELFARE SYMPOSIUM
## ASSESSMENT OF COMMUNITY WELFARE
## PROGRAMS FOR THE AGED

### ELLEN WINSTON

Over the last few years there has been growing momentum in social-welfare planning for our older citizens by both govern-

*Reprinted by courtesy of *Journal of Gerontology*, Supplement No. 2, Volume *13*:53-57, July, 1958.

mental and voluntary organizations. There are well-recognized reasons for this increasing emphasis. Foremost is the attention being directed in many areas to the growing number and proportion of older people in the population. The impact of population trends is being felt so widely that many organizations are focusing on the older age segment, much as other groups focus on children and youth. A second factor is the change in family patterns and living conditions so that aged individuals have a changing role in family life. During this same recent period there has been substantial development of social-welfare services geared to the older age groups under both public and voluntary auspices. Particularly important in this connection has been the development of programs for greater economic security for older individuals, as employment opportunities have been declining. Because of the widespread interest, the literature has been increasing rapidly. Books, articles, pamphlets, and reports of conferences and statistical summaries are so numerous that one cannot pretend to summarize even the major contributions.

The public assistance program established under the Social Security Act in 1935 and as substantially amended, with the resulting large number of persons receiving Old Age Assistance, focused attention as never before upon the great numbers of older people with insufficient incomes. These people have come, and continue to come, to social agencies for financial assistance and other services. The program of Old Age and Survivors Insurance inaugurated at the same time set the age for beginning eligibility at sixty-five years, just as that age was set for eligibility for Old Age Assistance. Recently we have the sixty-two year option for women. Nonetheless, we have the very real problem of an arbitrary age limit with respect to income-maintenance programs. This, in turn, has affected our approach to other programs and services geared particularly to the needs of older people.

We have seen the OASI program increasing sharply in recent years in terms of numbers receiving benefits and the total amounts of money involved. Along with the expanded coverage of Old Age Insurance, there has been relatively lesser need for Old Age Assistance. However, because of population increases, the numbers receiving Old Age Assistance are expected to continue at substantially the same, or a slightly decreased, level for many years to come so that "five years from now, even with the increasing effectiveness of insurance, we will have nearly as many people getting some old-age assistance as we do now—perhaps 200,000 less than the 2.5 million today. The number of the aged will increase by 1.5 million, and as a percentage of all aged, the old-age assistance load may drop about 15 per cent, but the absolute number . . . will not greatly decline."

Actually, in terms of income-maintenance programs and other services to be discussed hereafter, the parallelisms are far greater than any differences between programs under social-welfare auspices for older people and those for the younger age groups. The most striking differences in the development of programs perhaps are in those which are focused specifically upon employment. From the point of view of social welfare, this similarity in types of services for various age groups is extremely helpful, since it means that what has been learned in the operation of programs for younger age groups frequently can be transferred as basic experience for a newer program focusing on the older ages.

## EVALUATION OF RESOURCES

In evaluating the adequacy of the social-welfare resources of a community, the total needs of the community must be studied in relation to existing programs, and appropriate plans made for meeting all social-welfare needs insofar as possible. We do not believe in segregating out a particular age group for attention, to the neglect of other groups or to the neglect of total planning for the community. Actually when there is emphasis upon a specialized program or upon a particular group quite apart from other community needs, the program is likely to have slender roots in the community or to stand out as an independent effort substantially unrelated to the ongoing pattern of community services. In general we make progress most effectively as we seek to strengthen all essential services and as we provide sound foundations for meeting varied community needs. We must be concerned about raising the level, as it were, of all welfare programs so that we make social progress on a wide front rather than concentrating in too specialized areas. This applies not only to the social-welfare field and its various interests and emphases. We find also that, unless we are concerned in community planning with health and education and recreation, we cannot make as effective progress as we would like in our own area of responsibility. This is not to overlook the practical problems involved and the necessity for priorities. A timetable based on an overview of community needs and resources is one thing; focus on a special group while failing to recognize other community needs, quite a different one.

## RECENT DEVELOPMENTS

So far as social-welfare programs for the aged are concerned, we are moving in a variety of directions. Reference has already been made to the two large-scale economic-security programs. In recent sessions the Congress has strengthened both of these programs so that payments to individuals receiving either Old Age Assistance or Old Age Insurance have generally been increased. Even with these increases, the income available to thousands upon thousands of our older citizens remains far below the amounts needed for a minimum health and decency level of living. In many states, due to lack of adequate state and local funds for matching purposes, Old Age Assistance payments continue to be far too low. Also OASI benefits for retired workers who had low earnings are at best insufficient to meet minimum needs. Hence more and more people are receiving funds through both programs. Continued study is being given by governmental agencies to the proportions of beneficiaries of Old Age Insurance who must have their monthly payments supplemented by Old Age Assistance—a trend which will become of increased importance in the years immediately ahead.

Another major amendment to the Social Security Act with respect to the aged, enacted in 1956, was provision for "a description of the services (if any) which the State agency makes available to applicants for and recipients of Old Age Assistance to help them attain self-care." While any number of state public welfare programs had placed some emphasis in this area, this was concrete recognition on the part of the Congress and the Department of

Health, Education, and Welfare that a broad service program is an essential concomitant to the program for financial assistance. Self-care can, of course, mean many things. Generally, however, it relates to those programs of state and local public welfare agencies which contribute to the overall well-being of the individual and help him to make as effective use as possible of his own resources. Impetus is being given through this amendment to more specialized services under public welfare auspices for older people in general, not merely those who are eligible for Old Age Assistance.

In still another direction the 1956 amendments to the Social Security Act crystallized directions in which we had already been moving with regard to welfare programs for the aging. I refer to the amendment with respect to medical or other types of remedial care, whereby the federal agency will help pay for such care up to one-half of $6.00 multiplied by the total number of individuals who received Old Age Assistance in a state during a given month. Making provision for medical care outside of the subsistence grant is stimulating the development of more adequate medical-care programs. We still have a long way to go before persons who must have financial assistance in meeting health needs receive all of the assistance required, but this amendment represents substantial progress. At the same time public health with respect to the chronic diseases and nutrition are being strengthened under federal and state impetus.

The several social-welfare programs briefly reviewed here are in effect in differing degrees in the states. At the same time specialized programs of many types are beginning to be provided under public welfare auspices. Because housing is one of the more serious problems for older people, particularly those with low incomes, there has been particular interest on the part of public welfare agencies in various types of domiciliary or sheltered care. These programs have usually been developed to meet the needs of persons who, no longer able to maintain their homes, need protected living arrangements. These programs have been developed also because of the demand for an alternative to institutional care for individuals not requiring active treatment programs. Since these are normally programs based upon state legislation, they have been developing at differing rates but with a substantial core of common objectives to meet common needs. In order that there may be adequate standards established for such care, the National Committee on Aging of the National Social Welfare Assembly has placed particular stress upon this area. With our current widespread interest in domiciliary care for older people, we fortunately can point to the pioneer examples of group care for the aging, which, for fifty years or more, and usually under religious auspices, have shown the way.

Also, taking cognizance of the demand for housing suitable for elderly persons in independent living arrangements at a price they can afford to pay, the American Public Welfare Association has issued a policy statement, "Public Welfare and Housing." This of course is but one illustration of increasing emphasis on this facet of the need. There will inevitably be growing emphasis by public and voluntary agencies upon better ways for meeting housing needs, whether in individual domiciles or in group care.

Slower to develop, but receiving increasing attention, are those specialized services which help older people to continue to live independently and more happily in their own homes. One of these developments is the emphasis upon homemaker service, upon providing, on a recurring basis, sufficient assistance with the activities of everyday living so that it is not necessary to uproot the elderly person. That we have not moved more rapidly in this area has certainly been due, on the one hand, to lack of funds to provide this specialized type of service. On the other hand, perhaps we have also been slow to catch the vision of what this type of program, already so well demonstrated with respect to children, can mean to the aged. However, this type of service has been made available to a sufficient extent through both public and voluntary programs to demonstrate convincingly its importance in comprehensive planning for services for older people. Until we help more older people remain in their own homes or return to their homes when able to do so, we shall have a tragic gap in our pattern of available services.

Also in the category of helping individuals in the older age brackets in terms of their adjustment are the day centers, particularly associated with the large cities such as New York, Cleveland,

Chicago, and San Francisco. Here too, while the activities and programs differ, we have a type of development which has a parallel in
our planning for day care for young children.

There are many types of specialized programs associated with
an individual community or a particular service group in a community that cannot be enumerated here. Those which have been
enumerated are, by and large, the major developments in the social
welfare field, especially under auspices, in terms of making available needed services for older people. Basic to their administration
and to their effectiveness in individual cases is the level of casework
service provided by the sponsoring agency. Providing financial
assistance, as well as all the other social services, should be seen as
individualized skilled services by qualified caseworkers, with the
use of other professional disciplines as required. That we have such
a shortage of really qualified staff to work with older people is a
major deterrent to program development.

## BASIS FOR PLANNING

The question has been raised: Do we need to plan for all older
people in a community, or must we learn to think more clearly
about the categories of people who need help? I would question
both approaches. If we plan for all older people, we have no sharp
focus as a basis for program development. If we focus on categories
of people, we are really acceding to the framework which law has
laid down. It is actually far sounder to think in terms of the various
types of help that people need and how these services may be made
available to persons with specialized problems. After all, aging is
an ongoing process, and persons at different ages may have differing needs which social-welfare programs should be set up to provide. One of the real dangers in attempting to provide more effectively for the needs of older people is that we focus so much on
the age group that we do not emphasize appropriately the particular
services we are set up to offer—services that are perhaps needed
most by persons in the older age groups and that hence take on
particular characteristics because of the groups which seek and use
such services. When we do not have the resources to meet the particular needs of older persons, certainly we need to establish new

programs and services or to expand existing ones. Such programs need to be integrated into a total community program as we strive better to integrate older people into the total life of the community.

Most of us in the social-welfare field are gravely concerned over the inadequacies of present services, both public and voluntary, that are available to meet the special needs of older people. While some workers have perspective over a period of years so that they see the tremendous gains that have been made, we realize the deficits in providing truly adequate services. The reasons are not new. We lack sufficient funds, whether the funds come through federal, state, or local appropriations or through voluntary contributions. We lack adequate staff, not only staff with generalized training in social work and in allied fields, but particularly staff who have some special knowledge with respect to the processes of aging and of how the older years bring special needs or an intensification of certain types of needs. As in other programs, too, we find barriers in terms of lack of public understanding, perhaps too little imagination in providing some types of services, and always questions of whether even existing resources are being used to the full. However, in none of these problems is there anything that is particularly characteristic of services to older people. We have the same problems around adequacy of services for all age groups. The fact that we have come more lately to recognize, or at least to plan constructively for, the special needs of older people has made the development of service programs to meet the demand a more recent phenomenon in most communities.

## MEASURES OF EFFECTIVENESS

As we look at the vast pattern of services now being provided to older people, we must constantly be concerned with measures of their effectiveness in meeting the particular needs they are set up to serve. For some of these programs the degree of adequacy can be very definitely measured. In those programs designed to provide basic economic security, we have only to look at the published data to realize in how many states average Old Age Assistance grants, and even Old Age Insurance payments, are insufficient to provide for an acceptable level of living. When we take into account medical needs of older people and how they are being met, we have another measure of inadequacy in many states, but also adequacy in a growing number of states.

In the field of housing we can also be quite specific in certain measurements. We know, for example, that when it comes to licensing standards for domiciliary care or in the nursing-home field, we have a great distance still to go in order to guarantee that adequate standards are met. In some cases this is due to lack of basic legislation or of competent staff, or it is due to standards that either do not exist or have been set too low.

Our position in the area of basic casework services is much the same as that in the total social-service field. How does one measure effectively casework services? Do our records show constructive movement in the individual case?

Another approach to measuring the adequacy of services is found in the fact that so many of the specialized programs are located in a few large urban communities, wherease it is reasonable to expect that these needs exist also in communities of comparable characteristics generally across the country.

## PUBLIC AND VOLUNTARY AGENCIES

In services to the aging, as in all other welfare programs, the question of the respective roles of the public and the voluntary agencies inevitably arises. Certainly there is no difference in this respect in terms of services available to one age group as compared with any other age group. The basic philosophy that now determines any distinctions in roles would, we believe, usually apply in any community concerned with services to the aging. We recognize that private agencies are in no position to handle the tremendous cost involved in financial assistance for subsistence and medical care of the aging. Also public agencies must administer licensing laws and other types of legal responsibilities. Hopefully, voluntary agencies will increasingly demonstrate nonfinancial social services and recreational and educational programs and, through experimentation, build up the knowledge and skills, the emphasis on good standards, and the community support which are essential to offering specialized services on a broad scale.

## A LOOK AT THE FUTURE

As we look to the future, we realize that the sheer impact of the sharply increasing numbers of older people will have more and more effect upon the demand for specialized services which are particularly geared to meet their needs. We may expect to see increasing supplementation of Old Age Insurance payments by public assistance unless there is a sharp increase in the benefit rates. Certainly persons receiving Old Age Assistance will grow continually older on the average than their present average of seventy-five years. With an increasing number of elderly people who are very old, the demands for medical care at public expense, whatever the method of payment, must have increased attention.

Present services—in which, by and large, we either help people who can continue to maintain independent lives in their own homes, or we remove them from their homes into some kind of group or institutional care—need to be supplemented on a broad scale by services which will give sufficient help to enable individuals to remain in their own homes. We must give more attention to such programs as homemaker service, meals on wheels, home nursin services, and day centers. We must place more attention upon strengthening the individual family situation so that the elderly person can remain in his own home, either alone or in a family group. Here we have made only the slightest beginning in terms of effective programs.

We may certainly anticipate a wide variety of specialized services undertaken by voluntary agencies or by various organized community groups concerned with contributing to the total pattern of services in their own localities. Since much experimentation, demonstration, and supplementation of large-scale programs is needed, this is a development to be actively encouraged.

The deficit in personnel with special training for understanding the particular needs of older people has been stressed above. We have not yet geared our formal training programs in social work to any extent to preparing people for specialized services to older people. If through specialized training and experience we can build up a large group of persons with special skills in this area, we shall be able to promote more realistic and effective programs to meet the wide range of problems faced by older people. We shall be in a far better position to help promote continued good health and independence, to foster individual dignity and well-being. We shall, in truth, recognize in our older citizenry not only a community responsibility but especially a challenging opportunity.

# NEW THEORIES AFFECTING GERIATRIC SOCIAL INSTITUTIONS*

### Jerome Kaplan

People live longer on the average than ever before. They are also living longer after the time when they are expected to give up major social and personal responsibilities.

The community must assume greater responsibilities toward old people, not only for their well-being but for its own. The later years of life should be made a fruitful period of growth and improvement in mind and character, a time of continued contributions by the old people to better themselves and their communities. A well-planned program within the community should attempt to anticipate those problematic situations which may confront the elderly and their families, such as potential deterioration of personality and character, loss of self-esteem, and withdrawal from the satisfactions of everyday living. One means to avert these effects is positive control of the environment in which older people live.

## LEISURE AND RETIREMENT

Age forces change upon old people, and successful adjustment to aging demands changes in every sphere of activity. Although some relaxation of activity may be necessary, mental and physical health can be maintained only through self-discipline. However, the older person must find or be provided with circumstances favor-

*Reprinted by courtesy of *Geriatrics,* Volume *17,* March, 1962. Prepared for presentation at the Iowa Welfare Association Annual Conference and Institute, October 5, 1959, Des Moines, Iowa.

able to that maintenance. He may find that he has time on his hands after he has passed the age when he is expected to give up his major social and personal responsibilities, and self-discipline is dependent on having responsibilities to meet.

Anyone who makes a sudden break from one way of life to another without adequate preparation often finds great difficulties of adjustment, and old people are subject to great distress because of the worries peculiar to old age. Ill health, fear of death, loss of relatives and friends, poor or inadequate housing, fear of losing work, financial insecurity or a reduced income, and their children's and the public's indifference are part of their lengthy list of woes. The aging person may make a favorable adjustment to his altered situation when, given good health, he is still able to be productive at work or at home, but, in addition to work, the older person must be capable of finding release from his burdens through leisure.

Retirement suddenly presents a great amount of leisure. That leisure which was once merely a period of refreshment must now become an end in itself. The recognition, status, prestige, self-expression, and friendship once afforded by work must now be derived from leisure.

The average American, however, lives in a culture that consciously manifests a distrust and suspicion of leisure; he is imbued with a puritanical faith that life without work is meaningless. But the traditional values of the past can only cause dislocation if they are not revised to be in keeping with present-day facts. Today, 15 to 40 per cent of total consumer expenditure is for leisure activity. The seventy-hour week has been reduced to forty, and a thirty-hour work week has been envisaged in some industries. For a person without household tasks, the whole day is leisure time.

Adjustment to retirement can be aided in part by becoming psychologically prepared for it. A further part, of course, involves the attitude and conception of what constitutes a worthwhile role. How leisure activity or recreation is defined by the older person is important. Some older people insist that they are so active as volunteers or as members of an organization that they have no time for leisure. This was borne out by a sixty-eight year old man, retired for three years, who insisted that he spent so much time working around his house, watching television, and taking an active part in a retirement club that he had no leisure time. For others, leisure time pursuits represent the uselessness to which society has relegated them. For example, retirement from work is difficult to accept as a normal phase of life by some farmers. This is readily understandable, since retirement then conflicts with their social values of usefulness and productivity.

The older person clings to a tradition of culture in which work is all important and in which success and achievement are correlated with work. A part of this tradition connects growth with the young. Hence, programs for people must give them a chance to realize growth through leisure and through recreational activities. New meanings for leisure must be discovered. Different ways must be found by which persons can use their free time to contribute to their community and be held in respect and dignity even though their contributions are not made through work.

Although organization is the rule in almost every phase of modern life, retirement is entered upon without adequate planning or thought. The relinquishment of work and the beginning of retirement cause significant changes in daily routine and a possible disruption of social relationships. An appropriate understanding of leisure may preserve dignity and respect for the older person even when his social status has changed.

## THE YOUNG AND THE OLD

A review of history shows that old people are most secure when society has developed a mutually supportive and intermingled relationship between the old and the young. Youth and age do much to complement and inspire each other. When specific activities for only the old are outlined, the proper relationship of these activities to youth should not be forgotten. For example, any program developed in a home for the aged should recognize occasionally the zest and enthusiasm which can be brought only by children and adolescents.

Often we forget the kindness, wisdom, and stories which the elders can bring to the young. *There is no absolute substitute for the common interests which bind youth and age together.* Although this is true, there are synthetics which, at times, serve to supplement and, if necessary, replace the "genuine article." Foster homes, the golden age recreation movement, aid to geriatric patients, and retirement counseling are only a small portion of the programs now under way.

Far oftener than is necessary or desirable, older persons are denied opportunities to share and contribute as much as they could or should. Ours is a culture which tends to exclude older people and emphasize opportunities for the young.

## COMMUNITY ATTITUDES

Just as the individual must face the changes introduced by older years, so must the community prepare for its older citizens. Each community must learn to produce an environment conductive to desirable changes. The American of today carries with it an attitude of ambivalence toward the older people and the aged. On one hand, they are regarded as figures of authority; on the other, as dependent and childlike individuals. *In the immediate years ahead, it is not inconceivable that the older person may be more fully equated with authority.*

An individual is seldom responsible for defining his place in the sun. Part of the social battle and part of the person's internal conflict arise from the gap between what an older person is allowed to do, what he is able to do, and what he thinks he can do. This kind of uncertainty is found more frequently in societies in transition that have not been able to prescribe different types of roles for persons in specific age categories. Feelings of security, prestige, opportunities for participation and interaction are dependent upon what a community considers normal at a particular time.

In a rapidly changing society, the opportunity for active participation by the old is disrupted. Rapid social change tends to inactivate the older person, while stable conditions may set the pattern of participation by him. Seniority rights aptly illustrate the latter; being overlooked by an organization which one has served faithfully in the past or suddenly being given an honorary membership to replace an active one are examples of the former. More times than necessary, the effects are devastating, for what is a well-intentioned act serves to cut older people off from the rest of the group. Henceforth they are "different."

More than one factor undoubtedly influences changes within an individual. Yet, more and more a person is considered old by his community when he loses his social competence, whether it be from individual failure or through community apathy.

On the other hand, numerous subcultural groups have developed ways of dealing with the aged or working with older persons that have not been fully explored. Successful aging rests upon the capacity of the older person to take advantage of opportunities which are made available to him by the society of which he is a part.

In our society, it is grossly difficult to equate prestige, respect, or the material securities with old age. Few roles have been reserved for the old that can be performed with dignity in the eyes of the community or with prestige in the mind of the individual. Even the grandparent baby sitter is not rated as high as the young baby sitter. More and more, older people in our society experience contractions in social relationships as their work group and family group are either substantially altered or become nonexistent.

Playing a role in the productive economy or within the household, when coupled with good health, is predictive of a favorable adjustment to aging. On the other hand, the family structure is less and less a unit except for parents and their young children. The present emphasis is upon the conjugal, or one-or two-generation family, which by definition precludes aged parents. The scattered family has become an accepted part of the "New America." Occupation or selection of another part of the country for other reasons lure many away forever from the parental home. The social roles of the adult in the family unit are altered and, in some instances, are changed from provider and housekeeper to dependent.

Isolation and loneliness are potential causes of problems. Such loneliness comes when family group relationships are greatly modified without compensatory relationships to take their place. Yet, as adults grow older, social relationships other than those associated with daily work activities are progressively restricted to relatives. We expect the young to break away from the old and the old not to live with the young, although an unmarried daughter may feel a psychologic push or be actually pressured by the married siblings to care for the old parent. More often than not, the traditional three-generation family in the United States causes conflict rather than harmony. A new type of family relationship of independence of both the older and younger generations has sprung up.

While the social roles of persons in family units change with age, increase in status, respect, or security is not always insured. It is good to cheer the older person and the aged by pleasant labels, by exaggeration of work capacity, by assurance of happy retirement years, and by minimizing biologic quiescence. However, both personal and community planning must face realism as to health, income, housing, social relations, status, and adjustment. Unrealistic optimism breeds disillusionment and neglect.

Aging to be personally acceptable must allow older people to find places in society whereby they believe that they are participating strategically.

## CHALLENGE TO PLANNING

Total community planning needs to give more consideration to its entire organizational structure. The variance between that which is socially expected and that which is socially available is a tremendous challenge. Although our efforts toward helping older people adjust to personal problems should not be abated, an immense effort should be exerted to eliminate the lack of opportunities within society which precipitate many individual difficulties.

The loss of associations which have disintegrated must be replaced with other equally satisfactory group associations. *The views and actions of the older person are greatly dependent on how useful he feels in relation to his surroundings.* It is difficult to realize that in old age there is at last time for intellectual, cultural, and spiritual activities. Only in very recent years has society through its collective organizations begun to guide older people and the aged to a full life in the later years.

It is important to older people to remain active participants in group affairs in either operational or supervisory roles. The other basic concerns or older people, such as a long life, protection from the hazards of living, safeguarding or strengthening the prerogative of seniority, and a comfortable and honorable withdrawal from life when physical necessity requires it, are constant permeating influences as the community makes opportunities available to elderly people.

Community planning geared to older persons' needs is basic for the urban community, the small town, and the rural environment. Regardless of geography, a concerted community effort is necessary. The older person may be just as isolated and discontented in a small community as in a city. We have been holding on to a sentimental belief that the small community is an ideal place to live in the later years of life. While small communities in the United States have more older people proportionately than the larger cities, it is probably due in large measure to the migration of the young and to the reluctance of home owners to move. This does not underestimate the importance of social ties but suggests other factors which cut down movement by many older people. When the husband or wife dies or when they are estranged, when the children move, when the number of old friends declines rapidly, and when there is no longer a job, the older person exists on the periphery of life rather than in the center of social relationships. He cannot turn to his mate, his children, or old friends. The number of friends an older person thinks he has may even be at variance with the opinion of those he considers his friends. This is a major factor limiting opportunities for informal participation. Consequently, any efforts directed toward individual adjustment must also be concerned with the opportunities available within our communities. We are faced with a two-fold challenge of great magnitude: *preparing the individual to adjust and accept his changing role within society and providing the climate and sources that allow new senior roles.*

Community planning on all levels must learn how to develop the basic resources. It must recognize the relationships introduced by aged people who live in concentrated areas in addition to reaching old people who dwell in independent households. For those residing within and without the institution, we must learn how to create stimulating and effective environments. Intelligent action programs must learn to discern between problems which are essentially caused by the personality of an individual and those caused by the personality of the community.

Certain prerequisites for an adequate program for the rural older people and the aged are largely beyond the scope of local community action *only*. In this category fall the need for retirement and health benefit systems; additional attention to the employment needs of older people in state employment services; more adequate old age issistance payments when needed; additional adequate medical facilities, including nursing homes; basic and practical research in all phases of aging; demonstration and pilot projects; and fellowships and stipends for continuous learning and training.

To measure a community's program to meet the social, emotional, and health needs of older people and the aged in city, rural, and small town communities, answers must be provided for the following questions.

*Social Needs.* Is there a special job finding service for older adults? Is there a need for this particular effort? Do employers, agencies, or organizations offer counseling programs to prepare workers and farmers for retirement? Are education courses for older people offered in schools or libraries? How many recreational outlets such as "senior citizens" clubs or "after-60" hobby shows are available for the older farmers and small town residents? Is housing provided which is designed to meet the special needs of older people on the farm or in the hamlet? Is there a well-balanced area program to preserve farm family life? Are social and therapy programs provided on a regular basis in homes for the aged, boarding homes, and nursing homes where some rural people reside? Do fraternal and civic groups carry on active programs for older people? Is there an organized community effort to give continued direction in planning for the aging?

*Health Needs.* Are there adequate public health nursing services? Do home nursing care services meet the needs of the aged? Are there sufficient nursing home beds which are fire-resistant and designed to allow for good medical and nursing care? How many chronically ill aged patients are being cared for in community hospitals who could receive care in a nursing home? Is the medical society organized and alert? Are there aged people in nursing homes or mental hospitals who could live elsewhere if facilities, such as those providing care for persons recovering from debilitatting strokes, were locally available? Is there an expressed interest in expanding and improving health facilities and services?

The soundness of this approach of people working out their own problems has been demonstrated with success throughout the years. If a community problem is to be solved, it will be accomplished through the cooperative efforts of its residents and organizations utilizing national and state resources geared to the latest theories based on research and experience.

## THE ROLE OF RESEARCH IN
## SOLVING THE PROBLEMS OF THE AGED*

### Nathan W. Shock

Everyone aspires to a long life, but no one wants to be old. These conflicting desires stem from the popular conception that old age is always associated with long periods of disability and increasing hardship. However, casual observation tells us that individuals differ greatly in the way they age. The stooped shoulders and measured gait, so adeptly portrayed by Red Skelton's pantomime of the "little old man," is unmistakable as the stereotype of old age. However, we know that many older people retain their vigor and are active even at advanced ages. The accomplishments of Toscanini, Adenauer, Churchill, Baruch, Grandma Moses, and many others remind us that advanced age is not necessarily associated with disability and decreptitude.

Why do some individuals retain their capacities while others lose them? What can an individual or society do to assure a long, active and healthy life? These are important questions which ultimately will be answered by research. However, useful answers can seldom be obtained to broad general questions. It has been said

*Reprinted by courtesy of *The Gerontologist*, Volume *1*:14-16, March, 1961.

that there is an inverse relationship between the social importance of a question and the degree of scientific rigor that can be brought to bear upon it. That is, precise answers can be obtained only to small specific questions. There is a certain amount of truth in this statement, but it should not be inferred that socially important questions are inaccessible to scientific research. However, it does mean that the complex questions which are socially important must be broken down into many simpler questions which can be answered by carefully controlled research.

If we are to maintain health and vigor into advanced age, we must understand the processes and mechanisms involved in the phenomena of aging. The concept of aging, like that of truth, beauty, or liberty, may be glibly used, but defies a precise definition which will be acceptable to everyone. One definition is that aging represents the changes that take place in a cell or an organism with the passage of time, with particular reference to life following the cessation of growth.

Research on aging covers a wide range of questions. The questions fall into three major categories:

(1) What is the basic biological process that constitutes aging?
(2) What is the influence of aging on the psychological and behavioral characteristics of humans?
(3) How do social customs and institutions influence the behavior of aging people?

Thus research in gerontology extends from the investigation of fundamental problems in biology through the physiological, mental, and personality characteristics of humans to the broad social and economic factors that contribute to the full and meaningful life of man. The research design, materials and methods will differ in terms of the questions asked.

Since aging and death are properties common to all living animals, much may be learned about the basic biological processes of aging from studies on lower animal forms. Many important questions can be answered only by experiments on animals where careful control of genetic and environmental factors can be maintained. In simpler forms of animal life we may find the answer to the question, "Why do cells die?" Ingenious experimenters choose an animal species with qualities particularly adapted to the question being investigated. Thus, if one wishes to test the hypothesis that the rate of living influences longevity, one may study the lifespan of the fruit fly at different environmental temperatures. The fruit fly is well suited to these studies because of its normal lifespan of approximately seventy days and because its body temperature is the same as the environment in which it lives. By increasing the temperature of the environment, the chemical processes taking place in the fruit fly will proceed at a more rapid rate. By altering environmental temperatures the experimenter can alter the "rate of living." Current experiments show that lifespan of the fruit fly is reduced at higher temperatures.

Even the lowly cockroach can add to our knowledge about aging at the cellular level as shown by experiments conducted by Dr. Dietrich Bodenstein in our laboratories. Under normal circumstances the growing cockroach can regenerate a new leg if one is lost. However, after the final moult and the attainment of maturity, the animal no longer grows a new leg to replace one experimentally removed. If artificial Siamese twins are prepared by experimentally joining a young and old cockroach, and a leg is removed from the old one, it will now go through a moult and regenerate a new leg. Thus it has been shown that the cells in the old cockroach have not lost the ability to divide, since they are able to respond to the hormonal stimulus provided by its attachment to the young growing animal. These experiments lead us to question the generalization that adult cells lost their capacity to divide and form new ones. Perhaps it is simply a matter of providing proper stimulus or cellular environment.

Lower animals such as the rat and mouse are invaluable for studies on aging, since they have a relatively short lifespan and can be subjected to a wide range of changes in diet or environmental conditions. Tissues, cells, and cellular components may be obtained and studied biochemically to find out what changes occur with age. The rat has been used to show that caloric restriction with prolongation of the growth period can significantly increase the lifespan. A large share of our knowledge about age changes in enzyme activities of various tissues has also come from the rat.

In addition to providing answers to biological problems, basic research often yields unexpected contributions to the cure and control of the ills of man. The remarkable success we have attained in combating infectious diseases was aided by laboratory scientists working on basic biological or chemical problems which at the time seemed to have little direct relationship to human disease. For example, the conquest of malaria was possible only because many entomologists had carefully observed and classified innumerable species of mosquitoes as a study in basic science with no reference to the practical use of the result. With this information it was possible to show that only mosquitoes of the genus *Anopheles* transmitted the disease.

The discovery of penicillin stemmed from the sharp eyes of a laboratory investigator who noticed that bacteria failed to grow in cultures which became contaminated with certain molds. Scientific curiosity led Fleming to examine further the phenomenon and ultimately to isolate the active component, penicillin, which has proved so effective in controlling infectious diseases in the human.

Development of the Salk vaccine for poliomyelitis was greatly aided by laboratory investigators who developed methods for growing animal cells in test tubes outside of the body in connection with studies far removed from a direct attack on the dread disease itself. These methods were applied to growing cells from monkey kidneys, which provided the basic method for determining the safety of the vaccine preparations for use in humans.

By the same token, major advances in our understanding of aging may come from the laboratory of the experimental embryologist or geneticist working on isolated systems far removed from man.

Gerontological research is also concerned with assessing the physiological and behavioral characteristics of aging man. At present a large share of our knowledge about aging humans is based on average values for measurements made on individuals living in institutions. Since less than 5 per cent of the population over sixty-five years of age fall into this category, general conclusions about the total population may be biased.

Examination of average curves brings to light a number of sig-

nificant generalizations. First of all, we now know that the char‑
acteristics of the blood plasma which require close regulation for
the effective functioning of the cells of the body are adequately
maintained even into advanced ages. Other physiological func‑
tions, especially those which involve the coordinated activities of
more than one organ system, show gradual decrements in function‑
al capacities over the lifespan. The average age decrement differs
widely among organ systems. Thus the decrement in speed of con‑
dition of the nerve impulse is only about 10 per cent between the
ages of thirty and ninety years, whereas the cardiac output or maxi‑
mum breathing capacity falls by 40 and 60 per cent, respectively,
over the same age span. There are also wide individual differences
in the effects of age on any physiological system. We have observed
some individuals who, at the age of ninety, showed kidney function
as good as the average for fifty year olds. Age changes also become
most apparent when the subject is exposed to some form of physio‑
logical displacement. Older individuals show greater displacements
and slower rates of recovery from a standard stimulus than do
young. Many additional studies lead to the conclusion that aging is
characterized by a loss in reserve capacities which has its basis, in
part, in the gradual loss of functioning cells from key tissues.

Perhaps one of the most useful contributions of gerontologic
research has been the demonstration that aging is not necessarily
associated with deterioration and disease. In many studies, both in
the physiological and psychological areas, it has been shown that
many of the common beliefs about the impairments of older people
are without basis in fact. For instance, it has been shown that, with
adequate dietary intake of protein, calcium, and vitamin D, older
people are still able to form new tissue and to accumulate calcium
in their bones. In the psychological area, it has been shown that the
decrement in intellectual performance with age is much less than
had been previously supposed and that in superior adults the fall
in intellectual capacity is scarcely measurable.

It is essential that research programs must be expanded to in‑
clude observations on individuals who are leading active lives in
the community. We must also obtain information on age changes
in the same individual as he ages. Because of wide individual dif‑

ferences in most measurements, average values based on different subjects in each age decade may conceal what is happening in an individual. It is obviously impossible to know what a group of sixty year olds was like at age forty. Similarly, observations on a group of forty year olds may be biased because they include individuals who will die before the group reaches the age of sixty. The only solution to this dilemma is to obtain repeated measurements on the same individual as he ages. This longitudinal method is time consuming and expensive, but a number of laboratories are beginning such studies. In addition, follow-up studies of individuals who have been studied during childhood and adolescence offer a rich opportunity for gerontological research.

Research on the social aspects of aging presents special problems. In the first place, the social scientist is seldom able to experimentally alter the environmental conditions. He must often choose groups of subjects from different social or cultural groups for comparisons, but it is difficult to find populations which differ with respect to only one variable. Thus studies on the effects of dietary fat on the incidence of coronary artery disease which compare the South African Bantu with residents of the United States include racial, occupational, and social differences, as well as differences in fat intake. However, research on the influences of social factors on aging must be expanded.

Solution of many of the practical problems of employment, income maintenance, activities, and housing depends on expanded knowledge about behavioral characteristics and, the social interactions of aging people. Social scientisis must be concerned with an evaluation of the effectiveness of action programs provided for the elderly. This means that research must be combined with community programs. Because of the special training needed for effective research, it is unrealistic to assume that the research can be conducted without staff research positions which are built into action programs.

Research in the social science area has already contributed important information about age distributions of the population with future projections to aid in planning for the future. Surveys of the health status and needs of the population also represent essential research activities. It is apparent that the time has come for social scientists to look more closely into the impact of social and cultural factors on the aging human.

The rising tide of public interest in the problems of an aging population has focused attention on many unanswered questions. Although many of the questions arise from practical problems, final answers will come from an understanding of the basic nature of aging. Hence, we must expand research at all levels if we are to meet the challenge of an aging population.

# BIBLIOGRAPHY

## BOOKS

Barron, M. L.: *The Aging American*. New York: Thomas Y. Crowell Company, 1961.

Birren, J. E. (ed) : *Handbook of Aging and the Individual*. Chicago: University of Chicago Press, 1959.

Bond, F. A., et al.: *Our Needy Aged*. New York:

Burgess, E. W. (ed.) :*Aging in Western Societies*. Chicago: University of Chicago Press, 1960.

Cabot, N. H.: *You Can't Count on Dying*. Boston: Houghton-Mifflin Company, 1961.

Cavan, R. S., et al.: *Personal Adjustment in Old Age*. Chicago: Science Research Associates, 1949.

Donahue, W. and Tibbitts, C. (eds.) : *Politics of Age*. Ann Arbor: The University of Michigan, 1962.

Drake, J. T.: *The Aged in American Society*. New York: The Ronald Press Co., 1958.

Gernant, L.: *You're Older Than You Think*. Kalamazoo: Western Michigan University, 1960.

Gilbert, J. G.: *Understanding Old Age*. New York: The Ronald Press Co., 1952.

Havighurst, R. J., and Albrecht, R.: *Older People*. New York: Longmans, Green & Co., Inc., 1953.

Menche, A. J.: *Successful Pension Planning*. Englewood Cliffs, N. J.: Prentice-Hall, Inc, 1949.

Pollak, O.: *Social Adjustment in Old Age*. Social Science Research Council, Bulletin 59. New York: 1948.

Shock, N. W.: *Trends in Gerontology* (2d ed.) . Stanford: Stanford University Press, 1957.

Simmons, L. W.: *The Role of the Aged in Primitive Societies*. New Haven: Yale University Press, 1945.

Soule, G.: *Longer Life*. New York: The Viking Press, 1958.

Stieglitz, E. J.: *The Second Forty Years*. Philadelphia: J. B. Lippincott Co., 1952.

Steiner, P. O., and Dorfman, R.: *The Economic Status of the Aged*. Berkeley: University of California Press, 1957.

Tibbitts, C. (ed.) : *A Handbook of Social Gerontology*. Chicago: University of Chicago Press, 1960.

————, and Donahue, W. (eds.) : *Aging in Today's Society*. Englewood Cliffs, N. J.: Prentice-Hall, 1960.

Tuckman, J. and Lorge, I.: *Retirement and the Industrial Worker* New York: Columbia University Press, 1953.

Williams, A.: *Recreation for the Aging*. New York: Association Press, 1953.

Wolff, K.: *The Biological, Sociological, and Psychological Aspects of Aging*. Springfield, Illinois: Charles C Thomas, Publisher, 1959.

Woods, J. H.: *Helping Older People Enjoy Life*. New York: Harper & Brothers., 1953.

## ARTICLES

Adams, M. E., and Vedder, C. B.: Age and Crime. *Geriatrics, 16:*177–181, 1961.

Albrecht, R.: The Social Roles of Old People. *Journal of Gerontology, 6:* 138–142, 1951.

————: Social Roles in the Prevention of Senility. *Journal of Gerontology, 6:*380–386, 1951.

Alvarez, W. C.: The Neglected Art of Diagnosis by Eye and Ear. *Geriatrics, 12:*542–548, 1957.

————: The Management of Persons with Little Strokes. *Geriatrics, 12:*421–425, 1957.

————: More About Little Strokes. *Geriatrics, 10:*556–562, 1955.

————: Is Life More Strenuous Today? *Geriatrics, 13:*611–612, 1958.

Arnhoff, F. N.: Research Problems in Gerontology. *Journal of Gerontology, 10:*452–455, 1955.

Arnold, E. T., Jr.: Some Fundamentals of Geriatric Practice. *Geriatrics, 12:* 612–615, 1957.

Barkin, S.: Jobs for Older Workers. *Journal of Gerontology, 7:*426–430, 1952.

Beard, B. B.: Are the Aged Ex-family? *Social Forces, 27:*274–279, 1949.

Bettag, O., Slight, D., Wenig, P. W., and Sorenson, W. H.: Mental Illness in the Aged Population. *Geriatrics, 10:*595–598, 1955.

Bluestone, E. M.: Thoughts on the Geriatric Goal. *Geriatrics, 12:*553–556, 1957.

Bortz, E. L.: Stress and Aging. *Geriatrics, 10:*93–99, 1955.

Bowman, K. M.: Mental Adjustment to Physical Changes With Aging. *Geriatrics, 11:*139–145, 1956.

Britton, J. H.: Assessment of Services for the Aged in Rural Communities. *Journal of Gerontology, 13:*36–41, 1958.

Brown, G. T.: Never Too Old to Learn: A Gerontological Experiment in General Education. *School and Society, 74:*279–281, 1951.

Burns, R. K.: Economic Aspects of Aging and Retirement. *American Journal of Sociology, 59:*384–390, 1954.

Burstein, S. R.: The Cure of Old Age: Codes of Health. *Geriatrics, 10:*328–332, 1955.

——: The Quest for Rejuvenation. *Geriatrics, 10:*536–540, 1955.

——: The Historical Background of Gerontology. *Geriatrics, 10:*189–192, 1955.

——: The Foundations of Geriatrics. *Geriatrics, 12:*494–499, 1957.

Busse, E. W.: Treatment of the Nonhospitalized, Emotionally Disturbed Elderly Person. *Geriatrics,* pp. 173–177, April, 1956.

Cavan, R. S.: Family Life and Family Substitutes in Old Age. *American Sociological Review, 14:*71–83, 1949.

Chandler, A. R.: Attitudes of Superior Groups Towards Retirement and Old Age. *Journal of Gerontology, 5:*254–261, 1950.

Covalt, N. K.: The Meaning of Religion to Older People. *Geriatrics, 15:*658–664, 1960.

Cowgill, D. O.: Trends in the Ecology of the Aged. *Journal of Gerontology, 12:*75–80, 1957.

Dean, L. R.: Aging and the Decline of Instrumentality. *Journal of Gerontology, 15:*403–407, 1960.

Dinkel, R. M.: Attitudes of Children Toward Supporting Aged Parents. *American Sociological Review, 9:*370–379, 1944.

Drake, J. T.: Some Factors Influencing Students' Attitudes Toward Older People. *Social Forces, 35:*266–271, 1957.

Ebaugh, F. G.: Age Introduces Stress Into the Family. *Geriatrics, 11:*146–150, 1956.

Eisdorfer, C., and Altrocchi, J.: A Comparison of Attitudes Toward Old Age and Mental Illness. *Journal of Gerontology, 16:*340–343, 1961.

Feifel, H.: Older Persons Look at Death. *Geriatrics, 11:*127–130, 1956.

Filer, R. N., and O'Connell, D. D.: A Useful Contribution Climate for the Aging. *Journal of Gerontology, 17:*51–57, 1962.

Freeman, J. T.: Gerontology and the Gerontological Society. *The Gerontologist, 1:*161–167, 1961.

Friedsam, H. J.: Inter-regional Migration of the Aged in the United States. *Journal of Gerontology, 17:*51–57, 1962.

Granick, S.: Personality Adjustment of the Aged in Retirement Communities. *Geriatrics, 16:*381–385, 1961.

Hale, M. P.: Foster Home Care for the Aged. *Geriatrics, 13:*116–119, 1958.

Havighurst, R. J.: Old Age—An American Problem. *Journal of Gerontology,* pp. 298–304, October, 1949.

——: The Sociologic Meaning of Aging. *Geriatrics, 13:*43–50, 1958.

——, and Shanas, E.: Retirement and the Professional Worker. *Journal of Gerontology, 8:*81–85, 1953.

Hollander, J. L.: Treatment of Osteoarthritis in the Elderly Patient. *Geriatrics,* pp. 394–395, June, 1957.

Hopkins, E. H.: Gerontology: The University's Opportunity and Challenge. *Geriatrics, 13*:60–62, 1958.

Horwitt, M. K.: Nutritional Problems in the Aged. *Geriatrics, 12*:683–686, 1957.

Hoyt, G. C.: The Life of the Retired in a Trailer Park. *American Journal of Sociology, LIX*:361–370, 1954.

Hurwit, S., and Guthartz, J. C.: Family Life Education With the Aged. *Social Casework, 33*:382–387, 1952.

Jarvik, L., Kallmann, F. K., and Falek, A.: Psychiatric Genetics and Aging. *The Gerontologist, 2*:164–166, 1962.

Jeffers, F. C., and Nichols, C. R.: Attitudes Toward Death in Older Persons: A Symposium Relationship of Activities and Attitudes to Physical Well-being in Older People. *Journal of Gerontology, 16*:67–70, 1961.

Johnson, W. M.: Arthritis—Hypertrophic Versus Rheumatoid. *Geriatrics*, pp. 500–501, August, 1957.

Kaplan, M.: Pressures of Leisure on the Older Individual. *Journal of Gerontology, 13* (Supplement): 36–40, 1958.

Kent, D. P.: The White House Conference in Retrospect. *The Gerontologist, 1*:4–7, 1961.

Kleemeier, R. W.: Moosehaven: Congregate Living in a Community of the Retired. *American Journal of Sociology, 59*:347–351, 1954.

Kulowski, J.: Motorist Injuries Among Persons Over Sixty. *Geriatrics*, pp. 425–427, September, 1955.

Kuplan, L.: California Moves Ahead. *Aging, 17*:1–3, 1955.

Kutner, B.: The Social Nature of Aging. *The Gerontologist, 2*:5–8, 1962.

Lansing, A. I.: Experiments in Aging. *Scientific American, 188*:38–42, 1953.

Laurence, M. W.: Sources of Satisfaction in the Lives of Working Women. *Journal of Gerontology, 16*:163–167, 1961.

Leeds, M.: The Role of the Professional in Working with the Senile. *Geriatrics, 17*:116–122, 1962.

Levine, H. A.: Community Programs for the Elderly. *The Annals of the American Academy of Political and Social Science, 279*:164–170, 1952.

Linden, M. E.: The Older Person in the Family. *Social Casework, 37*:75–81, 1956.

Lipman, A.: Role Conceptions and Morale of Couples in Retirement. *Journal of Gerontology, 16*:267–271, 1961.

Lockie, L., Maxwell, M. D., and Cooper, R. G.: Gout, the Rediscovered Disease. *Geriatrics, 15*:497–502, 1950.

McConnell, J. W.: The Impact of Aging on the Economy. *Journal of Gerontology, 13* (Supplement): 42–47, 1958.

Michelon, L. C.: The New Leisure Class. *American Journal of Sociology, LIX*:371–378, 1954.

Moberg, D. O.: The Christian Religion and Personal Adjustment in Old Age. *American Sociological Review, 18*:87–90, 1953.

Mullen, H.: The Personality of Those Who Care for the Aging. *The Gerontologist, 1:*42–50, 1961.

Nathan, T.: Social Activities for Older People With Special Reference to the Needs of Immigrants From Different Cultural Backgrounds. *The Gerontologist, 2:*32–36, 1962.

Neugarten, B. L., Havighurst, R. J., and Tobin, S. S.: Measurement of Life Satisfaction. *Journal of Gerontology, 16:*134–143, 1961.

Novotny, G. B.: Age and Automotive Accidents. *Geriatrics,* pp. 271–277, June, 1961.

O'Dell, C. R.: Employment Services for Older Workers. *The Annals of the American Academy of Political and Social Science, CCLXXIX:*171–179, 1952.

Omachi, C.: Gerontology Practiced in Japan. *The Gerontologist, 2:*74–76, 1962.

Orbach, H. L.: Aging and Religion. *Geriatrics, 16:*530–539, 1961.

Peterson, Robert L.: A University Extension Course in Gerontology. *Journal of Gerontology, 6:*39–42, 1951.

Posner, W.: Adapting and Sharpening Social Work Knowledge and Skills in Serving the Aging. *Social Work, 2:*37–42, 1957.

Pressey, S. L.: Certain Findings and Proposals Regarding Professional Retirement. AUUP *Bulletin, 41:*503–509, 1955.

Richardson, I. M., and Weir, R. D.: Age and Disability. *The Gerontologist, 1:*185–190, 1961.

Rosow, I.: Retirement Housing and Social Integration. *The Gerontologist, 1:*85–91, 1961.

Ross, M.: Current Treatment of the Emotional Problems of Elderly People. *Geriatrics, 12:*603–606, 1957.

Sagal, Z.: Insomnia in the Aged. *Geriatrics, 13:*463–466, 1958.

Sandelius, G.: Ninety-nine Year Old Monozygotic Twins. *Journal of Gerontology,* pp. 171–174, 1955.

Scott, F. G.: Factors in the Personal Adjustment of Institutionalized and Non-Institutionalized Aged. *American Sociological Review, 20:*538–546, 1955.

Seven, M. J.: Current Concepts in Diagnosis and Management of Osteoarthritis. *Geriatrics,* pp. 327–332, May, 1958.

Shanas, E.: Family Responsibility and the Health of Older People. *Journal of Gerontology, 15:*408–411, 1960.

Sheeley, W. F.: The Family Physician, the Community and the Aged. *Geriatrics, 16:*321–327, 1961.

Sheps, J.: New Developments in Family Diagnosis in Emotional Disorders of Old Age. *Geriatrics, 14:*443–449, 1959.

Shore, H.: The Application of Social Work Disciplines to Groupwork Services in Homes for the Aged. *Social Service Review, 26:*418–422, 1952.

Smith, W. F.: Housing Preferences of Elderly People. *Journal of Gerontology, 16:*261–266, 1961.

Sommer, R. T.: Displaced Persons: The Elderly Patients in a Large Mental Hospital. *Geriatrics, 13*:653–661, 1958.

Strassman, G.: Unrecognized Intracranial Lesions in Mentally Sick Patients Over 60. *Geriatrics,* pp. 350–354, June, 1957.

Thumin, F. J.: Reminiscence as a Function of Chronological and Mental Age. *Journal of Gerontology, 17*:392–396, 1962.

Tibbitts, C.: Retirement Problems in American Society. *American Journal of Sociology, LIX*:301–308, 1954.

Tobin, S. S., and Neugarten, B. L.: Life Satisfaction and Social Interaction in the Aging. *Journal of Gerontology, 16*:344–346, 1961.

Tuckman, J., and Lorge, I.: Attitudes Toward Older People. *Journal of Social Psychology, XXXVII*:249–260, 1953.

Vance, R. B.: The Ecology of Our Aging Population. *Social Forces, 32*:330–335, 1954.

Whiskin, F. E., Dibner, A. S., and Rhudick, P. J.: Psychological, Cultural, and Health Characteristics of Aging Smokers and Non-smokers. *Journal of Gerontology, 17*:69–74, 1962.

Wiggins, J. W., and Schoeck, H.: A Profile of Aging. *Geriatrics, 16*:336–342, 1961.

Wilson, H. S.: University Programs in the Field of Aging. *Geriatrics, 15*:665–669, 1960.

Wolfbein, S. L.: The Outlook for the Older Worker. *Personnel and Guidance Journal, 36*–80:86, 1957.

Wolff, G. E.: Geriatric Mental Patients and How We Can Help Them. *Geriatrics, 14*:94–98, 1959.

Zola, I. K.: Feelings About Age Among Older People. *Journal of Gerontology, 17*:65–68, 1962.

Zborowski, M.: Aging and Recreation. *Journal of Gerontology, 17*:302–309, 1962.

————— and Eyde, L. E.: Aging and Social Participation. *Journal of Gerontology, 17*:424–430, 1962.

# NAME INDEX

# SUBJECT INDEX